THE GUERNSEY HOUSE

End-papers, front and back:
Extracts from the Legge Survey of 1680, reproduced respectively by courtesy of The British Library and the National Maritime Museum, Greenwich.

King's Mills' Farm (506): the tourelle stairs— 'We passed through King's Mills. It lies sequestered in a rural vale, and all its little cottages are uniformly neat and covered with the grateful vine, which spreads its branches with great luxuriance.' — *A Trip to Guernsey in 1798* by W. T. Money.

THE GUERNSEY HOUSE

by

John McCormack

with illustrations by
Carel Toms,
George Bramall and Robert Hardwick

Phillimore

First published 1980

Reprinted 1987 by
PHILLIMORE & CO. LTD.,
Shopwyke Hall, Chichester, Sussex

ISBN 0 85033 380 6

© Text: John McCormack, 1980, 1987
Line Drawings: George Bramall, Robert Hardwick
and John McCormack, 1980, 1987
Photographs: Carel Toms, 1980, 1987

Printed in Great Britain
at the University Printing House, Oxford

CONTENTS

Chapter		Page
	Foreword	ix
	Preface and Acknowledgements	x
I	Introduction	1

PART ONE: 1400–1625

II	The two-storey longhouse (Type 1)	22
III	The one-storey longhouse (Type 2)	42
IV	Les grandes maisons (Type 3)	46
V	The three-bay house (Type 4)	54
VI	Early alterations and additions	57
VII	La Maison de Haut, Pleinheaume	66

PART TWO: 1625–1787

VIII	The two-storey house with cross-passage (Type 5)	72
IX	The one-storey house with cross-passage (Type 6)	92
X	The house with integral byre but outside access (Type 7) ...	96
XI	The low-loft house (Type 8)	100
XII	The split-level house (Type 9)	103
XIII	Other eighteenth-century houses (Types 10 and 11)	106

PART THREE: ST. PETER PORT

XIV	St. Peter Port within Les Barrières de la Ville, 1400–1625 ...	112
XV	St. Peter Port, 1625–1787	120

PART FOUR: DATING, DERIVATION AND DESIGN

XVI	The need for a dating sequence	134
XVII	Inscriptions	136
XVIII	Legal documents	142
XIX	Private diaries and account books	144
XX	Livres des perchages	146
XXI	The French connection	151
XXII	House types	153

Chapter		Page
XXIII	Walling	156
XXIV	Woodwork	161
XXV	Arches and doorways	167
XXVI	Windows	179
XXVII	Fireplaces	184
XXVIII	Staircases	199
XXIX	Éviers and bénitiers	207
XXX	Merchants' marks and pelicans	219

PART FIVE: DETAILED STUDIES

XXXI	La Grande Maison, St. Sampson	226
XXXII	Les Poidevins, St. Andrew	233
XXXIII	Le Marais, Castel	237
XXXIV	The Guernsey Savings Bank, St. Peter Port	245
XXXV	Les Granges de Beauvoir Manor, St. Peter Port	252
XXXVI	Le Grée, St. Martin	261
XXXVII	Le Chêne Cottage, Forest	265
XXXVIII	Les Câches, St. Pierre-du-Bois	269
XXXIX	Les Prevosts, St. Saviour	276
XL	La Seigneurie, Torteval	283
XLI	Bordeaux House, Vale	290

PART SIX: THE DUKE OF RICHMOND MAP — 296

PART SEVEN: THE SCHEDULES

The First Schedule	320
The Second Schedule	326
The Third Schedule	327
The Fourth Schedule	327
Index of names and places in text	397

LIST OF ILLUSTRATIONS

COLOUR PLATES

King's Mills' Farm *frontispiece*

(between pages 20 and 21)

1. Les Grandes Mielles
2. Le Variouf de Haut
3. Le Grée, Le Gron
4. La Rocré
5. La Bellieuse Farm
6. Les Reveaux
7. St. George
8. Les Blancs Bois

HALF-TONE PLATES

(between pages 116 and 117)

1. Les Câches
2 & 3. Le Variouf, Forest
4. Le Bigard
5. Les Granges de Beauvoir
6. The Old Farmhouse, La Mare
7. Maison d'Aval
8. Maison de Haut
9. Bordeaux House
10. La Bouvée Farm
11. La Rocque Balan
12-15. La Houguette
16. La Forge
17. Les Maindonneaux
18. La Petite Câche
19. Les Reveaux
20. Les Tilleuls
21. La Carrière
22. Le Tertre
23. Galliot Cottage
24. Maison d'Aval
25. La Grande Maison de la Pomare
26. Le Bourg
27. Les Adams
28. Les Hamelins
29. Le Gélé
30. Le Moulin de Haut
31. Le Colombier
32. Le Marais Cottage
33. Le Camptréhard
34. Le Camptréhard
35. La Maison du Mont Bai
36. Le Pollet
37. Cornet Street in 1932
38. Le Gron Farm
39. 37, Glategny Esplanade
40. 26, Cornet Street
41. 10, Hauteville
42. Woodlands
43. Plaiderie House, Le Pollet
44. La Fosse Equerre
45. Retour au Nord
46. Le Truchon
47. Initials and date on Type 5 'Guernsey' arch
48. King's Mills' Farm
49. Le Haut Chemin
50. Les Merriennes Cottage
51. Pleneuf Court
52. Les Câches
53. Le Villocq
54. La Rocque Balan
55. Les Grands Moulins
56. Tertre Farm
57. Le Groignet
58. Le Gron
59. Les Blancs Bois
60. Old Farm, Brock Road
61. Carriaux Cottage, St. Andrew
62. Maison de Haut
63. The Elms, Pleinheaume
64. La Maison d'Aval
65. Female head on fireplace corbel, Le Chouet de Roche, St. Andrew
66. A 14th-century window head, Les Câches
67. Trough outside Castle Church
68. Finial over entrance arch, La Haye du Puits
69. Trough from Les Fontaines

70.	St. George		81.	Les Câches
71.	Window lintel, La Maison Guignan		82.	Saints Farm
72.	Les Câches		83.	Fireplace lintel, Castel Rectory
73.	Old Farm, Brock Road		84.	Crest or merchant's mark: EN 1596 CH
74.	La Maison de Haut		85.	De Sausmarez arms
75.	La Forge		86.	Unidentified mason's mark
76.	House at Le Mont Saint		87.	Jean Briard's merchant's mark, Guernsey Savings Bank
77.	La Vieille Sous L'Eglise			
78.	La Moye		88.	R. Briard's merchant's mark, Guernsey Savings Bank
79.	Saints Farm			
80.	Le Pavé		89.	Pelican feeding her young, Les Vallettes

LINE DRAWINGS

1.	The Channel Islands, the Brittany Coast and the Cotentin	2	23.	Split-level houses	104
2.	Guernsey—geological map	3	24.	Shops in St. Peter Port, 1400-1787	122
3.	The Angevin Empire	15	25.	Not allocated	
4.	The 5-bay longhouse	23	26.	Dated keystones	139
5.	Longhouses	25	27.	Le Grée, Le Gron	140
6.	Cobo Farmhouse	39	28.	Types of Guernsey masonry	158
7.	La Maison des Pauvres	40	29.	Moulded chamfers on main beams	162
8.	Plans of one-storey longhouses	43	30.	Early roof trusses	164
9.	Les Grandes Maisons	48	31.	Norman and Breton arches	168
10.	Three-bay longhouses	55	32.	Arches: types 1 and 2	168
11.	Le Tertre, Vale	62	33.	Arches: types 3 and 4	170
12.	Bordeaux House	64	34.	Arches: types 5, 6 and 7	171
13.	Maison de Haut	67	35.	Les Grands Moulins	179
14.	Maison de Bas	78	36.	La Rocque Balan	180
15.	Les Adams, St. Pierre-du-Bois	80	37.	Le Chêne Farm	182
16.	Arrangement of 1st-floor rooms, 17th-18th centuries	83	38.	Fireplaces and chimneys, 1400-1750	186
17.	Croissettes at the foot of roof copings	90	39.	Les Quertiers: fireplace	196
			40.	15th- and 16th-century tourelles	200
18.	One-storey houses with cross-passages	93	41.	17th- and 18th-century staircases	205
			42.	Eviers, and chamfers stops from arches and fireplaces	208
19.	17th- and 18th-century roof construction	94	43.	Le Frie: évier	210
20.	Les Cottes	97	44.	Bénitiers	213
21.	Le Camptréhard	98	45.	Les Grandes Maisons: arch and bénitier	215
22.	Low-loft houses	101	46.	Merchants' marks	221

ENDPIECES

Les Effards: bénitier	53
Rue des Landes: initialled and dated lintel	65
Les Blicqs	69
Les Mourains: lintel	105
Sausmarez manor: inscription	109
Newbourne, Petit Bouet: door hinge	131
La Haye du Puits: window head	135
Sausmarez manor: raised inscription	141
Le Douit Farm Flats: window seat	143
La Haye du Puits: angle turret loophole	150
La Rocque Balan: tourelle loophole	152
Les Hamelins: initials and date	155
Casa Seda: window head	166
Le Vallon Cottage: pelicans	223

FOREWORD

I am pleased to have the opportunity of saying why I think that this book is important. I have always maintained that conservation is an integral part of planning, and this book well illustrates that fact.

Over the past twenty years it has sometimes seemed as if a tidal wave of 'Development', much of it avowedly prestigious, has threatened to sweep away most remnants of our Island heritage. It is a curious reflection of our times that this admirable word has in so many parts of the world become considered a term of reprobation.

It may be, in the face of increasing protest, that this particular wave is receding and it will be for future generations to decide whether those of us who, in whatever capacity, have fought to withstand its excesses, have contributed or detracted from the future integrity and well-being of our Island home. Here I should like to pay a special tribute to the Guernsey Press for the free weekly publication over the years of a comprehensive list of all planning applications and for highlighting the important ones, thereby inviting healthy public participation in our sustained efforts to preserve the environment.

In the heat of discussion—and where multi-million pound investments have been at stake the discussions have sometimes been hot indeed—it has not always been easy quietly to demand an answer to the simple questions: Who benefits? and how?

It is possible that if this had been asked a little more persistently throughout the United Kingdom and in Europe, the catastrophic degradation of so much urban, rural and coastal development might not have occurred.

Some would disagree and would speak very confidently of progress. But such progress will only be possible if our future generations are allowed the opportunity, and if they go to the trouble of taking it, to learn from what they are trying to progress.

It seems to me that if we look unsentimentally at the history of this small Island we may discover traditions and values of which we must be proud, and insofar as the legacy of these values may be kept alive through preserving the best of our architectural and rural heritage in trust for our future generations, this is surely work well done.

It is for this reason that we are grateful for the time and meticulous care that has been devoted to the preparation of this excellent book, and that I feel honoured to have been asked to comment on it.

CONSEILLIER T.D. OGIER,
President, Island Development Committee

PREFACE AND ACKNOWLEDGMENTS

The idea of studying Guernsey's vernacular architecture in detail is one that has been with me, on and off, ever since I first came to live in the island, 19 years ago. *The Guernsey Farmhouse*, compiled by the Guernsey Society in 1963, spurred on my interest, and Joan Stevens' book, published two years later, on *Old Jersey Houses*, Vol. 1, whetted my appetite still further. However, it was not until many years later that I began to think how I could best start on such a project. By that time, the Archaeological Section of La Société Guernesiaise had asked me to organise the recording of 19th- and early 20th-century houses and commercial properties in St. Peter Port and St. Sampson, in areas ripe for redevelopment. It was while engaged in this task—a task which has never been completed—that I was finally convinced that a systematic study of the much older buildings everywhere to be seen would be a far more worthwhile enterprise.

In 1976, *The Guernsey Evening Press and Star* had decided to publish, in sections, *The Duke of Richmond Survey* of 1787, and I had carefully cut these out of the newspaper and put them away. It occurred to me one day that this *Survey* could be invaluable in the project I had in mind. For, *inter alia*, it marked every building already standing at the end of the 18th century. It could therefore provide a watershed between earlier houses and those which had been built since that date. During the summer of 1978, then, armed with my newspaper cuttings, I set out on my bicycle to look at the island's farmhouses and cottages in a systematic fashion. After two years at it, I now know my way around Guernsey better with a 200-year-old map than I do with a modern one!

Those first 18 months spent investigating every building marked, or the site of every building, served to establish many of the criteria necessary in making sense of what I saw. And, as always, the more I understood what I was looking at, the more I noticed all manner of things that had often enough been passed by, uncomprehending, before. At the end of it, the total number of houses 200 years old or more, in 25 square miles—over one thousand—seemed staggering.

It was at this stage that Carel Toms convinced me that I ought to think in terms of publishing the material I was collecting. His knowledge of the publishing world and his reputation in it smoothed the way considerably, and it was mostly in his company that the next part of the project was undertaken: gaining access to the 1,000 houses I thought were there in 1787. The tedious process of knocking on all those doors, sometimes several times, was undertaken largely during the winter

PREFACE AND ACKNOWLEDGMENTS

of 1979-80, and only on one occasion was a carving-knife brandished in my face. Overwhelmingly, our efforts were rewarded with tremendous generosity. The hospitality and goodwill we met will never be forgotten. This book is mostly due to the unselfish way in which people gave up their time to show us all they could of their houses; homes of which they are justly proud and on which they lavish a great deal of care and thought. Recent vandalism, where we met it, was mostly of the kind perpetrated by the insensitive application of legislation designed to ensure the proper construction and resistance to fire of new buildings: it is my earnest hope that one result of this present publication will be the realisation of the value of our heritage in vernacular architecture, and its vulnerability, so that as new legislation is drafted in the years ahead, special allowance may be made for houses not built to 20th-century specifications but whose construction has so far seen them through 300, 400, or even 500 years.

Most of the photographs in this book are by Carel Toms. They are but a fraction of the ones he has taken these last two years. Others reproduced are well before his time and show some of our houses when they were still thatched or unaltered: I should like to thank many people who sent in old photographs, and all those who have corresponded in answer to our queries on a variety of topics. George Bramall, B.Arch., A.R.I.B.A., whose concern for the island's architectural heritage is also well-known locally, has contributed the magnificent plans, elevations and drawings in Part Five, and also a sketch of Les Quertiers fireplace, Figure 39.

I should like to thank all those other people who have accompanied me on visits during the past three years, especially Marie Toms, on whose photographs some of the drawings in this book are based. Another of them, Robert Hardwick, has drawn Figures 26, 42, 44, 46, and has helped with Figure 43. Figure 45 was provided by the States Technical Services Department. All other line drawings and maps in the text are the work of the author. The end-papers are from the Legge Survey of 1680, that at the front of the book by courtesy of the British Library, and that at the back by courtesy of the National Maritime Museum at Greenwich.

In the spring of this year, Carel Toms and myself visited Normandy and Brittany in order to study the French parallels to our island architecture. We met with unfailing courtesy and enthusiasm, and yet again, a quite unforgettable hospitality on the part of householders whose properties we visited. Particular thanks must go to M. Gildas Durand, of Rennes University, who gave up much valuable time on our account, and to the *Inventaire Général des Monuments et des Richesses Artistiques de France* in Rennes, who allowed us access to the detailed lists they are compiling of all Breton buildings, in town and countryside. We were given every encouragement.

Here in Guernsey, I should like to thank the Priaulx Library and the Guille-Allès Library for every assistance given with research, and the curator and staff both of The Candie Museum and Art Gallery and of Castle Cornet. I am also very grateful to Conseillier T. G. Ogier, President of the Island Development

Committee and concerned, more than most, to preserve the island unspoilt in recent years, for consenting to write the Foreword. I am indebted to numerous authors of papers published in the Transactions of La Société Guernesiaise and the Quarterly Reviews of the Guernsey Society. Where I have drawn heavily on any one particular article, due acknowledgment has been made in the text. However, any conclusions drawn are entirely my own opinions.

For his infectious enthusiasm, for sharing his unrivalled knowledge of medieval Guernsey, and for many fascinating evenings elucidating Livres des Perchages, with a potted biography of every individual encountered in them, thrown in, off the cuff, I am particularly indebted to Mr. Hugh Lenfestey. The more tedious burden of proof-reading has been eased by Carel Toms. Finally, many thanks to all my friends who have put up with me during the last two years as I have become more and more obsessed with houses: I promise them I shall mend my ways in future. At least I hope my patient subscribers will not be disappointed.

JOHN McCORMACK

St. Peter's Valley,
St. Martin's,
Guernsey.

November, 1980

Chapter I

INTRODUCTION

OF ALL THE ATTRACTIONS Guernsey has to offer residents and visitors, the charm of quiet lanes and mellow granite houses ranks high. Often just a few steps away from the traffic of the 20th century, these houses maintain a quiet dignity, encapsulating the efforts and aspirations of generations of islanders, whose way of life is now fading fast.

And yet, although it is obvious enough that many of these buildings are of great age, even the most careful study of the exterior will often fail to give any indication of their original use or of the way of life of those who designed them. To understand our vernacular architecture, that is, the 'everyday' constructional methods and disciplines of islanders over the centuries, concerned with basic shelter for themselves and their belongings, it is necessary to look behind these homely façades. It is necessary to understand the climatic conditions from which they sought shelter and what materials were available to achieve this. It is also necessary to understand their ethnic origin, their political and religious background, and of what their livelihood consisted.

Guernsey is the second largest of the Channel Islands, a small group of islands lying off the French coast between the Cotentin Peninsula of Normandy to the east, and Brittany to the south. Jersey is about twice the size of Guernsey, but the other inhabited islands—Alderney, Sark, Brecqhou, Herm, Jethou and Lihou are considerably smaller. Guernsey itself barely covers 25 square miles, forming a right-angled triangle roughly six miles from north to south, six miles from east to west, and 12 miles along the hypotenuse, south-west to north-east. It is 70 miles south of the English coast of Dorset, 15 miles west of the Cotentin, and 25 miles north of Brittany. It is also the most westerly of the group, and is thus exposed on all sides to the fury of the Atlantic gales, though it enjoys mild winters because of the Gulf Stream which surrounds it. This mild weather is emphasised by the very high humidity, while this same humidity and the sea on every side prevent summer temperatures reaching spectacular levels. The rainfall is an average of 30 inches a year, and falls mainly as drizzle or comparatively light rain from depressions, rather than as torrential downpours from thunderclouds, for these rarely build up over such a small area of land. Thus, for the housebuilder, extremes of climate are not a problem, the basic concerns being to provide shelter from the winds, often very high winds, and from an all-pervading dampness.

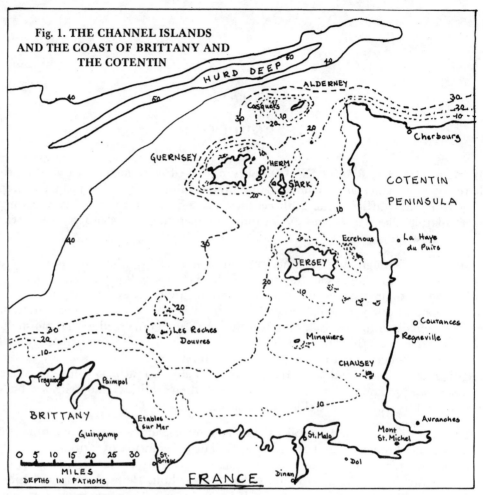

Fig. 1. THE CHANNEL ISLANDS AND THE COAST OF BRITTANY AND THE COTENTIN

What materials were at hand with which to achieve this? In the south of the island, the land forms a plateau between 200ft. and 350ft. high, much broken up by steep-sided stream valleys. Almost all of this area is geologically either Icart or Perelle gneiss, metamorphic rocks of poor quality as far as the builder is concerned. They are foliated and cleaved, and thus very difficult to fashion into a flat surface or tool into a straight line. The many fractures and joints tend to make them microporous and rather permeable, often giving damp walls.

The Icart gneiss is an attractive stone, because the cleavage faces are often iron-stained, giving walls a pleasing rust-brown colour, but the texture of the surface is variable, depending whether the joint face or the fracture face is used, and this can sometimes break down with continuous weathering. It therefore provides suitable material only for walls of a random rubble construction, the quoins of all houses after the mid-17th century being of some other stone. However, Icart gneiss was easily and cheaply quarried in the southern parishes where it was

INTRODUCTION

widely used, even after better quality stone became available last century. It is readily identified by the features described and by the tendency towards large and irregular mortar joints where the stone cannot be trimmed to a straight line.

The Perelle gneiss is much tougher, resembling a granite, except for the weak foliation, seen in aligned crystals. The overall dark grey colour is due to a preponderance of black horneblende. Although it will not trim as well as the granites, it was widely used in the Perelle and Rocquaine areas, and for quoins

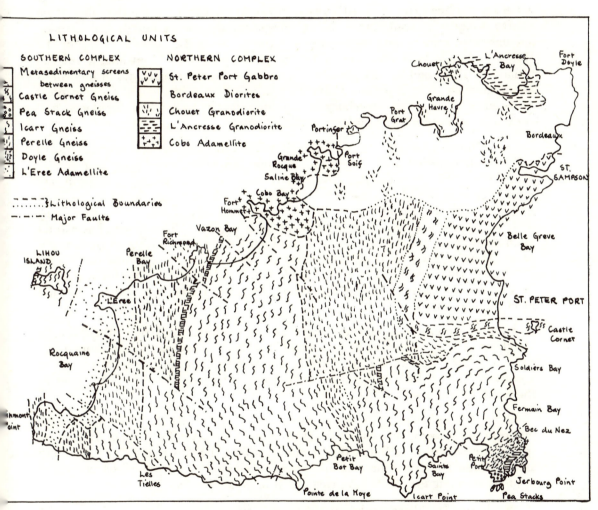

Fig. 2. SIMPLIFIED GEOLOGICAL MAP OF GUERNSEY

throughout the southern parishes from the 17th century onwards, when it was first quarried.

The northern half of the island is low-lying, rarely rising more than 50ft. above sea level, but here the rocks are mostly of volcanic origin. Around Vazon, Cobo and Saline Bay, the very limited outcrops of Cobo granite were much favoured by the early builders as providing a particularly attractive orange-pink stone which was also suitable for use as quoins, lintels, fireplaces and arches. Unfortunately, the coarse crystalline texture and the breakdown of felspar crystals tend to weaken it, so that it sometimes weathers quite badly, even indoors, giving a hackly surface after 300–400 years. However, it can vary considerably from quarry to quarry, some stone being comparatively unweathered, still with an angular appearance, although used *c.* 1600, as at Le Marais (493) or La Hougette (528). It is very similar to the Jersey granite of Mont Mado, but can usually be identified by the greater number of small black markings or inclusions about an inch or two across. Cobo granite was very widely used from earliest times until after 1600, especially for quoins, lintels, arches and fireplaces, and for the entire house, if the builders could afford it.

The Chouet granodiorite and the Bordeaux diorite of the extreme north were much quarried from the 18th century onwards. The diorite is generally older than the granodiorite, and partly dissolved by it, so that both are intimately intermixed in quarries. Being much younger rocks than the southern gneisses, they are largely uncleaved and consequently much easier to quarry in large stones, and are capable of being well trimmed. The diorite has a finer grain than the granodiorite, which is a much lighter grey. Although both types of stone were used in small quantities in early houses, it was not until after 1750 that their use became widespread. Much re-fronting of houses was done in the diorite, which, having no grain, was easy to fashion into ashlar and nicely-tooled lintels.

Another similar rock is the L'Ancresse granodiorite, quarried near Fort Le Marchant. The introduction of potassium into this rock, or potash metasomatism, gives it a khaki colour. Strong jointing allows it to break into angular blocks of a convenient size for small quoins, and it was extensively used in later times in the north of the island.

Along the coast near St. Peter Port, and slightly inland, there are several outcrops of gabbro, an almost black and coarsely-crystalline rock. It can be trimmed moderately well and it was much used in the Town and Bellegrève Bay areas, producing very sombre buildings, only relieved by a little off-white, where the felspars along the joints have weathered to cream kaolin.

In addition to these rocks, there is also stone from dykes which intersect the older formations. Most of these are useless for building, either because they fracture along multiple joints, like the felsite and aplite, or because, like the lamprophyre, being rich in mica, they rot quickly. However, the vein of quartz at Jerbourg—Pied du Mur (Marble Bay)— has provided stone sometimes found in early houses, though like a good deal of other building stone, it was not obtained by quarrying, but directly off the beach. In almost all early houses, huge boulders as well as smaller stones of all sizes show by their rounded shape that they were picked up from the foreshore, or at best, prised away from outcrops.

Stone from the black dolerite dykes criss-crossing the southern cliffs was also used in this way. But it was chiefly prized in the 18th century because, being free of quartz, it was comparatively soft and was found extensively on the shore as flat, rounded beach pebbles, ideal for the decorative galleting so favoured at that time. This was a form of pointing in which these pebbles were pushed into mortar joints, providing lines of contrasting colour.

These, then, were the types of stone most readily available. But it was quite possible, as the wealth of the island increased, to look further afield. The granite of the Chausey Islands, to the south-east of Guernsey and very close to the French coast, was much used by medieval church builders, and stone from Mont Mado, in Jersey, also appears here and there. In the second half of the 18th century, when the export of Guernsey granite to England began, ships returned to the islands with ballasts of Swanage or Portland stone, and sometimes of chalk. The former became popular for sills, lintels, steps, and for the paving of hallways, while the latter was used for puddling the floors of the warehouses and vaults lining the quay in Town. Red sandstone from Alderney also appears in some walls.

The use of Chausey stone is particularly interesting and a good deal more work needs to be done to ascertain at which periods it was available. For many years during the Hundred Years' War Chausey was under English control, but it seems likely that stone from the quarries there, used chiefly by the monks of Mont St. Michel for building their abbey, was available in Guernsey after the wars for as long as the ecclesiastical ties lasted with France. However, further study might indicate that this is not so and that it was only in the 14th and 15th centuries that it was used here. Compared with most Guernsey stone available at that time—that is to say the Icart gneiss and Cobo granites—it had the advantage of being easily trimmed although, having a high mica content, it weathers badly. Thus, though it was possible to carve grotesque animals on the gargoyles of the Town Church, and have other animal and human figures as label stops on the doorways, it is now almost impossible to make out most of those carvings. Examination of the chancel arcades in that church will show the various shadings of this stone, but in general it appears as a light brown, verging on grey when newly-cut, with the mica glittering in strong light. It was used at The Guernsey Savings Bank (756), at Les Quertiers (919) for the fireplace and for the arch since moved from there to St. George (586), for the arch from La Grande Maison de la Pomare (317), now lying at Les Vicheries, and much of the other better-quality work in the island, apparently in the second half of the 15th century.

It was then that the techniques involved in quarrying stone are said to have been introduced here by masons settling from Chausey and Brittany. Importation of stone from elsewhere is evidence of considerable wealth and might be expected to be associated with relatively advanced quarrying methods. The Chausey stone was almost certainly shaped to size before leaving the quarry. This accounts for the uniform sizes of blocks of stone in the Town Church and at The Guernsey Savings Bank. It might also be that this sort of standardisation was followed in the better quality stone quarried locally at the same time. The fireplaces at Les Caches (237) and Les Raies de Haut (251) might be used as evidence for this, if they are of Cobo stone and not stone from Mont Mado. Of course, if they are of Jersey granite, blocks might have been cut to a few standard sizes at those quarries in the same way as seems to have been done in Chausey.

From the foregoing, it is quite clear that, whatever his means, there was no shortage of suitable materials for the local builder in his efforts to provide himself with basic shelter and a comfortable home. Indeed, from the 15th century onwards, dwellings were of such a permanent nature that they have lasted until the present day. But the use of stone at all implies either that sufficient timber for wooden buildings was not available, possibly because of the intensive settlement pattern, or that the island was already sufficiently prosperous to enable a man to spend considerable time building a substantial house, or to pay someone else to do so for him. Whether early farmsteads were ever built in timber is a matter we shall return to later, but it is clear that the great variety of stone available, coupled with the wealth of the community, in practice made it possible for a man not only to provide a basic shelter, but also to express certain aspects of his beliefs and aspirations in the decoration and design of doorways and other features. We must therefore see who these people were and in what their wealth consisted.

Recent excavations are confirming, year by year, the sporadic finds of the last two centuries which show that Guernsey has been inhabited from very early times. From the pottery of the Bronze Age and Iron Age found here it seems certain that the island was already well-established on the shipping routes from the Mediterranean around the Atlantic coast of Spain and France and across the Channel to the great trading post at Hengistbury Head, near Bournemouth, well before the Roman conquest of Britain. Perhaps traders from Scandinavia and the Baltic also occasionally found their way here. Although evidence of Roman occupation is scanty, it might be inferred from the finding of a Roman vessel wrecked near the harbour mouth. For if the old-established trade routes were even better used in Roman times, coastal shipping in these waters would have been likely to call into the good harbour at St. Peter Port for revictualling, if not for local trade, and a local community would have existed to provide these facilities.

It must be remembered that if *Les Chroniques de Coutances* are correct, Jersey and Chausey did not become islands until the year 709. Before that time,

INTRODUCTION

marshland and forest stretched from Avranches to Chausey and as far north as Regneville, and Jersey was part of the mainland. But in that year, the sea broke through and inundated the whole region, the marshlands and forests gradually being replaced by the great stretches of sand which now engulf Mont St. Michel, the higher land of the present islands being cut off from the neighbouring coastline by a shallow sea continually deepened by the 40-foot tides of the area.

If this is so, Guernsey in Roman times would have provided the only good harbour between Cap de la Hague and the Breton peninsula, the island lying off a treacherous coast of sand-dunes and shallow beaches stretching from around Carteret almost to St. Malo. The extremely shallow waters between Jersey and France, often less than 10 fathoms, even now discourage shipping from passing that way. In early medieval times the seas around Jersey were no doubt even shallower, and the difficulty of using the harbour at St. Helier would alone have influenced the main trading routes towards Guernsey. But if those medieval shipping routes had been established even before Jersey became detached, it is easy to see why Guernsey was so important.

In Roman times, then, this island, if not politically significant, provided a useful stop on the long voyage between Britain and the Mediterranean, and for coastal traffic along the English Channel. During the 200 years following the withdrawal of Roman forces from Britain in the first half of the fifth century, the whole area saw enormous changes. Britons pushed towards Wales and Cornwall by the advancing tribes of Anglo-Saxon invaders in England, eventually fled southwards by sea to Armorica, or Brittany, where Roman rule had not yet quite broken down. They settled in the province of Gallia Lugdunensis, where they must have been more in the nature of refugees than invaders, escaping to their Romanised cousins from the heathen hordes overrunning Britain. Guernsey was probably settled by these refugees before the end of the sixth century and certainly well before 800, when Guernsey is known to have been inhabited by Britons, or Bretons. These islands were by that time included in the Frankish Kingdom of Charlemagne, and formed part of the province of Neustria at his death in 814. After that the Bretons pushed steadily eastwards, even beyond the historic boundaries of Brittany, until in 867, Charles the Bald, King of West Francia, ceded the Cotentin to Salomon, King of Brittany. From that time until the 10th century the Channel Islands were part of a Breton kingdom whose eastern border stretched from Caen to the Loire. Settlement of the Cotentin by the Bretons from the west of Brittany after 867 almost certainly would have meant even more Breton immigrants to the islands.

By 900, then, Guernsey had been effectively Breton for 400 years, during which time trade and travel continued. The continent still needed various goods produced by England, and the Anglo-Saxon ports along the south coast gradually took over from the older trading stations of pre-Roman times. The great burst of missionary activity from Ireland and South Wales included the Channel Islands in its evangelical work, the connections of Guernsey, Sark and Herm with St. Sampson, St. Magloire and St. Tugual dating from the early sixth century. We were almost certainly part of the diocese of Coutances by 867, and the parish system in the islands may well date from about that time.

This period of Breton rule came to an end in 939, though Breton influence continued long afterwards. In 911, a force of Viking adventurers, under the leadership of Rollo, penetrated along the Seine, and were allowed to settle around Rouen on condition that they accepted Christianity. For the next 20 years they extended their territories westwards, keeping up a constant pressure on the Kingdom of Brittany in combination with another group of Norsemen who had established themselves in the Loire Valley and were pushing north. The latter were wiped out about the year 930, and the Rouen Vikings' advance towards the St. Malo area was halted in 939 by a decisive victory by the Breton leader, Alan Barbetorte, at the Battle of Trano. This battle, near Portorson, established the boundary between Brittany and the Viking lands—or Normandy—at the River Couesnon, where it has remained ever since, and it meant that in theory, at least, Guernsey was now a western appendage of Normandy, rather than a northern appendage of Brittany. However, the consolidation of the Norman duchy, very loosely dependant on the French kings, the formation of an administration based on Frankish law, and the re-establishment of the church in Normandy so that it reflected Norman ambitions and ideas, was a process which was probably not completely accomplished for another 100 years.

But by the time of Duke Robert I (1027-1035), this island was effectively part of the Norman administration. The formation of a military aristocracy at various levels had by then become embodied in the feudal system of land holding. This system involved the granting of lands, or fiefs, by the duke, in return for various services usually including the provision of men-at-arms in time of war, and the administration of local justice. Guernsey was divided between two of the more important officials on the mainland of Normandy, the Vicomte of the Bessin and the Vicomte of the Cotentin, and thus became a small part of very much larger estates across the water. The revival experienced by the church at this time involved the acquisition of parishes by abbeys, rather than their remaining in lay hands: here, the island churches were divided between Marmoutier, near Tours, and Mont St. Michel.

For a further reference to medieval fiefs in Guernsey, see Chapter XX, page 146. A detailed account of the island from earliest times will be found in the excellent article by J. Le Patourel, in the 1975 issue of the *Transactions* of La Société Guernesiaise, pp. 453-461, from which much information for this chapter has been taken. The complex development of fiefs in the Channel Islands, though fascinating, must not be examined here. This brief survey of the island between the Norman conquest of England in 1066 has been undertaken in order to demonstrate that long before that, the original inhabitants had been swamped by a tremendous influx of Britons, *c.* 450-600, and that these new settlers were probably augmented by more Bretons, as they had now become,

INTRODUCTION

after the treaty of 867. And even after the Battle of Trano in 939, the inhabitants must have remained predominantly Breton, the Norman rule only having gradually become effective by the imposition of a military and administrative élite on the indigenous population. This early British settlement, the Breton rule 867-939 and the continued residence of the Breton population thereafter under Norman domination, is of the utmost importance to our study of vernacular architecture. For those Britons fleeing from the Anglo-Saxons would undoubtedly have continued their old way of life in a new land. Not only, therefore, might their settlement patterns be similar to settlement patterns in parts of Devon and Cornwall, Wales, Cumbria and Brittany, but their houses might also be basically similar to those from these areas.

It is well known that in other Celtic countries the settlement pattern is that of scattered homesteads spaced fairly regularly across agricultural land, for these people were predominantly farmers, without any attempt at forming a nucleated village such as is so characteristic either of the Anglo-Saxon or the Norman peoples. The contrast is well-marked in Pembrokeshire, 'Little England beyond Wales', where the southern half of the county was under Norman control and the northern half was Welsh. The latter has scattered farms and simple churches, without bell-tower and often with a double nave, situated near the sea or on the site of some even older pagan sanctuary or holy place. The former has villages, groups of houses around a central point, often the church, which is a building with single nave and embattled tower. In the Welsh part, the churches are frequently at the very edge of their parish: in the Norman or English part they are as near the centre as is possible. What is the position in Guernsey?

An examination of the 1787 map will show that there were very few nucleated settlements, even by the 18th century, and that where they occurred they are not usually associated with a church. The churches of the Vale, St. Sampson, and the Castel are virtually isolated at the extreme edge of their parishes, the first two being very close to the sea. Both St. Sampson's church and the Town Church were built, in fact, at the water's edge. The Castel church has an older statue menhir, a mother goddess, on the site, and so has the church of St. Martin, in its circular churchyard at the source of a stream. The churches at Torteval, St. Saviour and St. Pierre-du-Bois are equally dissociated from any nucleated settlement, only those at St. Andrew, the Forest, St. Martin, and St. Peter Port being surrounded by anything like a grouping of houses. St. Peter Port, with its harbour, is in a class of its own, and as for the others, it is only astonishing that after 800 years of Norman, or English, rule, there are no better examples of nucleated settlement. Moreover, the groups of houses around these churches are no larger than the other hamlets in those parishes. There is, in fact, nothing typically Norman about the siting of any island church. As for the structure of these churches, the towers belong to rebuildings from the 12th century onwards, but even then, remarkably, the churches at St. Martin, the Forest,

St. Andrew, the Castel and the Vale retain their Celtic double nave, as did Torteval before the 19th-century rebuilding.

The 1787 map, then, shows a Celtic settlement pattern of scattered hamlets. But some of these are individually almost as big as an early medieval nucleated village. What has happened is that the isolated farmsteads of the British or Celtic settlers have each become the nucleus of a later Norman agricultural system within a feudal society. By the 11th and 12th centuries no doubt an original farm had already become a small collection of three or four buildings, additional houses being built as the family expanded. In this connection it is significant that many such groupings are still known by a family name—for instance, Les Pages, Les Martins, Les Jehans, Les Prevosts. However, it is equally significant that the rural terracing of houses so common in Brittany does not often happen here. There are a few examples, such as at Les Fosses (61 and 62), or Les Fries (604 and 605), but the vast majority of farms and cottages are detached: and this is a Norman characteristic. The houses along Saints Road (66-69), for instance, each built gable to the road instead of being terraced along it, are typical of the villages of the Cotentin. We have, then, a fascinating mixture: an original Celtic settlement pattern of scattered farms afterwards being expanded each into little hamlets like Norman villages, the houses being detached in a fashion not exclusive to Normandy, but at least not particularly typical of Brittany, while the houses themselves, as we shall see, are of an exclusively Breton or Celtic type. The imposition of the Norman fief system on the existing pattern of things also led to the development of many *petit manoirs,* by the 15th century, each the centre of one of the numerous fiefs into which the estates of the Vicomtes of the Bessin and the Cotentin had been sub-divided. This did not always imply the residence of a seigneur, for various reasons, but the land-holding was clearly arranged as far as existing farmland would permit, on the Norman system, of open fields for the growing of crops, with individual strips in one field belonging to different farmers, and of large amounts of common land for the pasturing of animals. Place-names still preserve memories of this way of life. Les Landes and Les Mielles refer to areas of rough pasture unsuitable for the growing of crops, while Les Camps indicates an open-field system, still shown unenclosed in St. Martin's parish on sheet 19 of the 1787 map. And although by that time almost all farmland had been enclosed, the long narrow fields radiating from each hamlet or bordering the straighter roads reflect the sub-division of larger fields by early strip-holdings. Where other roads dog-leg their way around the corners of these enclosures, they are likely to have grown up later as tracks winding their way around the head furrows of strips in open fields. The field system therefore seems to indicate a Norman system, but it might well be that further research would indicate that this in turn is but the medieval rationalisation of much older Celtic fields.

In Brittany it is reckoned that the orientation of a house is of great importance and that the front of the older farmstead always faced south. This cannot be held to be so in Guernsey. Even where the topography did not impose any apparent

INTRODUCTION

restriction, there seems to have been little concern about orientation. Thus, in the Clos du Valle, La Rocque Balan (1007) faces south, but nearby, The Old Cottage (1005) and Les Mielles (1001) face north. At Bordeaux, Bordeaux Haven (982) faces east, while Amorel (983) and Bordeaux House (984) face north, and the houses around La Grève (1012) face north-west or south-east. Most of these houses were built before 1625 and some are much older. It therefore seems unlikely that orientation is of any importance in this island. But certainly a good number of farms do face south, and it could possibly be that detailed research on this matter would provide criteria for suggesting not that any existing houses are necessarily pre-1400, but that certain sites aligned in this way could be recognised as being very much earlier settlements, dating back to the Dark Ages. However, such evidence is at present entirely lacking, and we can only say that between 1400 and 1600 houses do not seem to have faced south more than in any other direction.

So much, then, for settlement patterns. But what of the houses themselves?

The earliest dwellings in Guernsey of which we know anything at all are the Iron Age hut circles excavated recently at Le Tranquesous, near Les Prevosts in St. Saviour's parish. They indicate that here, as in England and northern France during the first few centuries B.C., the houses were circular, never rectangular, the conical roofs resting on low walls of stone and turf which formed the perimeter of the hut, and supported inside by various props and posts. After that, there is a very large gap in any evidence of domestic building, indicating, of course, not that no settlements existed, but that they have not yet been found or that all traces of them have been obliterated by later building on the same site. Furthermore, it is likely that they were not stone structures, but built mostly of timber, reflecting not only the well-wooded nature of the land in those days, but the comparative poverty of the inhabitants—especially in the case of British settlers fleeing southwards in the sixth century—and the futility of building really permanent structures in the face of continuous Scandinavian raids in the following centuries. It may be that the temporary barns built until recently in the Grande Brière area of Southern Brittany may be a memory of Dark Age dwellings in the whole region settled by the Britons. Iorweth C. Peate, in *The Welsh House*, has made out a good case for the occasional circular stone pigsties in some Welsh farmyards being survivals of a technique formerly reserved for house-building. There, the beehive-shaped sties resemble in form if not in size the stone dwellings of the seventh, eighth and ninth centuries found in Ireland and also known from excavations to have existed in Wales itself. The construction and proportions of the Grande Brière buildings is such that on a slightly larger scale they, too, would represent a very satisfactory house. Indeed, the examples that remain are often as large in ground plan as some of our smaller stone-built houses, one visited by the author recently being 28ft. long by 18ft. wide. There was a central door in one side, 4ft. 6ins. high, under the eaves, and the roof was supported on 'kingposts' with collar and purlins. A ridge pole rested in the forked top of the 'kingposts', which stood on the *terre battue* floor. The height from floor to ridge was 16ft. All the walls, as well as the roof, were thatched with reed, tied on to hurdling or poles used as rafters. Of course, this building was of no great age, having been built by the present owner about fifty years ago as a cider barn, a function it still performs. However, the techniques used show every sign of having been handed down from generation to generation, surviving in this area where building stone is difficult to come by, when in other parts of Brittany they had long been replaced by more substantial structures. The suggestion that these timber-built stores have a history going back 1,500 years cannot at present be substantiated by any research and may prove to be misleading. They may have been derived from later stone houses rather than being a prototype of them. But at any rate they are remarkable in that they have a central doorway in the long wall, not in the gable-end, that they are approximately the size of a small house and that they are rectangular.

There has been a good deal of discussion as to the origin of the rectangular shape in house forms. As we have seen, the usual shape of dwellings in the Iron Age and onwards into the first century A.D. was not rectangular, but circular. This is ideal for a single-cell house, but has many drawbacks as soon as two or more rooms are required. It is certainly possible to join together a number of circular huts into one building, as is the case with the beehive-shaped stone buildings at Paradis, between Les Eyzies and Sarlat in the Dordogne region of France. But the construction is clumsy and there are severe limitations on the size of rooms. Admittedly this is less of a problem with wooden buildings than with stone, since the span of a timber roof is greater than a corbelled stone vault. But even so, it is much easier to extend a rectangular building lengthways without increasing the size of roof timbers needed, a consideration just as relevant whether the walls were of wood or of stone; and most people requiring more complex housing have preferred to build in stone, whenever it was available.

Rectangular houses and halls are known to have been used in Scandinavian countries from the earliest times. If, however, we are right in saying that our settlement pattern and our house form were already well-established in Guernsey long before the Norman administration of the 11th century onwards could have disseminated Scandinavian building techniques here, the rectangular form must already have been practised to the exclusion of all others for many years. Indeed, it may well have been introduced by the British settlers in the sixth century. But it is more likely that even by that time the rectangular house was known in Guernsey. We have seen that the harbour of St. Peter Port, as it was to become, is very likely to have been an important port of call even in Roman times, and it was the Romans who seem to have introduced the rectangular house not only to Gaul, but to Britain, their own houses being almost exclusively of this shape.

Gwyn I. Meirion-Jones, in a recent article on Breton houses in *Vernacular Architecture* (Vol. 10, 1979), quotes a principal of interpretation first put forward by V. G. Childe in the *Transactions* of the Glasgow Archaeological

Society in 1933, that 'the oldest types will be those most accurately reproduced in the greatest number of distinct regions; types localised in specific regions will be later inasmuch as they represent variants on the original type or types'. As will be shown in the next few chapters, the house-type universal in Guernsey during the later medieval period was the longhouse, that is, a dwelling in which man and beast lived under the same roof, and it is a type that occurs in all those regions occupied by the British, or Celtic, people, after the Roman withdrawal from Britain. It has been studied in detail in Wales and Monmouthshire, Cumbria, Devon and Cornwall, and has been identified throughout Brittany. If Childe is right, the longhouse must therefore represent a very ancient building tradition indeed and a way of life in existence before these various peoples were dispersed to the western extremities of France and the British Isles.

The Guernsey variant of the longhouse must also, judged by Childe's principle, be a later variation on the already widely distributed house form. For the longhouse in this island, although it has more affinities with Breton types than with Welsh, Cumbrian or Cornish examples, is in some ways different from all of them. Unfortunately, it is impossible at present to say when this island development took place, but it seems to have been complete by 1450. The great rebuilding of houses which seems to have gone on from around that time for the next 150 years, petering out soon after 1600, adhered almost exclusively to a type of longhouse that will be examined in detail in Part I of this book. After 1600, Childe's principle can equally well be seen to operate within the island itself. Whereas before that time, the Guernsey form of longhouse was almost universal, the next phase of house-building, from about 1650 until 1750, representing the last proper expression of a vernacular tradition here, witnessed considerable experimentation in house-forms, yet all of them related to the original longhouse pattern. By 1750, the real vernacular architecture was to all intents and purposes dead, swamped by the more formal classical ideas introduced first into St. Peter Port and gradually into the countryside from about 1700 onwards. Certain traditional techniques persisted, some even after 1900, but the period 1750 onwards must be regarded as a sort of afterglow of the vernacular tradition at its most vigorous and flourishing, which must in Guernsey be considered to be the years $c.1400-c.1625$.

The only link we have, apart from the deductions made in the preceding paragraphs, between the hut circles of the Tranquesous and the earliest houses now standing, which seem to be of 15th-century date, was the discovery of the remains of an early house at Cobo in 1966. Unfortunately, the results of the excavation carried out under the direction of Mrs. Le Patourel have never been published, and the plan of the building now housed at the Candie Museum in St. Peter Port is difficult to make head or tail of in the absence of a detailed explanation. The house has been called 'The Cobo Longhouse', but the plan at least is insufficient to substantiate this, although of course a longhouse is exactly what we might expect to find in the 11th or 12th centuries. Since the site was a sand-site, and partly overlaid by a modern road, it was no doubt difficult to work and necessarily incomplete: a great pity, because it would have been very valuable indeed to know whether it was a true longhouse with an entrance for men and animals in one of the long walls only; whether there was any evidence of a cross-passage; and what the exact position of the hearth was. At that time there must have been some sort of central hearth, with smoke escaping through vents in the roof, or holes at each gable end, since the fireplace and chimney were amenities which were only then appearing in the most important castles of north-western Europe. However, we shall have to wait patiently for another 'missing link' to be discovered. At present, all we can do is to infer backwards from existing structures.

In the foregoing pages we have suggested that the basic settlement pattern and house-form in the countryside of Guernsey was Celtic, introduced here from the fifth and sixth centuries onwards: and that this basic pattern was to some extent modified by the Norman seigneurs and landowners as their authority was established in the island during the 10th and 11th centuries. Parts I and II of this book will study the development of that vernacular tradition in farms and cottages from 1400 until 1787. But we must now turn to the development of St. Peter Port in the later Middle Ages and the political importance of the island during that period. For if the countryside showed the continuity of its Celtic links long after Norman domination had become complete, the more cosmopolitan atmosphere of the port and growing commercial centre of St. Peter Port was also to produce a profound influence on Town architecture and on the quality of many of the other buildings throughout the island.

Professor Le Patourel's survey, already referred to, of the fortunes of the islands at this time should be read in full for a proper understanding of the complexity of the factors involved. He shows that after the Norman invasion of England in 1066 until the islands were seized by Geoffrey of Anjou, probably in 1142, Guernsey must have been a relatively unimportant part of the Norman Empire. Although some trade no doubt still passed this way, and links with Brittany and Cornwall might have been maintained, new cross-Channel trade routes were developing between Barfleur and Southampton, and between Wissant and Dover. Estates in the island were but parts of far larger estates in Normandy and England, administration both judicial and ecclesiastical being a part of the government of church and state in the rest of the duchy. After 1153, when Geoffrey's son, Henry II of England, became ruler of an even larger Angevin Empire, its territories and dependencies extending from Scotland to Toulouse, an even smaller percentage of north-south trade passed through the islands, for it was possible to convey all goods overland except for the much shorter distances across the English Channel further east. But this state of affairs lasted for only 50 years, for the growing strength of the French kings at last enabled Philip Augustus to act against his English vassal, King John, in 1202, when all the English lands from Normandy to the north of Aquitaine were confiscated and became part of the French kingdom. Between 1202 and 1204 Guernsey and the other Channel Islands were also overrun by the French, but

INTRODUCTION 15

Fig. 3. THE ANGEVIN EMPIRE, 1153-1202

were rapidly regained by England, and their strategic value immediately recognised, to judge by the intensive programme of fortification undertaken by John. It was clear that if constant disputes about lands in France were to deprive the English of overland routes to the territories they still retained in Gascony, the establishment of a garrison in the Channel Islands and the retention of a safe harbour off a potentially hostile coast were vital. And although Jersey, being closer to France was more vulnerable, and was thus also strongly fortified, it was Guernsey's good harbour, as in earlier times, that determined its greater importance politically and commercially in the 13th to 16th centuries. For not only was it important to be able to maintain the sea route around a friendly Brittany, in order to administer Gascony and to transport an army there in times of trouble: it was also necessary to look elsewhere for a source of wine formerly imported into England from Angevin territories now lost. This gap was filled by the rapid development of the wine trade with Gascony, at first through the port of La Rochelle, but soon through Bordeaux, which, after 1224, became the chief outlet for trade with England. On the English side, the port of Southampton was the end of the long and difficult journey by ship up the French coast, around Brittany and across the Channel via Guernsey.

This was an extremely lucrative trade, both for those merchants involved, and for the Crown itself, which extracted considerable sums as customs dues at that city, and also from foreign ships using St. Peter Port.

Although there had to be major alterations in land ownership after the events of 1202-4, and island estates owned by Norman families were confiscated, there was still very considerable contact between Normandy and Guernsey for at least the next 200 years.

Ecclesiastically, too, the see of Coutances still included the Channel Islands, and French monasteries retained their estates and other interests here. The latter effectively came to an end in 1414, during the Hundred Years' War, but Guernsey remained part of the diocese of Coutances (except briefly during the Great Schism, when we were transferred to Nantes) until 1568. But to these traditional contacts with the neighbouring mainland was now added the tremendously increased contacts with Gascony and also the Mediterranean. Gascony exported wine, but had to import corn and fish from the West of England, Brittany and the Channel Islands. Some Gascon merchants settled here in order to look after their Channel Island interests, in the same way as Guernsey families in later centuries were in the habit of sending one son to Southampton or Lyme, Poole or Bristol, to supervise their affairs. The fish-drying grounds, or *éperqueries*, are known to have been a particular concern to the Gascons even as early as 1195, when Vital de Biele, a citizen of Bayonne, was farming them in Guernsey under a grant of Richard I. But the traffic through the island, recorded in various documents only in terms of campaigns or commerce, might legitimately be supposed also to have been responsible, too, for a constant interchange of ideas and skills. For the policies of the Plantagenet kings in their French dominions involved a constant struggle to retain their territories not only by force of arms but by many other inducements. One such, used by both sides, was the formation of bastide towns in the eastern parts of the Dordogne region, where the jurisdictions of the French and English kings interlocked in a puzzling fashion, and settlers in these new towns were given considerable privileges in return for their allegiance. It seems very possible that the administrative growth of St. Peter Port in the 13th and 14th centuries mirrored that of these bastide towns much more closely than that of contemporary towns in England or France. The strange proportions of the nave arcade at the Town Church and the similar ones at St. Sampson's bear a striking resemblance to the arthitecture of Montpazier and others of these bastides which possess arcaded central squares. It will also be suggested that one house in Guernsey may also show a tenuous link with a house-form common in that area (see Chapter VII).

However, the burgeoning wealth of St. Peter Port was undoubtedly reflected mostly by the development of a type of urban architecture native not to Gascony but to all the towns of northern Brittany and the boundaries of Normandy close by. No doubt there as here, the 14th- and 15th-century buildings we now see were partly rebuildings on more substantial lines of

INTRODUCTION

forms developed much earlier. How far these earlier urban forms were even more international is a matter that need not much concern us now. Clearly, during the Angevin Empire one might expect that merchants' premises in England might look much the same as those in Normandy: that houses in Lincoln and Dol might have similar characteristics. It might therefore be reasoned that Guernsey might once have had a few 12th- and 13th-century town premises such as have survived in Southampton. But until St. Peter Port produces evidence of buildings of that date the point is academic. What is of interest is that when, by the 15th century if not long before, styles had diverged; Guernsey followed the fashion of the Breton and French side of the Channel, rather than the English, though our political allegiance to England never wavered. The features of the urban architecture of St. Peter Port will be dealt with in Part III of this book. It is enough to say here that styles presumably introduced first into town houses quickly spread to the countryside, so that details of fireplaces and arches, where they have survived, in town and country can be taken as roughly contemporary.

In spite, or perhaps because, of the constant expectation of French attacks, Guernsey's prosperity steadily increased during the 400 years from 1204 to 1600, especially after the Channel Islands were declared neutral territory in time of war by a Papal Bull promulgated in 1483. From the time of Henry III, in 1254, when the future Edward I was assigned the Channel Islands, the English Crown showed a personal interest in them. No doubt this partly reflected the dues that could be collected from taxes and duties levied on shipping, but it also ensured that the welfare of the islands was the intimate concern of those in high places. Humphrey, Duke of Gloucester, fourth son of Henry IV, was Lord of the Isles in 1439, and he was succeeded by Henry Beauchamp, Duke of Warwick, known as the Kingmaker, who was crowned King of the Isle of Wight and also styled himself King of Jersey and Guernsey. He died in 1446. By that time the town's commerce was very diverse, its imports and exports affecting the whole island. This is shown by the growth of the wool trade here.

For by the end of the 15th century the exportation of home-produced knitted goods was well-established, and was to be an item of importance until the end of the 17th century. In 1740, Thomas de Havilland was granted privileges concerned with knitting, enabling him to set up a commerce with Normandy and Spain that continued for more than 100 years. Throughout the 16th century, royalty used stockings and other knitted goods produced in Guernsey. An indication of the early importance of the industry is found, too, in Pierre Bonamy's diary. He gave his daughter 12 spools of wool on the occasion of her marriage in 1505 to Thomas Carey, and his ship, *La Pitié*, carried cloth, wool and yarn for general use. Raw wool and cotton yarn was imported here throughout the next two centuries, and in return we sent away knitted and woven goods, stockings, guernseys and linen cloth. However, although the wool trade was an important item, it was the wine trade which was most vital until well into the 18th century.

Enough has been said to show that by 1600 considerable prosperity over at least 300 years must have enabled the island to build houses, both in town and country, on a scale that might seem surprising without some mention of this background. By 1621, the population, compiled from militia records, is estimated at about 9,400, of whom 3,000 lived in St. Peter Port. In 1727, the total population was 10,246. This is a very high density in a predominantly rural population, probably more than 300 per square mile, excluding St. Peter Port: and accounts for the number of houses already existing at that time. In 1615, there appear to have been 1,439 houses in the island, the number in individual parishes being as follows:

	Houses in 1615	Buildings shown on 1787 map
St. Sampson	77	122
Vale	156	226
Castel	166	300
St. Saviour	138	279
St. Andrew	151	179
St. Martin	151	284
Forest	72	149
St. Pierre-du-Bois	126	298
Torteval	55	108
Total	1,092	1,945

In 1615 there were 347 houses in St. Peter Port, and the 1787 map shows 325 separate buildings in addition to the continuous blocks of shops and houses in the centre of Town. There is no way of knowing, of course, which buildings shown on that map were barns and which were houses, but the ones that remain seem to indicate that few farms had separate, detached barns. We might expect that it will have been the smaller houses in general which have disappeared or been replaced since 1787, so that it is fair to think that about three-quarters of the total number were, in fact, houses.

It will be shown, in due course, that there was a very distinct contrast between the types of house in the town area of St. Peter Port in the 15th and 16th centuries and those outside. Chapter XIX assumes that the town walls ordered to be built by Edward III in 1350 were actually built, and that the stones placed about the town in the 18th century accurately mark the position of gates in those walls—Les Barrières de la Ville. There is, however, considerable doubt as to whether town walls, as such, did ever exist, or if garden boundary walls performed much the same function. It is certainly strange that medieval and Tudor contracts make no mention of walls as obvious boundaries. But whatever the truth of it, the sharp contrast in house types, within Les Barrières and without, certainly suggests that the distinction between the town itself and the rest of the parish was more palpable than just a legal definition.

INTRODUCTION

By 1650, if not rather before that, the town did burst through its medieval boundaries, but even in 1680, the illustrations in the survey of the islands prepared by George Legge show a distinct difference between the older centre of town and the suburbs. It also shows that, by then, most of the houses in Town were roofed with tile or slate. In 1695, thatch was forbidden in Town and tiled roofs became the rule. However, most farmhouses and cottages were thatched until well after 1800. Legge's survey, designed to strengthen the defences of the island after the destruction of the keep at Castle Cornet during a thunderstorm in 1672, spells out the importance attached at the time to the strategic significance of Guernsey. Its suitability as a base for harassing French shipping was recognised during the next 100 years by the official registration of many privateers in the island, whose profits from the capture of enemy shipping brought even greater prosperity than its legitimate trade during the 18th century. Legge refers to 'the island of Guernsey' as 'a place of great consequence, lying in the very heart of the Chanell haveing a good roade for considerable shipps'. It 'lyes off the Harbor of St. Maloes, and is by the French themselves esteemed the Key of that Port, being the best Roading without it'.

He also describes in detail the repairs necessary in Castle Cornet, the cost of £413 0s. 0d. for a two-storey house there being of particular interest. ('For a Stone house 50 foot long and 25 foot broad to be two stories high, and a Garrett, the two Lower Rooms to be for Stores and the Garrett for Provision Debouche'. The cost also included a lead cistern.) In another house, 'an Oven, 2 foot 8 inches broad and 3½ foot long to bake Bread for the Garrison', cost five pounds.

Legge's illustrations of Jersey are also enlightening, for they show a new half-timbered house, not in St. Helier, but in the countryside. In Guernsey, the use of half-timbering in 1680, or at any time after about 1400, as far as we can tell, was restricted to the gable-ends of town properties. The house in Jersey may have been an exception or we might say that as a faithful recording of architecture was not the purpose of Legge's survey, too much emphasis should not be placed on the details of his illustrations. However, his impression of St. Peter Port and Castle Cornet is extremely convincing.

At that point we shall leave this historical background. No comprehensive historical survey has been attempted here, the subject being far too complex to be compressed into such an introduction as this. Large facets of the island's development have been entirely omitted, for instance its legal and administrative arrangements, which are extremely interesting and also show how closely we have been linked with parts of France as well as England. The excuse for these omissions must be that they have been written about often enough and very ably. Although we have been very selective in the material covered so far, it is not, hopefully, a distorted picture we have shown: but will serve to emphasise the close racial, linguistic, political and ecclesiastical ties which bound Guernsey both to Brittany and Normandy in early times, as well as the more obvious strategic and trading advantages that led to its importance and wealth from the 14th century onwards. For all its trade with England, the basic style of living remained firmly rooted in its Breton origins, modified chiefly by Norman influence. All manner of materials might be imported from England, even the memorial slabs in churches, once inlaid with brasses, being of English and not Continental origin, but when it came to fashion in houses, the influence was firmly from France.

Returning to Childe's principle, not only the farmhouses, but the town houses too, show the distribution of a common type throughout the coastal towns of northern Brittany and Mont St. Michel, arguing a common origin in even older buildings than those we now see. The development of distinct characteristics in Guernsey farmhouses does not put them outside the general longhouse types of other countries: it shows a participation in a way of life where the commerce and wealth of the port played a far more intimate part in the prosperity of the countryside than elsewhere. This is to be expected in a small island community, for as we shall see, those engaged in commerce also farmed land and often lived outside St. Peter Port. Thus the conservative traditions of a farming community whose way of life went back nearly a thousand years by 1400, was enriched in a way that set its vernacular architecture apart even from the majority of Brittany, with whose culture it had nevertheless, a common origin.

Bearing all this in mind, we must now turn to the houses themselves in their scattered hamlets, surrounded by their open fields divided between neighbouring farmers, all owing dues on various fiefs, but enjoying a fair amount of independence. In Part I, from 1400-1625, the houses show Breton or Norman influence almost exclusively; in Part II, from 1625 until 1787, though French influence was still strong, the acceptance of English ideas gradually brought a decay in the vernacular tradition. Part III examines building traditions in St. Peter Port throughout the period 1400-1787; while Part IV attempts a chronology based on comparison of fireplace types, and so on. Part V deals with 11 houses in detail.

1. **Les Grandes Mielles** (966): a large 18th-century house and barns, showing early form of guillotine sashes.

2. **Le Variouf de Haut** (180): a 16th-century house, refronted 1729. Note older walling at far gable end.

3. **Le Grée, Le Gron** (436): a 15th-century single-storey longhouse, refronted, probably in 1739. Note the thatch ties.

4. **La Rocré** (598): a low-loft house, with bedroom windows under eaves almost at floor level.

5. **La Bellieuse Farm** (94): a 15th-century farmhouse with doorway added *c.* 1600.

6. **Les Reveaux** (258): a pleasing refronting in grey granite and red gneiss, probably carried out in 1751.

7. **St. George** (586): Arch with hood mould. Brought from Les Quertiers (919) in 1840, when house was refronted. Lintel above unconnected with arch.

8. **Les Blancs Bois** (576): the 17th-century entrance arch, in Cobo granite.

PART I

1400–1625

Chapter II

THE TWO-STOREY LONGHOUSE (Type 1)

BY THE 15th CENTURY, as we have seen, Guernsey, outside St. Peter Port, was divided into many hundreds of holdings, each the home of a 'yeoman' farmer. It was necessary for him to build a house where he and his family could live, his cattle could be stabled, and his produce kept under cover. Also it must be easily heated and well insulated, making best use in a small island of available fuel. Both for this reason and for purposes of construction it must be compact, using local materials as economically as possible. In fact, it was necessary to import nothing. There were beach boulders and quarried stone for building walls; clay and straw for plastering them and for puddling floors; timber for ceiling joists and roof trusses from local oak and elm—or from shipwrecks; and hand-threshed corn for thatching.

But although the need for shelter was a prime motivating force, the homestead must also exemplify the beliefs and traditions of the community. Concentration on the important features of the house, such as its doorway and its hearth, led to strong preferences in taste, a strong conservatism always at odds with the desire of an islander to be abreast of the latest fashions. Thus, although the basic way of life changed slowly, if at all, between 1400 and 1700, the expression in vernacular architecture of the prevailing styles of the time, produced very different designs as the centuries passed.

The longhouse met all these needs. It was a simple rectangle, capable of greater or lesser length depending on the requirements of individual families, but of fairly constant width. The larger houses could be as much as 42ft. long, and the smaller ones 27ft., but the width was always between 18ft. and 22ft. In Wales and Ireland, longhouses are usually single-storey dwellings, and while there are a handful of these in Guernsey, the type seems to have become developed as a two-storey house at least by the middle of the 15th century, so that these will be described first.

The essential feature of a longhouse is that, unlike any other house type, it provides under one roof, and without separate access, accommodation for man and beast. In Guernsey the invariable plan was as follows. The ground floor was divided by a cross-passage, running between roughly central front and back doorways. On either side of this cross-passage was a room, on the one hand the byre, on the other the living room or kitchen. Cattle and family used the same

THE TWO-STOREY LONGHOUSE (Type 1)

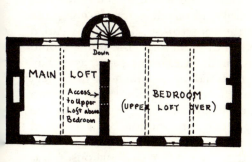

FIRST FLOOR

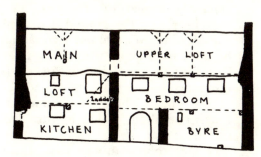

SECTION TO SHOW ARRANGEMENT OF ROOMS. Note slope towards byre end, reflected by change in floor levels upstairs.

Fig. 4. THE 5-BAY LONGHOUSE

Based on Les Belles (460)

Fenestration conjectural

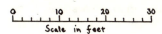

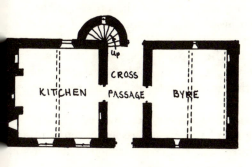

GROUND FLOOR

doorway. From the cross-passage, stairs led to a first floor, also divided into two, but with no cross-passage. Over the kitchen was an unceiled loft, open to the thatch of the roof, and over the byre was a ceiled bedroom, above which was another loft. There is no exception to this pattern in the two-storeyed longhouses of the island: kitchen with loft above, on one side of the house; byre, bedroom and loft on the other. Fig. 4 should make the arrangement clear.

Within this general framework, however, there was scope for a surprising amount of variation. There was always room for experimentation within the traditional way to build a house, and while the size of a building might depend on the number of cattle to be housed, the finish denoted the wealth of the family who lived in it. The two chief variables were the position of the main cross-wall, and the size of the byre. It is convenient to refer to the sizes of compartments in a house in terms of 'bays': a bay being the distance between one cross-beam or cross-wall and another, or between these and the gable end of the house. The byre was normally either of one or two bays, depending upon the number of animals to be housed. Very exceptionally, it was of three bays.

The kitchen was almost always of two bays, and the lofts and bedroom of either two or three. The cross-passage occupied one bay. The width of the house was chiefly governed by the sizes of timber easily obtainable for forming the cross-beams of the ground-floor ceilings and the roof trusses. The height varied considerably. Most rooms were about 7ft. high, but commonly the house would be built on a slope, with the byre at the lower end. In extreme cases, as at Fay Dell (54) or Les Bailleuls Cottage (638) there could be as much as three feet difference between the byre and the kitchen, the rooms sloping from one end to the other. Where this happened, a loss of headroom in the loft over the kitchen resulted, which in turn led to a different construction being adopted for the collar of the last roof truss. On the other hand, several houses have very high rooms, though it is arguable that these are not true longhouses, but derivatives.

The divisions between the cross-passage and the rooms on either side were sometimes of wood, sometimes of stone. In Brittany, it is common to find that longhouses have had no partition at all between the byre and the cross-passage, while in Wales, the cross-passage was often used as a feeding walk for the cattle. Guernsey houses provide no examples of this sort. There seems always to have been at least a plank division between the cross-passage and the byre. An interesting difference of construction emerges at this point between the south-eastern corner of the island and all the south and west coast parishes. In the south and west, the division between rooms is of stone, for instance at Le Marais (493), for detailed plans and elevations of which see Chapter XXXIII. Here, the main cross-wall between the kitchen and the cross-passage extends up to the ridge of the roof. But between the byre and the cross-passage, the wall terminates at bedroom ceiling level.

Taking the typical five-bay longhouse first, that is, a house with a byre of two bays, it is interesting to see what differences arise, depending upon which side of the cross-passage the main cross-wall is built. Let us assume that the cross-wall is built on the kitchen side of the cross-passage, and that the house has a tourelle staircase, as shown in Fig. 4. The main wall, running through the house from top to bottom, creates a two-bay kitchen on one side, with a loft above of the same size, while at ground-floor level on the other side, the cross-passage and byre occupy one and two bays respectively. Above them, the bedroom occupies three bays, and so does the upper loft above it. An example of this is at Les Belles (460).

But supposing the main cross-wall were built on the byre side, although the ground floor plan stays exactly the same, the main loft upstairs is now three bays long, and the bedroom and upper loft only two. De Bertrands (60) is an example of this sort.

In fact, a good many houses had two cross-walls, one on each side of the cross-passage. But in these cases, one wall, normally that on the byre side, finished at bedroom ceiling level, as at Le Marais (493). Here, at first-floor level, the bedroom

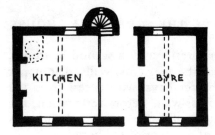 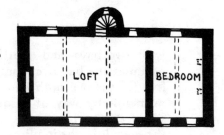

DE BERTRANDS (60)

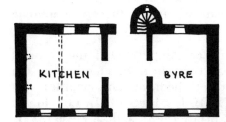 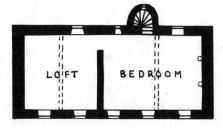

LES PAAS (233)

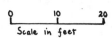

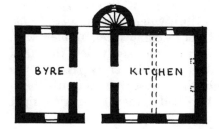 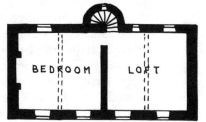

BALDERSTONE (113)

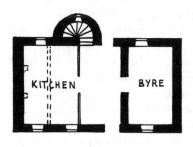 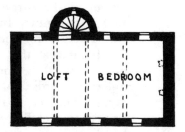

Fig. 5. LONGHOUSES — showing variable position of cross-walls: much simplified, with upstairs partitions omitted for the sake of clarity.

LA COUTURE HOUSE (893)

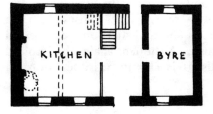 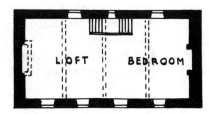

LES VILLETS (196)

is of two bays, and another unheated chamber, presumably a second bedroom, occupies the bay over the cross-passage, between the two cross-walls. The upper loft runs above both bedrooms, and is thus of three bays, with access from the main loft by way of a square opening in the cross-wall. Before restoration, the sill of this opening was provided with a good piece of stone on the side towards the main loft, the implication being that the top of a ladder rested here.

In the case of houses where the stairs are inside the cross-passage and not in a tourelle, the arrangement is either as at De Bertrands, or as at Le Marais. It is clearly not possible to contrive a three-bay bedroom unless there is a tourelle staircase.

However, the internal arrangements are further complicated if the house is of four bays—that is, if the byre is of one bay only. In most such houses, the main cross-wall is on the kitchen side, so that both bedroom and main loft can still be two bays long. This is so at Les Paas (233), Les Islets (307), Les Houets (364), L'Etiennerie (488), Wisteria (502), The Cottage (543), and La Fosse (331).

At Balderstone (113) there are two cross-walls, but that on the byre side is not carried up beyond the ground floor ceiling level, and hence does not interfere with the dimensions of the bedroom above. La Câche (314) and Le Bigard (207) are other examples. At Les Villets (196), where the only cross-wall is on the byre side, this also ceases at ground-floor ceiling level, though with internal stairs, the bedroom must always have been of one bay, unless the stairs opened into a corner of a second bay extending over the cross-passage. The same must have applied at La Câche, though the house has recently been altered. Of the two cross-walls, that on the byre side was not carried right through the house. La Couture House (893) with a tourelle, had the cross-wall on the byre side, again reaching only to ground floor ceiling level.

The position of the cross-wall is therefore clearly a determining factor in the layout of the entire house. Often quite massive in its proportions, it is obvious that 15th-century builders considered that it provided great stability, just as it was a common belief that the gable ends supported all the weight of the roof. So it was that they did not always think it necessary to bond it into the front or back walls, a somewhat disastrous mistake that has allowed many houses to bulge outwards along their whole length. We now know that a great deal of thrust from the roof bears on these walls, and just where it could in fact have helped to stabilise the structure across the centre of the house, the lack of bonding often makes the main cross-wall, for all its impressive thickness, structurally superfluous.

In the south-eastern corner of the island, and occasionally elsewhere, this fact seems to have been readily grasped, for here we find houses with no cross-walls at all. Their place is taken by a cross-beam, and divisions are created by wooden partitions slotted into these beams. Although again the ground plan is not affected by this lack of stone walls, it is clearly possible to obtain

THE TWO-STOREY LONGHOUSE (Type 1)

flexibility upstairs between the relative sizes of bedroom and loft, whether or not there is a tourelle, without all the difficulties encountered by having to negotiate the cross-wall. But since wooden walls are more often subject to renewal than stone ones, original panelling has in many houses been replaced, perhaps with later woodwork, with modern studwork, or Victorian brick walls. However, it has not been usual until the present century to remove entire stone walls when a house has been renovated, so that where none are encountered at present it can usually be inferred that the original partitions were wooden—unless there is clear evidence to the contrary. Often a comparatively modern wall has been built underneath an older beam, which would once have housed the top of the original woodwork.

If panelling has survived, it is often of great interest. For a fuller discussion, see Chapter XXIV. There is very fine oak panelling at La Rocque Balan (1007), La Maison de Haut (240), Les Granges de Beauvoir Manor (834 and Chapter XXXV), and Les Câches (237 and Chapter XXXVIII). This all dates from the 16th or early 17th century. Later panelling, of the post and panel type, sometimes known as 'in-and-out' planking, appears for instance at L'Echelle (649) or La Ville Amphrey (44), though it is perhaps better seen at Les Quertiers (676) or in 17th-century houses in St. Peter Port. Nineteenth-century tongued-and-grooved replacements are omnipresent.

While the cross-walls, or the lack of them, determined the internal layout of the longhouse, the cross-passage itself was also of great importance. For it was only by passing through this passage that access was possible between the two parts of the house downstairs, or between them and the bedroom or lofts. It was also the first part of the house seen by a guest, and was thus of some visual importance. From the practical point of view, a wide cross-passage was necessary because of the inflexibility of a cow's backbone. So it was almost always at least six feet wide and more commonly eight, to give plenty of room for manoeuvre. Particularly wide examples are at Le Marais (493) and La Maison d'Aval (241), where it is 10ft. across. The doorways into the kitchen and the byre were opposite each other, half-way along the sides of the cross-passage. This position combined the practical aspect of being half-way between front and back doors, and thus equidistant between the way outside or the way upstairs from either kitchen or byre, with the supposed advantage of allowing the cattle to see the fire—which would have been in line with both doorways and thus visible if both doors were open.

The central placing of these doorways also allowed room, though only just, for a staircase in the cross-passage itself. But a great deal more room was obtained by constructing a tourelle staircase that did not impinge on the space indoors at all. In most houses, the great width of the cross-passage also conveniently provided enough space for both back door and the tourelle door to go side by side. An inevitable exception is at Le Marais (937) where, although ample room exists for this arrangement, the tourelle opens out of an alcove at the back of the cross-passage, and pride of place, by the side of the back door, is given to a niche which would have been the first thing seen by a visitor on entering the front door. But this is a house where some considerable attention was paid to the visual appearance of the 'entry'. The oak ceiling joists of the cross-passage are very finely moulded, some having rosettes reminiscent of a Tudor rose on their undersides.

Another house with a niche, or bénitier, opposite the front door is La Forge (509). Here, a much finer recess occupies the unusually large space between back doorway and tourelle doorway. More will be said about the tourelle of this house in Chapter XXVIII. The usual position for a bénitier inside a cross-passage is on the front wall, next to the front door. Usually it is an integral part of the doorway arch. A bénitier in such a position necessitates the front door being offset to one side or other of the passage, rather than being placed centrally. Where a doorway is offset but there is no bénitier apparent, it may well be that one lurks below the plaster, or that it has at some time been removed.

As we have seen in our introductory survey, the land attached to each farm in the island was very small and constantly subject to partage between sons and daughters on a father's death. In most cases it provided enough pasture for only a few animals. Consequently, many longhouses were constructed to house only a maximum of five animals in the byre, and in the Brouard house at Les Islets (though the living end of the house had not been inhabited for many years), five cows could be tethered facing the gable wall, using rings let into a plank set about three feet off the ground and running right across the wall. A drain then ran across the byre from back to front, and out through a hole in the front wall, underneath the window inserted in the 19th century.

The original ventilation 'slit' or byre window—termed 'le pour' in Brittany— survives blocked with brick, to the right of the inserted window. Similar drainage arrangements have been noted at Les Queux (555) and Les Blicqs (610), in each case the hole being in the front wall. Byre windows remain in many houses. At Le Marais (493), the front elevation on page 240-1 clearly shows two such windows blocked with stone, the 17th-century parlour window opening having been inserted between them. In most cases, however, modernisation of the house when a separate stable was built for the animals in the 17th, 18th or 19th centuries, involved the destruction of the byre window. It was clearly simpler to enlarge an existing opening than to create a new one. They have survived at Le Marais because what is now the front of the house was originally the back, and in the 17th century it became fashionable to have only one window in the back wall of each room, with two in the front. At Les Islets, the window remains because it was clearly too close to the gable to fit into any regular façade envisaged in the 19th century. At Les Blicqs the tiny window next to the back door has been partially blocked with brick until it now resembles an arrow-slit. There must have been just such a window in the front wall of the byre at Le Marais (937), since there is no sign of any window at all at the back. A modern doorway now

THE TWO-STOREY LONGHOUSE (Type 1)

occupies this position, but the adjoining barn, built on at right-angles to the house, is early 19th century, arguably older than the doorway, and seems to have been constructed so as not to obscure the vanished byre window. If Les Blicqs were originally entirely without an opening in the front wall, it is easy to see why a total re-fronting was undertaken in 1720, though at some stage there has been an unusual central opening, now blocked, in the byre gable end. Only at Les Islets has a byre window survived at the front of a house, though it is likely that other such blocked openings may from time to time be revealed as 19th-century—or later—rendering is removed from façades.

However, at the back of a house they have frequently been recorded. At La Madeleine (306), the window was found during alterations. It had been blocked up, complete with its central oak bar, when a Victorian lean-to had been put along the back of the house. At Malator (892) the tiny window was in the process of being enlarged into a serving hatch in 1979, while at L'Echelle (649), the original byre window was no more than nine inches high by six inches across. Such windows would never have been glazed. In bad weather it is possible that an internal shutter may have been provided, as with other windows in the house, but if so, no evidence has survived.

The walls of the byre were left unplastered. Between the stones, some houses might have large knuckle bones built in, for hanging harness, and many small recesses, or keeping-places, were provided for placing a light or for setting down any other object that would otherwise be trampled underfoot or lost in the straw and muck on the floor.

The floor itself was of *terre battue,* or puddled clay, laid by wetting the clay until it obtained a pudding-like consistency, treading it across the room until it became fairly dense, and then levelling it off. The resulting surface was surprisingly durable, with a semi-polished look, so that it was quite possible to sweep a room without the *terre battue* breaking down.

The byre ceiling, if it were of one bay, would originally have been constructed with roughly-cut branches spaced about a foot apart and running between the cross-walls or cross-beams and the gable end. Rather than letting these joists into a cross-wall or a gable end, they were usually supported by another timber running against the wall, in turn resting on a number of small corbel stones. Then across the joists would have been laid smaller sticks, then a matting of reed, and finally the bedroom floor, again of *terre battue.* The only relic we have of this technique is at Le Gron Farm (435), where a much later cart entrance is covered in this way (see Illustration 38).

Floorboards have everywhere superseded this medieval arrangement, but it is interesting to compare this humble method of providing an earth floor upstairs before boards were easily produced—having to be sawn by hand from comparatively wide timbers more efficiently used elsewhere—with the floors of French châteaux, where baked clay tiles were laid straight onto the closely-spaced floor joists below.

Headroom in the byre was frequently lower than in the kitchen end. This had the effect of allowing space for fairly large windows in the side walls of the bedroom above by the simple expedient of lowering the bedroom floor, rather than by building the side walls higher all along the house, when the lighting of the main loft at the other end was not necessary. However, subsequent levelling up of the ground floor in most cases where the house was built on a slope, often exaggerates the lack of headroom in a byre that originally just followed the lie of the land.

If it was possible to build the house on a slope, the byre was commonly at the lower end, as it always is in Welsh longhouses. This ensured that when 'mucking out', the drainage did not run away in front of the main entrance and past the kitchen. Les Bailleuls Cottage (638) and Fay Dell (54) are extreme examples of this practice. But it was not the invariable rule. For instance, Les Queux (555) is built into a fairly steep slope, but the byre is at the upper end, partly underground. In Brittany, it is clear that the demands of elementary hygiene were not a consideration, and indeed in many of our longhouses, especially those built on the level, it can be assumed that in the absence of a separate drain, the byre was swept out through the cross-passage.

It is likely that nearly all of our four-bay houses were built as longhouses with a one-bay byre, although certainly a few later two-storey buildings, such as Les Issues (440), of four bays only and dating from the latter half of the 17th century, were unlikely ever to have been used for housing cattle. With five-bay houses, it is more difficult to be precise. Later alterations have so changed many of them, and particularly at the byre end, that no evidence at all remains. However, it can be fairly assumed that all houses that retain any of the other features of a longhouse did at one time have a byre. There is equally no way of discovering the arrangement of stalls in a two-bay byre. At Les Câches (190), where the entire house is now used for cattle, it can be seen that there is not enough width to have cows along both side walls, but there is room for calf-boxes and dairy.

Tradition persists in strange ways. We have already noted that after the family had left Les Islets for a grander house next door, cattle were kept in the byre, but not in the former kitchen; that was used for hay. At Le Clos de Bas (264), the byre has never been used as living accommodation. Instead, another doorway was created in the front wall, c. 1900, to give separate access, and the byre was used first as a horse stable, and then as a general store. The back of the byre was partitioned off, an opening created in the gable wall, and a 'modern' kitchen built against the original house. So the family lived with the stable almost in the middle of the house, the new kitchen on one side and the old kitchen, now a parlour, on the other.

Thus the byre was an integral part of the house, and, occupying half of the ground floor, might be regarded as of equal importance to the living room. Clearly, it was perfectly natural for a medieval farmer to consider his livestock as a sort of extended family. Then, the farmyard and the farmhouse were all part of the same community. A man lived with his children around him, and his parents; if necessary with his mother-in-law as well. Equally, he lived with his livestock at similarly close quarters. Just as the cattle were housed under the same roof, and were cheered, albeit at a distance, by the same fire, so the pigs and the hens pecked and rooted where they could around the farmyard, unenclosed, able to find some food for themselves and very much an integrated part of the farmstead. Such a way of life has been re-visited by the author only this year (1980) at Choucan-em-Paimpont, a tiny hamlet in the Forêt de Broceliande, in Brittany. Here, the unity of the countryside was still intact. Around a farmstead which might very well have been in Guernsey, roamed, as they pleased, the farm animals, moving, when they were in the way, but otherwise undisturbed by the intrusion of visitors. Opposite the front door, in a row, were the huge *chaudron* or *bashin,* cooking the pigswill over a wood fire; the outside bread oven, still used when a large meal was to be cooked; and the muck heap. The *grenier* or granary was over the kitchen; a barn at the back contained barrels of cider, made on the farm each year. And the inhabitants, alert and contented, might be illiterate, but were quite capable of running the business side of a youth hostel.

Here, in this little hamlet, two ways of life confronted each other. For just around the back of this 16th-century farmhouse, the son had built himself a fine new 'Breton' house. Reared up upon its subterranean garage, the countryside was surveyed at a distance. Certainly it was a wider view, an educated view, but the unity of the countryside was broken. A great barrier between man and beast was established. No longer could an inquisitive animal come and look in, for a minute, over a half door, before being shooed away. When pigs are in pigsties, cows in separate sheds, chickens in mucky pens (or worse), they become just a compartment of a farmer's life. Only when animals are at a sufficient distance, perhaps, are we so sentimental about them that we become vegetarians. Equally, perhaps, when our mothers-in-law are comfortably installed elsewhere, can we afford to become sentimental and patronising towards the elderly.

However, in medieval life, this dichotomy was not apparent. In everyday living, Chaucer's *Nun's Priest's Tale* with its evocation of life as it was in a 14th-century cottage, and as it is still lived in Choucan, is borne out in Guernsey by the will of Pierre Bonamy, who built the house at Les Câches Farm (112) in 1498. Furniture, livestock, clothes and jewellery are equally important and listed in an indiscriminate order, all part of his life, even though his prosperity depended mostly on his shipping and trading interests.

For the family, the kitchen was the communal living-room. It was dominated by the large open fireplace, *la grande cheminée*, built at the gable end. This fireplace was almost always a particularly splendid piece of design, reflecting the wealth and taste of the owner and perhaps bearing his arms on its lintel. It will be dealt with in detail in Chapter XXVII. Its size, often exceeding seven feet across, was not in order to accommodate an enormous blaze, though no doubt this was enjoyed on festive occasions, but to provide space for two or three small fires simultaneously, each cooking the contents of one pot. Of course, when a meal was not being prepared, only one fire would be maintained. The efficiency of such a fireplace is greater than might be supposed and may be experienced by a visit to one of the houses at St. Fagan's Folk Museum, near Cardiff, when the fire is lit. A large hood collected smoke from the fire, without concentrating the draught or making it burn too fiercely, and without creating an uncomfortable flow of air across any one part of a room, such as often happens with smaller, Victorian grates. At the same time, while the fire was alight, no cold air could come down the chimney, so that a fair amount of heat was dispersed on all three sides of the large hearth.

There was no bread oven associated with these hearths. No 'furze' oven, or *grand four,* in any Guernsey house is earlier than the 17th century, nor was it ever a part of French tradition to do the baking indoors. Baking was either done in a separate oven outdoors, or in earlier times, more usually in pots, directly over the fire.

Within the fireplace were usually one or two small recesses. In these would be kept the salt and no doubt anything else which needed to remain warm and dry. A much larger keeping place was often provided to one side of the fireplace, usually at the side which was towards the front of the house, leaving room for a bed to stand in the other corner, towards the back. This larger niche was square-headed, and in the nature of a cupboard, but without doors in its original form. Another such niche is usually found in the cross-wall, to one side or other of the kitchen door, and is also almost square but rather smaller than the one in the gable end. In some houses, a proliferation of keeping places occurs. At Les Queux (555), there are several in the cross-wall, and one in almost every window splay, not only in the kitchen, but everywhere else in the house. At Les Granges de Beauvoir Manor (834) and Le Variouf de Haut (180) they take the form of pigeon-holes, two above and two below. The need for such a large number of built-in storage places was due partly to a lack of furniture, and partly no doubt in order to leave the room uncluttered so that there was as much space as possible available for family and friends to use. Objects could also be put out of reach of children and dogs, and off the beaten earth floor.

The front wall of the kitchen would contain two windows, sometimes large, sometimes small, again depending on the family's means and their tastes. Where they bore arms and wished to impress neighbours, the lintels of these windows might well display a shield, as in the chamfered lintel bearing arms now lying neglected at the side of Burton's in the High Street. Another lintel with a shield has been re-used upside-down in a re-fronting of 1725, at La Maison Guignan (92), a superb house at present in a very sorry state. More magnificent than all of these, however, is the early 16th-century lintel now displayed in the garden at St. George (586). Its central mullion is preserved inside the old house. In an elaborate design, a double accolade is surmounted by swirls and a garland enclosing a coat

THE TWO-STOREY LONGHOUSE (Type 1)

of arms, showing Renaissance influence. It probably came from the house demolished soon after the present large house was built in 1824, and it equals any of the workmanship to be found in the larger houses of the Norman-Breton borders.

At Carriaux Cottage, in Candie Road, St. Andrew's, the finest 15th-century window we possess has been built into a gable wall (see Illustration 61). It is particularly interesting, in that it more closely resembles the English Perpendicular style than the Flambuoyant that dominated French architecture of the period. It consists of a four-light window, the upper lights with ogee heads, and is divided by stone mullion and transoms. This window, as well as a fine fireplace, whose corbel bore a large head, was illustrated by F. C. Lukis, in 1845, in the Sarre House between Les Adams and L'Erée, in St. Peter's. The fireplace corbel has vanished (see Illustration 47).

Even older are the two window heads at Casa Seda (896), in the Water Lanes, St. Peter Port, and the one now over the front door of the cottage at La Haye du Puits (583). The former has a fine ogee roll-mould, the point terminating in a cusp enclosing a head. It is from the first part of the 15th century. On this lintel, a shallow arch forms a sort of tympanum, enclosing a head in low relief very similar to those found in Jersey.

It cannot be too often emphasised that although such ornamentation was undoubtedly the prerogative of the more wealthy, the type of house in which they lived would have differed only in finish from those of their humbler neighbours. As in Brittany, where many a *petit seigneur* was no more than a yeoman farmer, so in Guernsey, a family's position in society might well be indicated by such ornament, while their everyday life differed little from that of other folk. So much for the kitchen windows. In Brittany, the *pour* or ventilation slit of the byre was often chamfered like the windows of the kitchen or bedroom. This does not occur in Guernsey.

In Brittany and in Wales the invariable practice was for the *lit clos,* or cupboard bed, to be placed at the back angle of the kitchen next to the fire. Very probably in Guernsey houses some members of the family might still have slept downstairs in this way, leaving the bedroom upstairs for the head of the household. It cannot be a coincidence that in the 18th and 19th centuries, this angle, at the side of the fireplace, was the position where the Guernsey green bed or *joncquière* always stood. However this may be, while the front wall of the kitchen usually had two windows, lighting the central table—*la table de cuisine*— the back wall commonly had none, or only one, giving room not only for a bed, but for the kitchen sink.

This kitchen sink, commonly called *un évier* in Brittany, was rather different from what we associate with a sink, but nevertheless fulfilled the same function. Only at The Elms, Pleinheaume (946) and at La Rocque Balan (1007) is there any kind of trough. Usually the évier consisted of a large round-headed or square-headed recess, more or less the height of the room, about 30ins. across and 12ins. deep, and with a large slab of stone forming a shelf at waist height. Below this shelf is a smaller, splayed recess, whose stone base slopes to form a drain through the wall. The drain itself, where it pierces the wall, is usually only about three inches in diameter, and on the outside, a small dripstone is sometimes provided, as at La Ville Amphrey (41). Such holes have, of course, been blocked in later times to discourage vermin, always by a small stone which is indistinguishable from the rest of the wall outside. Clearly the 'slop-stone', as it was vividly called in parts of southern England, had provision for a bowl to stand on the shelf, and allowed waste water to be disposed of below without having to carry the bowl to the back door. Twenty-five round-headed éviers survive and 17 square-headed ones. These are not to be confused with bénitiers. In no instance does any kitchen sink possess a drainage channel in its shelf, as most bénitiers have, nor is it so highly ornamented.

Indeed, our éviers are usually simpler constructions than those found in Brittany. But we have four and perhaps five examples of the usual Breton type in Guernsey. The most elaborate of these is at Le Frie (303). Under a large arch of dressed stone there are slots for two wooden shelves, and below them, a stone shelf on each side with a central drain between. This must have combined the function of kitchen dresser with that of a kitchen sink. Fortunately, when half of this building was pulled down in the 19th century and replaced by a really fine house at right-angles whose façade has few rivals in the country parishes, the kitchen was retained as the back kitchen for the new house and so this splendid évier has survived. A very similar one is at 5 Berthelot Street (808), and a slightly less ambitious one, though still with a slot on each side for a shelf, is at St. George (586). Another nicely-fashioned one is at Les Grands Courtils (388). It is possible that the arched recess at La Grande Maison (945), was once another kitchen sink of this sort, in which case it would have been alongside the fireplace as at Berthelot Street, but it is equally possible that in this house, and very likely at Les Quertiers (919) and Le Tertre (1026), the sink recess was broken through to provide access to a back kitchen added early in the 17th century, by which time this medieval arrangement had presumably gone out of fashion, since no other similar provision seems to have been made in any of these three well-preserved houses.

Although these éviers were almost invariably in the back wall of the kitchen, some exceptions to this rule occur. In what is listed in the First Schedule as Type 3 houses (see Chapter 4), the tourelle, the back window, and sometimes the bénitier as well, often occupy the entire back wall. The sink is therefore sometimes found in the front wall, as at Bordeaux House (984). Elsewhere in a few longhouses of standard type, it is found in the cross-passage. This is so at La Ville Amphrey (41) and at Rocquaine Villa, Le Coudré (285), while at La Houguette (321) it occupies an extraordinary position at the back of the cross-passage next to the tourelle, which is built behind it. This position necessitated an enormously elaborate drain, six feet long, constructed like a miniature passage tomb and curving slightly to the right so that it eventually

THE TWO-STOREY LONGHOUSE (Type 1)

emerged out of the side of the tourelle. When either the back or the front door of the house was so close at hand, it does seem strange that an évier was constructed in the cross-passage at all. At La Houguette, one can hardly avoid thinking that they just liked building drains, and what practical considerations dictated this particular positioning we shall never know, since the rest of the house was almost entirely reconstructed in the 19th century.

So much for the different niches and recesses in the kitchen. In some houses, the keeping place in the gable was discarded in favour of a gable window, on one side or other of the fireplace. At Les Adams de Haut (326), La Bellieuse Farm (94), and La Porte (480), for instance, it is on the left; at La Maison d'Aval (241), Cobo Farmhouse (596) and New Place, Petit Bouet (904), on the right; while Les Grands Courtils (388), Les Grands Moulins (505), and La Villette (123) have a window each side of the fireplace.

We must now consider the bedroom. This, the only other heated chamber in the house, was usually at the opposite end of the house from the kitchen, so that the fireplace could be supported on the other gable wall. Only at La Maison d'Aval (241) is the bedroom fireplace immediately above the kitchen. Usually, the upstairs fireplace was slightly smaller than the downstairs one, mostly because it would not have been necessary in the bedroom to have more than a single small fire burning at a time. By having a smaller fireplace, it was also easier to construct the tapering chimney hood above, and to reduce it to a size where it could run into the thickness of the wall, which in turn could then support the weight of the chimney, if it were of stone. In many 16th- and early 17th-century houses where the kitchen chimney hood seems to have been of wattle-and-daub, in order to avoid supporting the great weight of a stone hood, the bedroom one was still of stone, being, of course, only half the height. This was so at Les Fontaines (544)—where a third fireplace and chimney are a later insertion—and can perhaps best be seen at present (1980) at Les Blicqs (610), where both chimneys are complete. The bedroom hood was of stone, but the wattle-and-daub construction of the kitchen chimney hood once supported a circular clay chimney, such as still exists at La Ronde Cheminée (929), and is of great interest. However, see p. 188 for an alternative explanation of the wattle-and-daub-hood.

Fireplaces inserted or rebuilt after c. 1625 always have a wattle-and-daub hood. In the valet's quarters at La Houguette (528) it is very clear that an original stone hood has been supplanted by one of wattle-and-daub. The stones bonding the original into the gable end now project all down the side of the 'new' hood, whereas the supports for a wattle-and-daub hood would have taken the form of pairs of stones inserted through the wall at four or five foot intervals. These support stones, and the great shoulder stones of the fireplaces themselves, frequently project outside beyond the line of the gable, and have become known locally as 'witches' seats', but as usual, there was a rather more practical reason for their existence. Their function was to support the weight of the chimney hood, stone or otherwise, and in order to achieve this, they often extended through the entire thickness of the gable wall, so that they obtained the maximum stability. The two shoulder stones recently removed to Les Queux (555) from Les Hêches (446) were six feet long. In choosing the stones for this job, it was no doubt considered better to allow one to project on the outside, if it happened to be a little longer than the other one of the pair—since they must each project exactly the same amount inside—rather than risk breaking too much of the stone by trying to shorten it by a few inches. And maybe a witch would perch there anyway.

Inside the bedroom in many houses, the fireplace, central in the gable wall, might be flanked on either side by a window such as we have noted in the kitchen, or even by an évier, part window and part shelf, as at Bordeaux House (984). In addition, some early houses had a shelf built high up on one or both sides of the fireplace, obviously designed for ornament as well as use. A pillar type of fireplace was often chosen for the bedroom, though, unfortunately, very few have survived *in situ*.

In other respects, too, trouble was taken to make the bedroom, or *chambre*, as attractive and comfortable as possible. From the outside of the house, you could see how highly it was regarded by the comparative grandeur of the window, even at the back of the house. Sometimes, as at La Houguette (528), De Bertrands (60) or Le Grée (125) it would be exceptionally wide: sometimes adorned with a moulded sill, as at Saints Farm (83) and Les Tilleuls (563). Simpler sills exist at Le Chêne Cottage (154), and crude ones at La Villette (124), Le Grée and Le Catillon de Bas (292). The re-positioned sills at La Pompe (117) are similar to the one at Saints Farm, and are illustrated by F. C. Lukis (*c*. 1850) before this house was rebuilt, in 1863, when they were possibly re-cut. Another illustration among Lukis's papers shows the de Havilland house at La Fosse, St. Martin's, where the upper windows had even more elaborate sills. In some houses, the bedroom window might have a little window seat incorporated on either side of the wide-splayed opening. One of these has survived at Le Douit Farm Flats (499), almost identical to La Logis Tiphaine at Mont St. Michel.

The gable windows too might also have moulded sills, as at La Forge, King's Mills (509). But the upstairs gable window in the derelict house above La Bigoterie in Berthelot Street (815), like the kitchen one at La Bellieuse Farm (94) is not only undecorated, but appears to make no provision for glazing, though very probably diamond-shaped panes of leaded lights would have been clipped on to the outside of the window-frame, as in the window recently uncovered at La Forge, La Croix des Marchez (221) or that of horn found *c*. 1962 at Les Marchez (218). Most windows would in fact have been glazed by 1500, certainly in almost all the houses that have survived. After all, men who could afford to import stone from Chausey or from France for their front door arch and their fireplace, would also have afforded the sort of glass, perhaps on a humbler scale, that they donated to their parish church to the greater glory of God.

As for furnishings, by 1500, the more prosperous families seem to have possessed the sort of four-poster bed which we would recognise today. But while for some households the bedroom might well have been regarded also as the equivalent of the earlier castle 'bower', where the ladies could escape the proximity of the farmyard and sit sewing or weaving without so much of the hustle and bustle of the household about them, for many other families less well-off, the bedroom would rather have been partly an extra storeroom, as well as a place to sleep.

Inventories of the period, quoted in *The English Farmhouse and Cottage* (M. W. Barley), list all manner of items which we would hardly expect to find in a bedroom. There might very well be an odd chest with a cross-bow and breastplate rather than a gown, not to mention a sack of corn or spare scythe for which, for some reason, there was no room in the loft.

The bedroom ceiling was constructed in the same way as others in the house. The main beam, or *pouttre,* supported the lateral joists, which until the end of the 17th century always ran over it. Only where floors and ceilings have been replaced, from the 18th century onwards, are the lateral joists notched into the main beams. Above them was the planking of the upper loft floor.

A most interesting form of insulation, laid above this planking, has survived in a handful of houses. For not only was the bedroom kept warm by the heat generated from the animals in the byre below, and by the fireplace in the chamber itself, it was also insulated above by a three-inch layer of beaten earth made of puddled clay and straw laid on top of the planking. In this way the entire house was lined by a thick and efficient layer of clay. There were beaten earth floors; thick layers of clay plastered on the walls; and, finally, this layer overhead, laid on the planking of the loft floors, or the bedroom ceilings. It remains at the single-storey house at Le Tertre (601), and the two-storey houses at Les Issues (440), La Ruette (406), and Les Hamelins (294). However, Le Tertre and Les Issues are later houses continuing an earlier tradition.

A second, but unheated, chamber upstairs is created in some houses by the carrying up of the two stone cross-walls through the first floor. Presumably this was another sleeping-place, but it might equally have been used as a separate store for some particular crop or equipment. The structure gives no clue as to its use, and, of course, whatever its original purpose, it invariably served in later years as an extra bedroom.

The window in the upstairs passage, between the tourelle and the bedroom, is of all the windows in the house, the one most likely to have survived unaltered. Insignificant in size as it is, by the standards of later centuries, it was clearly thought unnecessary by 18th- and 19th-century improvers to alter or enlarge it. Early 15th-century frames remain at Les Câches (237) and La Rocque Balan (1007), while at Les Blicqs (610), there is an unglazed window, with diagonal oak mullion, which may have had leaded lights, or simply been closed by a shutter on the inside.

The last parts of the longhouse to consider are the two lofts. The main loft was over the kitchen, and from it there was access by steps or by ladder, into the upper loft. The only house where this layout has remained unchanged is Le Marais (937) at Baubigny, though another Le Marais (493), at Le Gélé, clearly showed the same arrangement before restoration in 1979. At L'Echelle (649) and Le Bigard (205) the main loft also remains unchanged. It would probably be more correct to refer to this main loft as *le grenier,* for it is to this use that it is still put in many parts of Brittany. But although chiefly a store for grain, it would undoubtedly be used for other things, though not as a furze loft. The storage of furze under cover was not necessary until the building of indoor bread ovens, from about 1700 onwards, and by this time both corn from the granary and animals from the byre had been moved out of the house into other farm buildings.

Direct access to the main loft or granary was never through the gable end. The gable end openings are always later insertions—often demonstrably so because of the brick used at their sides—or are to be found in later houses, and always associated with the storage of furze. The original access was at the front or back of the house, through an opening the size of a modern window at the level of the loft floor. A good example of this, adapted as a window, is at the Brouard House at Les Islets (307), where it is to be hoped that building regulations will be flexible enough to ensure its retention when the house is restored. Another example at the back of the house, still with its door, is at Le Bigard. There are naturally few other survivors, for later conversion of the loft into a bedroom has obliterated all but a handful.

The most noticeable feature of this main loft, open to the thatch—or later the pantiles—of the roof, is the great hood of the kitchen fireplace, tapering as it reaches the base of the chimney. In some houses it tapered very rapidly and then continued up almost straight, as did both hoods at Bordeaux House (984), one now unfortunately removed, and one at Le Grée (125). A single-storey house whose hood is of this shape is La Forge (924). Other, possibly later, houses, taper more continuously. The hoods at Le Catillon de Bas (292) and Les Villets (196) were of this second type. Both have been recently removed. Others remain at the Old Farm (925) and La Rocque Balan (1007).

Overhead, the truss is often of a different construction from those in the remainder of the roof. Elsewhere, an upper cruck with collar and upper kingpost and windbraces, was the common design, or later the simple 'A' frame, the upper sides of the triangle being morticed and pinned with wooden dowels. But over the main loft the base of the triangle was omitted. Instead, the thrust of the roof was transferred on to the walls and the truss prevented from spreading by a cleat carried down the inside face of the wall. A collar sometimes supported a kingpost with windbraces, as at La Porte (479), but kingpost and windbraces are

THE TWO-STOREY LONGHOUSE (Type 1)

normally absent, as at Le Marais (493), La Bouvée Farm (24), Les Bailleuls Cottage (638), and many other places. Especially where the floor of the loft was higher than that of the bedroom, to give headroom in the kitchen, and the eaves consequently lower, this simple variation of the roof trusses gave more freedom of movement, more headroom perhaps for winnowing, and more unencumbered storage space.

The upper loft, approached, as we have seen, by ladder through the opening in the main cross-wall or by steps from the main loft, was presumably an area where storage was available for those items which were not constantly needed, since they were that much more inaccessible. However, a photograph of Les Naftiaux (665), taken *c.* 1900, shows an 'eye-brow' opening under the thatch, giving direct access by ladder to the upper loft from the back of the house. How many such openings were lost when the irregularities of a thatched roof were replaced by the straight lines of the now ubiquitous pantiles and slate, it is impossible to say. In single-storey houses that once had no internal access to their lofts, a great many such openings have certainly been swept away by re-roofing and such access replaced by later staircases indoors.

Otherwise, the upper loft was just a smaller version of the main one, but its ventilating slits, either side of the bedroom chimney hood, a little higher than at the other end of the house, in order to be above the bedroom ceiling.

Outside, the two-storey longhouse would have differed in many ways from the same houses that we now see around us. Most of them have been altered, often with loving care and attention to detail, over the centuries, into homes now boasting far more living rooms and bedrooms than their builders ever intended. More about such alterations will be said in Chapter VI. These alterations have chiefly affected the façade and of all the early houses now left to us, The Old Farmhouse at La Mare (928) most preserves its ancient appearance (see Illustration 6). Irregular window openings, much wider than they are high, look very strange to us, used as we are to thinking of the 'traditional' Guernsey house complete with all its inserted and enlarged windows. Another building disused as a house, possibly when King's Mills' Farm was erected beside it in the 16th century, is the barn in King's Mills (505), whose gable abuts the main road. The low lines of the roof and the meagre window openings are typical of the proportions of an early 15th-century house. Upstairs, at the back, an original oak window frame has survived. At Cobo Farmhouse (596), known to have been built before 1470,

Fig. 6. COBO FARMHOUSE (596)
showing irregular window arrangement. Later additions omitted and stonework of gable conjectural.

the windows clearly show the different ceiling heights of kitchen and byre, loft and bedroom.

A longhouse roof would have been thatched with hand-threshed corn. After this was unobtainable in Guernsey early this century, it was brought over from Sark, but now no house is thatched, and the one remaining thatched barn at Duvaux Farm (936) is rapidly falling into disrepair. In some houses, for instance at La Maison D'Aval (975), projecting stones on front or back walls, often at different heights so that the ropes could be interlaced, show how the thatch was tied down to protect the roof from damage in high winds. Similarly, the gable ends were protected by stone copings, rising above the thatch, which would have been attached to them by a flashing of clay plaster. Around the granite chimneys more 'witches' seats' are actually dripstones, projecting from the granite stacks so that the thatch is pinned underneath them and the rain running down the stack is directed onto the surface of the roof. There is a unique set of dripstones at La Maison des Pauvres (308) where a row was built into the gable to cover the roofing of the lower and later house adjoining. The ridge of the roof would have been sealed either by a heavy layer of clay, or more probably—as often in Normandy still—by a sod ridge; that is, a layer of turfs cut and placed over the apex of the thatch. Such a 'roof garden' may sound comical, but is really quite practical, for the ridge, far from letting the rain in, depends upon it in order to grow, but, of course, being grass, sends out only shallow roots that cause no damage to the timbers underneath.

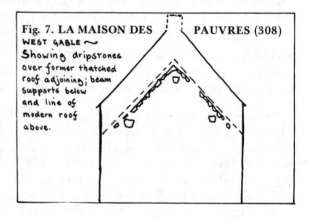

Fig. 7. LA MAISON DES PAUVRES (308) WEST GABLE — Showing dripstones over former thatched roof adjoining; beam supports below and line of modern roof above.

The chimney stacks would usually have been fairly low and built mostly in Cobo stone. Many of the taller, grey stone stacks we see now are later replacements from the 18th or early 19th centuries, though some are undoubtedly older, for instance those of Les Granges de Beauvoir Manor (834), from about 1600. La Houguette (528) has no fewer than five stone chimneys remaining, apparently from the same period. No doubt a good many of the brick stacks built in the 19th century, often when thatch gave way to pantiles or slates, replaced quite humble stacks of clay. Two of these have survived, at La Ronde Cheminée (929) and La Moye (999), while the base of another has already been noted at Les Blicqs. There is an old photograph of another in an old house at Le Mont Saint, now demolished. (See Illustration 76.) The front door arch from this house is now built into La Jaonière, just below the dam of St. Saviour's reservoir. Circular chimneys were also built in stone. There is a fine one at Les

THE TWO-STOREY LONGHOUSE (Type 1)

Fontaines (544), and there was one at La Vieille Sous L'Eglise (475) which has now been replaced by a prefabricated one of curious shape.

From a distance, the 15th-century farmhouse would have appeared to lean inwards, the 'batter' of the walls being due to their tapering from a minimum of 2ft. 6ins. at the base, where they rested on a row of huge boulders placed on the levelled ground, to about 1ft. 6ins. at the top, this construction giving considerable strength and stability. The roof, because of the thatch, would have been very steeply pitched, at between 45degs. and 55degs. from the horizontal and the walls would have been left as natural stone, unplastered and without any colour wash. By the front or back door was often a large stone, such as F. C. Lukis's papers illustrated at La Contrée de Saint (69), c. 1850, and such as still exists at Le Marais (493—see Chapter XXXIII). This might well have served any purpose from killing the pig to scrubbing the washing.

Usually at the back of the house was the well. Most of the well-heads that can still be seen are 18th- or 19th-century replacements or covers to wells formerly open. At many houses, the proximity of the well to the back door has enabled the builder of a later back kitchen to enclose the water supply, which has then been connected to a pump. At La Houguette (528) is a superb grouping of well-head, with shelves on which to stand a pail or jug, a trough for watering the animals and alongside it a huge scrubbing stone (see Illustration 13).

Around the farmyard there might also have been a number of temporary buildings, constructed entirely of timber, with thatched roofs and sides, such as those still surviving in the La Grande Brière region of Brittany. These simple, but effective shelters would have provided room for additional stores and stables. Long since replaced by stone buildings, they would have surrounded the yard as the present stables do at Les Câches (see Illustration 1); but always dominated by the longhouse itself.

Such, then, was the most widespread type of house built in Guernsey between 1425 and 1625. That all the houses still remaining on the Fief Le Comte and the Fief Blanchelande, which date from before 1470 and 1488 respectively, are of this type, a fully-developed two-storey longhouse, indicates the great prosperity of this island in the 15th and 16th centuries. Nowhere else does the longhouse so consistently attain this form, and where related examples occur in Brittany, they are from the very end of the period.

Chapter III

THE LONGHOUSE (Type 2)

INEVITABLY, it is misleading to draw conclusions about the numbers and types of houses existing, say, in 1450, or in 1650, from a survey done in 1980, which is why there are no distribution maps in this book. There may well have been a far greater variety of house types then standing than now remain. There is no way of knowing. More than half the buildings shown on the 1787 map have since been lost or rebuilt, and in only a very few instances do we know what those buildings were. But where we do, they seem almost invariably to have been two-storey houses, and of the longhouse type. The First Schedule lists 286 houses with clear evidence of a byre existing, or which closely resemble in other ways those where such evidence has survived. Although some of these may in fact be one stage removed from a true longhouse, as will be explained in Chapter VI, there is no way of proving this and they date from the period when the longhouse was almost universal in the countryside, that is from about 1400 to about 1625.

From the same period, just 11 single-storey dwellings remain. It is tempting to argue that a one-storey longhouse must be a more primitive type and therefore earlier than a two-storey one, and while this conclusion is indeed logical there is no evidence to support it in any of the buildings that we can see. Neither arches nor fireplaces seem to be of any earlier pattern than those which can be found in their somewhat grander neighbours. So either there was, in fact, no progression in the island from the one-storey longhouse so popular in Brittany, Wales and Ireland to those two-storey ones we have just been examining, both sorts always being known, but the one vastly more popular than the other: or else there was a time when the single-storey type was universal and what we have left are just a handful, perhaps built when the style was already becoming unfashionable, the only survivors of a type of building demolished at any time between 1480 and 1980. The question is still open and could well repay further study.

Of those 11 houses, only two possess a byre window, or *pour*, which makes it possible to assert with a fair degree of confidence that they were longhouses. Neither seems earlier than *c.* 1500, from the style of its fireplace. Le Grée, Le Gron (436) has been re-fronted and has had a back kitchen added, probably in 1739, at which date the bread oven was almost certainly built to the left of the fireplace, re-using some of the earlier chamfered stone to form its angle. La

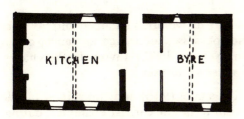

LA COCQUERIE
(408)

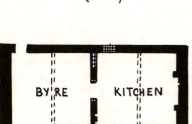

THE ELMS, PLEINHEAUME
(946)

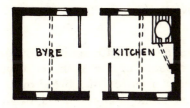

LA CORBIÈRE
(215)

LE PETIT JARDIN
& THE COTTAGE,
LE VARIOUF (178-9)

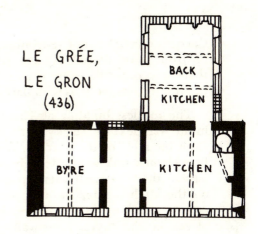

LE GRÉE,
LE GRON
(436)

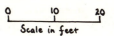

0   10   20
Scale in feet

Fig. 8. SIMPLIFIED PLANS OF ONE-STOREY LONGHOUSES

■ Original building

▦ Later additions and refronting: single inserted windows are not shown.

▦ Blocked doorways

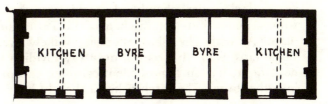

Cocquerie (408) is not re-fronted, but has had its windows enlarged and possibly its front door altered. At any rate, neither possesses an arched entrance, nor is there any other dateable material in them. Neither do the Livres des Perchages, the fief records, help us with dating any of these 11 houses.

The roofless building at The Elms, Pleinheaume (946) and the ruined façade in the wall next to Dalgary Cottage (992) seem to be the earliest examples, dating, from the style of their arches, from the early 15th century. The Elms has a very fine kitchen sink with a trough instead of a shelf. One side of the trough forms a part of the front wall outside, to the right of the doorway. No cross-wall remains on the kitchen side, and it is possible that there never was a kitchen cross-wall, even of planking, in this house, as there is a remarkably complex set of keeping places in the 'byre' cross-wall, facing the kitchen fireplace, and it could be asserted that these would have been more likely to form part of the kitchen accoutrements than the furnishings of a cross-passage. Certainly there are no such keeping places in a similar position in any other house, one- or two-storeyed: but then we have hardly any one-storey ones to compare with. The 'byre' at The Elms had already been converted to living accommodation before it fell into ruin, so it can only be inferred that it ever housed cattle. The present back door opens directly into the byre. If this is the original position, then this may not be a true longhouse, but perhaps should be regarded as a house where cattle were indeed housed under the same roof, but where there was alternative external access, as well as internal, by the doorway in the cross-wall. The remaining peculiarity is that the position of the doorway in that cross-wall has been altered. It is at present in the usual position in the middle of the wall, but the original opening was in the extreme back of the wall. A somewhat similar arrangement exists at Les Cottes (951), for details of which see page 96, under the section on Type 7 houses.

The houses at La Corbière (215); La Houguette (529); La Chaumière (594); and La Forge (924) all possess good fireplaces, probably of the 15th century, that at La Corbière altered as at Le Grée, by the later insertion of a bread oven. That at La Forge, as already noted, preserves its fine stone chimney hood, of an early design. La Houguette has been altered so as to form a range of cowsheds. None of these houses retains any other clues as to its original use. But their proportions are those of longhouses.

The two houses at Le Variouf, Le Petit Jardin (178) and The Cottage (179) provide a further puzzle. They adjoin each other, and if not built together, are of much the same date. At present, the arch, which is a version of the 4R type— i.e., a single order, chamfered, in this case the arch itself consisting of only two stones—opens into the kitchen of Le Petit Jardin, which possesses a fine fireplace. As with The Elms, there is unlikely ever to have been a cross-passage, a single cross-wall with central doorway dividing kitchen from 'byre'. The Cottage, next door, has an almost identical plan, except that there the front door opens into the 'byre'. The kitchen has a slightly later type of fireplace. As both houses

THE LONGHOUSE (Type 2)

are built into the bank, neither has or could ever have had a back door. It is possible that, in fact, these were not originally two single-storey cottages, but houses of two storeys that have suffered the same fate that has befallen the fine house at St. George (586), where a two-storey building has later been reduced to one storey and a loft, by the expedient of taking down the front and back walls to the level of the bedroom window-sills—perhaps because of deterioration in the fabric—and putting on a new roof at this lower level. At St. George it is fairly clear that this has happened, because the positions of kitchen sink, bénitier, byre keeping places and so on are exactly where they would be in a two-storey house, and a cart entrance now occupies the space that would have been taken up by the back door and the tourelle doorway. Both at St. George and Le Variouf the front and back walls are far higher than in any of the other single-storey houses of the 15th and 16th centuries. However, at Le Petit Jardin and The Cottage, the positions of doors and cross-walls, even allowing for evident alterations in the façades, seem to show that these could not have been typical two-storey longhouses, but might perhaps have more closely resembled Les Cottes, both in proportions and interior arrangement. In that case, The Elms and these two houses could perhaps be seen as ancestors of the late 16th century Three Bay Houses.

We are therefore left with nine true one-storey houses from this period, the last of which is the building now known as La Mottes Cottages (73). This house has been greatly altered over the years, but retains its kitchen sink in the back wall. It is, perhaps, the latest of the series.

Since every one of these nine houses has been considerably changed, for better or for worse, since it was built, one can only speculate upon the original layout. Probably there was a kitchen of two bays, a cross-passage of one bay and a byre of one or two bays, a single loft running from end to end of the house with access through an 'eye brow' opening under the thatch and over the front door. The kitchen would then have contained beds for all the family as well as supplying all their daytime needs. But the evidence will take us no further.

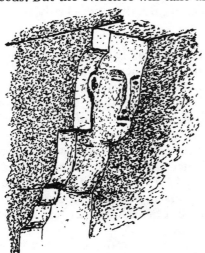

'Corbel in a Chimney Sarre's House near Les Adams, St. Saviours Guernsey'
After a sketch by F.C. Lukis, May 1845.

Chapter IV

LES GRANDES MAISONS: Type 3

AN ALMOST equally select group, of 21 houses, comprises the next variation on the longhouse pattern. But here we are on far firmer ground, because these 19 include some of the finest houses in Guernsey, aptly termed *les grandes maisons* in the Livres des Percharges. They will be referred to by this name throughout the remainder of the book. Two of them, Les Câches (237) and Bordeaux House (984) are examined in greater detail in Chapters XXXVIII and XLI.

These houses exhibit a greater individuality than any other we have to deal with. But they form a group because they have one element in common: in plan they all consist of kitchen, cross-passage, 'byre', and one additional room. In two cases, this additional room is between the byre and the cross-passage—at Les Bordages (452) and Les Fauxquets Farm (482). In all the other houses, it is behind the kitchen, but on the same line; never at right-angles, like a later back kitchen. Internal access is always provided, but a separate doorway, either in the front or the back of the house, gives external access to this extra room, except at Le Marais Farm (1008). At Les Bordages and Les Fauxquets Farm the external access is to the byre rather than to the intermediate room. These two examples, therefore, are not true longhouses, because the cattle would not have used the same door as the family, but for convenience they are dealt with here, as in every other regard they are clearly related to the other houses of this group.

What was this extra room? Certainly it was not what has become known in Guernsey as a 'widow's third'. By Guernsey law a widow is entitled to one-third of the house after her husband's death, and in the 19th century it was common for the next generation to solve the problem of a parent in continued residence by building on a small wing, half the size of the original house and therefore one-third of the whole. But there is no evidence that this was the practice in early times, and from everything we know of medieval society, the widow would have continued living with her children and grandchildren. In any case, not one of these rooms ever possessed a fireplace. King's Mills' Farm has the remains of an inserted 18th-century fireplace, recently repaired with stone from the ruins of an earlier building nearby, but here, too, the room was originally unheated.

LES GRANDES MAISONS: Type 3

If we suppose that in fact it was the byre, built behind the kitchen just so that it was unnecessary for animals to use the central door, then, of course, none of these houses could be classed as longhouses, and the room to one side of the cross-passage, where the byre is found in Type 1 houses, would be an embryonic parlour. But while, in some cases, this is possible, it is not probable, because where byre windows occur, in each case, except for those already mentioned, they are in the part of the house where we would expect the byre to be. This is so at Le Marais Farm and La Rocque Balan (1007), where cattle are said to have been kept at the 'byre' end of the house until the present century, and the earth floor remained until recent times. At Bordeaux Haven (982) and St. Magloire (996), the byre window is in the usual place. Both Les Bordages and Les Fauxquets Farm, incidentally, are known to have had byres, though, as we have seen, these have separate access. Evidence of a byre in six out of 21 houses is a very high proportion, and the possibility that byres existed in most of the others when they were built cannot, therefore, be lightly dismissed. Again, at Les Câches and nearby Les Raies de Haut (251), although there is no surviving byre window, the insertion of a later fireplace, at the end of the building where the byre should be, provides at least some reason for thinking that one previously existed. At King's Mills' Farm (506), although the 'byre' end is of one bay like so many byres in the four-bay longhouses—the additional room behind the kitchen is of quite exceptional length: at least three bays.

On the other hand, the large windows in Bordeaux House (984) and Les Tilleuls (563) at the 'byre' end give every appearance of being the original ones and were clearly intended for a living-room. At La Houguette (528) there always appears to have been a second fireplace at this end, the very fine panelling and fireplace surround of an 18th-century modernisation masking earlier stone corbels behind.

The remaining houses throw no particular light on the matter, one way or the other. They are: Les Villets Farm (189)—much altered; La Mare (239); La Haye de Puits (582); Les Naftiaux (665); La Ronde Cheminée (929); The Old Cottage, L'Ancresse (1005); Le Tertre (1026); and La Carrière (1028). Maison d'Aval (975) is probably of this type, but the original layout downstairs is very difficult to decide, due to later divisions into two or three dwellings. La Haye du Puits and Le Tertre will be fully discussed in Chapter VI, p. 57.

The most likely explanation of the extra room in all but Les Bordages and Les Fauxquets Farm is that it was a service room for the kitchen adjoining and that in these two houses it was thought more convenient to place the service room between the byre and the cross-passage.

At Le Marais Farm, where there is no external access, it was ideally placed as a buttery or pantry, a cool storage room for the food and drink as well as of other provisions for the household. In this house the room was only one bay wide, and seems to have had only one window, in the back wall. It is entered from the kitchen by a very fine ogival doorway. Bordeaux House also boasted a good

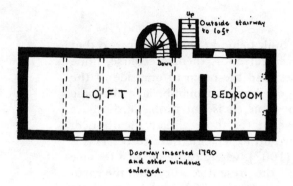

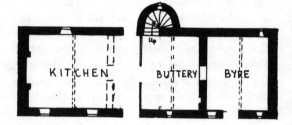

LES BORDAGES (452)

Fig. 9. LES GRANDES MAISONS

LA ROCQUE BALAN (1037)

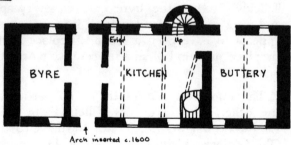

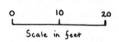

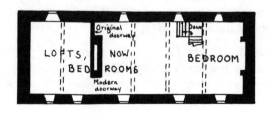

BORDEAUX HAVEN (982)

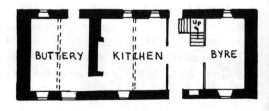

KING'S MILLS' FARM (506)

Below - LA HOUGUETTE (528)

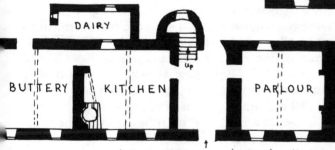

Arch replaced by doorway with flat lintel, 18th century.

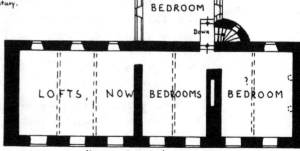

House refronted in 19th century

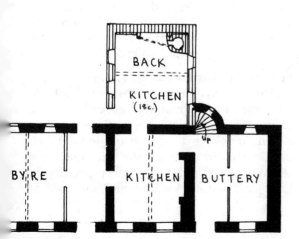

LA MARE (239)

doorway to its back room, but elsewhere there was no extra care lavished on this opening. In any case, the doorways in Le Marais and Bordeaux House probably indicate more the quality of the kitchen than the importance of the room to which they gave access. At Les Raies de Haut, the position of the window in the back wall, between buttery and kitchen, is of particular interest.

However, the suggestion that we have here the equivalent of an English buttery or pantry is only offered on the basis of what is known about the larger farm-houses of England and France at that time. The fabric we are faced with really offers few clues.

But perhaps the best indications are at La Mare and La Haye du Puits. In these houses, the tourelle is entered from the buttery, almost at the extreme end of the house. When there was plenty of room to build the stairs elsewhere, it is inconceivable that they would ever had been built out of a byre, whereas the construction of the tourelle out of a storeroom would have been quite acceptable and would have had the advantage of avoiding the draughts that must often have whistled up the stairs when they were entered from the cross-passage.

In date, these houses appear to span two centuries. Les Câches, with its delightfully ornate window in the upstairs passage, and its fine fireplace, and La Rocque Balan, with its scarcely less ornate window in the same position, and its two ogival doorways, cannot be much later than 1450. La Contrée de Saint (69), a four-bay longhouse with a similar doorway, was standing in 1488. La Carrière has a round-headed doorway upstairs. Bordeaux House has its splendid fireplaces, both with shelves, and Les Raies de Haut has the remains of a fireplace which would have been a facsimile of the early downstairs one at Les Câches. All these houses date from around 1450. Bordeaux Haven may be as old, especially if it be granted that its downstairs fireplace, covered, but patently of the same strange pattern as that at Le Catillon de Bas (292), is earlier than the 1606 incised on that at the latter house. If not, then it must be c. 1600. The form of the arch at La Ronde Cheminée suggests the late 15th century, and St. Magloire is at least that old: while La Mare, King's Mills Farm, La Houguette, Les Tilleuls, and The Old Cottage are 16th century. Les Villets Farm, Les Naftiaux and Les Fauxquets Farm are perhaps at the end of the series, soon after 1600. However, a far closer comparison of all these houses is necessary before a really firm dating sequence can be fixed. The attempt is made at this stage in order to give the reader at least some idea of the period involved.

If the practical purpose of the extra room downstairs in *les grandes maisons* now provides us with a puzzle, the building of it certainly provided the 15th- or 16th-century owner with much more choice in designing the rest of his house. The extra element introduced by the ground-floor plan was the compulsory inclusion of at least one stone cross-wall, in order to construct the kitchen fireplace and its chimney-hood. As we have seen in dealing with the usual form of two-storey longhouse, it was not always considered necessary, especially in the south-eastern corner of the island, to have a stone wall forming one side or

LES GRANDES MAISONS: Type 3

other of the cross-passage. One can imagine many an argument, 500 years ago, between a man from St. Martin's parish, and one from St. Pierre-du-Bois, about how to construct a house. The man from St. Pierre-du-Bois would have insisted that you needed 'the main wall', while the other would have said that in his parish they were not built, and were superfluous. The result was that the bedroom, in the usual longhouse form, had to be at the opposite end of the house from the kitchen, because only here was there another wall to support a fireplace, and although we know from La Maison d'Aval (241) in Guernsey, from examples in Jersey, and from many a small chateau in Brittany, that men knew how to built one fireplace above another, their flues running side by side, it was clearly easier to put the kitchen fireplace against one gable and the bedroom one against the other.

However, in *les grandes maisons* (with the exception of Les Bordages and Les Fauxquets Farm), the kitchen fireplace was not against the gable wall, since it was the 'buttery' that occupied one end of the house. And as the extra room which we shall call the 'buttery' was never heated, it followed that at least two walls were available upstairs for a bedroom fireplace. If there were cross-walls on one or both sides of the cross-passage as well, there could be a maximum choice of four different places for the bedroom fireplace, though, in fact, where there are two cross-passage walls in these houses, only one is carried up beyond the ground floor, thus reducing the choice upstairs to three. For all that, most houses still had their bedrooms over the byre, where it would have been in smaller houses. This is so at Les Câches, King's Mills' Farm, Les Tilleuls, Les Naftiaux, Bordeaux Haven, Bordeaux House and Le Marais Farm; and almost certainly so at St. Magloire, though road-widening has removed the bedroom gable. But at Les Bordages, The Old Cottage, La Rocque Balan and La Carrière, the bedroom was at the opposite end. At Les Bordages, therefore, it was in effect, still over the byre, because of the exceptional positioning of the byre below; at the others, it was over the buttery. Only at La Houguette was the full potential of all the cross-walls realised. Here, they seemed to think that wherever there was a wall, there must be a fireplace. There are two upstairs, and two downstairs, arranged alternately, from left to right, bedroom; kitchen; bedroom; and parlour. Together with the unusually early fireplace above the stables in the detached barn nearby, these fireplaces provide the most complete range of original stone chimneys we have in Guernsey—five splendid granite stacks.

In the other nine houses, the position of the original bedroom is difficult to establish accurately, and while we have been thinking in terms of a single bedroom, so that the variation on the usual longhouse arrangement can be more readily grasped, it is clear that these houses usually had more than one, but that only at La Houguette was more than one heated. Both La Rocque Balan and Les Câches might always have had additional unheated bedrooms, though at both houses it is quite likely that considerable alterations were carried out between 1550 and 1625, perhaps 150 years after they were built. It is probably at about this time that the upstairs panelling, which in both cases is of the highest quality and resembles that at La Houguette, was installed, thus sub-dividing into separate rooms part of the open granary such as is still found occupying most of the first floor of the larger fortified farmhouses of the Norman-Breton border, for instance at Le Manoir, Carnet, of 1581. Certainly the internal tourelle staircase to the loft over the bedroom at Les Câches is of this date. The exact arrangement of bedrooms and loft (or *grenier*) on the first floor of *les grandes maisons* prior to about 1550 must therefore remain in doubt. While there may possibly have been at least one additional unheated bedroom included in the original design, this cannot be proved, and it is not until the end of the 16th century that we can be certain that standards of comfort in these larger houses dictated the provision of more than one bedroom, in the case of La Houguette the provision also of a second upstairs fireplace.

Instead of the usual ventilation slits in the gable ends of the loft, La Rocque Balan and The Old Cottage originally had a larger central opening, similar to the unique example downstairs in the byre at Les Blicqs (610). The upstairs ones, about three feet wide and two feet tall perhaps gave outside access to the loft. These two houses are the only ones in Guernsey with any evidence of early access to the main loft through the gable end.

There is no need to elaborate on the fireplaces and other fittings of these larger houses, since they are of exactly the same shapes and forms as are found in the Type 1 longhouses. It is only in the layout that *les grandes maisons* differ from the usual longhouses. Methods of construction, external appearance and so forth, were the same.

One final peculiarity, however, remains to be described, and that is the position of the tourelle staircase. In the 'standard' longhouses, as we have seen, the tourelle, where it existed, invariably opened out of the cross-passage. Of the 21 *les grandes maisons*, 13 have tourelles: the remainder a straight flight of stairs. Of those with tourelles, in only one case—at La Houguette—does it open from the cross-passage.

Almost everywhere else it is entered directly from the kitchen, and there seems no rhyme or reason to the direction in which it turns. In nine cases it turns towards the kitchen fireplace, leaving three houses (for what it is worth, all in the west of the island—La Mare, Les Câches and Les Bordages) where it turns away. Looking at it another way, in four cases certainly and maybe four others, it turns in the direction of the main bedroom, and in four cases it turns away. Or, for the benefit of those who may still insist that these houses were built by right-handed or left-handed warriors defending their bedrooms to the last, seven turn to the right and five to the left. The general effect of their positioning was that they appeared roughly central along the back elevation of the house, but whether this was a consideration cannot be known. Unlike tourelles in the Type 1 longhouses, the top of the staircase did not emerge on one side or the other of a cross-wall, so that this was not a determining factor.

LES GRANDES MAISONS: Type 3

In spite of all ingenious reasoning, it seems most likely that in these larger houses, they quite simply built the tourelle where they wished.

As for the upper loft in these houses, there is no way of telling by what method it was originally entered, but as it would have been twice the size of the upper loft in the usual longhouse, it would no doubt have been well-used. It was of sufficient importance at Les Câches to warrant the construction of a separate staircase, presumably, as has already been noted, after the main loft had been turned into bedrooms.

LES EFFARDS BENITIER (552)

Chapter V

THE THREE-BAY HOUSE: Type 4

HAVING DEALT WITH *les grandes maisons,* we now turn to what the Livres des Perchages refer to as *les petites maisons.* Whereas *les grandes maisons* were from six to eight bays long, these little houses were always three. And since the term *la petite maison* has acquired other connotations, this type of house will be referred to as the 'three-bay house'.

Unlike the houses dealt with so far, the 13 three-bay houses that remain all seem to date from the period 1550 to 1700. Whether they were ever longhouses —and applied to those buildings the term would be particularly inappropriate—is very doubtful. Although a few seem to possess a 'byre' window, it may well be that the room was used rather more as a store, for in all of these houses the cross-passage is far too narrow for a longhouse. But in every other regard, the plan is that of a longhouse telescoped. On one side of the cross-passage is the kitchen, on the other, a second room (byre or store): over which is the bedroom, with lofts opposite and above. Incredibly, in such small houses, a stone cross-wall was sometimes built, as at Galliot Cottage (72) and La Vieille Maison at Le Villocq (580), though this is only carried up to bedroom floor level. With the exception of La Petite Maison, at Le Monnaie (660); Grove Hill House (847); Shrubwood, St. Jacques (887); the wing at Vrangue Manor (902); and Galliot Cottage, they all possess fine stone fireplaces with shaped corbels and, often, stone chimney hoods. Grove Hill House and Shrubwood almost certainly did have similar fireplaces, but these houses have been altered during the last century. La Petite Maison probably dates from the last half of the 17th century, and the wing at Vrangue Manor was probably built in 1674, when the main house was re-fronted and considerably altered. (Here and at the main house the tourelles are square additions of the 19th century, and none of the three-bay houses possesses a genuine tourelle staircase.) However, although fireplaces with shaped corbels clearly exist at Les Taudevins (231), Le Grand Douit (383), and Beaucoin, Le Camptréhard (653), the form is uncertain, as they are covered over. The earliest fireplace among those now visible is at Les Grandes Maisons (922), which cannot be much later than 1550. Les Simons (340) has two fine fireplaces and is known to have been built by 1592. La Vieille Maison; Cruchbrée, Etonellerie (968) and Belle Vue, Ville-ès-Pies (993) must also date from the second half of the 16th century.

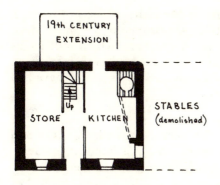
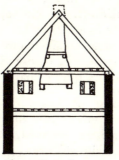
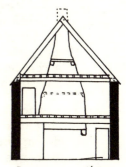

LA VIEILLE MAISON, LE VILLOCQ (580)

West gable wall: store with bedroom above.

East gable wall: kitchen with loft above, showing blocked doorways to stable and further loft, now demolished.

Fig. 10. 3-BAY HOUSES

Simplified plans omitting upstairs partitions for the sake of clarity.

Scale in feet 0 10 20

■ Original walling
▨ Later walling

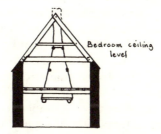

Section A–A, showing kitchen with loft above and low tie-beams of roof.

GALLIOT COTTAGE (72)

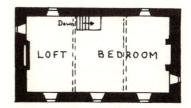

LES SIMONS (340)

La Vieille Maison once had a two-storey wing to the right of the house, with internal communication from kitchen and loft. At Beaucoin a similar door by the side of the kitchen fireplace gave access to the barn which still exists alongside, and the same arrangement may since have been altered into living accommodation at Grove Hill House. The other houses do not seem to have had any sort of contemporary byre or barn.

The three-bay house at Les Simons, now disused, is the one where the characteristics of this group can most clearly be seen. Both the upstairs and downstairs fireplaces have survived, the latter modified by a later bread oven. In the course of inserting this bread oven, the left-hand corbel has been removed and re-used as a seat on the right of the fireplace. The whole house is typical of 16th-century work. But at Galliot Cottage the bread oven is integral and there is an unshaped corbel at the other side of the hearth. A loft above has an opening for unloading furze into it through the gable end. These are 17th-century features. We are thus dealing with a group of houses which span a very important change of emphasis in house-building. It has already been noted that none of them possesses a tourelle. Only that at Le Grand Douit has an arched door, of late 16th-century design (Type 5). But it is possible that this house was not always of three bays, but was originally a longhouse of four or five bays shortened when the new house was built alongside in 1778 at which time its doorway was moved, as at La Seigneurie (367—see Chapter XL). However, the complete removal of doorways, as we shall see, was a common pastime in later centuries, so that their presence or absence in these houses is not, by itself, proof of anything. But with the exception of Les Grandes Maisons, where the door-head with its arms of the Le Marchant family is almost certainly a fireplace lintel re-used, there happens to be little sign of re-fronting. It cannot be argued, since so many had 'good' fireplaces, that the builder was too poor to afford an arch, and so one is left to ponder whether arches went out of fashion just about a generation before fireplaces with shaped corbels. In these houses we are almost certainly witnessing a transition in styles. They are also very intimate buildings, their proportions and such details as the low tie-beams of the roof trusses that cut across the upstairs at Galliot Cottage making them attractive inside as well as outside.

Chapter VI

EARLY ALTERATIONS AND ADDITIONS

WE HAVE BEEN EXAMINING the features of houses built between 1400 and 1625, and have now, in considering the three-bay house, reached beyond the end of that period. By 1625, perhaps as many as one hundred of our oldest houses had already been standing for 150 years. It is natural that during that time, succeeding generations should want to extend their homes, or at least adapt them to changing needs and incorporate in their work the latest fashions. Of course, some houses were built as the result of the prosperity or the energy of a single generation. When the fortunes of a family waned, their house remained untouched. We must be thankful that in almost every family there are periods of stagnation. Most houses have had an owner who for one reason or another did nothing to his property. If this were not so, it would be quite impossible to weave in and out among the layers of alterations and improvements of the last 500 years, or those which are still going on today. What knowledge we can gain about the homes of our forebears depends upon examining features that remained unaltered because people could not afford to keep up with the latest fashions. Conservation is a modern religion.

But we must now look at some of the houses which had already been extended by 1625. They are fascinating because they foreshadow the sort of thing that was to happen on a much greater scale during the two centuries that followed. The strong conservatism and clinging to old tradition that made many families continue to live in longhouses when they were well able to afford other accommodation for their animals is well-known in all those parts of England, Wales and Ireland where such a way of life has persisted until recent times. A few longhouses are still used as such in Brittany to this day, and the reference in Chapter I to the way of life at Choucan clearly demonstrates this sort of attitude. In Guernsey, as we have seen, there is reason to believe that the longhouse tradition persisted until the beginning of the present century, and certainly well into the 19th century. But already by the middle of the 16th century, there were some families who were leaving this way of life, and we have already noted that there is some doubt that *les grandes maisons*—Type 3— were really longhouses, providing as they did a range of rooms and, by implication, a degree of comfort, far greater than a longhouse of the standard pattern could afford.

Even some of the houses built on the longhouse plan were clearly never intended to house animals. All new two-storey houses erected after *c.* 1625 are of this type: and some are earlier. One of the earliest and best examples we have is La Maison de Haut (240), one of two properties which adjoin each other and formerly belonged to the Le Messurier family. Before giving a description of it, we should note that the entire complex is of quite outstanding importance. Already we have noticed the phenomenon of two fireplaces, contrived one above the other, at the older house, La Maison d'Aval (241). Dating from no later than 1450, only the kitchen side of this building survives, the remainder having been pulled down in 1866 to make way for a very fine Victorian house that retained the excellent 15th-century work at its side as a back kitchen. But long before 1866, in the 16th century, the original house must have been one of the first to build on a back kitchen proper, and to this we shall return later on. But while dealing with this complex of buildings, two other unique features at La Maison d'Aval must be mentioned. One is the seventh or eighth-century cross re-used as a quoin stone in the 16th-century back kitchen. It may well once have marked the grave of a missionary saint from Wales or Ireland, and in design links up with other crosses in those countries and in Scotland. The re-use of this stone here as building material is not only instructive when thinking of the sources of stone found in our houses, but is also indicative of the tremendous religious and social changes in Guernsey from the 1560s onwards, when for 100 years a Calvinistic Presbyterian régime turned the Catholic tradition of the island upside-down. Only at such a time could this cross have found its way into a house. The other feature unique to La Maison d'Aval is less spectacular but of considerable interest. On a barn opposite the house, a door has the raised inscription in wood, 'ILM : M : 1685' (see Illustration 64). Not only is the survival of this wooden inscription outdoors in itself remarkable: it helps to date the 'in-and-out' planking of which the door is made, and which we shall meet elsewhere.

La Maison de Haut, next door, is the later of the two houses. From its enormously impressive arch and its fireplaces, so similar to that in the back kitchen at La Maison d'Aval, it should belong to the last decade or so of the 16th century. It was then, as will be argued in Chapter XXV, that this type of arch achieved its most extreme form, as exemplified here and at The Old Farm, Brock Road (925).

The dimensions of the house are generous, and all internal divisions are of panelling, a form of construction unusual in St. Pierre-du-Bois. Most of this original woodwork survives, and is of the highest quality, similar to that at Les Câches (237) nearby. The cross-beams, too, are uncommonly elaborate, with double hollow chamfers reminiscent of the *sablières* of 15th- and 16th-century jettied houses, and perhaps a little later than the similar fine beams at Les Reveaux (259). While it may seem a pity, in such a splendid house, that the roof timbers were completely renewed early this century, we must undoubtedly be thankful that this action has helped to keep the rest of the house below in such a good state of preservation. We can hazard a guess at the shape of the original roof. In the usual way, the main beams of the bedroom ceilings also formed the tie-beams of the roof-trusses, and from the slot remaining in the upper side of one of them, we may conjecture that the roof was of king-post form, probably with collar as well, and windbraces.

To return to the layout of the house, immediately inside the front door arch and integral with it, to the right, is a fine bénitier, with an 'accolade' top: that is, a flattened and later form of the ogee arch. The wide cross-passage gives room both for the back door and the entrance alongside to the spacious tourelle staircase. On the right of the cross-passage is the kitchen, with its massive fireplace, and on the left, a room originally unheated, but whose fenestration is the same as that of the kitchen and bedrooms. Here is no hint of a byre. It is clear that this house was designed purely as a dwelling for the family, and that animals were housed in the very attractive barn, in front and to the left of the house. The pigeonnier in the gable end of this barn is the best example we have of its sort. Keeping of pigeons provided an important addition to the diet of our forebears. In feudal times, only a seigneur might have a building designed especially for this purpose, and known as *le colombier*. Behind the farm of that name in Torteval (336—see Illustration 31) is the only surviving colombier in Guernsey (though the ruins of another were noted on Lihou in 1909): a circular tower with openings for the pigeons to enter, and rows of nesting places inside. But the present tower is almost entirely a 20th-century reconstruction. For other families, the keeping of pigeons was restricted to the provision of nesting places in the walls of their barns and houses. Examples are frequent, for instance at Le Colombier farmhouse itself, in the disused house at King's Mills (505) and in the main house and the back kitchen wings at La Vieille Sous L'Eglise (475). These at La Maison de Haut occupy almost all the gable end (see Illustration 31).

There are clear remains to the right of the house of another wing beyond the kitchen with internal communication by way of a doorway to the left of the kitchen fireplace, in the same position as those giving access to the buttery in *les grandes maisons*. Although this wing was certainly two storeys high, there does not appear to be any similar internal access at first-floor level from the bedrooms. If this extra part of the building had served the same purpose as the buttery at *les grandes maisons,* it is extremely unlikely that such an integral part of the house would have been allowed to fall into ruin, especially when the remainder is so splendidly preserved. We must therefore assume that this had been a store, with access from the kitchen and with an upper floor entered only by ladder from below. A much later addition was the 19th-century back kitchen, behind the kitchen and entered by a doorway enlarged from a window in the usual manner (see Chapter VIII).

Over the kitchen, the entire space appears to have been used for a range of bedrooms, divided from each other, and from the passage along the back of the first floor by the fine wooden partitioning already mentioned. There is no main loft, and, unlike Les Granges de Beauvoir Manor (834), the tourelle is not carried up to give access to the loft above. We are looking, therefore, at a house where two of the chief constituents of the longhouse are absent, though the construction is exactly the same as the traditional form already used everywhere in Guernsey for 150 years. There is no byre, and there is no loft. These elements were accommodated in separate buildings, and extra rooms for the family occupy the vacated space. We shall meet many houses of this pattern in Chapter VIII.

Another way of achieving more living space for the family was to build on a wing at right-angles, usually at the kitchen end, the effect of which was to create a house of the same size as *les grandes maisons*. But there is no house in the island where the original building was L-shaped in plan: in every case the wing is a later addition. At Saints Farm (83) the wing is probably 16th century, though later alterations make it difficult to decide. It has a pair of gable windows, now blocked, which were probably at either side of a bedroom fireplace. Les Mainguys (969) has an exactly similar arrangement, and here the corbels of the bedroom fireplace, as well as the windows, survive. Neither of these houses has an external tourelle, but at the remaining houses where such extensions were carried out, the tourelle stairs have been cleverly adapted to give access to the newer wing as well as to the older part of the house. La Ruette (406) preserves a very fine 16th-century door at the top of its tourelle, opening into what was almost certainly a bedroom, with a storeroom beneath. At this house and at Les Sages Villa (272), the wing is built at the byre end of the house, and at Les Sages Villa, as at La Maison d'Aval, it is at the front of the house. At La Maison d'Aval, the intention was clearly to create a back—or perhaps one should say a front—kitchen: there is no sign that the space above was ever a bedroom. But except at Les Sages Villa, the extra wing in other houses was designed to provide an additional heated bedroom with an unheated service room for the kitchen below.

Three houses where this occurs are so similar in detail that they must surely have been copied, one from the other. They are Les Quertiers (919), La Grande Maison (945), and Le Tertre (1026). La Grande Maison will be fully described in Chapter XXXI. This house and most of the other houses mentioned in this section have been completely re-fronted in the 18th or 19th centuries, and at first sight do not give the impression of being particularly old. But Les Quertiers, as well as being six bays long, has the largest chamfered window openings in the island, at the back of the house; the finest fireplace in the island in its kitchen (see Chapter XXVII); and two very good arches, very similar to those at both Les Grandes Maisons and Le Tertre. There is one on each side of its tourelle staircase: one is the back door of the original house, the other gives accesss to the downstairs room in the new wing.

Le Tertre is perhaps the most fascinating of all these houses, because it was once a small fortified farmhouse, or manor. In Normandy and Brittany there

EARLY ALTERATIONS AND ADDITIONS 61

are many such *petits manoirs*. One which once must have been exactly like Le Tertre is La Ville Durand, on the outskirts of Etables-sur-Mer, in Brittany. Another, rather different, has already been mentioned: Le Manoir at Carnet, near Fougères. This house was defended by an *eschaugette,* over the front door: that is a projecting chamber supported on machicolations through which could be poured or pelted anything to deter anyone from forcing the door below. In the farmyard is a charming chapel. Les Annevilles Manor (948) must once have been just such a fortified farmhouse and chapel, but earlier, probably of the 13th century. Very little of it remains beyond some pointed arches, probably from the chapel of St. Thomas, and an arrow slit. The house appears to have been pulled down and rebuilt at a higher level at right-angles in the 16th century, on a longhouse plan, re-using the superb pointed arch of two orders that now forms the porch, as well as various other stones from the older building. The medieval *garenne,* or rabbit warren, however, does survive: a moated enclosure with earth bank, where rabbits bred and were killed for the kitchen as required. This was probably constructed by Sir William de Chesney, who was granted the right of free warren on this manor in 1260, by Edward, Lord of the Isles (afterwards Edward I). There are two other and larger buildings in Guernsey which were defended in the same way as Le Tertre. They are Les Granges Manor and La Haye du Puits. The tourelle at La Haye du Puits is carried up beyond the roof and battlemented. Perhaps it is no coincidence that this turret, octagonal like the 15th-century stair turret (1466) at the Town church, is of a form more common in Normandy than in Brittany, for in the area of La Haye du Puits in Normandy, as well as in such towns as Valognes, are many such octagonal tourelles. The doorways at Les Quertiers, La Grande Maison and Le Tertre are also of Norman rather than Breton design.

The original entrance at La Haye du Puits in Guernsey was through a fine wide arch, its hood mould terminating in a finial that encloses a head (see Illustration 68). The arch once opened directly off the road which used to run past the entrance wing at a slight angle: hence the strange shape of the gable end. The wedge-shaped space left inside the arch, between the entrance and the road, was no doubt a porter's lodge, from behind which a high wall would have run along to the stable wing opposite, enclosing a courtyard. In the last century the arch was blocked and the road moved some distance away, so that it now passes the other side of the garden. These, and many other alterations have obscured the original form of this house, but it was probably one of *les grandes maisons* type, the tourelle opening from the buttery, as at La Mare (239), and a 16th-century entrance wing projecting from the buttery at right-angles. The re-used stone in some of the older buildings clearly shows that there was an even earlier house of some importance on the site.

The fortified house at Le Tertre was rather smaller, but its entrance arch was earlier than that at La Haye du Puits. Some of it has been removed and the entrance itself completely blocked. But enough remains to show that of all the cart or carriage entrances we have in the island, this was the earliest.

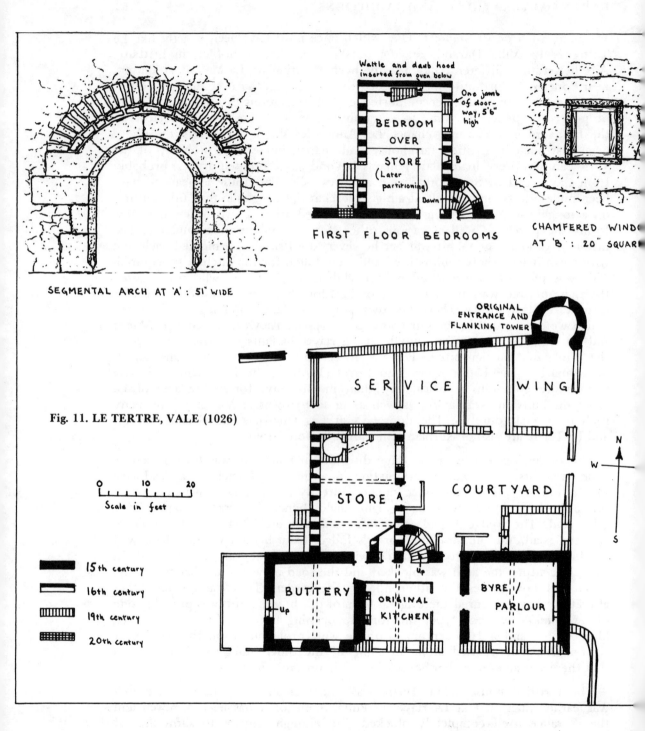

Fig. 11. LE TERTRE, VALE (1026)

EARLY ALTERATIONS AND ADDITIONS

Unlike all the others, neither the side of this arch nor the arch itself were chamfered. It was built of small, squarish blocks of Cobo granite, and must date from about 1450. The double entrance to the driveway at Le Groignet (517) is a little later, but there the carriageway has never been arched. To the left of this entrance at Le Tertre—looking from the outside—is a defensive tower forming the angle of the courtyard (see Illustration 22). There are known to have been three arrow slits in it, two of which survive. It is unclear whether or not the tower ever had an upper floor, but the various holes around the masonry inside could well have housed joists, and it is probable that a range of buildings existed in early times from this angle, across the entrance arch and beyond. These have been replaced by much 19th-century work. From the other side of the turret a high wall ran to the back angle of the main house. Thus the courtyard was—as at La Haye du Puits—entirely enclosed, the various patchings and piercings of the wall being modern. The main house was one of *les grandes maisons* type, but whether or not a longhouse originally cannot now be determined, due to a 19th-century re-fronting and to a considerable amount of good quality 17th- and 18th-century work indoors. This re-fronting has been carried out in such a way as to make the house appear as though symmetrical with a wing to the left. Compare Les Câches (237—Chapter XXXVIII). The original front door arch is probably the one now built into the gable end of the buttery on the left. It is a very wide arch, and has been inserted very curiously at about two feet above ground level.

There is one cross-wall on the 'byre' side. The tourelle originally opened out of the kitchen, as in most of *les grandes maisons,* and turned to the left. Late in the 16th century, the first alteration to the house was made by building a wing on to the back, at the kitchen side, in exactly the same way as at La Grande Maison and Les Quertiers, except that those houses were of simple longhouse type and their tourelles opened out of the cross-passage. At Le Tertre, because the tourelle was so far along the house, it was only possible to provide access to this new wing from the kitchen by making an extremely narrow doorway— only 29ins. wide, in the back wall, to the right of the fireplace where the doorway to the buttery already pierced the thickness of the fireplace cross-wall. Perhaps this new doorway was achieved by lengthening an existing window such as we have noted at Les Raies de Haut (251). The new wing also had a fine arched doorway into the courtyard, against the back of the tourelle. This arch is of two orders, springing in the Norman fashion from shoulder stones that form an angle with the sides. In other words, it is not truly semi-circular. Between the two orders is a narrow row of small stones about the size of thin bricks, purely decorative. La Grande Maison has two arches of this type, beautifully restored.

Why was it necessary to have this extra service room, in a *grande maison* that already possessed a buttery? Clearly the function of the room was closely associated with the kitchen, or so much trouble would not have been taken to provide internal access in an inconvenient corner. But perhaps, as in most of these early extensions, the chief desire was for extra bedrooms. Certainly the new downstairs room was not intended to be a new kitchen or to be heated in any way. The wide chamfered window, now blocked, in the gable end is sufficient proof of that.

As at Les Grandes Maisons, Les Quertiers, Les Sages Villa, Les Mainguys, La Ruette, and probably Saint's Farm, the fireplace was in the bedroom above. And a very fine fireplace it is, too, complete with its stone hood, and preserved intact, though at present well-nigh inaccessible, by a curious chance. For round about 1700, the room

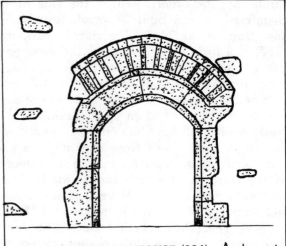

Fig. 12. BORDEAUX HOUSE (984) Arch as at present exposed. The 'spotted dog' effect is due to bad modern plastering. Note similarities with Le Tertre arch: dimensions are identical.

below was converted into the main kitchen. The old kitchen became a parlour and a passage was created in post-and-panel partitioning along the back of the house, so that the new parlour no longer had direct access to the stairs, to the old buttery or to the new kitchen, which was fitted with the latest amenity—a bread oven. At the same time, the ceiling was raised, so that the bedroom above was at a higher level. And because storage for furze was required, as near to the bread oven as possible, one end of the 16th-century bedroom was partitioned off as a loft. So the fireplace was left stranded in mid-air and the wattle-and-daub hood from the new kitchen fire below somewhat ignominiously inserted underneath its lintel up inside the older stone hood, so as to use the same flue. This extraordinary arrangement, like so many things at Le Tertre, is unique.

A further surprise looks out from the upstairs wall of the 16th-century bedroom wing on the courtyard side. This is a line of vertical stones 5ft. 6ins. high, the base 7ft. above the ground. It must be a doorway, for a charming chamfered window to the left of it is minute by comparison: but what is it doing here? Inside the room, the doorway would be in the angle by the fireplace: a strange place for a door. And why would external access be necessary when there was perfectly good internal access from the tourelle stairs? It is all very puzzling. However, if this is the side of a doorway, there must have been a flight of steps up to it, and such an outside staircase would have been one of the very few known to exist in Guernsey at such an early date. Illustrations of the old buildings at the Vale Priory show a similar outside staircase, but the only one now remaining on a building of c. 1600 is at La Houguette (528), leading to its detached barn with its shaped fireplace corbels. In 17th-century barns, such outside staircases always stuck out at right angles, as at La Houguette, Les

EARLY ALTERATIONS AND ADDITIONS

Bordages (452) and Les Prevosts (467), whereas in the 18th century they ran along the wall of the barn. Perhaps at Le Tertre this extra bedroom fulfilled the same function as that at La Houguette: at Le Tertre it was possible to join the wing on to the main house, while at La Houguette it was built separately, a barn beneath and a chamber above. In the 18th and 19th centuries such rooms were the quarters of the valet, or chief farmhand. We do not know whether La Houguette and Le Tertre are our earliest examples of this arrangement, but it is possible. If so, it was probably not the case in any of the other 16th-century extensions we have mentioned.

RUE DES LANDES (160)
Faint initialling and date on lintel in gable end of barn

Chapter VII

LA MAISON DE HAUT, PLEINHEAUME

BEFORE WE LEAVE the period 1400–1625, it is necessary to describe one building which does not fit into any category. This is La Maison de Haut (974), whose antiquity is obvious, but whose use is baffling. As it stands, it consists of two rooms on the ground floor, divided by a cross-wall. Each room is entered from the outside by an arch of early type, one of them a doorway of the usual width, the other a cart entrance. Between these two doorways is a third, of similar design, but smaller, and this opens directly upon an internal tourelle with stone steps. There is also access to these stairs from the room on the right. The bulge of the tourelle wall is on the inside of the building, the cross-wall between the two rooms running into it.

The upper floor has been adapted in the 17th or 18th century as a one-storey cottage, with cross-passage, kitchen on one side and bedroom on the other. Above them runs a continuous loft with no original timbers in the roof. Since the whole structure is built into the side of the valley, ground level on two sides is one storey higher, so that the front doorway of the cottage above was over the back wall of the storey below, and entrance to the loft was possible by constructing a straight stone flight of steps against the gable end. These run along the gable end at right-angles, due to the lie of the land, but in other respects resemble the flight at Les Bordages, noted in the previous chapter.

Whatever was originally above ground-floor level we shall never know, because although the outer walls are 500 years old or more, all else has changed. However, there is enough on the ground floor to provide food for thought. Especially in the left-hand room, along the gable wall that is underneath the outside entrance to the loft—two floors above—the foundations of the wall are formed of quite massive stones, several of them up to four feet high and as much wide. They look exactly like a dismantled cromlech. About half way along this gable end, and between two of these stones, a small entrance at ground level is formed, 26ins. high and 18ins. wide. Emerging from the tunnel-like entrance behind the wall, one enters a tiny oval room, stone-built and about six feet high, the corbelling of the roofing forming a dome. It is entirely subterranean, and appears to be contemporary with the rest of the ground-floor layout. If so, it cannot be later than 1450, and may well be considerably earlier.

There appears to have been no appreciable change in floor levels anywhere, and even if the opening to this little chamber had been higher, it would have been

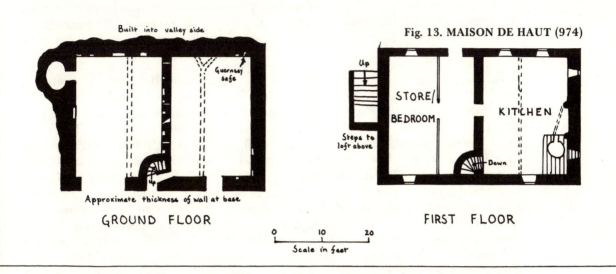

Fig. 13. MAISON DE HAUT (974)

too narrow for a doorway, especially when one considers the very wide arched entrances in the outside walls, and the very ample proportions of the building overall. It cannot have been any sort of bakery, because although superficially it resembles the bread ovens of 300 years later, it has never been associated with a hearth. In fact, there is no sign of a fireplace in either of the two ground floor rooms, and that in the cottage kitchen above has an unshaped corbel and is patently part of the later alterations.

The most likely explanation of this tiny structure is that it was a pig-sty. None of the ranges of pig-sties associated with Guernsey farmyards is of any great age: most are 19th century. We have no clear idea where pigs were housed before that time. But these later pig-sties all consist of a small house, built of stone, with a low doorway and a little walled yard in front. The chamber at La Maison de Haut is of exactly the right size; it, too, has a low doorway, and as for a yard, that is a recent idea preventing animals from wandering around the farmyard and digging up the garden. As at Choucan (p. 31), the pig who lived in this little house could wander where he wished. Support for this theory is supplied, perhaps, by Iorwerth C. Peate in *The Welsh House,* pp. 42-45. Here he notes the existence of about twenty circular pig-sties, mostly of stone and with corbelled roofs, associated with Welsh farm complexes. In this part of the book he is producing evidence of a round house as the earliest form of human habitation in Wales, and shows that the circular pig-sties may have employed building techniques once reserved for houses. Neither that argument, nor the actual shape of the pig-sty need concern us here; but the existence of a comparatively ancient form of corbelled stone sty on Welsh farmsteads gives some clues as to the type of housing provided for a pig before Victorian regimentation, even for animals, became the rule.

The massive beams of the ceiling and the plethora of keeping-places around all the walls in the room from which this 'pig-sty' opens provide further interest; the cross-wall also possesses a squint, rather like an ecclesiastical hagioscope, into the adjoining room. At present it seems to be angled upon nothing in particular.

In this second room, to the right of the internal tourelle, or newel staircase, the timbers are similarly massive—one is a forked tree trunk roughly squared, with both ends of the fork let into the wall, a peculiarity which also occurs at The Old Farm, Rue de la Passée (953), and occasionally elsewhere. There are more keeping-places, and in the back wall, near the right-hand angle, about four feet above the floor, is a 'Guernsey safe', as it has been called, consisting of a pottery jar built into the masonry, its neck pointing slightly upwards and towards the room. The mouth of the jar is blocked by a small piece of granite, which, of course, looks like all the other stone in the wall. This was a hiding-place for valuables and is one of very few examples that have been found. Maybe there are many more, still safely concealed. There is one in a wall halfway up the stairs at Les Fontaines (544), and another was discovered in 1924 when demolishing an old house at La Moye, L'Ancresse, for road widening. In that case it was in the wall at the side of the bedroom fireplace, and about four feet off the floor. One was also recorded under a floor-slab in a barn at Les Vardes Farm Hotel (955).

Such is the strange building called La Maison de Haut. What was it used for? Clearly it was not a house; at least the ground floor was not. There is no hearth, and no sign of there ever having been one. The most likely possibility is that we have here the only example in Guernsey of a former first-floor hall house. *The English Farmhouse and Cottage* (Barley) gives examples of such buildings, which were common in Anglo-Saxon England, being shown in the Bayeux Tapestry, where King Harold's Manor at Bosham, near Chichester, is of this form. The type was also found in many of the earliest houses at Oxford and Thetford. However, it is not suggested that La Maison de Haut is 11th century; merely that it has a credible pedigree. The type was widely used by merchants and by monks. In many monasteries the refectory or the dormitory was placed above a range of storerooms. More to the point, perhaps, is the presence of similar farmhouses on Dartmoor. These very closely resemble our Guernsey example, having a byre below and a division into two rooms above. An example is at Neadon, in the parish of Manston, which dates from about 1500.

But this type of house was also widespread in France, where first-floor halls remain from the 13th century onwards. At Figeac, L'Hotel de la Monnaie is a free-standing example, and it is a form commonly used in most of the new bastide towns of the 13th century in the Dordogne. In case this sounds a ridiculously remote connection, it must always be remembered that it was with Gascony, where the interchange of ideas was so important for both French and English traditions, that much of our wine trade was carried on. It was also to and from Aquitaine that ships were calling at Guernsey during the entire period when the English claim to large territories in France was constantly being pursued. And only in these new colonising towns of the Dordogne—the bastide towns built by both French and English—will you find arches with those strange proportions that we see in the nave of the Town Church, and in St. Sampson's church, too. So it is quite possible that a first-floor hall house might be found in Guernsey. The only wonder is that there are not more; that our house-forms are so incredibly consistent. The longhouses outnumber La Maison de Haut at least 250 to one.

It should be noted, finally, that the layout of a first-floor hall house is very nearly that of a longhouse upside-down. Instead of a byre and a kitchen on the ground floor, and a bedroom and loft above, you have byre and storage on the ground floor, and a bedroom and loft above. The provision of such a substantial staircase then makes good sense, and a pig-sty under the bedroom becomes more than a remote possibility. It is intriguing to speculate upon the details of the original first-floor plan at La Maison de Haut, but there, at least, we shall never know what was supplanted by a cottage in about 1700.

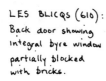

LES BLICQS (61b): Back door showing integral byre window partially blocked with bricks.

PART II

1625–1787

Chapter VIII

THE TWO-STOREY HOUSE WITH CROSS-PASSAGE (Type 5)

THERE WERE FEW HOUSES built between 1625 and 1700. During this time the prosperity of the islands waned, and political bitterness eventually culminated in civil war. When times are unsettled, people feel less inclined to build new houses, and it was not until after the restoration of the monarchy in 1660 that confidence returned. As the 18th century progressed, Guernsey once again became wealthy. Although the 1462 Bull of Neutrality that had so contributed to prosperity in the 16th century was now effectively a dead letter, trade increased, protected, too, by privateering, which in itself brought vast sums of money into the island. By the end of the 18th century, Guernsey was again a very thriving community, the commercial activity of its port reflected in the economy of the countryside. Other factors were also affecting the way of life in the islands.

By 1625, a couple of generations of social and religious separation from France, and a greater exchange of ideas with England, brought totally new influences to bear upon vernacular architecture. While in Brittany the shadow of the Gothic Age and the Renaissance lingered on well into the 18th century, in Guernsey a new set of ideals began to affect house-building. The basic plan might often remain the same as that used 200 years before, but the late 17th and the whole of the 18th century witnessed a gradual acceleration in experimentation, both with regard to different house forms, and the finish of a new building.

During the whole period 1625-1787, the vernacular tradition weakened, as the ideas of formal architecture began to affect building styles. Although the year 1787 is, of course, a totally artificial finishing date for the period, chosen because the Gardner map enables us to survey the island easily at that time, it happens to come within a couple of decades when building techniques changed considerably. The exploitation of local stone as the quarrying industry developed provided greater quantities of good material for building: the Revolution in France and the Napoleonic Wars that followed made Guernsey ever more dependent upon Britain, and in due course upon the Colonies, for trade and the cross-fertilisation of ideas. The Georgian and Regency architecture that was already making its appearance in St. Peter Port and occasionally in other parishes even by 1787, eventually led to the death of the vernacular tradition. The period between 1780-1800 is thus a watershed, and 1787, when

THE TWO-STOREY HOUSE WITH CROSS-PASSAGE (Type 5)

the old Manoir ès Marchants in Town gave way to the present Constables' Office, happens to epitomise the changing attitudes.

For all that, the farmhouses and cottages of the late 17th and the 18th centuries appear to shade into the Victorian era almost imperceptibly. Why is this? It is not wholly that the farming community of the country parishes comprised that part of the social structure which changed least during this period, though that may certainly have been a factor to take into account. Rather it was that when elegance and fashion began to demand symmetry, there by chance, as it were, was the longhouse plan to supply it. For the ground plan of two rooms divided by a cross-passage was exactly what was being built for the first time in country towns and villas by the English upper-middle classes. All that was necessary was a very different attitude to the façade.

So it was that the most popular type of house built between 1625 and 1787 remained the two-storey, five-bay house. But the two-storey four-bay house was also not unknown. There are 25 such houses. Sometimes, no doubt, the lack of funds or the limitations of a site were responsible for this, the 'small-parlour' house, as it has been called. But equally, it might represent a transitional period, at least in attitudes, it not chronologically, towards the way in which the ground-floor rooms were used. Although most are 17th century, four-bay houses appear occasionally throughout this period, and indeed, beyond.

Social pretentions might require the possession of a parlour, but when conditions of life in some families were such that it was probably never used as this, not surprisingly it was sometimes decided to place less emphasis on the room on that side of the cross-passage than was accorded the kitchen—still the main living-room of the house. Many an early 'parlour' was probably used much more as a store and for that reason was not heated. Many houses continue to have only one fireplace downstairs, in the kitchen: and one upstairs, in the bedroom at the opposite end of the house. As time went on, more houses had a fireplace in each downstairs room, and, as brick became used after 1750, thus making chimney flues much easier to build, both bedrooms and downstairs rooms were supplied with fireplaces. But the house of 1750 was very different from that of a hundred years before. In 17th-century inventories, it is well-known for the contents of a parlour to be anything other than what we might expect, and the phenomenon of rooms being called by names quite alien to their use is well-documented from the earliest times. Thus the term 'parlour' first occurs in Chaucer's *Troilus and Criseyde*, in 1374. Other interchangeable terms—when applied to farms—were bower, solar and chamber, in the order in which they gradually went out of use. But in early times rooms known as parlours were often additional chambers for sleeping—the word 'chamber' originally denoting the innovation of a separate sleeping place. Equally, the ground-floor storage room, which was commonly called a 'cellar' in England, though it was not below ground, might also be called a parlour. The contents of one such parlour in England included tods and barrels of eels and salmon, as well as equipment for making bow-strings. That was in the late 16th century. It is likely that a similar confusion of use was common in Guernsey throughout the 17th century at least, and that in many houses built then, or adapted from longhouses when the cows were ousted, the second room downstairs was no more than a glorified store, becoming only gradually the parlour proper, as known in the 19th century.

It is for this reason that no distinction will be made in this book between four- and five-bay houses. In many cases, houses which appear to be 'small parlour' houses from the outside, because the parlour has been provided with only one window, turn out to be five-bay constructions inside: for instance, Les Issues (440) of 1764.

These four- and five-bay houses depend greatly upon their façade and their furnishing for effect. Gone are the fine features that attract in the earlier houses. Arched doorways, carved fireplaces, bénitiers and tourelles—all were unfashionable by the mid-17th century. And if a dated lintel leads you to think that a house with a tourelle is 17th-century, beware! This period was nothing if not efficient with its face-lifts.

But though the details are different, the basic form is familiar. The kitchen was of two bays, the cross-passage of one, and the other room usually of two. In some cases the cross-passage might be divided from the kitchen by a stone wall and from the other rooms by panelling, but usually there was either two cross-walls, both rising to the ridge of the roof, or none. An example with two is Les Vieilles Galliennes (353), and it is interesting that King's Mills' Lodge (519), a house with a tourelle, also had two cross-walls rising to the ridge. King's Mills' Lodge can be dated between 1584 and 1636 and has all the appearance of being nearer the latter date than the former. Perhaps this practice of building both walls to the very top of the house, above the bedrooms and apparently dividing the loft quite unnecessarily, was a sort of rationalisation of the earlier house-building, where two cross-walls might be included downstairs, but only one would be carried right up, as the division between upper and lower lofts. Now the two walls were built of equal height, not for any practical reason, but out of habit. By the end of the 18th century, comparatively few houses were being built with any stone cross-walls. More and more it was presumably realised that if wooden partitions were adequate upstairs, they could be employed on the ground floor as well.

The kitchen in all these houses was still dominated by its hearth. But whereas the 15th and 16th centuries had lavished much thought and money on creating beautiful fireplaces with carved corbels and delicate chamfer stops, the 17th and 18th centuries preferred totally undressed stone, had no chamfering whatever at the sides of the fireplaces, and dispensed completely with stone lintels. Indeed, the corbels underneath the shoulder stones were usually omitted, just the shoulder stones being inserted through the gable wall to provide support for the wooden lintel and the wattle-and-daub chimney hood above. The general appearance was thus considerably rougher, ironically, than in the earlier houses.

THE TWO-STOREY HOUSE WITH CROSS-PASSAGE (Type 5)

But the evidence is quite indisputable, as reference to the First Schedule will show. Of the many houses with such fireplaces, Les Profonds Camps (58) and Côte ès Ouets (964) are examples from opposite ends of the island.

From about 1700 onwards, many new houses incorporated a bread oven into the design of their kitchen fireplace. This was constructed in one of three ways. Perhaps the earliest idea was to put the door of the bread oven at the back of the fireplace, piercing the gable end, so that the oven itself was built outside and projected in a beehive shape beyond the house. The first oven inserted into the fireplace of the back kitchen at La Maison d'Aval (241) was formed in this way, though it was later dismantled and another oven built to the left of the hearth. The same thing happened at Le Douit Beuval (267), where the earlier oven survived until 1978. At both houses, and at La Vieille Sous L'Eglise (475) the oven in fact projected into adjoining barns, and in each of these examples was constructed in the back kitchen. An example—though in a Type 8 house—where it was constructed from the main kitchen and still survives, is Les Niaux (539). In all these cases, the oven door surround is of stone rather than brick. The type is occasionally encountered later, as in the 'new' house at Les Bordages, 1790, where a particularly fine example projects from the back kitchen and is protected by a lean-to roof in exactly the same way as some of the outside ovens of detached bakehouses in Brittany and Normandy. Les Vinaires possesses an even later, though rather better-constructed, external bread oven.

The second, and by far the most common method of construction was to build the oven at one side of the fireplace, normally towards the back of the house, but not always, for instance at Les Mielles (1001). Here, the oven was built at the same time as the house, in 1727, and is a very good example of its type. The oven occupies the front angle of the room to the left of the fireplace, and the oven door is thus at the left of the hearth. To fuel the oven, bundles of furze were pushed inside and set alight, leaving the door ajar. The smoke would therefore join that from the fire on the hearth itself, and in order to collect the smoke from the oven more efficiently, the wattle-and-daub hood was usually brought further forward on that side than the other. A wooden lintel placed diagonally is the almost invariable rule. One end was supported by the masonry of the oven itself, the other rested further back on the usual large shoulder stone. By this device, it was thus only necessary to use one, instead of two, shoulder stones to support the lintel and the chimney hood. It should follow that houses where a shoulder stone can be seen at each side of the fireplace did not originally possess a bread oven, whereas in those in which only one shoulder stone is apparent, the oven is contemporary with the house. But the matter is not as simple as that, because in the course of building ovens into earlier houses, shoulder-stones—and corbels where they existed—were often displaced. Where the insertion has been into a pre-1625 house, it is obvious enough, because the jamb of the original fireplace, on the other side of the hearth, will always be carved and chamfered. But where an oven has been inserted into a house that is itself post-1625, it is not always possible to tell whether the oven was part of the original equipment or not.

The oven door, in most examples of this second type, has surrounds of brick, but a few are of stone, as in the inserted oven at Bordeaux House (984). The use of brick for the door surrounds and for the dome of the oven itself is probably the earliest use of this material for domestic purposes: earlier than the brick chimneys that almost everywhere replaced stone or clay stacks. Stone chimneys were still being built even up to the end of our period, whereas many of our furze ovens certainly date from before 1787. Brick was extensively used in the Married Quarters at Castle Cornet, in 1750, and in the building or extension of various town premises between 1750 and 1787. The many 18th-century brick vaults of the period indicate how much more suitable it was than stone for this sort of construction, quite apart from its greater resilience when exposed to intense heat in a bread oven.

Above the brick dome, the oven was often further insulated by a layer of sand up to nine inches deep. But this was not invariably so. In some ovens, there was a door close to the ceiling, so that bundles of furze could be passed into the kitchen from the loft above. Sometimes a separate chute was provided for this, on the other side of the fireplace, as at Duvaux Farm (936), though here, and probably elsewhere when it occurs, this feature is 19th-century rather than earlier.

Indeed, of all the features we are dealing with, furze ovens are the most difficult to date with any accuracy, because their construction remained basically the same until they went out of fashion, around 1900. As with the fireplace itself, the period did not call for any ornamentation, and a comparison of styles is therefore impossible. Certainly some superior examples in nicely-dressed stone are clearly 19th century, and those ovens built entirely of brick are also comparatively modern. But with many it is impossible to tell whether an oven was built or inserted in 1750 or 1850. All are therefore recorded, for the sake of completeness.

The third way of placing the oven may well be an entirely 19th-century characteristic, since it often seems to depend upon the existence of a back kitchen of that period. In this instance, the oven was still placed in the angle to one side of the kitchen fireplace, but the oven doorway was built through the back wall of the house, so that the oven was fired from a back kitchen. The advantage of this method was undoubtedly that it caused less chaos in the kitchen when the oven was in use, the kitchen in these houses having probably become more of a dining-room. Smoke presumably escaped up a separate chimney hood in the back kitchen. Two ovens of the sort can be found in both houses at Le Truchon (245 and 246). One of them has been half demolished, leaving the oven exposed in section (see Illustration 46). The method of constructing a dome of slightly tapered bricks used vertically, is clearly visible.

THE TWO-STOREY HOUSE WITH CROSS-PASSAGE (Type 5)

The method of using a bread oven, or *grand four,* as it was known, was as follows. The most common fuel was the furze that grows so easily on banks and cliffs in the island. Every farm had its furze-brake or *jaonière,* sometimes quite a long way off. The *jaonière* belonging to Les Fauconnaires (674), for instance, was at La Corbière, on the south coast (while the *sécage* for this farm, or place where vraic—seaweed—could be laid to dry before being carted home for fertiliser, was at Richmond, on the west coast). The furze, *la jaon,* was cut in the spring while it was green, and after being left to dry, was tied into bundles— *jibbes de jaon*—and brought home to be stacked in the furze-loft, or *schnar.* Special leather gauntlets were used for this prickly operation, and the furze was cut with special hooks which can be seen at the Guernsey National Trust's Folk Museum in Saumarez Park.

Baking of bread, gâche—a sort of fruit loaf rather like the Welsh *bara brith*— and Guernsey biscuits—a kind of bread bun—would be done once a week or once a fortnight, depending upon the size of the household. The dough would be kneaded on the scrubbed kitchen table, in the centre of the room, and then placed in wooden trays on the Guernsey green bed—*la jonctierre* (one of several names)—to rise overnight. The green bed was formerly to be found in every farmhouse at the side of the hearth opposite the bread oven. It consisted of a large wooden 'tray', on short legs, roughly the size of a bed. This tray was filled periodically with dry bracken and covered with a quilt to provide a soft and warm bed or couch on which the farmer could relax, perhaps in the evening. It was a forerunner of the modern settee, an easy chair being unknown in 18th-century farm kitchens, as in many French houses even today.

When the bread had risen in its tray on the green bed the oven was lit with a couple of bundles of furze. Different families had different methods of testing the heat. Some would see if the oven was ready by putting a hand inside; some would place a brick in the oven and wait until it gave off sparks. When it was ready the ashes would be raked out with *la rotarre* and the bread carefully placed inside, using a long wooden shovel, known as *la palette.* Then the door would be shut and the food would bake from the heat already absorbed by the brick lining.

After baking, the bread would be kept on a rack. At Le Tertre (1026) there were two racks in the back kitchen: one for cooling the bread and one for storing it. At La Rocque Balan (1007), the bread rack is unaccountably upstairs, opposite the top of the tourelle. But the usual position was above the door to the cross-passage, where it is at Duvaux Farm. This house undoubtedly retains the best evocation in the island of life in the late 18th and early 19th centuries. The earlier farmhouse there was almost entirely re-modelled, and a back kitchen built on in the 1820s, and not only the kitchen but the entire house has kept its fittings and furnishings of that date.

Along the back wall of the kitchen would be the dresser—cupboards below and shelves above. Sometimes it was built into the corner, with a settle adjoining it, against the cross-wall. Several dressers and settles survive, some with the end of the settle shaped into a hat-stand, or, at L'Echelle (649) elongated into a wig stand. The most magnificent dresser is to be seen at Duvaux Farm, while just opposite, at Le Marais (937) is a much humbler and probably earlier version.

Suspended from the ceiling in front of the fireplace was the pork rack, on which were kept sides of pork ready for use, and no doubt other meat as well. Light would have been from a cresset lamp—*le crasset*—a somewhat smelly device using oil rendered down from fish livers (conger, cod, and ray fish being set aside for this purpose). A twisted cotton wick, singed to keep it together, would require fairly frequent trimming with a wick cleaner called *l'amichet*. By using the hook at the end of the handle (*la tanque*) the crasset could be placed in any position. It could be stuck into holes in the masonry so that it gave light when bread was being taken out of the oven; suspended by means of a lath over the table, *la table de cuisine,* in the centre of the room; or over *le jonctierre* to give light for sewing or reading. It could also be supported on a metal stand, or *vilaine,* enabling it to be moved about the room. Large double lamps would be used at festivals, when the house was filled with people, and probably at other times by families who could afford the extra oil. One such lamp remains at Duvaux Farm, together with the lath for suspending it over the green bed. The lath is hinged onto one of the ceiling joists, against which it folds back when not in use. There are

Fig. 14.

two examples of laths for *le crasset* at Maison de Bas (973) above and another at Les Messuriers (158). While engaged on this survey, only three green beds were seen still in position, pork was on the rack in only one house—Les Champs, Les Jehans (334)—and *le grand four* or bread oven was regularly used (at Christmas in 1979 for five families), only at La Fosse (300). The only terpied still in occasional use—the open hearth taking its name from the tripod used for cooking over the fire—was at Les Romains (944), for making jams and marmalade in a large brass *bashin*; and very good the jam is, too!

It will be apparent that apart from the green bed, very little of the way of life described above, or of the kitchen layout, is peculiar to Guernsey. A Guernseyman from a farm in St. Andrew's parish might have felt pretty much at home visiting a small farm in Surrey or Cornwall or Yorkshire, in about 1750. Just as 200 years earlier his way of life had been close to that of his Breton or Norman neighbours, so by 1750 many of the elements of his existence had

THE TWO-STOREY HOUSE WITH CROSS-PASSAGE (Type 5)

been greatly influenced by English traditions and customs. Nothing emphasises more succinctly this switch of allegiance, as it were, from France to England than the all-popular bread oven. Normandy and Brittany had very few of these indoor ovens and those there are seem to be later than 1800. The insertion of the bread oven into almost every farm and cottage here between 1700 and 1900 indicated an acceptance of English ways; and the incidental desecration of many a fine medieval fireplace in the process seems almost symbolic.

From the 18th-century onwards there is almost an embarrassing quantity of written material recording intentionally or otherwise, life in all its aspects in this island. Much has been published, one way or another, already. And as the purpose of the present book is to examine the vernacular tradition as it expressed itself in architecture, rather than in belief and traditions or social customs, space must not be taken to delve into these matters more deeply than is necessary to explain the construction and arrangement of the houses we see around us.

We have seen, therefore, that by 1750 the kitchen was a rather more sophisticated place than it was in 1550. The kitchen sink recess was no longer built, and to the simple furnishings of earlier times, consisting very likely of little more than a long wooden table and two benches, a green bed and an armoire or large cupboard, much more was added. The dresser implied the accumulation of crockery, including some good pieces used chiefly for display. It also meant that the wealth of keeping places all around the walls of medieval buildings was no longer required. Although the earth floor was still very common, the better-off could afford a paved kitchen and entry (or cross-passage), either of local stone or the fine limestone slabs brought over from Dorset as ballast in the holds of the ships that returned to England laden with granite.

At Le Bourg de Bas (162) and Les Adams (328), however, there is reason to think that we have examples of an alternative way of organising the kitchen and its oven. These two houses seem to possess separate bakehouses, on the same principle as the *boulangeries* outside many a farmhouse in Normandy and Brittany, though the Guernsey examples are much more similar to detached bakehouses known in England, as far as their internal arrangement inside is concerned.

The whole complex of house and farm buildings at Les Adams is of outstanding interest. The early 19th-century façade of the main house belies its age, for it was certainly there before 1625, as were some of the row of barns and stables opposite. Late 17th-century improvements include a unique double entrance, the carriage way having sloping sides and the pedestrian way a flat lintel; a *prinseur* or barn containing the cider press; and the detached kitchen. This detached kitchen later became attached by the interpolation between it and the main house of a 19th-century back kitchen very ingeniously contrived. And at this time the tourelle was rebuilt, and ranges of pig-sties provided.

The detached kitchen looks from the outside like a small house, being 23ft. long by 20ft. wide. But it is clear that it was never intended to be more than a

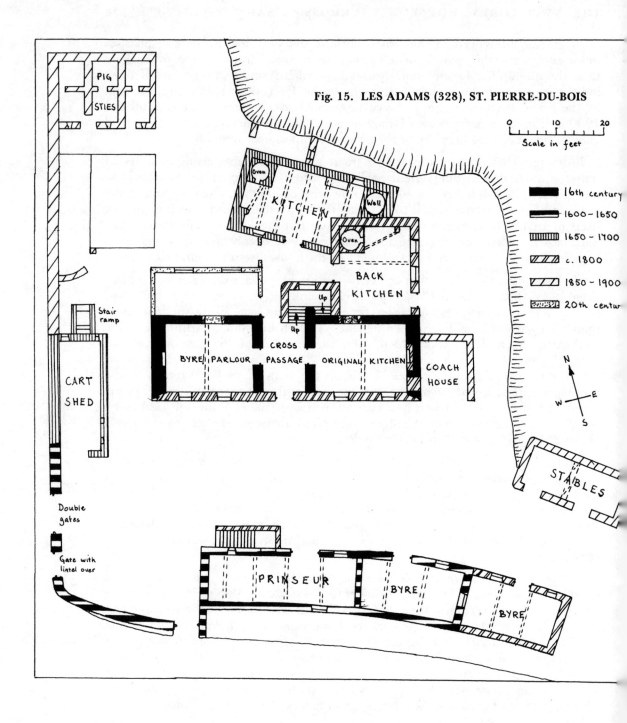

Fig. 15. LES ADAMS (328), ST. PIERRE-DU-BOIS

THE TWO-STOREY HOUSE WITH CROSS-PASSAGE (Type 5)

kitchen below and loft above. There is a central doorway with one window to the left and none to the right. The only other window is at the back on the right, alongside the well which occupies all of that corner. At the opposite end, to the left of the door, is the large hearth, with a furze oven to the right of it. Together, these occupy almost the entire gable end. Along the back wall, between oven and well, is a large built-in cupboard, which has the appearance of being contemporary with the building.

The ceiling beams are arranged as in a barn or warehouse, rather than a dwelling, fairly close together and without intermediate joists. There is no sign of there having been any sort of internal sub-division. Above, the loft was no doubt used partly for the storage of furze. The wattle-and-daub chimney hood tapers to a stone stack built of red granite and of somewhat stumpy proportions, as all early stone chimney stacks are, and the building must date between about 1680 and 1710. As well as being the only detached bakehouse known, beside that at Le Bourg de Bas, it has one of the earliest ovens, and it is at the side of the hearth. Further work at dating the different types of oven construction may well come to the conclusion that those which pierce the gable wall to bulge externally, and those built beside the fireplace are merely alternative designs of the same date.

The other detached bakehouse at Le Bourg de Bas is a much smaller building, still standing detached from the main house, and dating, if one is to take the inscription on the beam inside as evidence of its construction, from 1770. A low ceiling provides the floor for a small loft, and the fireplace and bread oven occupy the entire gable end.

Whether these two have always been the only examples is impossible to tell. It is equally difficult to decide whether they are elaborate ways of combining the facilities of a back kitchen with the tradition of an outside bread oven, once, no doubt, as common in Guernsey as it still is in Brittany: or an innovation from England that never became popular.

After this extended discussion of the kitchens of the 17th- and 18th-century houses, we must now examine the rest of these dwellings. The room across the passage from the kitchen, as we have seen, gradually evolved from being virtually a store in the majority of houses, in 1625, to becoming a parlour or withdrawing-room in many of the better houses built or altered after 1750. The fine panelling that became fashionable by the middle of the 18th century was often reserved for this room and for the best bedroom. Such was the case at La Porte (526), a new house; at La Houguette (528) nearby, where the parlour was embellished in this way; and similarly at the Moulin de Haut (486).

But between 1625 and 1750 most houses with wooden partition walls had the post-and-panel, or in-and-out planking that we have met at La Roque Balan (1007) in the 16th century. There was, however, a difference in detail. The earlier and later forms of this walling can most easily be compared at 11 Cliff Street

(717), a house where the ground floor and first floor date from the 16th century, but the top floor was added in the first half of the 18th century. The same technique of post-and-panel partition is employed throughout, but the earlier work is of narrower timbers of different widths, while the later work is regular, with a simple moulding. Whereas early panelling was usually in oak, the later, 17th-century building was always pine. Although there is some post-and-panel work to be found in a good many houses, undoubtedly the best examples, which have preserved their original 17th-century partitions intact, are Les Quertiers (676), built before 1684 and also possessing some of its early windows, and The Cottage, Hauteville (695) which also has some of the Georgian panelling. Another house, like the two previous examples, where these features have been carefully retained and treasured, is Havilland House (685), one of a small number of three-storey houses, c. 1675–1700, with very similar characteristics, found on the outskirts of St. Peter Port, as they were then: the two others being Chateau de la Montagne, in La Charroterie (697) and 3 Back Street (733). (No. 3 Back Street is almost certainly earlier than 1747, the date on the door lintel.)

In all of these houses, the first-floor bedrooms, and, where they exist, the second-floor ones too, are separated by post-and-panel partitions. Both in town and country, the arrangement of the first-floor accommodation in the period 1625–1787 differed significantly from the layout in the longhouse. Instead of the bedroom over the byre and the loft above the kitchen, there was now a whole range of smaller rooms. Sometimes the large two-bay bedroom remained, above the parlour as at 3 Salter Street (858), but more frequently, in a five-bay house, four bedrooms were made, each a bay wide and of different sizes due to the necessity of having the upstairs passage along the back of the house, and to the need to provide headroom for the stairs. The final bay, at the gable above the kitchen, was left unfinished. Although the façade might well include a window to preserve symmetry, this last bay formed the furze loft, and a square doorway at floor level was almost invariably provided in the gable end, so that the furze could conveniently be unloaded from a cart driven up alongside. As has been noted above, the furze could then be used from the kitchen below without having to carry it through the rest of the house. However, where the bread oven was built in a back kitchen wing, the loft above it would be used for the furze, and all of the main house could be given over to bedrooms.

Almost invariably, the staircase to the bedrooms was set at the back of the cross-passage. In many cases, a short flight of about eight stairs led to a tiny square landing, from which two or three more stairs went up on each side. By this device, it was just possible to fit such a staircase into the space between the central doorways in the cross-wall of kitchen or parlour and the back wall of the house. The stairs ran along either kitchen or parlour wall (or partition). It was also just possible to find space for the back door beside the stairs, underneath the top two or three steps. Above the back door and slightly to one side of it, a window set a little lower than those of the upstairs passage on either side, marked the position of the little landing. A curious feature in a few houses

THE TWO-STOREY HOUSE WITH CROSS-PASSAGE (Type 5)

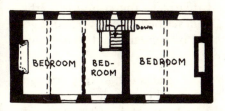

MAISON VILLOCQ (577): an older house refashioned in the early 18th century. Two large and one small bedroom.

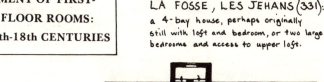

LA FOSSE, LES JEHANS (331): a 4-bay house, perhaps originally still with loft and bedroom, or two large bedrooms and access to upper loft.

Fig. 16. ARRANGEMENT OF FIRST-FLOOR ROOMS: 17th-18th CENTURIES

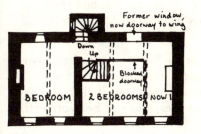

MOULIN DE HAUT (486): an older house refronted in the late 18th century. Tourelle rebuilt, and stairs added to loft bedrooms in the 19th century

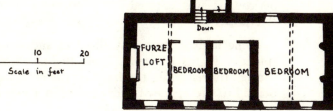

LES HAMELINS (294): loft reduced to one bay when house refronted and tourelle rebuilt in 1743. One large and two small bedrooms in 18th century, covered by clay insulation on floor of upper loft.

is that the back wall was cut away into a small hollow on this landing, presumably to allow more space to manoeuvre furniture. An example is at La Planque Farm (897) and in 17th-century buildings in Town, it is found, for instance, at 23 and 25 Mill Street (745/6). At La Bellieuse Farm (94) a similar hollowing of the wall accommodated a curved but strangely elongated staircase built *c.* 1625 against the front wall, and, incidentally, blocking an earlier kitchen sink below.

The staircase at La Bellieuse Farm is a variant of a type of staircase common in Brittany and Normandy from about 1550 to 1650 and found occasionally in Guernsey between the same dates. In a way, it links the tourelle tradition with the wholly internal staircase. Its distinguishing characteristic is that the stairs, whether in a projecting tourelle or otherwise, turn around a central, wooden newel, in some cases very probably a re-used mast from a ship. Only the very late tourelles are built in this way, for instance the very fine example at Les Granges de Beauvoir Manor (834); that at 2 Coupée lane (723); and almost certainly the staircase, now vanished, from the tourelle at 28 Le Pollet (793). Where the stairs are completely internal, the outside wall is always hollowed out to house them, as at Saints Farm (83) and at Les Câches (237), where the inserted stairs to the upper loft are of this type. So the progression seems to be from tourelle with stone steps to tourelle with wooden stairs around a newel post, from this to an internal newel staircase and thence to the common 17th- and 18th-century form of 'split' staircase already described. However, though there may be some truth in this conclusion, it must be remembered that many of the earliest houses had internal straight staircases.

At least two 17th-century houses in the parish of St. Andrew had very strange staircases. The disused house, now a barn, behind the other two houses at Les Poidevins (662), and the former house, now also a barn, at Le Camptréhard (656), had solid straight stone staircases in the cross-passage, rising towards the front of the house. The example at Le Camptréhard will be dealt with more fully in the section on Type 7 houses, but both here, and at Les Poidevins, which had two cross-walls rising to the ridge, there are clear signs that the bedroom (or bedrooms) was entered by a doorway in the cross-wall right at the front of the house.

Some houses, especially those in and around St. Peter Port, have rather more splendid flights of stairs, short flights arranged around three sides of a square formed by regarding the back of the cross-passage area as a stair-well. They really belong to the types of stairs found in Town shop premises, and will be dealt with in that section (Chapter XV).

From the description in the previous four pages, it can be seen that a much larger and more flexible area of accommodation for the family was provided in the farmhouse of 1750 compared with what had been available in the longhouse of 1550. In addition to the main house, there was very frequently an extension, in the form of a back kitchen, built either at the back or against the side of the existing kitchen. Mostly they were of two bays only, but there are a few examples three bays long, for instance, at Les Reveaux (259) and Les Quatre Vents (108). We have seen in Chapter VI that the earliest back kitchens appeared as early as the 16th century. In the 17th, 18th and 19th centuries they multiplied all over the island. They were particularly popular in the parish of St. Pierre-du-Bois as a means of accommodating a bread oven without altering the original kitchen fireplace. But in a good many houses, both new and old hearths were given furze ovens, as at Le Haut Chemin (311) where one side of a particularly fine 15th-century fireplace was destroyed for this purpose, while on the other side of the same wall, there is a later *terpied* and oven (see Illustration 49). Maybe this happened when the institution of a 'widow's third' began, so that the various parts of a family could each have an oven. Later on, if a property deteriorated into tenements, a similar thing occurred with the proliferation of Victorian cooking ranges in every room.

No doubt it was often necessary to arrange the back kitchen behind the house rather than at the side, either because the main kitchen was at the upper end and was already built into the valley side, or because by the 18th century many

THE TWO-STOREY HOUSE WITH CROSS-PASSAGE (Type 5)

houses already had a range of stabling attached at one side or the other, or both. These byres and barns housed the animals and provisions that in a longhouse would have been kept within the house. In some cases, as prosperity increased, they also no doubt replaced more flimsy temporary storerooms, such as those we have noted at La Grande Brière (Chapter II). It is not proposed to discuss very fully the farm buildings which grew up as the farm expanded. As well as stabling, they usually included a barn where cider was made, called *le prinseur,* a particularly good example of which is at Les Mourains (575). Here, the barn is dated 1722 and the cider press inside, 1735. They also included, on many farms, a room for the cowherd, who was often a young man employed to help generally about the farm, and called *le valet.* The valet's quarters were usually above the cowshed, as at Les Portelettes (355) and innumerable other places. Although the heat from below was quite considerable in winter, the valet's room was always provided with its own fireplace, but not usually with an oven— naturally, since the baking was the duty of the woman of the house. The earliest remaining example of a valet's room, with a fine early fireplace has already been noted at La Houguette (528). Elsewhere, these later upstairs fireplaces with their rough, unshaped shoulder stones and wooden lintels are a feature of 17th- —and even more commonly—18th-century farms. And the straight stone staircase leading to the valet's room is often a very picturesque feature of the farmyard. The shallow flights of steps, at right-angles to the buildings, that we have described in Chapter VI, gave way by 1700 to the sort which can be seen everywhere, running alongside the back wall of the building, or sometimes against a gable end. Some of these steps bridge the entrance to the byre below in ingenious ways. Those at Les Massies (421) and Les Hêches (375) use massive slabs of granite. Other flights of steps include a hole for the dog underneath, a later 18th-century example, recently carefully rebuilt, being at La Vieille Sous L'Eglise (475).

Returning to the house itself, much thought and expenditure were lavished on the exterior. Clearly it was desirable, by possessing a fine façade, to impress one's neighbours who were still living in longhouses with irregular windows and unfashionable arched doorways. For as the ideals of classical architecture trickled through to the countryside, 'Gothic' ornamentation did indeed begin to seem barbaric, as its name was meant to imply. Coupled with this basic change in taste came the availability of stone very different from the warm, red Cobo granite used by their forebears. Quarries at Perelle and in the north of the island began producing grey granite (grey rather than the even later 'blue' stone quarried in the 19th century), and the quarry near La Salerie in St. Peter Port provided an almost black gabbro. Whereas pieces of every sort of stone had been used in earlier houses, the source had been usually the seashore, or an outcrop from which a quantity of rock could be prised off; or a small quarry, opened for one specific job. For the first time, large quantities of grey stone were now available, and the colour appealed to house builders. Especially in the Forest parish, the use of this new and probably expensive stone for quoins and lintels produces very effective façades. Since there was an unlimited supply of local gneiss here for the rubble building of walls, both types were combined, the good quality stone being reserved to emphasise the symmetry of the elevation. The result is a very pleasing contrast in red and grey, of which a good example is the large house at Le Bourg (165). It dates from the first half of the 18th century and replaces an earlier house whose arch is re-used as quoins in the wing to the left. The similar house at La Villiaze (202) also provides a very pleasing composition. Here the dated stone inserted in the outer wall of the back kitchen cannot be relied on as evidence for the building of the present house, which is not much earlier than 1740. It does, however, possess a very strange fireplace, in the original kitchen, that gives the impression of being an educated effort to copy the fine workmanship of earlier carved corbels and shoulder stones. The tooling is very fine, and whatever the reasons for its existence, it is unique.

Red rubble walls with grey quoins and lintels can be found in most parts of the island, the combination of colour being far more satisfactory than in modern granite walling, where different stone used haphazardly often produces a rather blotchy effect. Later on in the 18th century, the entire front of a house might be built in grey stone. The more formal appearance of a grey granite façade seemed at the time infinitely preferable to the rather rustic look of the red stone. St. Briocq (277), was re-fronted in 1799 completely in grey stone, and the new house at Les Bordages is very similar (1790).

Undoubtedly the formality of these late 18th-century façades was affected by the public and military buildings erected at Castle Cornet and in Town from the middle of the century onwards. The Town Hospital of 1743 and The Married Quarters (1036) of 1750 were the forerunners not only of many fine houses in St. Peter Port, such as Moore's Hotel (795); but also influenced new house-building all over the island. In them we can see the final metamorphosis of the vernacular longhouse tradition into the symmetry of the Georgian and Regency town house and villa.

The result of all this new workmanship was, in fact, not only to impress the neighbours, but to make them wish to acquire large windows in their own houses, and to emulate on their own properties the balanced façades that had suddenly become so fashionable around them. The re-fronting of old houses was the consequence: a phenomenon that affected almost every 15th- and 16th-century house in the island at some time between 1700 and 1900. However, it was not a phenomenon confined to Guernsey. There are a good number of French manors whose ashlar front belies their true age: for instance, the fortified Manoir du Dur Écu, near Valcanville in Normandy. In the town of Valognes the houses almost all present frontages of the 18th century, and it is something of a surprise to find a 15th-century tourelle behind almost every one of them. In England, too, many a medieval farm and manor house was given a new façade at this time, complete with parapet and stucco front. Jettied timber houses in towns often had a new wall of brick built on the ground floor under the projecting upper floors, so that they could become more elegant, their woodwork covered over with plaster, and presenting a flat façade to the street.

THE TWO-STOREY HOUSE WITH CROSS-PASSAGE (Type 5) 87

Here in Guernsey it was clearly cheaper to upgrade an old house than to build a new one. There might also have been considerable reluctance to leave the family home. As far as we can tell, it was uncommon to abandon an old house for a new one until the 19th century. Not until Victorian times were old houses partly demolished, in the way we have noted at La Maison d'Aval (241), where a new house was built in 1866, keeping half the old one as a kitchen wing. Neither until last century were houses re-used as barns or stabling, such as happened at Les Islets (307).

Rather it was the practice to modernise the existing house. This might consist perhaps of building a separate cowshed, so that the cows no longer used the main house. It might include the building on of a back kitchen, providing a bread oven, or buying a pump to save drawing water from the well. The upstairs bedrooms might be re-designed, as we have seen, using the latest panelling for the walls, But, above all, the house would be re-fronted.

No other activity of the house-builder of previous centuries has been so misleading to the students of local architecture. For a house that was re-fronted in 1700 has now weathered sufficiently to look superficially very similar to the original. If a matching stone was chosen, as for instance at La Forge (221), it is often necessary to look twice to realise, as here, that the superb ashlar of the front is of a different period from the equally superb arch. More confusion occurs because in totally new houses of the 18th century it was often the practice to copy the effect of re-fronting an old one. Thus at Le Bourg, for instance, the fine façade in contrasting stone is far more splendid than the back, which is mostly red gneiss with much rougher grey lintels. Re-fronting carried out in the 19th century is easier to spot, even when it is not ashlar, because most masonry erected after *c.* 1790 was coursed rubble, rather than the uncoursed or semi-coursed masonry used until then.

One wonders how this major alteration was achieved. Presumably the idea was to support the front end of all the main beams while the entire operation took place, so that the fabric of the rest of the house was disturbed as little as possible. In many cases, caution (or cheeseparing) prevented the old walls being taken down as far as one might have thought necessary. Often the original frontage was removed only to the level of the new window-sills, and many of the gable-end quoin stones were left *in situ*. Admittedly, to have removed some of the larger stones used at the angles of old houses might seriously have weakened the gables. But the effect of not doing so does, at its worse, produce a very strange effect. A house where the renovators seem to have done as little as possible when inserting the new frontage is La Contrée de L'Eglise (632), re-fronted by Pierre Le Lacheur in 1746. The grey stone chosen for the new work shows up clearly how much of the older wall was left. The new work looks, in fact, like a very large patch. Other houses where re-fronting has been only to ground-floor window-sill level are Le Douit Farm (498) and La Grande Maison (945), though there are many other examples.

In general, if there is doubt about re-fronting, the hallmark of the 18th-century builder is the grey stone used in so many houses as quoins and lintels; and also the proportions of those quoins themselves. Unlike earlier masons who used stones large or small, but many quite massive, at the angles of the gable ends, the 18th-century workmen usually chose stones that were all of a size, and in the 19th century quoin-stones were even more regular, being exactly the depth of one course (or layer) of walling.

If nothing else indicated its period, the pointing at La Moulin de Haut (486) would reveal it. For during the 18th century it was often the practice to push little black beach pebbles into the clay mortar when pointing between the larger stones. This technique is known as 'galleting' and can be highly ornamental where it is done systematically. At La Moulin de Haut they form very straight lines producing an ashlared effect. At La Fosse (63)—one of very few properties inadvertently omitted from the 1787 map—fairly large pebbles in all the rubble-walling results in a web of black dots.

Wisteria (502) in King's Mills, is treated similarly, but not in quite such an exaggerated way. La Tanière (550) is the only house in the island where galleting is done with the stones inserted on edge, instead of flat, into the mortar.

Such obvious efforts at decoration often date an entire wall. But elsewhere, a little galleting may mean no more than a bit of re-pointing carried out on much older masonry. Surface coatings of any kind, as evidence of dating, must always be used with caution.

The 18th century witnessed a rapid change in window design. In the longhouse the windows had been mostly small and of various shapes, but tending to be much wider than they were high. When the first regular façades appeared, from about 1580 onwards, arches and carved fireplaces were still in fashion, and so the chamfers and chamfer-stops of these fireplaces and arches were applied to the fine regular windows of which the owners were very justly proud. Window proportions might sometimes be nearly square, but usually they were still wider than they were high. This is most clearly seen on the three-storey house at Les Granges de Beauvoir Manor (834), but other fine houses with chamfered windows of the same type are Le Tourtel (129), La Carrière (208) and Le Chêne Cottage (154). Throughout the majority of the 17th century, proportions remained the same, the window being divided usually into six lights—three above and three below—by heavy square mullions and transom. In France, windows divided in this way are termed *fenêtre à meneaux*. In Guernsey, the six-light windows were glazed with diamond-shaped leaded lights of bluish, thin glass, like the example at La Forge; or sometimes of horn, like that found nearby at Les Marchez (218). Each of the six lights was protected by a vertical bar of iron, set firmly into top and bottom of the window-frame and transom.

By the end of the 17th century the proportions had changed. Windows were now square, or almost square, as in the delightful re-fronting at Les Prevosts

THE TWO-STOREY HOUSE WITH CROSS-PASSAGE (Type 5)

(463), where grey window surrounds contrast with red ashlar (see Chapter XXXIX). At La Vrangue Manor (901), one original surround of red stone, now enclosing the arms of De Beauvoir and Carey, remains from an earlier façade, but in 1674, the front was re-fashioned with extraordinary new window surrounds, of a design only found elsewhere at Normanville (883). Each jamb was monolithic, like the lintels and sills, forming a fine array of square windows. But what we see at La Vrangue Manor now has been altered yet again, in the 19th century, when the fashionable square windows of 1674 had become unfashionable, and were the wrong proportions for the guillotine sliding sashes that were coming into use. So the window-sills were all taken out, broken in two, and re-used to elongate the sides.

Elsewhere, all through the 18th century, window shapes tended to lengthen. And while the larger windows sometimes threw a whole house out of proportion—as the insertions of last century at Les Picques (445), curious as they are—we must be thankful that Guernsey followed the English fashion of guillotine sashes rather than the French style, which favoured even larger casement windows. Downstairs, a favourite way of accommodating the new sliding sashes that were used here from about 1750 onwards (and earlier at Sausmarez Manor), was to elongate the downstairs windows by removing the sills, just as at La Vrangue Manor. It is not often realised that many houses with 19th-century sashes would originally have resembled Le Bourg, the same sort of fine grey sill below the window, matching the lintel which remains over the top. Upstairs, an opportunity of enlarging the windows came when the thatch was removed. The window lintels upstairs had usually been wooden, since they carried comparatively little weight. Since neither a pantile nor a slate roof needed to be at such a steep pitch as thatch, it is common to find that both front and back walls of houses were raised by at least one foot when re-roofing, thus accommodating new guillotine sashes with the minimum of alteration, and achieving more headroom in the bedrooms, in many houses at the same time getting rid of the slope at the sides of the bedroom ceilings, where the thatch had come down low over the eaves. The upstairs windows at La Villiaze were altered in this way, while, curiously, the downstairs ones were left square, with their casement sashes. At Les Mauxmarquis (669) and in many other farmhouses, it is possible to guess at the original height of the house itself by comparing it with that of the barn alongside. No doubt, before the re-roofing and enlargement of windows, both formed a continuous line.

All these improvements to the façade were characterised by the desire to reserve any ornamentation in stone, formerly so popular inside the house, for the exterior. Thus we find that the corbel shapes so commonly associated with 16th-century fireplaces, now appear in the *croissettes* of the roof-coping. Most roof copings that remain are not much earlier than 1650, and this line of large stones, necessary to protect the thatch of the gable from the elements, was often terminated, where it projected slightly over the front or back walls at the base of the gable, by a carved stone or *croissette*. There is an unusually

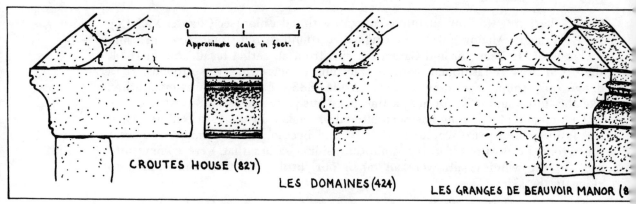

Fig. 17. CROISSETTES AT THE FOOT OF ROOF COPINGS

complicated example at Les Domaines (424) and simpler ones at Les Hamelins (294) of a type fairly widespread. Chimney stacks also became grander: taller and usually of grey ashlar construction.

At the same time as the fireplace corbel became a *croissette*, as it were, the front door arch was often removed one stage further away from the house to form a garden gate: that is, where it did not find its way into the pig-sty. At Les Graies (268), the bottom half of a very fine arch is embedded in the pig-sty, while the top half is at a respectable distance across the road. Another variation on this theme is represented by Les Tilleuls (563), where the bedroom fireplace lintel has been re-used over the front door, and the front door arch is at the garden entrance on the roadside, probably in a desire to emulate the double entrance arch to the drive of Les Blancs Bois, not far away. At Le Chêne Cottage (154), Le Cas Rouge (210), and Le Tourtel (129), the fireplace lintel itself was used to span a garden entrance, though at Le Tourtel the lintel has been restored to its proper place this year (1980).

The very idea of a front garden was an indication of changing ways. A longhouse with a garden would have been almost a contradiction in terms. But the 18th-century front garden with its flower beds and gravel paths was all part of an effort to show how prosperous and how civilised the family had become. Our earliest front garden walls date from the 18th century, and their flat tops, formed usually of large grey stones on a red rubble wall, use exactly the same building technique as the copings of the gable end. Just as the house itself was a harmonious composition of red and grey stone, so the low garden wall at La Villiaze is built of red stone below with grey capping above: a nice detail. Les Grandes Meilles (966), however, is probably more representative of most farms of the period, with its range of pig-sties running from the house towards the road. Somehow, the concept of a noisy, bustling farmyard in front seems in no way to detract from the simple dignity of this house behind.

Whatever the social pretentions of the age, we have seen that it was the four- or five-bay house of two storeys which most people chose for their homes. Two

THE TWO-STOREY HOUSE WITH CROSS-PASSAGE (Type 5)

hundred and ninety-seven are listed in the First Schedule, far outnumbering any other house form found in the island before 1787. But the years from 1625 to 1787 also witnessed a far greater diversity in the types of houses built than the sorts which survive from previous centuries, and are described in Part I of this book. However, to understand the other types of houses produced in the 17th and 18th centuries, it is very necessary to bear in mind the developments noted in their two-storeyed cousins, for naturally many characteristics re-occur, perhaps in humbler form.

Chapter IX

THE ONE-STOREY HOUSE WITH CROSS-PASSAGE (Type 6)

THE DIVERGENCE from one basic house-type which we noted in Part I, where the variation was on the longhouse theme, accelerated during the 17th century, but with one important difference. Whereas the earlier variations of house plan seem mostly to have been at the upper end of the social scale, while the poorer or more conservative families remained in single or two-storey longhouses, in later times the layout of the more important houses seemed to crystallize into one almost invariable form, while it was the smaller buildings that provided the variety.

The simplest type of house-plan, clearly dependent upon the two-storey cross-passage house for its inspiration, was the single-storey house with cross-passage. Of these, 113 remain, of which 17 are four-bay structures, and almost all the others are five-bay; although there are occasional six-bay cottages, for instance, that at The Cottage (212).

In essence, the layout is exactly like the ground floor of the two-storey house. But whereas in the larger houses the parlour occupied the room on one side of the cross-passage, in these it became the bedroom and was usually unheated until *c.* 1750. The kitchen contained bread oven, racks, dresser and settle, and differed only in the quality of its fittings and furnishings. Just as in the larger houses, there might be two cross-walls, one or none. But because these dwellings are so much smaller, a family produced twice as much wear-and-tear on the fabric. Moreover, in the last 100 years they have been even more continuously improved than their larger counterparts. Consequently, they contain hardly any early panelling. All is now 19th-century tongued-and-grooved planking, or matchboarding, or modern studwork.

The lofts of these cottages were clearly of importance, since there was no farm complex of barns and cartsheds in which to store things. Although many cottages have an opening in the gable-end for the storage of furze above the oven, as in the two-storey houses, the most important outside access—and probably in many cases the only access—would have been by a doorway above the front or back door, tucked under the thatch, which would have formed an 'eye-brow' above it. Such attractive loft openings and upstairs windows so often found in thatched houses everywhere are lost when a pantile or slate roof is put on. It is more difficult to produce a waterproof roof around curves with tile or slate, and so

THE ONE-STOREY HOUSE WITH CROSS-PASSAGE (Type 6)

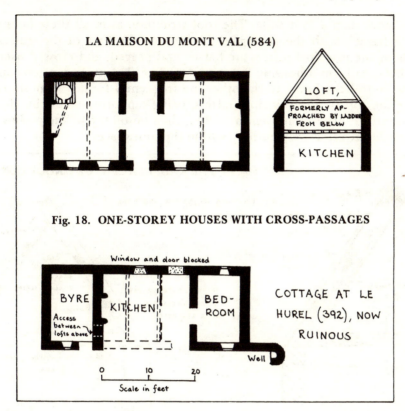

Fig. 18. ONE-STOREY HOUSES WITH CROSS-PASSAGES

the eye-brow opening becomes a dormer window. The presence of original loft openings as eye-brows under the thatch is amply documented in old photographs, which show them perhaps with a ladder against the sill, or a cart outside, such an opening being within easy reach for pitching in furze or whatever else was required.

Some of these houses, especially in the Cobo area—though Tangela in Les Croutes is another example (829)—have higher front and back walls, so that there would have been sufficient room for a square loft-opening at loft-floor level without the need to raise the thatch in an eye-brow over the top. Whether these buildings did in every case include such a loft opening, however, is doubtful, that at La Maison du Mont Val (584), for instance, having only an opening in its gable end. Le Guet (597) and Les Petits Cherfs (571) are others built higher in this way, Les Petits Cherfs clearly retaining its front loft entrance as a window.

Internal access to the loft was often completely lacking, though almost all lofts have been converted into bedrooms in recent times. However, a most interesting and unique survival of a stone staircase to the loft from the cross-passage was noted in 1980 at the Rue des Vinaires (302). Its continued survival is in the balance. Boxed into a later Victorian cupboard, it consisted of large flat stones built into the structure of the cross-wall, forming a set of narrow steps no more than a foot wide. The roof structure, as in all these houses, was a simple 'A-frame', with the ceiling-beams forming the base of the trusses above. The tops of the principal rafters are halved and pegged, and crossed over, in the earlier roofs, to form a housing for the ridge-plate. The purlins, often continuous from one end of the house to the other and frequently formed from ships' masts, run over the top of the principal rafters, being supported below by cleats. The common rafters, little more than branches, then lie on top of the purlins, so that the principals are effectively entirely within the roof space.

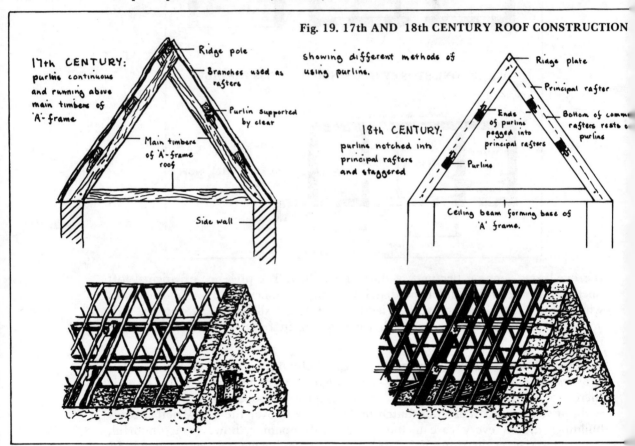

Fig. 19. 17th AND 18th CENTURY ROOF CONSTRUCTION showing different methods of using purlins.

In later roofs—and certainly in most houses after 1750—it became the practice to notch the purlins into the principals, alternately above and below each other from one bay to the next. The top of the principals was thus on a level with the common rafters. And whereas in 17th-century roofs the timbers might be almost unshaped (though there are exceptions where they are carefully squared), by 1750 both principals and purlins were almost regular. However, the curve of the tree trunk is usually visible on parts of these 18th-century timbers whereas it is not on 19th-century work.

THE ONE-STOREY HOUSE WITH CROSS-PASSAGE (Type 6)

Although internal access to the loft was probably rare, there are very occasional signs that it was used as a bedroom before the end of the 18th century in a few cottages. One such is at Mount Pleasant (585), where an original wattle-and-daub flue for an upstairs fireplace can be seen in the loft.

Additional space was sometimes achieved by building a little stable or store often only one bay wide, at one end or other of the house. At Newlands, Le Monnaie (663), it adjoins the bedroom: at the ruined cottage near Le Hurel (392) it was at the side of the kitchen. This cottage, whose front has been entirely removed, is of considerable interest, as it clearly shows how access from the loft over the main house into the loft above the stable was achieved by squeezing in a narrow, lop-sided doorway beside the wattle-and-daub chimney-hood, in between it and the slope of the roof. At the other end of the building, a nice detail is the continuation of the house wall along a few feet to enclose a well-head, which is still intact.

The external appearance of almost every single-storey house built between 1625 and 1787 has been altered drastically, either by re-fronting or by the insertion of large 19th-century windows. The original appearance of such cottages is perhaps best conveyed by the single-storey back-kitchen extension, c. 1675, at Le Grée, Le Gron (436); a much older house that has preserved, on its 1739 re-fronting, a row of original thatch-ties (see Colour plate 3). It will be noticed that these stones are set too low to have been the supports for a guttering, quite apart from the fact that a guttering is not needed with a thatched roof and would be very difficult to fix because of the overhang of the foot of the thatch.

La Maison du Mont Val is one of the few houses where the original façade survives: a very pleasing composition of Cobo stone, with Perelle stone used as contrasting lintels and window-sills. One of the earliest groups of fishermen's cottages remains at Les Jenemies, some rather later than 1787. In fact, of all the other cottages along the bays of the west coast hardly any had been built by that date.

Chapter X

THE HOUSE WITH INTEGRAL BYRE BUT OUTSIDE ACCESS
(Type 7)

TYPES 7, 8 and 9 in many respects shade into each other, and the separation into three groups is done only to highlight particular characteristics. They also span the arbitrary division of 1625, just as the three-bay house does. With the exception of Les Cottes (951), which is in some ways unique, there is no example of these houses in St. Sampson's or the Vale parishes, and only one in St. Peter Port. This is partly because split-level houses—that is, all of Type 9 and three of the four in Type 7—are obviously adapted to a site on a valley side, and are consequently found only in the 'upper parishes'. But it is also probably partly a matter of survival, for their proportions presented nothing of the fashionable façade favoured from 1700 onwards. Furthermore, when they were built of inferior materials, although picturesque while left untouched, they are very difficult to transform into acceptable homes without considerable alteration, as has been found recently at Les Niaux (539—Type 8).

There are four houses only which still show any signs of having been built with an integral byre, to which there was both inside and outside access. These are classed as Type 7. To them must possibly be added The Elms at Pleinheaume (946), though there the separate outside access to the byre may well be an insertion.

Of the other four, Les Cottes is undoubtedly the oldest. In the style of its fireplace and the provision of gable windows in the bedroom it greatly resembles the earlier examples of the three-bay houses, especially Les Simons (340). It probably dates, therefore, from the last quarter of the 16th century.

Its distinguishing feature is that it possesses no cross-passage; and that it has never done so, is proved by the unique positions of the front and back doorways. The front doorway opens directly into the kitchen, but at the extreme gable end, next to the fireplace. For a possible upstairs parallel to this arrangement, see p. 64. The back doorway opens directly into the byre, but towards the middle of the house, so that the doorway between byre and kitchen is right next to it. The cross-wall between byre and kitchen is only carried up to ground-floor ceiling level, so that the bedroom above could have been of three bays, extending over both byre and kitchen below which are of one and two bays respectively.

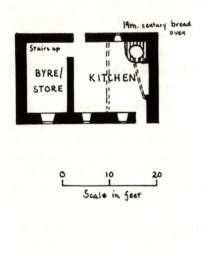
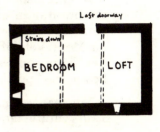

Bedroom fireplace corbel

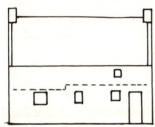

Front elevation

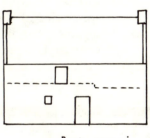

Back elevation

Fig. 20. LES COTTES (951)

West gable end: byre or store with bedroom above

East gable end: kitchen with loft above

However, if the downstairs ceiling levels are original, there was probably a one-bay bedroom with a wooden partition separating it from a two-bay loft. In any case, it is more than likely that the staircase was elsewhere, perhaps being moved when the bread oven was put into the kitchen. The low side walls of the bedroom are curious; no higher than those just noted in the 'Cobo' houses such as La Maison du Mont Val (584). But those later houses had no upstairs bedroom, whereas Les Cottes possesses a heated bedroom whose fireplace, like that in the kitchen below, has corbels of a design found nowhere else in Guernsey.

Whereas we may have here a truly transitional stage between longhouse and 17th-century farmhouse, it is more probable that Les Cottes is the product of a personal whim. It is also possible that it was built by an immigrant from Brittany—there were many Huguenot settlers here at that time—for it represents a type of house found in his native land, built here, as it were, in defiance of local tradition. Without other houses with which to compare it, there is no possibility at present of reaching a conclusion on the matter.

The remaining three houses are split-level buildings with a byre about four feet below the level of the kitchen. Clear evidence remains of stairs down from kitchen to byre. It may, of course, be that many of the older split-level houses were once of this type but that all sign of an internal staircase has vanished. For instance, the newel staircase from the cross-passage to byre once noticed at La Cour de Longue (442) no longer exists.

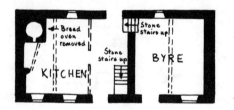 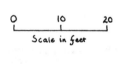 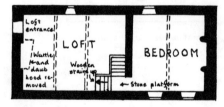

Fig. 21. LE CAMPTREHARD (656)

We are fortunate that the disused house at Le Camptréhard (656) has survived intact as a barn. For it shows to perfection the assimilation of the elements of the longhouse, adapted to a sloping site and to 17th-century needs (see Illustrations 33 and 34). At the front of the house there are two doorways, side by side, one to the dwelling and one to the byre. Comparison must immediately be made with many houses on the borders of Normandy and Brittany where pairs of doorways give access to the kitchen on one side and to the byre on the other. Some of them have arched doorways and some are later, with straight lintels of wood or stone. However, they are always built on a flat site, so that both

HOUSE WITH INTEGRAL BYRE BUT OUTSIDE ACCESS (Type 7)

doorways are at the same level, though the house one is frequently larger than that to the byre. Here, at Le Camptréhard, the byre doorway is a good three feet lower, and it is probable that the house doorway opened into a cross-passage rather than directly into the kitchen, although the wooden partition wall between cross-passage and kitchen has gone.

The one stone cross-wall, as at Les Cottes, served to separate house from byre, but at the back of the building, steps (now blocked) from the cross-passage gave access between the byre and the house part. Unlike Les Cottes, the cross-wall was carried up to the ridge of the roof, giving support to the straight stone staircase alongside it that rose towards the front of the house. At the top of that staircase, the cross-wall was pierced by a doorway into the bedroom over the byre. Presumably, wooden stairs then rose to the higher level of the loft above the kitchen. But the loft floor has now gone, so that the exact form of this staircase cannot be determined.

In both the bedroom and the kitchen were fireplaces of typical late 17th-century type with rough shoulder stones and wattle-and-daub hoods. The hoods have gone, but their supports are clearly visible. The kitchen fireplace also had an oven, almost certainly contemporary with the house. Consequently there was a gable opening in the loft above for throwing in the furze.

Using the slope of the land to produce this split-level house enabled the builders to economise on height while yet being able to achieve enough headroom for the bedroom windows to be a respectable size while slightly above floor-level. In the loft, on the other side of the house, a couple of low lights were squeezed in under the eaves, but as the chief external access was through the doorway in the gable end, no height was particularly necessary here on front or back walls.

Thus this compact little house had the kitchen with loft above, on one side; the byre with bedroom above, on the other. The only longhouse element omitted was the upper loft. No re-fronting has been carried out, and so it is possible to see in this interesting building the extra care that was taken, round about 1700, to make the front superior to the back, even in a cottage.

The remaining house in this group, Les Quatre Vents (108) is a rather larger version of Le Camptréhard. It was later extended by building on at right-angles a very long back-kitchen wing with stabling, and was re-fronted in the 19th century. At the same time, the cross-passage has been turned into another room, and the byre partly filled in, so that it is now barely five feet high. However, the former doorway down into the byre from the cross-passage is still possible to make out. Here, too, the bedroom was above the byre and was heated; and there was formerly a loft over the kitchen. The house probably dates from about 1700.

Chapter XI

THE LOW LOFT HOUSE (Type 8)

LES PIÈCES (150); Hillview, Le Variouf (181); L'Epinel (198); La Rocré (598); and Les Niaux (539) comprise the five houses of Type 8. Unlike most of Type 7 and all of Type 9, none of them is a split-level dwelling, all of them being built more or less on the flat. Nor does any of them show any clear signs of having had a byre inside the house, such as is found in Type 7 houses. On the other hand, each of them possesses an upstairs bedroom, unlike the houses of Type 9.

In other respects they differ considerably, but their unifying feature is their low loft. La Rocré and Hillview also happen to have a rather low bedroom, similar to that at Les Cottes (p. 96), but later. At Les Niaux, at present being rebuilt (1980), the bedroom walls were a little higher, to provide room for windows upstairs, while at L'Epinel and Les Pièces, the bedroom end of the house was raised to a full two storeys, the cross-wall forming a gable end against which the lower roof of the loft abutted.

La Rocré is clearly the oldest of the group, dating from early in the 17th century. Its tapering walls, rising from large foundation stones, and its former stone chimney hoods inside, are reminiscent of 16th-century buildings, but its two fireplaces have unshaped corbels, and none of the other features associated with earlier houses is present. There are two cross-walls, and the inserted bread oven takes up a good deal of the kitchen, which—extraordinarily—is of only one bay, while the other room is of two. The stone hood of the kitchen chimney was replaced by a wattle-and-daub hood when the oven was added. A split staircase leads from the cross-passage to loft and bedroom, and there are clear signs of low windows and loft openings under the eaves at the front of the house.

The kitchen is thus of the same dimensions as those in the three-bay houses, but the room across the passage, unheated parlour or store, allows for a two-bay bedroom above.

Hillview has only one cross-wall, and its kitchen is two bays long. It appears to date from the latter part of the 17th century and has not been re-fronted. Like La Rocré, the original windows upstairs were on floor-level, for in both houses the bedroom walls, as at Les Cottes, rose only about three feet front and back. The roof construction in both houses consists of upper collar trusses in order to give headroom underneath.

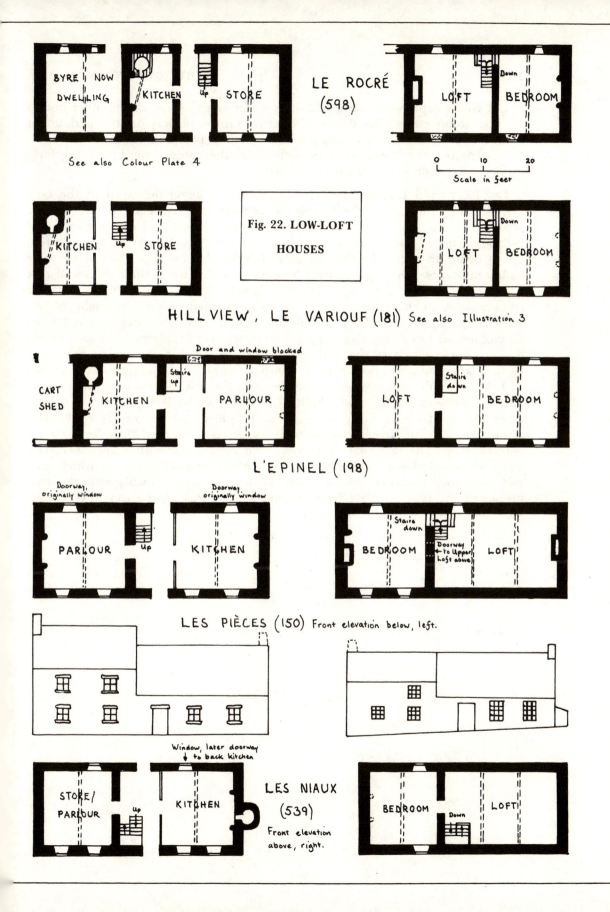

Les Niaux is probably early 18th-century in origin. As at all the other houses of this group except La Rocré, the single cross-wall was on the parlour—or bedroom—side of the cross-passage, the kitchen partition being of planking. In this house, the bread oven projects from the gable instead of being built inside, and is contemporary with the house.

Les Pièces and L'Epinel give the impression of being the latest of the Low Loft houses, from about the middle of the 18th century. They are much more regular in their lines than the others mentioned above, and in both cases the bedroom end of the house is raised so that front and back walls are carried up to bedroom ceiling height and there is room for an upper loft above. The bedroom at Les Pièces is two bays long, so that it is the parlour cross-wall that becomes an outside gable upstairs. At L'Epinel the bedroom extends over the cross-passage, so that it is the kitchen cross-wall that becomes the gable above. Whereas at La Rocré, Hillview and Les Niaux, only the kitchen was heated downstairs, at Les Pièces and L'Epinel there are two fireplaces (that at L'Epinel having been replaced in the 19th century), showing that the second room was used as a parlour, and no longer as a buttery or store. As was the fashion from *c.* 1750 onwards, the bedroom fireplace joins the flue from the fireplace in the parlour below in one chimney, built of fine grey ashlar at Les Pièces. It is clear from the construction both here and at L'Epinel that the family could have afforded a standard five-bay, two-storey house, perhaps of slightly less superior workmanship. The fact that they chose to have a house with a single bedroom and only a loft above the kitchen perhaps reflects the conditions to which they had been used elsewhere, in the early 1700s, and also probably indicates that houses of the type we have been dealing with in this section were a good deal more numerous then than they are now.

Chapter XII

THE SPLIT LEVEL HOUSE (Type 9)

THE 22 HOUSES in this group differ from Type 7 in that although there is a byre or store below the bedroom, no internal access was provided to it from the house part above. Looked at in another way, these are all single-storey cross-passage houses with the addition of a byre below the bedroom end. If the lower room was used for animals, and in some houses it might have been purely a store for fishing gear and so forth, this does again seem a continuation of the longhouse pattern, byre below bedroom, kitchen with loft above. But the equally strong reason for the popularity of this design, where the topography lent itself to it, must have been the ease of access to the loft. By building into the valley side, the loft entrance in the kitchen gable was easily reached from the lane or track running past the house. Drawing up in a cart alongside, furze and other stores could very conveniently be unloaded without the use of a ladder. However, while this second advantage was almost certainly responsible for the continuation of the house-type well into the 18th century, the longhouse association, of byre at the lower, and kitchen at the upper, end of the house seems likely to have been at least as much a consideration originally. For instance, in the case of La Bonne Vie (443), probably the earliest of this group now surviving, we know from the Livres des Perchages that this house was in existence by 1586, and it has many of the characteristics of a mid-16th-century house, with a fine fireplace at the kitchen end, and a bedroom, originally unheated, at the other, over the byre. The kitchen fireplace once had a stone chimney-hood, though this was altered when the bread oven was inserted. Another fireplace, with rough shoulder stones and a wattle-and-daub hood, was built into the bedroom during the 18th century. It follows that as the kitchen was originally without bread oven, the loft above would not have been required as a furze store. Moreover, the fact that the bedroom was not heated until the 18th century may indicate the presence of animals in the byre below until that date. And although there is no particular evidence in this house for a byre rather than a store, the walling of the building and the pattern of its early fireplaces are exactly the same as at Le Grée (436) nearby, a house built on the level and clearly a longhouse Type 2 with a ventilation slit for its byre.

Three other split-level houses date from the close of the 16th century; Les Ruettes Cottage (439) is a stone's throw from La Bonne Vie and had exactly the same fireplace arrangement. It is an excessively long house of seven bays, but

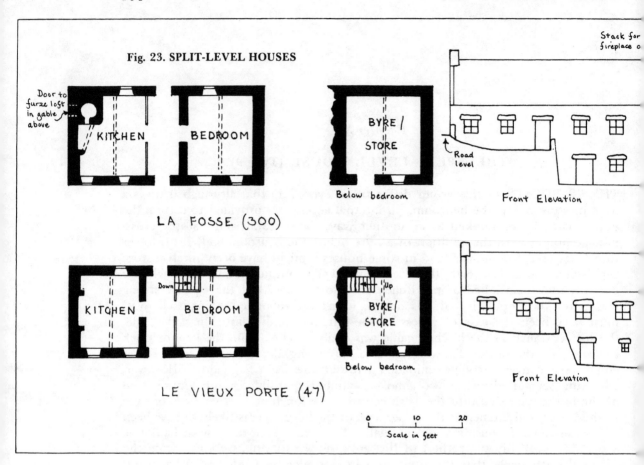

Fig. 23. SPLIT-LEVEL HOUSES

alterations have been made it difficult to see how these were sub-divided. Le Vieux Porte (47) also has one early fireplace and one late one, and may perhaps have been a house with internal access to the byre; in which case its nearest parallel would have been La Cour de Longue (442). As it is said to stand on the site of the old gateway to the priory of Martinvast, a dependency of the Norman monastery of Blanchelande—hence the name Le Vieux Porte—it must have been built after the Reformation in Guernsey, that is, after 1568. The third house, Le Rocher (495), was built between 1583 and 1634, but was considerably altered inside during the 19th century.

However, the majority of split-level houses are either from the second half of the 17th century, such as Caw Chapin (362), or the first half of the 18th century, like the derelict house at Les Galliennes (354). Both these have bread ovens contemporary with the house and an additional fireplace in the bedroom. Both also have two cross-walls, though many of the other houses possess only one, on the byre side, for instance, Vaux Douit (677) and Les Damouettes (684), a house that has been given an extra storey in recent times. These houses

THE SPLIT LEVEL HOUSE (Type 9)

all display the characteristics of other house-types of the period already dealt with. In general, they were humbler counterparts of the standard farmhouse of the time. In origin they combine the longhouse ideal of having the cattle under the same roof, with the improvement of having the byre quite separate from the house part. With the innovation of a furze oven, the loft arrangement ensured the continued popularity of these houses for a while, and perhaps it is no accident that in one of their number, La Fosse (300), the bread oven is still used every Christmas, lit in the traditional way with furze, the food prepared on the kitchen table the previous day, with all the happy commotion associated with a festival. Although recently pointed, the back wall of La Fosse shows what small stone was often used in these houses. Some of them are hardly larger than you could pick up after digging the garden. Any disturbance of a wall constructed with such material, held together with clay mortar, is bound to mean that it has gone for ever. Any patching means a rebuilding of that part of the wall. It is undoubtedly partly because of this that so few of these simple cottages remain—the improver has always found it far easier to demolish and start again.

Lintel over garden gate at Les Mourains (575)

Chapter XIII

OTHER EIGHTEENTH-CENTURY HOUSES (Types 10 and 11)

FROM THE HOUSES listed in the First Schedule, there now remain 19 to consider, 15 single-storey, and 14 two-storey houses. They are a heterogeneous group, put together here because they do not fit elsewhere into this survey. They were built at different times and for different reasons, Milnes, in Contrée Mansell (737) is a late-17th-century property whose internal arrangements have more in common with the houses at the bottom of Hauteville (707–710) than with the two-storey buildings of the countryside. When it was built, it was on the extreme outskirts of Town. Similarly, 99 Mount Durand (844) is the product of experimentation in building patterns incidental in a phase of great expansion, in this case at the very end of the 18th century. Rope Walk Cottage (867) and Hilltop, Les Canichers (874) were clearly built for specific purposes. Hilltop is an extraordinary structure, warranting considerably more research than has been possible here. It really consists of one square room at first-floor level, supported on four arches, one on each side of the square. Each arch is made up of dressed sandstone and limestone blocks, much weathered, the keystone of the seaward-facing arch dated 175(0?). From the Cobo granite pillars of these arches springs a quadripartite vault, the springers supported on undressed red granite corbels, and the vault constructed of brick-like pieces of yellow sandstone such as are found occasionally elsewhere in Town. (There is some patching with these little sandstone blocks in the alley beside Burton's in the High Street, and in early 18th-century shops in Mill Street.) A limestone string-course runs around the building at first-floor level, and above it, on the seaward side, there is a 'Venetian' window, that is, the central part higher and rounded, similar to the windows at the Constables' Office, Lefebvre Street (805), a Le Marchant house built in 1787. The most likely explanation of Hilltop is that it was connected with another Le Marchant house, Le Grand Bosq—now the Royal Hotel—possibly as a gazebo at the far end of the garden, or as a lookout, since the fine plasterwork device above the doorway upstairs includes an anchor.

These buildings, although of considerable interest, do not fit into this survey, and are listed only for completeness. Most of the others in the group are either small cottages or houses erected after 1750. (An exception is the cottage at Les Ruettes (678) now a pottery, which is no later than 1700, and built in two parts.) Taken as a whole, they are further evidence of the breakdown of the traditions of the past, and examples of the willingness to experiment that led

OTHER EIGHTEENTH-CENTURY HOUSES (Types 10 and 11)

to the even greater variety of 19th-century designs in house-building. In them we can see how architecture had begun to sever its links with custom and was reflecting in each house the needs and personality of the person who was to live in it.

Consequently, none of these buildings, compared with those of earlier periods possesses any feature of outstanding merit. The majority have a bread oven, but then so do most cottages built until 1880. However, the wooden supports for the wattle-and-daub chimney hoods at Le Variouf (184) and Les Niaux (641) are interesting, because they represent the final development of chimney hood design, before wattle-and-daub was replaced by brick. In Brittany it is fairly common to find chimney hoods supported on wooden beams set in the gable walls in the same way as the shoulder stones of earlier fireplaces: but in Guernsey, examples are rare, the use of stone for this purpose being preferred right through the 19th century. Occasional examples in wood do, however, occur in fireplaces built between 1750 and 1850, or supporting chimney hoods that were rebuilt at that time. At Les Niaux these supports passed right through the gable and were exposed to the elements until covered by a later lean-to. This healthy practice allowed the beam to dry out, so that rot was not encouraged by moisture trapped behind surface plaster. The practice is often encountered in France on buildings of considerable age, but is not often found in Guernsey. A barn where beam ends are exposed in this way is at Les Hêches (375). Other wooden supports for chimney hoods are at Flambie Cottage (692) and can be found in a good number of valet's quarters, such as those at Les Brehauts (243).

The three farm cottages at Le Variouf (184/6), together with the split-level house which is the lowest of the group (183), are in one of the most picturesque hamlets in the island, and one of the most interesting architecturally. The various houses, representative of several different types, span three centuries of building activity. There are two four-bay former longhouses of the 16th century; two cottages probably even older (see p. 44); a low-loft house of the early 17th century; a single-storey five-bay house of the 18th century; and a five-bay two-storey house from around 1600, which has an early example of re-fronting in grey stone of 1729. In addition to these houses there are the farm cottages which were the last to be built, and are on the edge of the hamlet, forming a delightful group on the bend of the lane. It is easy to see in this hamlet how the earliest houses occupied the best sites, sheltered and well-spaced. The later cottages filled the spaces in between or were built beside them, tucking themselves in close to the bank to keep out the wind, and with generous planting of elms to act as wind-breaks (see Illustrations 2 and 3).

Presumably these cottages were designed specifically for the people who were to occupy them. The split-level house nearest the farm is the largest. Next door, the cottage is of three bays, consisting of an entrance hall divided by a stone wall from the two-bay kitchen. The other two cottages are each of two bays. In all of them, the loft was used as a bedroom, though at the top cottage (186) it is entered from outside. Taken singly, none of these tiny cottages would be of great interest; but together they form a very instructive group of great charm.

The ruined building at Le Moulin de Haut (487) was a very curious structure. On the ground floor were two stables or byres, one of two bays, the other of one bay only, divided from each other by a stone cross-wall. A wooden staircase led out of the larger byre to a kitchen or living-room above, and this was separated by the cross-wall from a one-bay loft. The upper loft, in the roof-space, was floored and was probably sleeping accommodation. It is possible that the whole building represents no more than a valet's room of a rather unusual sort, detached from the farm.

Of similar proportions, the very pleasing little cottage in the Rue de L'Eglise (80) is, happily, still occupied, and still retains its beaten earth floor, covered with a cartload of sand from L'Erée, before the dunes became a car park. The house itself originally stood not on the edge of a lane, as it does now, but along a much narrower footpath, lined with hydrangeas (an even more suitable way from the rectory to the church). Inside the front door is a hallway running across the house like a cross-passage, but without a back door. From here, stairs go up to a two-bay bedroom with loft above. On the ground floor—in this house the term can be taken literally—the kitchen or living room is of two bays and has a fireplace with rough corbel on the left; bread oven on the right. As in a good many of these late-18th-century houses (since they are less than half the age of those built before 1500), the original windows remain, and the original plaster is on the walls.

An even smaller house stands nearby. Merriennes Cottage (102) is just two bays long, the front door opening straight into the living room. A similar house existed until *c.* 1970 at Le Varclin and was demolished in order to make a service road. Here again, a tiny two-bay kitchen with bread-oven, and stairs squeezed into a corner, occupied the ground floor; above was a bedroom, then a loft in the roof-space. However, the cottages of the same size at Le Mont Saint (412) and at Cheshunt, in Les Hubits, are barn conversions, and that at Cheshunt is 19th-century.

The three-bay houses at Les Petites Mielles (568) and at La Haye du Puits (583), as well as those at Pieds des Monts (921) and La Mare de Carteret (569) must have been much the same as the cottage in the Rue de L'Eglise. The first two distinguish themselves by incorporating part of a fireplace, and a very early window lintel respectively, from much older buildings. No. 1 Mauxmarquis Cottage (668) is built against a much earlier longhouse, and foreshadows the dower wings, or 'widow's thirds' of 19th-century houses.

These and the other little cottages labelled as Types 10 and 11 attract, if they attract at all, in their individuality. In all these later 18th-century structures, the vernacular tradition has become so diluted that one seeks about desperately for

OTHER EIGHTEENTH-CENTURY HOUSES (Types 10 and 11)

some evidence of individuality to make up, as it were, for the fine details that, however widespread, delight the eye with skilled craftsmanship in the earlier houses, springing from a thriving culture that had not yet become severed from its roots. The later houses also serve to emphasise the vastly more complex social structure that had evolved by the end of the 18th century. Influences outside the island were greater, for although our building tradition had always been susceptible to ideas, first from France, then from England, these had been absorbed slowly into a way of life that had continued relatively unchanged in the countryside for centuries. The burgeoning spread of St. Peter Port from 1750 onwards, the building of elegant villas outside the town, and the elegant façades of the houses constructed within it, were all elements of another way of life; a way of life available to islanders just because of the great prosperity of 18th-century Guernsey, but in its turn opening up horizons and opportunities undreamt of before.

Raised inscription (Matthew de Sausmarez), Sausmarez Manor (35)

PART III

ST. PETER PORT

1400–1787

Chapter XIV

ST. PETER PORT WITHIN THE BARRIERES DE LA VILLE
1400-1625

THE DEVELOPMENT of St. Peter Port as a town distinct from the other parishes of Guernsey was a process that had already begun before the 12th century, and to trace it in any detail deserves a separate book. But a brief summary is necessary here in order to understand the influences at work on Town architecture. The ports of St. Helier and Gorey in Jersey, and St. Peter Port in Guernsey, were well-established on the trade routes around the coasts of north-western Europe, and particularly on the shipping routes between the Mediterranean and England in early medieval times and arguably in Roman and pre-Roman times, too.

D. Trevor Williams in his excellent article in the *Transactions of La Société Guernesiaise* in 1927, pp. 175-186, has demonstrated that whatever its 12th-century status vis-à-vis St. Helier and Gorey, St. Peter Port rapidly outstripped them in the centuries that followed. Its superior harbour and its position at a comparatively safe distance from the French coast gave the town distinct advantages over its rivals. After the French had regained mainland Normandy from King John in 1204, England still retained its possessions in south-western France—as it has since become. Communications with Anjou, Poitou, Guyenne and Acquitaine were of very great importance, and the maintenance of friendly relations with Brittany, then a separate kingdom, was also a policy pursued consistently during the next three centuries, before it had become part of France. Edith Carey, notably in her article in the 1909 issue of the *Transactions*, has shown that the changes in the feudal administration of the island, brought about by the events of 1204, also led to the setting up of communal privileges that must further have enhanced the early status of St. Peter Port. For the seigneurs of many of our fiefs at that time were large landowners in the Cotentin. During the civil wars between Geoffrey of Anjou and King Stephen, 50 years before, their ancestors had forfeited their estates because of loyalty to the losing side. Now, in 1204, their estates escheated to the Crown because they had backed the winning side in Normandy. On the mainland they saw that their interest lay in loyalty to Philip Augustus of France, but as a result they lost their lands in Guernsey, which remained an English possession. The administration of justice, formerly a prerogative of their officers, had thus to be reorganised and so our system of jurats was first introduced.

At the same time, the imminent danger of attack from France, which might have restored to the Norman landowners their former interests in Guernsey, became a real threat. Fortification of Castle Cornet, Le Chateau du Marais, and the Vale Castle, was put in hand as an urgent measure. And from this time onwards, the Governors of the Isles were appointed from among the king's most trusted soldiers and counsellors. While these governors were not themselves resident in the island, their involvement, in various ways, in local affairs and in keeping the king and the English Court very much aware of the importance of the Channel Islands throughout the Plantagenet period and indeed up to Stuart times, must have been instrumental in the increase of wealth and the maintenance of prosperity during the four centuries after 1204. The De Chesney family, Sir Hugh de Calverley, Otto de Grandison, Warwick the Kingmaker, and in later times Sir Walter Raleigh are all names intimately connected with these islands, and indicate, not only the importance to the English Crown of Guernsey and Jersey from a strategic and political point of view, but of their importance commercially as a source of wealth and prestige to men high-placed in Court circles. For the duties that could be levied on goods passing through the Channel Islands, and notably through St. Peter Port, were considerable.

Whereas the ships of the 12th century had been very small craft, the next 100 years saw a tremendous advance in boat-building. By 1330, in addition to the great Venetian and Genoese sea-going galleys, there were ships of 100 tons or more using this island as a port of call, with rudders, compasses, pumps, and sails. This sort of equipment made it less necessary to hug the coast, keeping land in sight as had been the practice in earlier times, but trade routes set up with less sophisticated craft were maintained partly because of commercial interests that had grown up en route, and partly as providing ports for frequent re-victualling on the long journey between England and Bordeaux. For, apart from the political necessity of maintaining links with south-western France, it was the wine trade with Gascony which was all-important, a trade that was not permanently interrupted even by the Armada in 1588. The importance of this trade is illustrated by the fact that even in times of considerable tension, when war with France was in progress or in danger of breaking out, convoys of wine-carrying vessels were organised each year. Ships from Southampton, Winchelsea, Sandwich and Bristol assembled off the Isle of Wight and were then escorted to St. Peter Port across to Brittany and on by warships. They carried to France fish, metals, wool, meat and leather, on all of which the king of England levied taxes, and they returned with wine.

In this lucrative trade, Guernsey ships no doubt played an important part. In 1596, 32 of the 71 ships using the port of Southampton were from the Channel Islands, and for centuries before that, prominent Guernseymen owned ships.

In time of war, St. Peter Port was also a convenient base from which English pirates could operate against French shipping, and this might well explain the various punitive raids organised by the French against this island, for instance that by Du Guesclin in 1373. These raids culminated in its occupation for seven years, between 1456 and 1463. At St. Peter Port, too, enemy ships were intercepted and held up until they could produce guarantees that they were proceeding to an English port. Even in the time of Henry III, 1224-29, Geoffrey de Lucy held up vessels from Bordeaux, Normandy, La Rochelle and Bayonne in this way. From St. Peter Port, too, raids were organised against the French coast. Thus in 1425, 20 ships sailed from here to blockade Mont St. Michel, among them three Guernsey vessels. These were La Pitié, La Marie and La Trinité, owned by Denis Le Marchant, Pierre Nicholas, and Hémon (or Edmund) Henry, whose parents built Ste. Appoline's chapel in 1392. They had mustered 27 men-at-arms and 89 archers and sailors for this expedition, but fortunately took part only for one month. They were paid off by Le Vicomte de Carentan in the harbour at Chausey on 30 May 1425. At the end of June, the rest of the English fleet was totally destroyed.

These few glimpses, almost at random, into aspects of life involving Guernsey between 1200 and 1600 are perhaps enough to demonstrate that on various scores, Guernsey was a place of considerable importance, on one of the principal trade routes, and often a springboard for the wars with France. A thriving settlement must have existed at St. Peter Port before 1200, but after that time its prosperity was assured. Although it is first termed a town in 1275, when its harbour was rebuilt in substantial fashion, it was of sufficient importance by 1305 for dues to be levied on all shipping in order to finance rebuilding after a French raid. In 1331 there were 47 houses in and around Cornet Street— more than there are now—and the importance and vulnerability of this rapidly-growing community was further recognised by the king's command in 1350 that a town wall should be built for its protection. No doubt unwilling to bear the expense of such a costly construction, the townspeople did not carry out this order until it was reiterated later in the year. The wall enclosed the whole town as it existed then, and clearly shows us the size of St. Peter Port by the middle of the 14th century. Naturally, those responsible for the financing of the operation were hardly likely to enclose a larger area than was absolutely necessary, just in order to allow for any possible future expansion. And so it was that St. Peter Port, like so many towns and cities elsewhere, became constricted inside its walls until the changing times rendered them obsolete by about 1600. And since these medieval walls have entirely disappeared, it may be as well to follow their previous course in some detail.

In designing these fortifications, defence of town and harbour was provided by Castle Cornet, from the sea, and by strong towers at the northern and southern extremities of St. Peter Port, on land. At the northern end of the town stood Le Tour Gand, roughly where Plaiderie House now is, and at the southern end Le Tour Beauregard, on the site now occupied by St. Barnabas church. The wall itself began by the south transept of the Town Church, where a gate, or barrière gave access from the harbour to the bottom of Cornet Street and Fountain Street. From here it ran southwards along the low cliff between Cornet Street and the foreshore until it reached Cliff Street, which was probably a lane running under the shadow of the wall itself. Where Cliff Street joins Cornet Street was a second gate, and at this point it became part of the defences of Le Tour Beauregard, which had certainly been built by 1352. By 1373, this strongpoint was regarded as the next most important castle in Guernsey after Castle Cornet, and its captain was paid more than the bailiff. Apparently it consisted of a keep with a bailey around it, and in this bailey stood barracks as well as the gallows and the stocks.

From Le Tour Beauregard, the town wall went steeply downhill to Fountain Street, where there was another gate near the steps leading up to Rosemary Lane (Les Cottes). Running around the back of the rectory garden, thus crossing the present Market Square approximately by Les Poids de la Reine, the wall climbed steeply, cutting across Berthelot Street, which may have been a cul-de-sac, since there was no gate there, unless, as seems likely, there was a small postern. At Smith Street, a fourth gate stood by the present post office. From there the wall ran across Forest Lane to the back of La Plaiderie, where it turned towards the sea. The fifth gate was at Le Tour Gand, in the Pollet.

The appearance of St. Peter Port with its walls in the 14th century can perhaps best be imagined by looking at a town such as Conwy in North Wales, which preserves its medieval plan complete. At Conwy the walls run across similar steep slopes, enclosing a relatively small area between a strong castle and the small harbour, with little apparent regard to the topography. Here, too, the room occupied inside the walls by church and manor seem disproportionately large. In St. Peter Port, as has been mentioned, the rectory and its garden would have extended almost across the town from the wall on the west of the Town Church on the east, from which it would have been divided only by a few properties adjoining the mill. The 16th-century successors to these properties, and the mill itself, were demolished in 1870 to build the eastern end of the present Market Halls. But a mill on that site (by the present Arcade Steps) had been mentioned as early as 1048. The walls of St. Peter Port also enclosed a manor, Le Manoir de Haut, eventually acquired by the Le Marchant family. The house was where the present Constables' Office now is, and its Chapel of the Blessed Michael stood at the southern side of the comparatively modern arch into Lefebvre Street.

With a considerable amount of land inside the walls occupied by the manors and the church, it follows that space was at a premium. We must also remember that there were at that time no buildings on the seaward side of Le Pollet, which street probably got its strange name from a very similar street in Dieppe, well known to merchants, where the street ran along the top of a little cliff, or *falaise*, above the sea. Even as late as 1680, there were only three buildings shown on the seaward side of Le Pollet. An indication that in 1573 houses had not long been built along the harbour side of the High Street is the fact that these properties were at that time excluded from the Livre de Perchages as being *dedans les limites du grant Flo de Mars* (within high water mark of spring tides). Another indication that there was no building between the bottom of Berthelot

Street and the sea in 1601 may be read into the law-suit brought by the de Beauvoirs against Jean Briard for obstructing their view. (See Chapter XXXIV.)

Frontage was limited, and so, instead of the rooflines of houses running along the street, buildings were turned round so that they were gable end to the road. Perhaps the most striking example of the contrast within and without the walls is between 11 Cliff Street (717), a 16th-century house just outside the walls, and the remaining early buildings in Cornet Street nearby. No. 11 Cliff Street is a typical longhouse, in its plan, if not in its use, and no instances of this sort of house occur inside les barrières de la ville. Conversely, all the original shops and houses of the town were like those in Cornet Street, and none occur outside the limits of the town wall, except in the two early suburbs of Mill Street and the Lower Pollet, and also in that part of the top of Berthelot Street which might have been just outside the early boundaries. This is to be expected, because patterns traditionally followed for 300 years or more inside the town walls were naturally used when first those boundaries were burst through, as it were, in the 17th century.

The architecture which flourished in St. Peter Port in medieval times was not, of course, unique to Guernsey. The house-plan followed here was common to towns on both sides of the Channel, and can best be studied elsewhere. For town buildings in granite, we must look at Mont St. Michel, Vitré, Guingamp or Tréguier to see what St. Peter Port would have looked like in 1500. For an earlier period, we must visit Southampton, a port with which we were closely connected. Here have survived merchants' houses from the 12th century onwards. At Dol-de-Bretagne, too, there are a few survivals from this time. Of pre-15th-century town architecture in St. Peter Port, nothing recognisable remains above ground. The stone-vaulted cellars of the Guernsey Savings Bank (see Chapter XXXIV) may be 14th-century, and the cellars of Nos. 28, 30 and 32 Cornet Street are at least as old as that, much smaller and following different building lines from the 17th-century houses above them. But nothing else remains.

In fact, almost all of medieval St. Peter Port was swept away between 1740 and 1880, when the town was virtually rebuilt. By that time, the older buildings, deserted in favour of more fashionable residences by the wealthy families, had become tenements and were in an appalling state of disrepair. The picturesque buildings at the lower end of Smith Street, clearly 15th-century, were demolished in 1870. So were the old houses facing the west end of the Town Church. Medieval Fountain Street had already been rebuilt by John Wilson in 1822. Virtually our last medieval street, Cornet Street, was almost completely demolished in 1935, and the one Elizabethan house remaining (No. 24) was disgracefully removed in 1953. Just about all we have left to link us with our medieval past, are the narrower streets themselves, and even these are only 19th-century pavé. Road-widening in 1914, which began to remove the frontages of Le Pollet, was mercifully halted by the First World War, and by some extraordinary oversight of town developers, not continued afterwards.

(*above*) **Les Câches** (237): the ...stead. An enclos with house, ...es and prinseur.

(*right and below*) **Le Variouf**, ...: a hamlet tucked into a hollow ...e valley side.

65. Female head on fireplace corbel, pillar-type 'A' at Le Chouet de Roche, St. Andrew.

66. 14th-century window head outside Les Câches (2

67. Trough outside Castle Church, with two animal heads: probably an évier.

68. Finial over entrance arch, La Haye du Puits (582).

69. Trough from Les Fontaines (544), perhaps an évier, showing two mermaids holding mirrors; now at Castle Co

70. St. George: a 16th-century window lintel with double accolade and provision for central mullion.

71. Damaged window lintel re-used upside down at Maison Guignan (92). An accolade with shield and fleur-de-lys.

73. **Old Farm, Brock Road** (925): tourelle window with iron bar and stepped lintels.

Les Câches (237): 15th-century window-frame, *airs* passage.

75. **La Forge** (509): Bénitier, tourelle doorway and arrow slit.

La Fontaine (422): the tourelle staircase.

76. House at Le Mont Saint, now demolished, showing round chimney and 17th-century window frames.

77. **La Vieille sous L'Eglise** (475): round chimney in 1909, before being replaced by present one of curious shape.

78. **La Moye** (999): round chimney, showing drip-stone coping.

80. Le Pavé (523): Byre window or 'pour'.

Saints Farm (83): bedroom window sill with cable mould, 0.

Les Câches (190): the entry.

82. Saints Farm (83): kitchen door, *c.* 1600.

83. Fireplace lintel built into Castel Rectory (556), probably 15th century. 'Orate pro m' (Pray for me).

84. (*left*) Crest or merchant's mark; EN 1596 CH: from demolished house at La Greve, now at Le Cognon.

85. (*above right*) De Sausmarez arms with angel supporters: 16th-century fireplace lintel re-used at Soundtrack (753).

86. (*below right*) Unidentified mason's mark with angel supporters, 16th century: at St. George (586).

87. (*below left*) Jean Briard's merchant's mark, Guernsey Savings Bank (756). 'En Dieu j'ai mis mon appup' (In God did I confide).

88. (*below centre*) R. Briard's merchant mark, Guernsey Savings Bank. 'Et sa providence m'a conduit' (And He hath been my guide).

89. (*below right*) Pelican feeding her young: at Les Vallettes (447), 1596.

ST. PETER PORT WITHIN THE BARRIERES DE LA VILLE

The only exception to this wholesale destruction remain at the bottom of the High Street and in Berthelot Street. Here are our earliest town buildings, dating from the late-15th and the 16th centuries. Even here, no one building is complete or has escaped drastic restoration and alteration. But enough remains to show that our town architecture was exactly the same as that of Brittany and Normandy at that period.

The basic plan of a town house, between 1400 and 1625, was much the same as that of the farmhouse we are familiar with: that is, it was roughly 15ft. wide by 40ft. long, and of four or five bays. The fundamental difference was that the gable end faced the road, so that the fireplaces were all in the side walls, and the doors and windows all in the front and back gables. In order to leave as much room as possible for windows, it was usual to construct only the side walls of stone, building the gable ends of timber, often jettied out, so that successive storeys overhung the narrow streets, almost touching the upper floors of similar houses opposite (see Illustration in Chapter XXXIV).

Stretching back from the street, the house would be divided into two or three compartments, either by stone walls or by wooden partitions. No stone cross-walls have survived. In many French examples, access between floors is by means of an internal newel staircase of stone, entered from the back room. There is only one division, creating a front room or shop of two bays and a back room of three bays. This seems to have been the case at 5 Berthelot Street (808), where the back two bays on the first floor are occupied by kitchen sink and fireplace, side by side. It seems likely that the fireplace would have been symmetrically placed along the side wall, so that the évier on the left would have been balanced by a window on the right. The stairs must have been in the central bay, though their exact form in these buildings is impossible to say, since they have long since been replaced.

In four-bay premises, it is probable that the two-bay rooms were juxtaposed, the stairs being accommodated in a tourelle at the back of the building. This may well have been so in the house on the southern side of Smith Street, which is shown as a fairly shallow building, front to back, with a tourelle at the south-west angle, in a print of *c.* 1870. However, the Guernsey Savings Bank (756), and 5, Berthelot Street, both five-bay houses, show no signs of a tourelle and must be presumed to have had some form of internal staircase.

Sometimes the building would have been two storeys high, sometimes three. Where it was three-storeyed, the ground floor, and probably the cellars, too, would possibly have been let out as shops—the invariable arrangement in Southampton. The house above would then have consisted of a kitchen and another chamber on the first floor with bedrooms above and in the attics. This was certainly so at 5 Berthelot Street, where the very fine fireplace and kitchen sink already mentioned are on the first floor. Where there were only two storeys, the building would probably have been a private residence, with the kitchen on the ground floor. Several examples of this plan survive in La Rue Jerzual and elsewhere in Dinan, and in Tréguier. However, although such was likely to have been the plan at the former Maison des Pauvres in Berthelot Street, now part of the Savings Bank, it is now impossible to state this with certainty.

There is no real probability that the central portion of the first floor in these buildings would have been a hall, open to the roof, in the English fashion. The window arrangements would not seem to allow this, and it never occurs in any of the French towns mentioned above. Since the influences on our farmhouse architecture were wholly Breton and Norman at this time, and since our cultural, if not our political links were with Brittany and the Cotentin, it seems sensible to suppose that our town houses were much the same as the ones to be found, for instance, at Mont St. Michel.

The occasional displaced corbel or fireplace lintel are the only tantalising relics of the fine houses that once lined High Street, Berthelot Street, Fountain Street and Cornet Street. Two such lintels in Church Square are well-known survivors from a previous De Sausmarez house on this site, bought by them in 1444-5 from Lucas Effart. It seems probable that the property would have been rebuilt at about this time, and since fireplaces are not easily altered, the lintels are likely to be mid-15th-century. Since that time the house is known to have been rebuilt in 1608, and probably again about a century later.

A very fine lintel, known to have been removed on the demolition of one of the Cornet Street houses in 1935 has since vanished. It is said to have borne an inscription, and may very well have been similar to another lintel—if it was not confused with it—recorded at Le Couteur's stoneyard in 1953 as having originated at Les Lohiers, in St. Saviour's parish. The second lintel had the inscription 'La Paix de Dieu Soit Ici'. It is a great pity that these lintels have been allowed to disappear without proper record being made of their present position. They must have closely resembled the extremely fine lintel rebuilt into the Castel Rectory (556) over a modern fireplace (see Illustration 83). It is presumed that the Castel example came from an earlier rectory, but this is not necessarily so. The inscription 'ORATE - PRO M' (Pray for me) is on either side of a lozenge which encloses a device and two initials in Lombardic script. This is clearly the personal badge of the builder of the fireplace, and it is for him we are asked to pray. Identification of the badge would help in locating the property that originally possessed this magnificent piece of work. From the style of lettering used in the inscription and the type of lozenge, it, too, must be 15th-century, and like so much of the best work of that time, is of Chausey stone.

Such is our meagre remaining inheritance from medieval St. Peter Port. For a fuller description of the Guernsey Savings Bank see Chapter XXXIV.

The prosperity of Guernsey, developed during the Hundred Years' War partly because of our strategic importance and in spite of several disastrous French attacks, was assured in the 15th century by the making of St. Peter Port a free port in 1444, and by the Papal Bull of Sixtus V in 1483, which declared the

Channel Islands neutral territory in time of war and therefore safe for all shipping. The last serious threat of French invasion had passed in 1461 and the 16th century was a period of very great wealth, not seriously interrupted by the changed order under Calvinistic rule from 1568 onwards. St. Peter Port had already begun to develop outside Les Barrières de la Ville, with the founding of La Petite Ecole in 1513 in La Contrée de Glategny, just north of the old Chapel of St. Julian and the foundation of Elizabeth College in 1563. Several houses in Berthelot Street outside the walls existed by 1550, of which parts of two at least remain (811/812) and development had also begun in Le Bordage, though all has since been rebuilt. By the end of the century, the town walls had become obsolete and Le Tour Beauregard was in poor repair.

Chapter XV

ST. PETER PORT, 1625-1787

AS WE HAVE SEEN in looking at the houses of the countryside, stagnation was the hallmark of the first half of the 17th century. The wine trade continued to be the most important source of wealth, but the discovery of the New World and changing political and religious patterns in Europe directed commerce into new paths. The development of ocean-going shipping and greatly improved navigational aids also left Guernsey out of the mainstream of international trade routes.

The Civil War did nothing but aggravate this decline. And when the island began to awake once more, the world was a rapidly-changing place. More and more, the island looked to England both for its trade, and as new areas of commerce opened up, for new ideas in many spheres of activity, not least in architecture. Houses associated with the old order of things were naturally regarded as old-fashioned, and rebuilding or new building introduced concepts copied from the society that was arising after the Great Fire of London in 1666, or from fine architecture from even further afield, such as that of the great cities of Holland.

Although we have many more buildings in town whose origins are 17th-century than have survived from previous times, they have fared little better than their predecessors. For the new era ushered in by the Restoration in 1660 continued to create wealth on such an unprecedented scale throughout the following 200 years that houses which had seemed up-to-date in 1680 were already being drastically altered two generations later. Thus, for instance, among 34 17th-century houses, mostly in Hauteville, Mill Street and Le Pollet, not one original fireplace remains.

However, the general layout developed during the period 1650-1700 was followed during the whole of the next century and remained popular until 1850, even if the details of design changed considerably. This layout was itself related to medieval house plans quite closely, and the five-bay building, gable-end to the road, remained normal. But before we look at the typical five-bay plan, it must always be remembered that the limitation of a site, or the existing windows or tourelles of neighbouring buildings, or the proper regard for a long-established right-of-way, might all be important factors in determining the size of a new house. Nos. 21, 23 and 25 Mill Street illustrate this point (745-7). Here, the middle house is only three bays deep. The adjoining properties seem to have been designed with windows in their side walls which could not be blocked by the house between. A similar example involves Nos. 28 and 30 Le Pollet. Here, a tiny venelle, or alley opening off Forest Lane gave access to the base of a tourelle staircase at No. 28, and the site was further constricted by an existing house (being recently renovated for the Samaritans). Thus, No. 30 Le Pollet could not be extended without blocking the access to its neighbour's staircase, and both houses are only three bays deep.

The chance survival of the tourelle, though it has lost its staircase, at No. 28 Le Pollet (793), gives us an insight into the division between house and shop. For there seems to have been no provision for any access between the two, although later alterations may have removed an original flight of stairs. At any rate, the tourelle staircase begins on the first floor, where an outside doorway in it gave access from the venelle just mentioned. The shop was in all probability entered only from the street in front and was no doubt intended to be let out entirely separately from the house. In this case, there was a three-bay shop at ground floor level, probably with a small cellar below; and three-storey living accommodation above, one three-bay room on each floor. The tourelle was carried up to the eaves, but did not give access to the attic. That it existed at all, marks this property as being not later than 1650, probably contemporary with the only other property within Les Barrières to retain its tourelle, No. 2 Coupée Lane (723). Both tourelles were built to contain wooden stairs, both rise three storeys, and both are very narrow, quite unlike medieval tourelles. They are probably among the last tourelles built in Guernsey. The Legge Survey clearly illustrates No. 28 Le Pollet as one of a small group of houses at the corner of Forest Lane in 1680, by which time the construction of this sort of staircase had completely gone out of fashion. The survey also shows only three buildings on the seaward side of Le Pollet, between Smith Street and Le Tour Gand. One of these is almost certainly the property at present occupied by Keyho's (800). In common with Wyatt's (773), this retains a wooden staircase set inside a square timber construction projecting from the side of the shop and supported on wooden struts—a further development of the tourelle. Keyho's is probably the earliest building in Town not to be gable-end to the road. There are two reasons for this. First, until the middle of the 17th century, the seaward side of Le Pollet had not been built on at all. It was a low cliff behind the shore, and, of course, beyond the northern arm of the harbour. Keyho's property, being one of the first to be built, was therefore not forced to occupy the space between any existing buildings. Second, since there was very little space at all between the street and the sea, it would obviously have made most sense to build along the road. Not until this area became popular for shops and warehouses, after 1700, were retaining walls built in front of the old cliff-face so that it was possible to construct five-bay properties pointing out to sea.

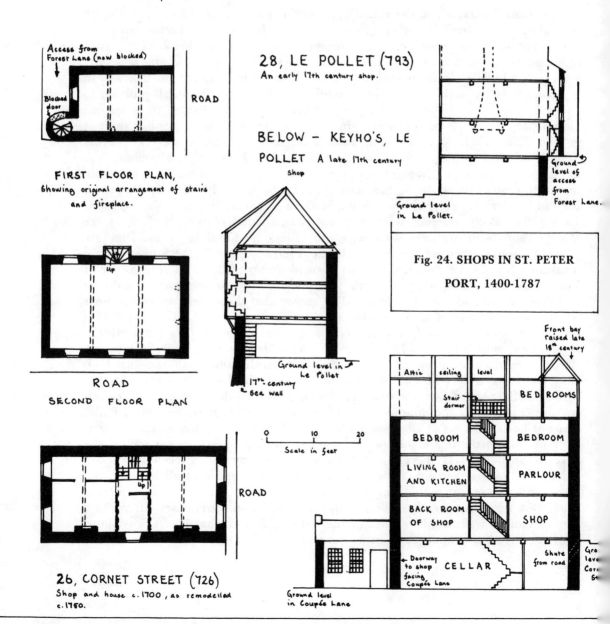

Fig. 24. SHOPS IN ST. PETER PORT, 1400-1787

The three Mill Street shops already mentioned were also the beginnings of development in an area that had been gardens in 1580, with a footpath along the mill-race. A hundred years later, the Legge Survey shows that the old settlement around Contrée Mansell and Back Street had been linked to the top of Fountain Street by lines of buildings on one or other side of the road for the whole of its length. Of these, Nos. 21-23 must have been some of the earliest, at least of those that have remained relatively unchanged. Their staircases also consisted of wooden steps around a central newel post. But unlike the Pollet examples, they projected into the shop, the only concession to the tourelle tradition being the way that the side wall was hollowed out a little to accommodate them, very like the quasi-tourelles at Saints Farm (83), La Bellieuse Farm (94), or with the split staircase at L'Echelle (649). These all seem to represent a type of construction common in the second and third quarters of the 17th century.

By about 1675, the pattern of Town building had become as standardised as that of the rural areas 50 years later—always excepting difficult sites. But in general the plan was the same: five bays, divided into three parts. There was a two-bay room at the front, a two-bay room at the back, and the central bay was occupied by the stairs at one side, with a small room against the opposite side wall if the property were wide enough to allow this. At first, the staircase rose around a central newel post, but by 1700 or very shortly afterwards it became customary to construct a staircase around a stair well. Short straight flights, with rather heavy balustrading, rose around three sides of a square between each floor, the fourth side consisting of the landing at each stage. It is interesting to compare the stair-well at Sausmarez Manor (36), of 1712, with that at 26 Cornet Street. During the 18th century the detail of the balustrading changed considerably, later examples imitating the very fine work at Moore's Hotel (795) and Plaiderie House (801), for example. Light for the stairs was provided by raising the roof-line above it and inserting a long, low dormer, running the whole width of the stair-well. After about 1750, this arrangement, which also allowed headroom enough to continue the staircase into the attic, became popular in houses outside Les Barriéres that adhered to the basic cross-passage plan. It is typical of almost all the town houses listed in the Third Schedule, and became the usual way of lighting the stairs in all 19th-century homes. The great advantage it had over the traditional low window in the back walls of farmhouses was just in facilitating the conversion of the old upper loft into extra bedrooms. In most instances, this was done, if it was done at all, when thatch was removed. A pantile roof with dormers for each attic bedroom can be seen everywhere in Guernsey, and it was almost certainly the innovation of the dormer for lighting the stair-well, common in Town by 1725, which made the conversion of farmhouse lofts possible and led to all new building adopting this method. At 11 Cliff Street (717), a tourelle has been raised in much the same way to give access to another storey, though here, strangely, a cupboard staircase gives access to the loft itself.

In panelling, too, Town buildings set the pace for the rest of the island. It is difficult to be precise, but gradually, between 1720 and 1750, the almost universal post-and-panel planking of the previous century was replaced by fine 'Georgian' panelling, often of a very high quality. Excellent examples remain, often with their original fire surrounds, above Creasey's (760), Bucktrout's (764), and Boots' (769). At 11 Le Pollet (776) there is also a Venetian window in the stair dormer, while 20 Le Pollet (788), Baker's Bazaar (799), and the United Club in Berthelot Street (810) have similar panelling of slightly varying dates. Of the earlier post-and-panel work, a good quantity survives at La Bigoterie (813) though the rear two bays of this house have been replaced by a Victorian addition. Unfortunately, there is hardly a shop in Town where the ground floor preserves its original plan. In many, the first floor has been altered out of all recognition as well. It is only by going even higher that the top two flights of a 17th-century staircase come to light, or Georgian panelling is revealed. Sometimes it is necessary to go down instead. At Pandora (785), one floor below ground level preserves its staircase and all its ceiling beams.

New buildings in and around the centre of Town from about 1750 onwards presented a façade to the street which was a complete break with tradition. The gable-end that is so typical of all earlier building was replaced by a flat façade, exemplified by Boots' (769) and Burton's (762). The elegance and fine detail of both of these façades and of the workmanship inside need not concern us here. But the new fashion was quickly followed, c. 1800, in humbler materials by raising the front bay of older buildings elsewhere. This curious device was adopted at La Bigoterie and at The Imperial Club in Berthelot Street, where the back bay was also raised so that the property appeared fashionable when viewed from Cornet Street or Fountain Street; it was done, too, at 1 Mill Street (751); and at 26 Cornet Street (726).

The house and shop at 26 Cornet Street is, by any standards, a building of outstanding quality, at present (1980) sadly neglected and in need of urgent attention. It is the only complete Town house we have left from the period 1680–1750, and in fact the earliest complete building of any age in St. Peter Port. Other places have some panelling, or a couple of flights of their staircase remaining: here it is all virtually complete.

The outside walls are from the last decade of the 17th century or the first of the 18th century. From this period there remain the spacious cellar, of six bays, almost the whole of the staircase from ground floor to attic, and a good quantity of post-and-panel partition everywhere except on the ground floor. Overall dimensions are 40ft. front to back, by 16ft. across. The cellar is just over 8ft. high, with the beams formed of tree trunks only very roughly shaped, and about one foot square. There are two alcoves in the back wall, such keeping places being very common in the cellars of all Town premises and being an average 24in. high and 18in. wide. There is a beaten earth floor.

The staircase to the ground floor from this cellar gives the impression of being a fairly late replacement of an earlier flight, but from the ground floor to the attic, the staircase is original, except that the first few steps run up against the side wall, so that the staircase can be approached from the 19th-century side passage rather than from the middle bay of the house. Apart from this, the staircase rises around a stair-well and is of the early, heavy type, lit by a dormer whose sashes have been replaced in the last 100 years.

The post-and-panel partitioning around the stair-well is complete on every floor and in the attics, but elsewhere it has been partly replaced round about 1750.

At this time, considerable work was done on the property. A small, lean-to shop, or workshop, was built against the back wall of the cellar, which is at ground level at the back. This shop was entered from Coupée Lane, and although almost ruinous, retains its guillotine sash windows, with their very thick glazing bars. This sort of window must have been inserted throughout the house, but except for the windows in the side wall, they have since been replaced. As the space between this house and the much earlier house next door (No. 24, demolished in 1953) could not have been more than a few inches, the middle rooms must always have been rather dark, and no doubt were not so well-used as the larger, lighter rooms at the front and the back.

However, the chief improvement achieved around 1750 was the fitting out of four rooms with splendid Georgian panelling and fire-surrounds, comparable with any elsewhere in the island, and are very similar to that at La Grande Maison (945). All of the first-floor rooms were treated in this way, and also the front room on the second floor. The older post-and-panel work can be found in the cupboards formed in the alcoves to each side of the fireplaces, and in one room it has inexplicably been allowed to remain in one other corner, perhaps because this was at the time concealed in some way with shelves or another cupboard.

The plan of both first and second floor is the same. A two-bay room 16ft. square occupies the front of the house; then the stair-well, 8ft. across, with a small room opposite, occupy the central bay; while the back two bays again provide a square 16ft. by 16ft., but sub-divided to make a small bedroom or dressing room, entered from a larger bedroom.

In the early part of the 19th century, the ground floor shop was re-designed, using tongued and grooved moulded planking to divide a side passage at the foot of the stairs, with its own front door, from the shop, thus giving separate access to the living accommodation above. The two cross-walls, dividing the shop into three sections were also re-partitioned, with handsome fanlights over the central doorways. The shopfront was fitted with a pair of bow-fronted windows on either side of the shop door, and these windows were provided with reeded shutters, opened and closed by some interesting machinery, which, like the entire shop fittings, at present survives intact and in working order.

Upstairs, good, if undistinguished, firegrates were inserted without disturbing the Georgian surrounds, and later on a 'Guernsey' range perhaps indicates the splitting-up of this fine house into tenements. Also, c. 1800, the front bay of the attics was raised to a full storey, thus turning the roof-line by 90degs. and producing a fashionable façade to the street. No doubt this indicates that at the time it was still a house of quality.

What modifications have occurred at 26 Cornet Street have been carried out with taste and a due sense of decorum. That cannot be said for the majority of St. Peter Port, where it is obvious that almost all the craftsmanship of the previous three centuries and more has been wantonly sacrificed to the commercial interests of our own. It is only now that some discerning individuals are restoring what little is left, possibly because it is considered picturesque by visitors. That is as it may be, but in many cases the workmanship of the 16th, 17th and 18th centuries was far superior to that which systematically obliterated it in the late 19th and 20th centuries. With the very honourable exceptions of such buildings as Maples in Smith Street, and the Jewellers' and Silversmiths' corner of the Commercial Arcade, there is little of quality from the last 100 years in the centre of Town.

In Hauteville and in Contrée Mansell we have two attractive areas where traditions of Town and country seem to meet. Here, the houses and shops were not built gable-end to the road, but neither were they of the traditional cross-passage pattern; or if they were, they were three storeys instead of two storeys high. Lower Hauteville, between Tower Hill and Pedvin Street is shown by the Legge Survey to have been built up by 1680, and although a few of the group have been rebuilt since then, most of the original houses have survived. Nearly all of them use the steeply-sloping site to combine three storeys above ground level, on the Hauteville side, with one or two below. Some open directly on to Tower Hill at the back, and rather like the contemporary shop and house at 18 Le Pollet, were probably designed to combine a separate shop or store underneath from Tower Hill, with living accommodation above, entered from Hauteville. Certainly in later times the ground floor on the Hauteville side has also in some cases been a shop. If this was the original arrangement there could well have been two shop levels, or a shop in Hauteville with store below in Tower Hill.

The majority of these premises are three-bay, and all of them had a wooden newel staircase of some sort, though the layout differed according to the size of the house. At Nos. 1 and 3 (709/10) the staircase was in the central bay; in No. 7 (707) on the left; and in No. 11 (706), a larger, five-bay house, it was at the back of a cross-passage.

Presumably the awkwardness of the site, tapering to a point where Tower Hill joins Hauteville, was responsible for the differing layouts as much as individual preference. In No. 1, the 10ft. width did not leave enough room for a proper cross-passage, while No. 11 was of more usual dimensions. No. 5 is the most interesting of the group, partly because it is the smallest, only two bays wide, and partly because it has preserved a good quantity of original woodwork, unlike No. 11, where the post-and-panel partitioning has unfortunately been recently plastered over. In No. 5, it is exposed, as are most of the ceiling beams and joists. No doubt because it was so small, the stairs are in the front corner, on the left, and the awkward modern insertion of another flight down to the stores below show that access to them from above was not part of the original plan. There is no stair dormer, and consequently the newel stairs do not extend to the attic, as they would have done in a house built after 1700. The windows are still square.

Across the road, 10 Hauteville (715) shows a very important development. The lower two storeys are of 17th-century origin, though not much of that date remains inside; but the top floor has been added in 1765, to judge by the date on the rainwater head, which by great good luck has survived. It is important, because this top storey is built in brick, and is one of the very earliest Town premises to use this material. Nearby houses at 11 Cliff Street (717) and 26 Cornet Street (726) have been heightened at about the same time or perhaps a little later, but neither employs brick, except for the extension to the tourelle at 11 Cliff Street—a similar use of brick is at 2 Coupée Lane (723). In Cliff Street the back wall has been raised in granite, and the front by lath and plaster.

A precedent for the brickwork of 10 Hauteville can be found at Castle Cornet, both the Married Quarters and the Main Guard (1036/7) using it extensively as internal window surrounds and for the chimney flues, 1745-50. This seems to be its earliest dated occurrence in the island, and the bricks were imported from Southampton. It is clear that their value was quickly realised and that they soon supplanted more traditional materials for the construction of chimney flues in Town, all premises built or altered after about 1750 using it in this way. By 1790, it appears in chimneys and window-surrounds on many new houses throughout the island, the new house at Les Bordages in St. Saviour's being a clear example.

To employ brick for walling is, however, rare, and the 1765 work at 10 Hauteville, where both front and back are raised in this material, is striking. The upper floor at Milnes, Contrée Mansell (737) may be of similarly early date, but is more likely to be nearer 1800, when a few other properties in Contrée Mansell and Mill Street used brick in their construction. However, it never became a popular building material in Guernsey, due to the great output of stone from the island quarries throughout the 19th century, and the consequent abundance of local building material.

The rainwater head in Hauteville is thus instructive, as well as being attractive. Similar embellishments must formerly have adorned the front of every property in the Town, but few remain today. Those which still do exist are often extremely fine examples of craftsmanship in lead, and are often encountered in unexpected places. Who, for instance, would expect to see one at the back of

Lipton's (761)? The cone-shaped head here, dated 1726, is typical of early-18th-century design. Later shapes are much broader and are in two parts. The upper part resembles a box with rounded angles flattened against the wall, and it fits into another ornamented section forming the top of the downpipe. Examples of the earlier form can be seen at La Frégate (875) with initials of the Dobrée family, 1721 and 1752; and in the country at Woodlands (533), 1769. Very fine examples of the later design are at Plaiderie House (801), 1763; and at Curry's, 15 Le Pollet (777), where the workmanship is of outstanding quality.

An area containing similar three-storey houses to those found in Hauteville is Contrée Mansell and the top end of Mill Street. More space for expansion than in the crowded ridge of land next to Le Tour Beauregard enabled these new houses to be of more generous proportions, though it is arguable that the picturesque triangle in Contrée Mansell is another example of the smaller premises built c. 1625-1675, and that the larger properties nearby are later. The exceedingly quaint 23a Mansell Street (740) occupies a most awkward corner site, but manages, in a most ingenious way, to cram in quite a lot of accommodation. It also preserves much of its 17th-century panelling.

Its neighbours opposite are mostly five-bay houses with a cross-passage, but three storeys high. This sort of house was quite common on the edge of the Town, for instance in Cliff Street (716) and at Le Marchant House (816). They merge with others, such as 3 Back Street (733), Chateau de la Montagne (697) and Havilland House (685), all three-storey houses, difficult to categorise. Perhaps rather annoyingly, they appear in each of the first three Schedules in this survey, a decision as to how to place them having been made on the basis of whether they seemed to be closely connected with vernacular styles and traditions, in which case they are in the First Schedule; whether they were in a Town context and also in other ways were typical of Town shops and houses 1700-1750, in which case they will be found in the Second Schedule; or whether they were examples of more stylish residences, like Le Marchant House in the Third Schedule. But cross-reference is widespread in all architecture, especially in a small community; and divisions of this sort are naturally artificial.

There are equally borderline cases everywhere. For instance, what does one say of the two-storey building on the corner of Cliff Street and Le Tour Beauregard (721)? Considered from the Cliff Street side it is a five-bay cross-passage house, its front door having a great base stone at each side, its staircase turning against the back wall. Looked at from Le Tour Beauregard, it is gable-end to the road, a two-bay shop in front, and a two-bay room behind, the staircase in the bay between. This corner site shows how clearly inter-related are our house-types. Comparison of this example with the façades of 16 and 18 Hauteville (711/12) also demonstrates with what ease they shade into fine Georgian frontages. We must not be dogmatic. To separate buildings into different types serves to emphasise certain facets of their construction or their finish: but it must always be remembered that they were inhabited by people who visited one another and exchanged ideas; who walked down the road with curious eyes when they went into Town, eager to see the latest fashion in these new developments that were gradually eating up the countryside, imitating them at home when they could. So longhouses shade into the later buildings with parlours; one cottage form looks suspiciously like another; Town shops, turned round, become five-bay farmhouses; three-storey Town houses in other contexts, are not much removed from gentlemen's residences. There is overlapping everywhere, but in considering the extremes it is easier to understand some of the reasons for whatever differences there are.

Before finishing with the Town architecture, brief mention must be made of the tremendous development of warehouses that occurred along the harbour and in Le Truchot during the 18th century. The Legge Survey shows that the houses built along the harbour in 1680 faced the High Street. They are raised up on a high wall, well out of reach of the sea at spring tides. An occasional tourelle overhangs the water, and there are no doorways at all on that side. Along Le Pollet, a sea wall, still to be seen in the basements of many shops, ran along the roadside. There was thus nowhere in the Town any way of unloading at a quay immediately in front of the warehouse where the cargo would be stored. In 1780, the first coal quay was built, and in 1783 the bridge over Cow Lane, linking the north and south arms of the harbour. This is clearly shown on the Duke of Richmond survey. By building this quay well out into the sea, it was possible to construct a whole new street of warehouses in front of the houses shown 100 years before. Where there had been only a beach, there were now spacious stores with two storeys of brick-vaulted cellars being included at quay level and below. Only at Marquand's (768) do the cellars below quay level survive; elsewhere they have been filled in. These great brick vaults often occupied the next floor above ground level as well, while at the back of Le Marchant House, in Le Truchot (804) is a two-storeyed range of warehouses built for the storage of wine before re-export. Here, there were five vaults, side by side, with a huge open hall rising another two storeys above.

Where they are not brick-vaulted, similar warehouses have just one link with the vernacular architecture of the island. Their closely-spaced beams, without intermediate joists, follow exactly the pattern of loft floors in barns, where the weight of the produce to be stored above demanded a construction of greater strength than that needed in a house. The saving of timber and consequently of cost by the use of ceiling joists in domestic buildings could not be risked in stores. The 28 great beams at Sheppard's in the Lower Pollet (802) are spaced at two-foot centres. Nearly 20ft. long, they are an average 12in. square in section. This building may, in fact, be a little later than 1787—and therefore technically outside the scope of this book—but it is the best example in the island of this construction, and also retains its original capstan, as does Brennan's warehouse in Le Bordage.

We can only speculate upon what form the cellarage of St. Peter Port took before this great 18th-century development. Only below the Guernsey Savings

Bank (756) do medieval stone vaults survive, perhaps even earlier than the 16th-century building above (see Chapter XXXIV). From later times, the barrel vaulting at Lloyd's (798) must be post-1680, as there is no sign of this house on the Legge Survey. Perhaps it was more usual to have cellars which were not vaulted, as those remaining in Cornet Street suggest, or perhaps stone vaults were destroyed when shops and houses were rebuilt or re-fashioned, between 1650 and 1750, or even later. Certainly there are no clues left to tell what preceded the brick vaults that are now so common in the Town.

However, the building of the Coal Quay in 1780; the rebuilding of Le Manoir és Marchants in 1787; the transfomation of La Plaiderie by the splendid house, now Moore's Hotel; all serve to close an era. Steadily the efforts of the Le Marchants, de Beauvoirs, Bonamys, Tuppers, Careys, Priaulx, and Dobrées to make St. Peter Port a fashionable place, where the High Street would be lined by their fine town residences, was beginning to produce some order in a congested town. But it is probably more evocative of the period we have been dealing with, to leave it with a description of High Street in 1670, visualising it overhung by all the houses shown on the Legge Survey. For the most part, the medieval street still remained at that time, at least as narrow as it is now. Houses since swept away almost filled the space now occupied by Town Church Square, and a pillory and a cage for the punishment of offenders stood between Cow Lane and Quay Street. The unfortunates who were thus confined, to be pelted with rotten fruit and eggs by passersby, were certainly within reach of plenty of ammunition, for the vegetable market was held in the High Street on Saturday mornings and the fish market on Saturday afternoons, and all round them was the meat market. On these market days the confusion in the narrow streets must have been complete, one writer, quoted by Edith Carey in La Société Guernesiaise *Transactions,* complaining in 1670 of 'a most beastly and inconvenient custom . . . introduced of hanging up . . . beefes and other slaine beasts for sale along the houses of the High Streete, and in the same streete they are cut out, divided, and sold; the fish likewise are laid out and exposed for sale in the same open streets, which, being narrow enough of themselves, are so straightened by it for divers houres of every day in the week, but the Sundays, that they are rendered in a manner impassable'.

No wonder that the town gates had all disappeared by 1684, and the town walls, too, and that St. Peter Port was rapidly growing outside Les Barriéres. The medieval fishing suburb—'La Contrée de Glateny'— stretched northwards from the early hospital at Le Bosq as far as the 'éperqueries', or drying grounds for fish, at La Salerie Corner. The 1680 map shows the almshouses of Le Bosq and the medieval buildings at St. Julien joined by a continuous line of houses round St. George's Esplanade. Mill Street and Lower Hauteville were the next areas to be built up, but accommodation problems must have remained acute. The population in 1670 must have been double that of 1450. A period of stagnation had allowed property to fall into disrepair and customs to grow up that disfigured the town, such as those described above. And when business flourished again, the additional sailors and merchants visiting the port, contributing to the overcrowding, created even more discomfort. Add to this the soldiers from the garrison, and it can be seen that the great advances in local architecture during the following century were not only a reflection of growing wealth and taste; the building of larger and better houses was a sheer necessity.

18th-century door hinge, Newbourne, Petit Bouet (890).

PART IV
DATING, DERIVATION AND DESIGN

Chapter XVI

THE NEED FOR A DATING SEQUENCE

THE PROBLEM OF DATING our houses is a complex one, for various reasons. First, vernacular architecture, being an expression of the lives of the people, was never in the forefront of fashion in the same way as was church architecture in the Gothic period, nor did it rigidly reflect the discipline of classical proportions in later times. Only insofar as Gothic ornamentation served to highlight the important elements of a 15th- or 16th-century house, or Georgian symmetry reflected the aspirations of the 18th century to taste and culture, did fashionable styles filter through to simple dwellings. And yet, in their way, house-builders through the ages attempted to keep up with the times; so far as money and manpower allowed they used the latest techniques and the best materials. It was a living tradition, so there was no nostalgic harking back to earlier periods, no educated reconstructions of previous styles.

Thus although the student of vernacular architecture is hindered on the one hand by the simplicity of his raw material, he is helped by its honesty. While he may not have the luxuriance of ornamentation in a cathedral or château on which to draw for comparisons, he knows that at least a 16th-century arch will be of one shape and an 18th-century one of another. That is the least of his difficulties.

The real problem is that when a house or shop has been in continuous occupation for centuries, the very improvements made during that time serve to mask its origins. Sometimes an alteration is clear enough, for many a piece of 18th-century panelling must conceal a medieval kitchen sink. But sometimes it is not at all obvious. Until one thinks about it, for instance, it is not easy to see that large 16th-century doorways have been inserted into the north walls of the Forest church, or the church at St. Saviour, because they are of very similar stone to those walls themselves and have by now weathered nearly as long. But they have, and if it is not obvious in the fabric of a church, how much less clear is it in a farmhouse, especially if the walls are colour-washed, or covered with a thick layer of 'Torteval stucco'.

For all this, it is very necessary to make an attempt at realistic dating. Otherwise, the building makes little sense. It is useless to describe a house as having one room right and left of a cross-passage without giving some indication of its age, for it will signify nothing. One wants to know whether it is an unusual building, or one of 300 like that at that time—and why.

THE NEED FOR A DATING SEQUENCE

Part IV is an endeavour to separate some of the threads that are woven into the complicated fabric of our houses so that they can be studied in greater depth, hoping thereby to arrive at a system of dating that may be provisional, but is better than nothing. However, it will be stressed continuously that though we may look at each element of evidence on its own, every available source must be taken into account in dating any one house. A conclusion arrived at on the basis of one kind of evidence alone is that much weaker, more suspect, than that which draws together again some of these threads. But, of course, in any one house, one piece of evidence is all that we may have. The intention of the Schedules at the end of this book is to try, whenever possible, to provide the raw material for comparison of each dwelling with similar houses, which perhaps have that feature present in the first one, but also two other details that appear in a third, fourth and fifth house, and so on. It is self-evident that however laborious this business of detailed comparison may be, the results are the surer.

There are two chief ways in which it is possible to begin this process of dating. One involves written evidence, either on the house itself or on documents concerned with it; the other involves an examination of the fabric, the layout, the construction and where possible, the details of ornamentation used in it. We shall deal with the written evidence first.

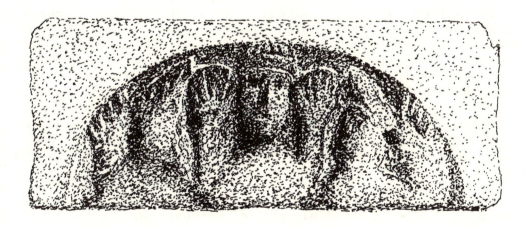

Window head at La Haye du Puits (583)

Chapter XVII

INSCRIPTIONS

MANY HOUSES have initials and a date inscribed over their front door, and occasionally elsewhere, such as on the window lintel at Les Prevosts (465) or on rainwater heads. Later on, they are frequently found on pumps, most of which were first installed in the 19th century. What is to be made of these dates? At La Contrée de L'Eglise (632), for instance, the door lintel announces 'PLLC 1746'. It seems clear enough. We know that Pierre Le Lacheur owned the house then, so presumably he built it (this, by the way, is a good example of syllabic initialling—Pierre Le La Cheur). But did he build it? If so, then the fact that it possesses a tourelle staircase must mean that tourelle staircases were still being built in 1746, or even later, if we take notice of a similar inscription of 1789 at Les Blanches (33). Clearly, this will not do. Why, then, did Pierre Le Lacheur put this date on his house? Fortunately, the answer in this case is all too clear, for he partially re-fronted it in grey stone, but made no attempt to 'cover his tracks', as it were. Plenty of the older red walling is visible on each side, adjoining the gable-end and barn, which he left untouched. (In other houses where the re-fronting has been more thorough, a quick look at the gable-end may be needed to show what the original walling was like.) What are we told, at La Contrée de L'Eglise, is that in 1746, Pierre Le Lacheur improved his house, so that you would probably never have recognised it as the same place. He would have thrown away the front door arch, got rid of the irregular tiny windows, and probably refurbished everything inside, making civilised bedrooms and a parlour where there had been old-fashioned loft and store. Such major work was clearly worth recording, so on the new lintel he put his initials and the date.

This practice was commonplace all over the island. Out of 25 houses in the parish of St. Martin alone, all with pre-1787 date-stones, only five can be relied upon to indicate the actual age of the house. Ten have been completely re-fronted, and 10 have had doorways and windows in the original walls inserted or enlarged. The date may tell us the age of the front of the house, or record some work done on it, but no more. Possibly lintels which have hearts between the initials may commemorate a marriage, or the acquisition of a property by a young couple; but much more research needs to be done, comparing the existing date-stones with marriage registers, before this can be definitely asserted.

INSCRIPTIONS

It is also necessary to bear in mind that a stone can be inscribed with any date, at any time. Occasionally, houses bear dates where the figures and lettering have been added in modern times, possibly after much study. But unless the date displayed is documented, it can be misleading, especially if the property changes hands a few times, and the origin of the educated guess is lost.

At times the authors have come across houses not included in this survey where the present owners have attached totally spurious dates to their homes for no other reason than that they thought it might be of that period. To cherish such an illusion is one thing, but to display it in a position where it is likely to become an accepted fact is hardly ethical. Les Hubits de Haut (6) has had the date 1639 added to a lintel inserted in the 18th or 19th century, though the house is almost certainly pre-1600. La Ruette (52) has also had a date added to its lintel—1586. The house is probably 16th-century, but where did 1586 come from? Is this the earliest documented reference, or has the date been 'dreamed up'? In these two instances, the calligraphy clearly betrays the modern origin.

From these examples, it follows that a date stone must be checked against other data, if it is to be believed. At La Fosse (63), the date stone is 1733. As it happens, this house is one of a very few inadvertently omitted from the 1787 map. The 1733 date is therefore immediately arresting, but careful examination of the structure shows that in this case it can be believed. This was a house newly-built in 1733, and is typical of its period, with very fine galleting, a form of pointing popular in the 18th century. At Retour au Nord (1017) a long and very curious inscription can obviously be relied upon to date a cart shed, stretching across the 10ft. 6in. lintel of the entrance (see Illustration 45). The lintel itself, the lettering and the actual phrasing are all clearly correct: it reads 'IL · EST · ECRIT · ICI · PIERRE · MOLET · CEST · MOI / FAIT : DE : PAR : PML : MARS : 17 : 1787'. One only wonders why he needed to be so emphatic.

There is also the problem that the stone on which a date is inscribed may have come from another house. It is in an effort to record the present positions of all displaced stones that the Fourth Schedule has been compiled. Naturally, from an archaeological point of view, any object removed from its source is far less valuable. That is to say, it can only appreciated as an object in its own right. It tells us nothing about the building where it now rests, neither can it tell us anything about the building where where it once was, for the good reason that its origin has usually been forgotten. Two striking instances where we fortunately do know the original situations come to mind. The arch illustrated in *The Jersey Farmhouse,* Vol. I, as a 'typical Guernsey arch' is at Le Cognon, Hougue Jehannet. The arch is indeed typical of Guernsey, but it has been built into a 19th-century house. Originally it was at La Grève.

The dust cover of *The Guernsey Farmhouse* illustrates Les Beaucamps de Bas with its fine doorway. Unfortunately, this house was dismantled soon after the book was published, and the arch is now at Le Pré de Merlin in Torteval. In other cases we are not so lucky. The collection of arches at La Falaise (144) and Pleneuf Court (631) only serve to remind us that in many other houses there were very fine arched doorways; but we have no idea where.

There is one sort of inscription, however, which can always be relied upon—that is, when it is in the right place. This is the sort where letters and figures are raised and not incised. Whereas it is possible to add a date to an existing arch at any time, for instance at La Petite Cache (959), where 1758 has been added, it is highly unlikely that the whole of an arch would be worked over in order for an added date to be raised above the surface. Two groups of such raised inscriptions are to be found in Guernsey.

One is on the type of arch just mentioned as having come from Les Beaucamps de Bas and La Grève. It will be argued elsewhere that this type of arch was both the culmination and the swan-song of such doorways in Guernsey. Of 13 closely-related arches, eight bear raised dates and initials inside a shield. All range between 1596, on the arch from La Grève, to 1614 at La Carrière (208). Another very similar arch at St. George (586) bears an incised date that appears genuine, and is our earliest date on a domestic building—1581. Since all of these houses have other features in common, and in every case the raised date is clearly genuine, it can be stated with almost complete certainty that the houses are contemporary with these arches.

The second group occurs much later, on a few 18th-century straight lintels. Again, initials and date are enclosed within a frame, all cut away so as to stand proud of the stone. But lintels of this sort were much more fashionable in Jersey than in Guernsey, where almost the only examples are on the old building at Sausmarez Manor, marking alterations to the 16th-century range. One reads 'M.D.S. 1777'; the other 'I.D.S. 1789'.

Even with raised inscriptions, however, care must be taken not to misinterpret the information. A fireplace lintel at Les Sages Villa (272) bears a shield with the date in raised figures of 1747. If a fireplace of this sort had actually been built in the 18th century, it would be unique in Guernsey. But a closer look at it not only reveals 15th-century heads on the corbels, but shows that the shield was cut into the earlier stone in such a way as to give the date the appearance of being raised when in fact it is merely level with the original surface.

As to dates inside houses, they must be regarded with even more caution than those on the outside. That they record something of importance is not disputed: rather, it is a matter of deciding what exactly that something is. Is it the renovation of a room, or the purchase of the house by a new owner, or what? It is doubtful whether any date found inside a house is meant to refer to the construction of the entire building. Usually it seems to record a later improvement, and often it is possible to make an informed guess, as at Les Reveaux (258). Here, very unusually, the wooden lintel of the fireplace is initialled and dated 'PBH:ABH:1751'. This fireplace is a 15th- or early 16th-century one,

Fig. 26. DATED KEYSTONES FROM TYPE 5 ARCHES

Le Repos au Coin (56)

Le Manoir (211)

La Pompe (117)

La Carrière (208)

St. George (586)

La Maison d'Aval (241)

Les Hamelins (294)

altered to accommodate the furze oven. It is therefore fair enough to infer that the oven must have been put in at this time, and as the house has been re-fronted with windows that would not have been common much after 1760, it might be supposed that major renovations to the entire house were carried out in 1751, though there is no way of proving it. Similarly at Le Grée, Le Gron (436), 'IDL 1739' has been delicately pricked out on the main beam in the kitchen. The beam itself is approximately nine inches square in section, the sort of weight favoured in the 18th century, and better finished than those of very old houses, unless they were of the highest quality. Le Grée is a comparatively small cottage. Like Les Reveaux, it has been re-fronted with almost square windows, and again it seems reasonable to suppose that in this case, a major

Fig. 27. LE GRÉE, LE GRON (436) Date and initials on kitchen beam

job involved renewing all the ceilings and roof-structure as well. Certainly this has all been done, and, yet again, a bread oven added to a medieval fireplace: but whether it was in 1739 cannot be proved. We can only say that it seems extremely likely.

The same applies to the date often to be found on the pump in a back kitchen. Strictly, it can only be held to apply to the pump itself. Sometimes it is possible to hazard the guess that the pump was installed when the back kitchen was added; but only rarely can we be absolutely certain of this.

Two examples where dates on barns can be taken as authentic are at the Rue des Landes (170) and at La Maison d'Aval (241). At the former, 'IVMD 1680 ♡ M ♡' is very lightly incised on a rather rough stone lintel over a loft doorway. At the latter, 'ILM:M:1685', in raised lettering on a wooden board is attached to the outside of a post-and-panel door, in a ground-floor stable. In each case the calligraphy, the form of the inscription and the weathering of the material on which it appears, combine with the construction of the barn itself to show that it is genuine.

The habit of dating either the whole house or any part of it was something that did not seem necessary to the medieval mind. The very earliest dating of work in this island is the inscription of 1466, at the Town Church, recording the building of the large south transept and other work carried out at the same time. To have such a date is highly unusual. It was only towards the end of the

INSCRIPTIONS

16th century in Guernsey, as in England and France, that a man would record the building of a new house by putting his initials and the date in a prominent position. Thus we shall look in vain for any date stones on our oldest dwellings, or, if we find them, they will record an 18th-century re-fronting. As we have seen, a small group of houses between 1580 and 1620 were carefully dated and initialled, but even then, the practice did not become widespread. Between the 1623 date added to an older arch at Les Grands Moulins (520), and that of 1674 at Vrangue Manor (901), there is only the strange stone let into the much later back kitchen of La Villiaze (202). This stone seems to include the whole family in a sort of alliterative formula, reading 'SAL:SIL:SAL/CAL:VA (?L): AL/IAL:DIA:(?)/1659.' A slump in house-building during the middle of the century is undoubtedly part of the reason for the scarcity of date-stones before 1700. After that, it became common practice to record new buildings and alterations in this way, and 18th-century dates are widespread.

To summarise, we may say that date-stones do not help in determining the age of any house earlier than 1580, for there are none; we can accept all dates in raised lettering on Type 5 arches; and dates from 1674 onwards can be regarded as genuine where the context allows. All 18th-century dating externally must be checked to see if it refers to re-fronting; and internally, a single dated object must not be held to give us the age of the whole edifice.

Raised inscription (James de Sausmarez), Sausmarez Manor (35)

Chapter XVIII

LEGAL DOCUMENTS

IN GENERAL, the deeds of a house, the legal division of an estate between inheritors (termed partage), and any other document from a court of law, all have one advantage and a great many disadvantages, when used to adduce the date of a building. The advantage is that the date of the document itself can be completely relied upon, and moreover, the situation of property is described in great detail so as to avoid any possible confusion or pretext that might result in a legal wrangle. That is a great help.

The first disadvantage is that in only a very few instances does any such document refer to the actual building of a house. That is not what it is concerned with. The business of a legal document is to ensure that already existing property is possessed in its entirety by its rightful owner, and to give that owner a written title to what he possesses. Thus, only rarely does it tell us that a house exists, nor does it tell us for how long it has existed. Neither can it possibly tell us that a house old in 1680, for the sake of argument, is the one we see there in 1980. It could well have been rebuilt twice since. There are major difficulties in accepting the earliest document in our possession as conclusive proof of the actual age of any house, even after we have established that we are dealing with the same site. And as many early house deeds have been lost, it is rarely that we have much evidence at all before the 18th century.

However, used with great caution, they can be of assistance. If an estate divided up in 1720 lists seven fields by name, and some other document of 1735 refers to a house bounded by six of those fields and apparently sited on the seventh, we may expect to find a house there now that exhibits various 18th-century characteristics. And if we do find such a house, we can feel confident in saying that it was built between those two dates.

Careful perusal of legal documents can also provide invaluable supportive evidence to a case that must be chiefly based on other criteria. It is, for instance, the practice to refer to someone in a legal document not only by giving his name, and where he lives, but also his parents' names and where they lived. A document referring to something quite unconnected with a house that happens to interest us might yet mention a man's mother or father as living there, or as having lived there, merely as a means of identification for another matter. We can then say, not only that a house, probably the one we are studying, was there at that time, but that it was possibly there for a generation before, since the father or mother in question was likely to have lived there for some years.

These documents also provide a great deal of incidental information on all sorts of subjects. A partage will tell us the size of a man's family, listing quite a few of his possessions, and a title deed will tell us the size of a farm and will name the buildings on it. And a whole host of miscellaneous documents, such as the 17th-century papers dealing with La Maison de Quay (768), now Marquand's, mention responsibilities for matters which we might otherwise have known very little about: in this case, duties concerning the management of the harbour, and responsibilities about a 'gallery' which might well be the wooden bridge-like structure shown on the Legge Survey. Records in the Greffe, and the almost completely untapped documents of the Ecclesiastical Court, as well as the many papers in private hands, all contain a vast amount of information of this sort. Painstaking research among them would undoubtedly provide much detail about our houses, but with a handful of exceptions, no amount of this kind of study will tell us when they were built.

LE DOUIT FARM FLATS (499)
Window seat in bedroom.

Chapter XVIX

PRIVATE DIARIES AND ACCOUNT BOOKS

OCCASIONALLY, a family has preserved the account books over a number of years dealing with the running of the estate. Even more rarely, a private diary has been kept or a bundle of letters: sometimes these turn up as part of a collection of other important papers. Where they exist, these more personal documents often throw immediate light on points that would otherwise have remained obscure. We can only be sorry that there are not more such documents to support our suppositions with facts.

Of these papers, perhaps letters must be regarded with rather more caution than account books and diaries, with allowance being made, where appropriate, for exaggeration. For instance, can the reference to Guernsey in the famous Paston Letters be taken as completely factual or not? Botoner writes to John Paston on 8 June 1454: 'The Frenchmen hafe be afore the Isles of Gersey and Guernsey, and a grete navy of hem, and VC (500) be taken and slayn by men of the seyd trew Isles'. Guernseymen and Jerseymen might in fact have killed 500 Frenchmen, but it could easily be an exaggeration. However, this reference records an incident not documented elsewhere, and exaggeration, if there is any, would be justified because it served to indicate to John Paston that we had inflicted severe losses on the invaders.

With account books, however, we are on firmer ground, because they naturally record expenditure accurately and show what the money was spent on. For our present purposes, the most valuable document to have come to light so far is the notebook of John Bonamy of Les Câches. This fascinating record of life around 1500 not only provides us with a complete account of a pilgrimage from Guernsey to Rome at that date, but also tells us in some detail about the building of his house in 1498; now Les Câches Farm (112). A full description of this notebook will be found in Edith Carey's article in the 1920 issue of La Société Guernesiaise *Transactions,* from which the following paragraphs are quoted:

'On May 14th, 1498, he began to build the house at Les Câches, St Martin . . . The stone was quarried at Albecq, and evidently work was then done on the co-operative system; neighbours lent their carts, horses, and oxen to carry his stone and to plough his fields, and were paid in kind as well as in money or corn rents. Thus we find that, while Colas Jehan, senior, was paid 10 gros, his son was paid 5 gros and two pairs of stockings (cauches) worth 6 gros, while Philipin Le Poitevin and Colas Tyquet, for quarrying his stone, were each paid two pairs of stockings. He also got some of his stone from "Lécluse Luet", namely, the Mill Pond behind the old water mill at Moulin Huet, and from what was then known as "Vieille Port", but what is now called "Moulin Huet Bay". In 1499 we find that he owed Thomas Cluett . . . "for his chimney piece". In passing, it must be said that the *mantell de cimeyne* at Les Câches Farm is unique and looks as though it was never finished. Perhaps Thomas Cluett was never paid, for it was in the following year that Bonamy went on his pilgrimage.

'Later on, various drafts of his will give us an idea of his worldly goods. Besides lands and money, "he leaves to his children his harness, carts, ploughs, livestock, spurs, farming implements, sheets, silver rings (annoz d'argent), pots, pans, plates and porringers of pewter, prayer books and psalter, clocks, silver cups and silver spoons, halebard and cross bows, and forty shields made of betony, worth two écus". To his daughter was to be given her mother's mantle; his own clothes (drapeaux) were to be given to the poor, except his three "bonnets" (probably the flat velvet caps worn by the men of that day), which his children were to have; and his last will directed that his fields on either side of the Bailiff's Cross should be let to a priest for seven years on condition that he said a weekly mass for his soul. John Bonamy died about 1510.'

Another Guernseyman who may have accompanied John Bonamy on his pilgrimage to Rome, 10 years before, also used this notebook in which he made an inventory of his goods before he set off. In 1500, Denis Ozanne possessed 'one bed, with curtains, coverlet, tester and pillow all complete; one Flemish chest, and a small metal coffer; one table complete and three benches; a little trestle and two bashins; a metal pot and two pewter pans; also a porringer, three candlesticks and two salt-cellars, a saucer and a pint measure of pewter, a bust of St. John and two bottles (probably the leather water bottles carried by all pilgrims); and seven skeins (eschevaulx) of écru thread, and two of white thread' (probably for stringing his bow).

The second notebook was continued by Dennis Ozanne's nephew, Jean Girard, and is known as the 'Manuscript Girard'. In 1510 he gives details of the expenses to which he had been put in rebuilding and re-thatching the two houses belonging to his uncle—'la grande' and 'la petite maison' after they had been burned down. It is obvious that there is room for a great deal more research among notebooks of this quality. They might well provide information about all manner of details which we should never find out in any other way. For instance, what instructions did a man give for the design of his fireplace? Did he specify what sort of stone was to be used? Whom did he employ to dress the stone? This is a fertile field for further study.

Chapter XX

LIVRES DES PERCHAGES

THE MOST COMPREHENSIVE lists we have available in Guernsey of houses during the last few centuries are the feudal records. As in most other parts of north-western Europe, land in this island was held on a feudal system from at least the 11th century onwards. For a further study of the subject readers should begin by consulting de Guérin's article 'Feudalism in Guernsey', in the 1909 *Transactions* of La Société Guernesiaise.

Before 1028 the island appears to have been divided into two great land-holdings, or fiefs, held by two of the great regional officers on the mainland of Normandy, the Vicomte du Bessin and the Vicomte du Cotentin. The former owned the parishes of the Vale, the Castel, St. Saviour and St. Pierre-du-Bois; the latter the parishes of St. Peter Port, St. Sampson, St. Martin and the Forest. By the time of William the Conqueror, parts of these territories had been assigned to the great abbeys of Marmoutier and Mont St. Michel. During the 12th century, especially during the wars between Geoffrey of Anjou and King Stephen, the seigneurs of these fiefs were expected to provide money and men for the king, and consequently the lay fiefs were forfeited when Geoffrey gained control of the island. In the time of his son, Henry II, they had already been in the possession of other families for two generations, though the fief that had formerly belonged to the Vicomte du Bessin kept its name of 'Fief Le Comte'. Throughout the next two centuries, the large fiefs of early times became sub-divided into smaller manors, most of them part of the larger estates of Norman landlords in the Cotentin or of religious houses on the French mainland. Many of the church land-holdings were again confiscated by the Crown in Henry V's reign, in order to finance his French campaigns, and have remained the Fief Le Roi ever since. By the 16th century Guernsey comprised 48 fiefs, all with their own organisation for the collection of dues and the administration of local justice. Many of the manorial court seats survive, for instance those at the Fief Beuval, in the front garden of Les Sages (270) and on the roadside by Les Pelleys (537).

The dues collected by the seigneurs of the various fiefs usually consisted of chef-rente, a payment in return for the holding of land by free tenants. Villein tenants also paid a tithe of their crops; the twelfth sheaf of their corn—champart; or on land uncultivated, the twelfth bundle of flax—revart de champart; two chickens for each house—poulage; pésnage for the right of running their pigs loose on the manorial common land; and moulage, or a tithe on all wheat ground in the manorial mill.

The collection of these dues was naturally a complicated business, and the amounts to be paid were often the cause of considerable bickering. It was therefore necessary to have a detailed list of all tenants and what property they held. Since land was measured in vergées and perches, the estate books were known as Livres des Perchages, and were brought up-to-date every few years by the officers of each fief, to take account of new houses that had been built, and all changes of ownership. In order to avoid arguments and to prevent litigation in higher courts, great care was taken, in the preparation of each new book, to refer to the previous one, to identify the tenants by their names and the names of their fathers. In the case of a property passing to a daughter, and thence by marriage into another family, that is carefully stated.

Thus these fief records are invaluable. But like all documentary evidence, they must be used with caution. On some fiefs we are fortunate that a succession of the Livres des Perchages has survived. Having established the 20th-century owner of a house and the area of land upon which it stands, it is thus often possible to trace that property back for centuries, during which time the area of land may well remain exactly the same; but it is also necessary to check the names of owners in each book, the order in which the entry occurs, and so on. It is a complicated but a fairly reliable process. However, where a succession of books is not complete, and there is a gap of 100 years of more, it is extremely hazardous to attempt identification of a property. Moreover, however good the records, they do not usually tell us exactly when a house was built, though they often bring us close to the date; and they can never tell us, any more than other documents, whether the house has been rebuilt, because they were only concerned to levy taxes on it, new or old.

Once again, the documentary evidence must be taken in parallel with the evidence of the buildings themselves. But in a way, the Livres des Perchages are like the Duke of Richmond's map. They tell us that there was a house on a particular site, say, in 1500. What we must determine is whether it is the same house as the one now standing. On the other hand, if there was no house there in 1500, then clearly any building on that site at present cannot be that old. In fact, looking through the books in sequence it should be possible to come to the point when a house has suddenly sprung up, on land where formerly only a field is listed. That house—if the actual details of the present building will bear us out—should then have been built at some time between the date of one Livre des Perchage and the previous one.

An actual example may help to clarify the method. La Tanière (550) is on the Fief de la Cour. Omitting the entries in recent books, which are reliable, the house belonged in 1750 to Nicholas Le Get; in 1729 to Rachel Breton, fille Jean; in 1707 to Abraham Moullin, à cause de Rachel Breton (i.e., it was his wife's property); in 1634 to Jean Le Jersiez fils Clement. But in the 1602 book it does not appear, and must therefore have been built between 1602 and 1634. This agrees well with the architecture of the present house, so there is no reason to doubt the evidence. It is interesting that within 100 years this property had changed hands twice.

Another example from a nearby house, Les Queux (555), this time on the Fief Le Comte, will show how far back these records can take us:

    1914—Les Queux Manor Vineries Ltd.;
    1894—Adolphe Jean Mahy, fils Nicolas;
    1873—Nicolas Mahy, fils Nicolas;
    1853—Nicolas Mahy, fils Nicolas;
    1833—Nicolas Mahy, formerly belonging to André Cohu;
    1798—André Cohu, fils André;
    1750—André Cohu, fils André;
    1729—André Cohu, fils André;
    1662—Thomas Cohu, formerly belonging to Hellier Marquy;
    1583—(H)ellier Marquy, fils Collas;
    1549—Perryne Le Queu;
    1471—John Caritey (Queritez), alias Le Queu.

As stated at the beginning of this chapter, the more evidence there is, the safer the conclusions we can come to. It is therefore particularly fortunate that the set of Livres des Perchages for the Castel section of the Fief Le Comte go back so far and are so easy to follow. The Fief Blanchelande, in St. Martin's, provides a similar sequence, back to 1488. Using these two sets of books, then, it is possible to see whether any houses from the 15th century, 100 years before date-stones became popular, may have survived to the present day.

Houses on the Fief Le Comte that were there in 1471 are:

    Le Marais (493)
    La Forge (509)
    Les Grands Moulins (520) almost certainly
    Les Effards (552)
    Les Queux (555)
    Old Cobo Farmhouse (595)
    Cobo Farmhouse (596)

On the Fief Blanchelande, those existing in 1488 were:

    Le Mont Durand (26)
    La Contrée de Saint (69)
    La Tourelle (76)
    La Maison Guignan (92)
    La Maison Godaine (131)
    Les Martins (135)

Three other houses on Fief Blahchelande in 1488 have since been rebuilt on the same site, since none show any characteristics earlier than the 18th century. On the other hand the 13 houses listed above which can safely be said to date from the 15th century are not, of course, the sum total for the whole island. Indeed, near neighbours, especially in the King's Mills and at Les Martins, may be equally ancient. They are not listed here because they cannot be satisfactorily traced, or are on another fief whose earlier books have been lost. Also, it must be emphasised that there are many houses that can be traced as far back as the first half of the 16th century, and in fiefs where the books are very awkwardly arranged, prolonged research might very well produce 15th- or 16th-century dates for other houses where we have had to rely on different evidence in this survey.

What use, then, is to be made of these early Fief Le Comte and Fief Blanchelande records? Firstly, they show us that we may well be right in suspecting that houses have survived from the middle of the 15th century, and secondly, they confirm that those houses contain the features which seem to be characteristic of early dwellings.

Without exception, these 13 houses adhere to the longhouse plan, and considering that only Old Cobo Farmhouse has kept its original fenestration, the number of early features still present is remarkable. They contain between them 16 carved fireplaces; seven tourelle staircases; eight arched doorways; seven gable windows: five éviers; three bénitiers; and no fewer than six byre windows.

Armed with this information, it is clearly worthwhile to look at all the other houses that possess some of these characteristics. Some of them, we find, do not go back beyond the late 16th century, even though they are on a fief whose books are easily understood and are therefore easily traced. It can then be supposed that the house-type remained popular for a long time. On other fiefs, whose 15th- and 16th-century books have been lost, it is at least encouraging if we find that houses similar to the 13 listed above occur in the first book we do have. By a process of comparison and elimination, a picture is gradually built up of the sequence of building styles. Even negative evidence is worth having. If the fief records do not completely contradict hypotheses worked out from other evidence, then at least those hypotheses are worth considering. And occasionally the Livres des Perchages produce a really useful piece of positive information.

An example concerning the Type 5 arches already mentioned in connection with their raised inscriptions will illustrate the point. There are few nicely-chamfered window-openings in Guernsey. Still fewer windows have chamfer-stops similar to those we find on arches and fireplaces. In every case where these arches with raised inscriptions remain in their original position, window openings with fine chamfer-stops or highly-decorated window-sills are associated with them, or are known from old illustrations to have existed previously. What about the houses with similar, but undated arches? Le Tourtel (129) is one such house, and it has a particularly fine range of chamfered window-openings completely unaltered. In tracing it back through the Livres des Perchages it was therefore particularly gratifying to find that it was not mentioned before 1580, in which year it is described as 'sa neuve maison' (his new house), just one year before the 1581 date at St. George (586) on an identical arch. With this in mind, it is all the more probable that Les Granges de Beauvoir Manor (834), another house with a similarly fine array of chamfered windows, must have been built between 1580 and 1620. And so the process of comparing and checking goes on.

The Livres des Perchages, then, are our most useful sources of supportive evidence because they give a total number of houses on a fief at any one time and because they are a systematic record, rather than a chance series of documents depending on whether the sale or division of a property passed through a court of law. All the same, they are not always easy to work, there are gaps where books are lost, and even at their best, they can never tell us as much as the house itself. It is therefore time to examine the fabric of the house.

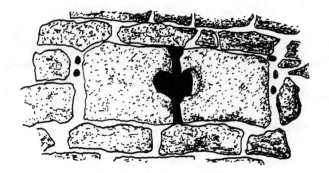

LA HAYE DU PUITS (582) Loophole in angle turret commanding entrance and former roadway: probably 15th century, with 18th century pointing and some galleting

Chapter XXI

THE FRENCH CONNECTION

FROM TIME TO TIME the importance of links with France have been stressed. To begin with, Guernseymen were of the same stock as the people of Brittany, very largely descended from the Britons fleeing from the west of England and Wales under the pressure of Anglo-Saxon invasion in the fifth, sixth and seventh centuries. The same Welsh and Irish saints evangelised our islands and Brittany, and England was in alliance with that country until it became part of France in 1498.

We also had trading ties with Gascony, an English possession until 1453, and the wine trade passing through these islands continued even after all English claims in France had come to an end. But for as long as England administered Aquitaine, Poitou and Gascony, our links with those areas were particularly close and maintenance of the sea-route between them and England was a vital part of English policy for nearly three hundred years.

Above all, we were inextricably bound up with Normandy, the land ceded to the Norseman, Rollo, in 913, to be held in fief by him in virtue of his homage to the French king, Charles the Simple, whose daughter he married. The former Roman province of Neustria thus became Normandy, and the Channel Islands, until then part of the kingdom of Brittany, were annexed soon after the Battle of Trans, 939, and became part of the feudal system under the Norman dukes. The owners of estates in the Cotentin also possessed land in Guernsey, their houses or granges here no doubt being built in imitation of the manor-houses they were used to on the Norman mainland. Ecclesiastically, too, we were part of Normandy, forming until 1568 a rural deanery of the diocese of Coutances so that our parish priests were appointed from France. The powerful abbeys of Mont St. Michel and Marmoutiers had important interests here, until they were confiscated during the French wars, and gifts of land from time to time had also linked us with other religious establishments in France. And while the English built the castles in Guernsey, it was the French who built, or influenced the building of churches. Above all, we spoke the same language.

Whatever the political implications of the protracted wars with France, we may be certain that trade continued, and that church-building was not seriously affected. And although a good deal of local stone was used, the best work was always carried out in granite from the isles of Chausey. In 1360, Michel du Port, Prior of the Vale, became Abbot of Mont St. Michel, and this Guernseyman vigorously encouraged the rebuilding and enlargement of his own abbey and of churches in his territories. It is probable that much of the best work here was stimulated by him or was inspired by the splendour of the abbey at Mont St. Michel. Certainly the quarries both in Chausey and near St. Malo were particularly active during the next two centuries. It is from them that the art of quarrying and dressing blocks of granite was introduced here at the end of the 15th century. But the fine ashlar work of the Town Church tower and, for instance, at St. Saviour's church, must have meant the employment of skilled masons here before that. While they were here the richer merchants and landowners would have engaged some of them for work on their own properties. And Chausey stone must have been even more readily available here in the second quarter of the 15th century, for then those islands were in English hands. Even as late as 1741-48, when Chausey was again held by England, 400 men were sent over from Jersey to quarry stone, much of which was used in Guernsey's fortifications.

So not only might we expect, for historical and cultural reasons, to find Breton and Norman house-types in this island, but also we might expect French stone to be used in our better houses. In fact, this is so. The Guernsey Savings Bank (756) was built of Chausey stone, probably in the 15th century (see Chapter XXXIV), and many of our arches and fireplaces were from those quarries. Occasionally, for instance in the construction of the évier at Le Frie (303), it is possible that stone from the Mont Mado quarries in Jersey, or from the area around St. Malo, was used, though it is somewhat difficult to distinguish it from Cobo granite.

Finally, the influx of Huguenot refugees into Jersey and Guernsey during the second half of the 16th century and the beginning of the 17th century, must have ensured the continuation of French influence on our way of life at least until 1600. Our political allegiance to England was unswerving, but strong links with France on other levels, from the earliest times until the 17th century, are indisputable. From then on, our ties with France became gradually weaker.

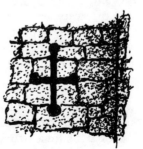

LA ROCQUE
BALAN (1007).
Loophole in tourelle
covering back doorway.

Chapter XXII

HOUSE TYPES

THUS THOUGH GUERNSEY is an island geographically, it is not isolated from architectural influences, and in trying to date our buildings it is necessary to compare their forms with houses in those areas most likely to have similar types. Our houses do not markedly differ at any time from contemporary buildings elsewhere. This theme has been fully developed in Part I. It is only necessary to say here that the longhouse form has been studied by Meirion Jones in Brittany, where its form is sufficiently distinct from the Welsh or Irish longhouse, and sufficiently similar to our oldest houses to show that the longhouse plan between 1400 and 1600 was part of a way of life that had already been followed for centuries both in Guernsey and Brittany. Our comparative prosperity, because of our political importance and our trade, allowed us to construct two-storey buildings here in great numbers at a time when only the more important farms in Brittany were of that size. It seems that although the island estates were not extensive enough to support such large manors as are found there and in Normandy, it was these that set the pace by the end of the 15th century and made the builder of many a medium-sized farmhouse aspire to arched doorways and fine fireplaces that must have been the prerogative of his betters a generation before.

The strange thing which seems to set apart the houses of Guernsey, between 1400 and 1600, from those of their Norman or Breton cousins, is their remarkable uniformity. Perhaps this is just the mark of a small community, where one type of house, answering local needs perfectly, might equally become popular and the fashionable sort to build. By the next generation it would be accepted as 'the way to build a house', and so it would remain, until a better pattern came along. On the French mainland, the great diversity of forms to be found in vernacular architecture are a reflection of the greater cross-fertilisation of ideas and traditions and the greater variation in local conditions to be expected in a large country. Within Brittany alone, the actual interpretation of the longhouse plan takes various forms, and houses differ significantly in their proportions, one from another. In detail, too, they offer much greater variety. It is therefore impossible to say that the Guernsey longhouse originated in this or that part of Brittany or Normandy, for while its plan may closely resemble houses to be found in Morbihan, its elevation is quite different. The tendency towards symmetry which was always characteristic of the Guernsey house is often quite lacking in Brittany. The houses that seem to be most akin to ours in their proportions, when seen from a distance, are the farms in the area around Tréguier. But, of course, their fenestration, as well as ours, has usually been altered and their façades will consequently look quite unlike ours; but the dimensions are the same. Many of their arches, too, are like our Type 4 examples.

On the other hand, they do not possess our low tourelles. These occur only occasionally, but if anything are slightly more popular in the area around Mur-de-Bretagne than elsewhere. However, nowhere in Brittany was any great number of houses equipped with this sort of staircase. Neither were they ever common in fairly small houses. They were usually reserved for the *petit manoirs*, and nowhere is there such a density as in Guernsey.

We shall see in a later section that our arches seem also to be derived from different sources. It therefore appears that the Guernsey longhouse is very much an eclectic design, adapted to local needs, to local resources, and reflecting local and sometimes individual taste.

In later times, the same house-type continued here, chiefly because it was so easily adapted to the complete symmetry of a classical or Georgian façade. It therefore seems unnecessary to examine English house types at all. The single greatest difference in layout between English houses and our own in medieval times had been the position of the chimneys: in England, almost invariably, a central chimney stack with rooms on either side showed its ancestry from the central open hearth, but in Guernsey as in Brittany, the fireplaces were always at the gable end—any others were later additions. We have no examples of the hall-house type that was so widespread in England, except for the possibility of a first floor hall-house at Maison de Haut (974, see Chapter VII). And since the proportions of 18th-century architecture both in England and France did not favour the central chimney stack, there is no reason to see the local house-plan of that time as in any way English. However, the phenomenon of building on a back kitchen was a fashion which certainly sprang from England, where the proliferation of service-rooms in small manor houses and the homes of the wealthy merchants and yeoman farmers is well-known from the 16th century onwards.

Our two examples of kitchens built separately from the house at Les Adams (328) and Le Bourg de Bas (162) may owe something to the *boulangeries* or bakehouses associated with the outside bread ovens of Norman farms, but the back kitchens added beside or behind the kitchen ends of our earlier houses reflect the first stage in that English development of the separation of the old kitchen into kitchen and living-room. The integral bread ovens of these back kitchens were also characteristic of England, though their usual position in Guernsey at the side, rather than behind the fireplace, is a local preference.

So much for derivation. The dating of these forms is only of general help to us in deciding the age of a house. The longhouse was popular in Brittany

HOUSE TYPES

for such a long period of time, certainly from 1400 to 1700, that it would be foolish to base our conclusions on comparison of the general form of the house alone; the building of back kitchens was a process that went on from 1600 to 1900 and consequently does not help either. It is to the details of house-construction that we must look.

LES HAMELINS (294)
Initials and date of refronting, with galletting

Chapter XXIII

WALLING

THERE IS NO REAL dry-stone walling in Guernsey houses. Sometimes prolonged exposure to the weather has led to the washing away of mortar so that a dry-stone effect is produced, but there is no surviving house which uses it as a technique. Neither do any cob houses remain.

Until at least 1900, walls were normally constructed with two faces of fairly good stone, though not usually of ashlar, with a rubble filling between, all held together with a clay mortar. Lime mortar was used here only for the churches and the castles. The strength of these walls was thus in the two faces, not in the middle. Thus it was necessary to build these walls at least 18in. thick to provide stability and in order to interlock the stones of the inner and outer faces. An 18in.-wall would allow stones averaging 9in. wide to be used. However, far larger stones were more usual, especially for the oustide walls, so that gable-ends 4ft. 6in. thick are often found.

These thick walls not only had to withstand the thrust of the roof, but in the case of the gable ends, to support the massive shoulder stones and corbels of the fireplaces and the immense weight of the stone chimney-hood above them. Even greater stability was often achieved in the oldest houses, and occasionally even after 1650, by tapering the walls, so that a front wall 2ft. 6in. thick at the base would be only 18in. wide at the top. This batter, or slope of the walls in most houses built between 1400 and 1600 produces an impression of great strength, clearly justified, since a good many have already lasted 500 years, and most of those that have gone had suffered generations of neglect or have been demolished, like the Ville-au-Roi Manor House in 1943, not because of structural defects, but to make way for other development.

Indeed, two at least of the houses listed in the 1471 Livres des Perchages of the Fief Le Comte, Old Cobo Farmhouse (595) and Cobo Farmhouse (596) are built directly onto sand and are clearly more enduring than the Biblical parable would have us believe.

These two houses, like all others of that period, have no foundations. When a house was built, first the site had to be cleared and levelled, perhaps to the accompaniment of pagan and religious ceremonies such as was the practice in Brittany—see *Architecture et Vie traditionelle en Bretagne* —François Pacqueteau,

p. 33. The intimate relationship of the people with the place where they were to dwell might be established by burying a bird under the kitchen floor, or a coin under a large corner-stone. A priest would bless the land on which the house was to stand and the family would keep a little of the earth so blessed to use in case of illness. The huge stones chosen to form the base of the walls would then be placed in position. It was often the custom to leave particularly massive corner stones projecting, perhaps to protect the corners of the house from the wheels of carts.

In many cases, small quarries were opened just in order to provide stone for a single house. Sometimes, if the site were sloping, the stone quarried in levelling the site would be used for the rubble filling. We have seen that in 1498, John Bonamy obtained his stone from two sources. The 'good' stone, which could be shaped up by a mason, came from Cobo and was used for the corner, or quoin stones and for the arches and fireplaces; the stone from Moulin Huet (Icart gneiss), close at hand, was used for the rest of the walling, being what is sometimes locally called 'rotten stone', because of the way in which the surface tends to break down into gravel. Especially in those houses near the coast, stone from the beach was used in great quantities.

Until the late 17th century the red Cobo granite was the stone almost universally employed for quoin stones and arches. Especially during the 15th and early 16th centuries, Chausey stone was also used occasionally, while some of the more unusual grey stone arches or the stone chosen at St. Clair (932) and The Elms (946) must have been quarried specially or fashioned from surface boulders or even dismantled megaliths. Then, at the end of the 17th century, new quarries at Perelle began producing much harder grey stone, making possible a systematic contrast of colour in the façade and serving to emphasise the larger, evenly-spaced windows. In the 18th century, other quarries were opened in the north of the island, heralding the start of the great granite-quarrying industry of the following 150 years, when vast quantities of stone were exported from Guernsey. The organisation of the quarrying industry led to a degree of standardisation and an improvement in the finish of stone used in the façade of a house. During the period 1650-1750, the size of quoin stones tended to diminish, and by the end of our period (1787) they were almost always totally regular, about 12in. high and nicely squared.

As the quoins became smaller, the average size of the stone used in the rubble walling became larger, so that both quoins and other stones were of equivalent height. The result was that throughout the 18th century many, but not all, walls were built almost in courses. By the end of the century, the properly coursed wall had developed. It is used, for instance, in the new house at Les Bordages in 1790 and became almost universal in the 19th century, when a stonemason was paid per foot length of wall built, the coursings being lined up between quoin stones of exactly equal height. The base of each new course was set slightly inside the top line of the preceding one, producing a definite 'banding' effect

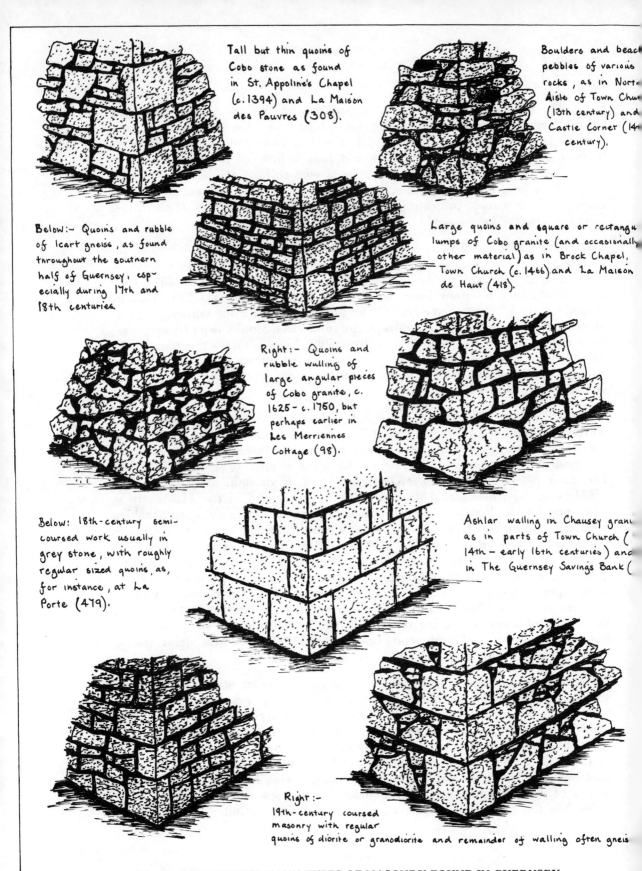

Fig. 28. SOME OF THE MANY TYPES OF MASONRY FOUND IN GUERNSEY

along the wall. Recognition of this 19th-century coursed walling is vital to the identification of pre-19th-century houses, for while some 19th-century walls were still uncoursed no stonework used this technique before *c.* 1780, at the earliest. We can therefore say that whereas no coursed masonry will be before 1780, some uncoursed masonry may be later.

Secondly, it is important to remember that a house might have been re-fronted after 1780, or some other patching carried out. The coursed masonry at the back of La Maison des Pauvres (308), for instance, does not mean the house is only 19th-century. It indicates a total change of use at that time, probably when the gable-end was taken down for road-widening and rebuilt further back, also in coursed masonry. Similarly, the eastern gable-end at La Grève (1012) was taken down and replaced in coursed work, probably in order to fit 19th-century chimney flues more easily. But La Grève is an exception. Almost always it is the gable ends which have survived change, for two reasons: partly because the concern of the 18th- and 19th-century re-fronters was mostly to achieve a harmonious façade; and partly because the gable-ends themselves were more massively built and it was unnecessary to disturb the structure of the chimney and the bread oven. So it is important to notice exactly which parts of a building are coursed and which are not. Coursed front or back walls, rebuilt so as to include large windows, might not have affected the gable-ends and cross-walls of a much earlier house.

Lastly, it is necessary to distinguish between the quasi-coursing and the coursing that succeeded it. This is not easy. In the former, the depth of the quasi-coursing along the wall tends to vary, and the depth of any two courses will also be different, according to the size of the quoin they are lined up with. The quoins themselves are not squared up so well as in 19th-century work.

However, these are only general hints. Wall-building is different in different parts of the island, according to the availability of good stone. Thus in one place a comparatively small house will use stones that resemble ashlar; whereas in another, a large house may use a good deal of Icart gneiss. Moreover, especially in houses built after 1650, there is often a considerable difference between the front and the back walls of a house. La Fosse (300) is a case in point. Here, the best stone has been reserved for use at the front of the cottage, while the back wall is made up of tiny stones that would have been used only for the rubble filling in a wall of larger farmhouse. At Le Haut Chemin (311) the very ancient back wall is made up in part of similarly small stone: in this house the different techniques used in patching, and the great variety of stone, are fascinating.

In some early 17th-century walling a patchwork of very angular stones was favoured. Parts of the front and back walls of Le Marais (493), rebuilt probably between 1625 and 1650, contrast with the lumpier stonework at either side, of pre-1470 date. The preference for horizontal slivers, reminiscent of 19th-century work, but not coursed, is probably no more than a reflection of the sort of stone produced by one quarry where the rock split more readily than usual along the bedding planes.

While it is not possible to be precise about the evolution of wall-building techniques because they tended to vary from one part of the island to another, and also, of course, according to the wealth or poverty of each individual, it is instructive to look at the island churches, which can be fairly accurately dated, and which exhibit quite a variety of styles. For instance, at the Town Church, the north aisle wall of the nave is 13th-century; the ashlar of the tower is 14th century; the rubble walling of the north and south transepts and Brock Chapel are *c.* 1466; while the east wall of the chancel and the west wall of the nave are early 16th-century ashlar. The ashlar work is all carried out in the brownish Chausey stone. The 13th-century wall is made up very largely of local gabbro and red Cobo stone mixed with occasional pieces of other material. Much of it is clearly from the beach, or prised away from outcrops: mostly rather small and with slightly rounded edges. The window embrasures are of dressed Cobo granite. The 15th-century work is also rubble walling of local origin, but quite small, rather square blocks of stone are used in irregular lines, a technique very characteristic of this period, widely-used elsewhere. Stand with the late afternoon sun shining against the north wall of the Forest church, and this sort of walling will not easily be forgotten. Here again, somewhat squarish stones are set almost in lines, which however, unlike the 'coursing' of 19th-century walls, are not really regular. An example in domestic architecture is at La Maison de Haut, Les Trépieds (418).

Ste. Appoline's chapel, built in 1392, shows another technique. Very tall but narrow quoin-stones of Cobo stone contrast with rubble walls of much smaller stones. The proportions of the quoin stones and the contrast is the same as that of the front façade at La Maison des Pauvres (308).

It is particularly instructive, too, to look at the walling in our churches and in the houses recorded in the 15th century in order to understand the effect of 500 years of weathering. A 15th-century wall of Cobo stone looks very different from an 18th-century one of the same material, mostly because the surface of the stone has been exposed to the elements for 300 years longer. This effect, once fixed in the mind, can easily be recognised in a good many buildings whose exact age cannot be accurately established; and it is of some importance when assessing the antiquity or otherwise of any house. This is true not only for the outside. The stonework of fireplaces indoors also changes over a period of time, merely from exposure to fresh air. It is impossible to match an old piece of stone with a new one, even from the same quarry, because one will be freshly-hewn, while the chemicals of the atmosphere will have been working on the other for centuries.

Thus, the general appearance of stonework, both inside and outside a house are worth taking into account as much as the actual techniques of building construction, for which the accompanying diagrams should help establish a tentative chronology.

Chapter XXIV

WOODWORK

OF ALL THE ELEMENTS used in house construction, the woodwork shows the greatest changes over the centuries. We can study this firstly in the structural features, that is to say the beams and ceiling joists, and the trusses of the roof; and then in the panelling and furniture. The beams and ceiling joists, and occasionally the roof-structure, are all that remain of the original woodwork in the oldest houses. We have no surviving doors earlier than the 16th century. However, a good number of beams and joists are 15th-century, and possibly even older. As a rough guide, the larger they are in cross-section, the older they are. The main timbers at Maison de Haut (974) vary from 12in. to 15in. square. They are only roughly shaped and one of them is a forked tree-trunk, with both forks inserted in the masonry. The beams at Bordeaux House (984) are equally massive. Making a virtue out of a necessity, it became the practice to chamfer the angles of a timber, taking advantage of the circular section of the tree to achieve as large a beam as possible. In the oldest houses, the chamfer is a simple one, with plain stops at either end. Gradually, it became the practice to produce moulded chamfers, with elaborate stops, some of the best examples being at La Maison de Haut (240) and Les Reveaux (259). However, it was in the horizontal beams helping to expose the jetties of town houses that this ornamentation was most exaggerated.

The 1870 print of Smith Street reproduced in MacCulloch's *Folklore* shows the overhanging storeys of the old house, where the Guernsey Press shop now is, supported on these highly-carved beams, or *sablières*. La Maison des Pauvres in Berthelot Street, now part of the Guernsey Savings Bank (756) and 5 Berthelot Street (808) also possessed these features, now unhappily lost. The even more decorative *sablière* from the High Street frontage of the Guernsey Savings Bank is, however, preserved in the Guille-Allès Library, and a facsimile of it will be replaced in the bank when alterations begin this year (1980). It bears the inscription *La Paix de Dieu soit ceans: fait le 18 Octobre 1578 de par André Monamy* (The Peace of God be among us: built by André Monamy, 18 October 1578). Though this is the only remaining *sablière* in Guernsey, almost every town in Brittany retains plenty of examples of similar fine wood carving. In Rennes, it is reckoned that such beams with undecorated chamfer-stops belong to the end of the 15th century, while those where an ornament based on a cauliflower

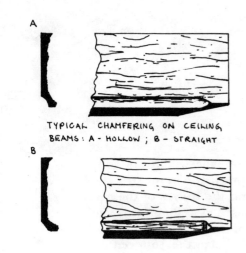

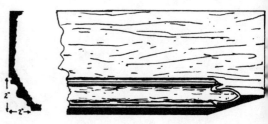

Fig. 29. MOULDED CHAMFERS ON MAIN BEAMS

leaf reduces the elaborate chamfering to a square corner at either end is 16th century. But some *sablières* have 16th-century chamfering without quite such an exaggerated stop. From the general shape of the mouldings, based on a comparison with this outside woodwork it would be reasonable to expect the fine beams inside at La Maison de Haut, Les Reveaux and Les Granges de Beauvoir Manor (834) to belong to the end of the 16th century. This accords well with the evidence of their arches and window-surrounds. The plainer work at Bordeaux House, clearly an important building, suggests a much earlier date; but in many less important farmhouses, plain chamfers were used from the 16th to the 18th century.

The fashion for elaborate chamfers faded together with the liking for fine fireplaces and arches. Seventeenth-century houses reverted to a simple chamfer with plain stops. As time went on, the timbers used for the main beams became smaller, rarely exceeding 9in. square in section. In the 18th century, the chamfer was either noticeably narrower than before, barely one inch across, or else again became ornamental, usually with an ovolo mould in association with panelled walls and cornices.

The joists between these main beams were at first very closely spaced, hardly more than a foot apart, and were roughly 4in. square. If they were not square,

WOODWORK

they were invariably laid flat, rather than upright; and until about 1700, all floor joists rested on the main beams and were never notched in. Usually, these early timbers were unornamented, the mouldings and the rosettes on the cross-passage timbers at Le Marais (937) being exceptional. Towards the end of the 16th century they were often chamfered to match the fine work on the main beams, but after 1750 there was a distinct change. Not only were the joists notched into the ceiling beams, but they were smaller, about 4in. by 3in. and set upright with a roll-moulding.

The type of wood used also changed. Whereas the 15th- and 16th-century houses always used oak or greenheart when they could afford it, and local elm when they could not, the 18th century saw a growing use of imported pine. This was more easily worked and less expensive, but not, of course, as hard as the other timber. The recent replacement of a huge 15th-century oak beam by a steel joist at Le Fleur du Jardin Hotel (508) seems particularly pointless, since that timber was as sound as the day it was put in, and almost impossible to saw. Many are the tales of blunted chain-saws after attempts to cut into these beams, and of 6in. nails that cannot be hammered in. The local elm, often used with its bark still on, might have its surface attacked by beetle, but while it is penetrating the green wood, the heart of the beam is becoming harder and harder.

Oak was also chiefly used in the oldest roof timbers we have left. Unfortunately the original roofs left from the 15th and 16th centuries hardly reach double figures. Most were destroyed when thatched roofs were replaced by slate or tile, in some cases, no doubt, because they were defective, but often because it was desired to raise the side walls of the house by a foot or more to insert larger windows in the bedrooms. The trusses, therefore, had to be disturbed, and were replaced by new ones of standard Victorian pattern. Those original ones we do have mostly seem to follow the contemporary roof patterns of Normandy and Brittany, where the usual form was to use the first-floor ceiling beams as a tie-beam either just with a kingpost, or, more often, with a collar, upper kingpost and windbraces. As on the Continent, some of our examples are associated with upper crucks. No true cruck form remains, and none was probably built, since it is a type more appropriate to a timber-framed house where the pairs of crucks, like an upturned 'V', support, not only the roof, but the walls. In Guernsey, the slightly-curved upper crucks usually sit on the inner face of the side walls and are notched and pegged into the tie-beams. At Les Câches (237, see Chapter XXXVIII), however, the upper crucks are notched into the tie-beams inside the inner face of the wall, and are also braced. Full kingpost roofs remain at La Rocque Balan (1007) and La Grande Maison (945), and can be traced at La Maison de Haut (240). Upper kingposts and collars exist at Le Carrefour (457) and Les Granges de Beauvoir Manor (834), almost the only example to have kept its windbraces.

Seventeenth- and 18th-century roofs were simple 'A'-frames, usually without kingposts or windbraces, and built in elm or pine, rather than oak. As the

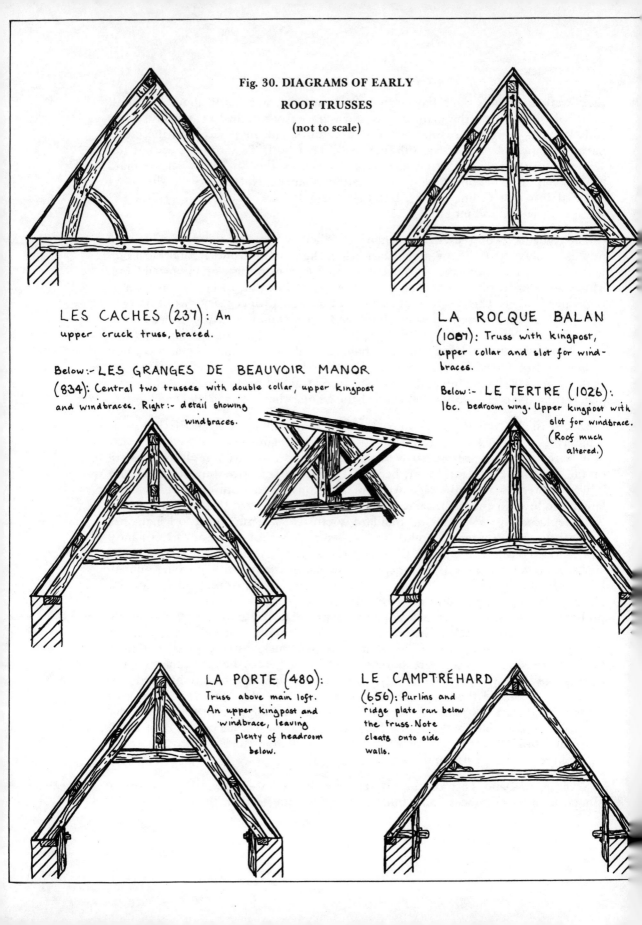

Fig. 30. DIAGRAMS OF EARLY ROOF TRUSSES
(not to scale)

LES CACHES (237): An upper cruck truss, braced.

Below:- LES GRANGES DE BEAUVOIR MANOR (834): Central two trusses with double collar, upper kingpost and windbraces. Right:- detail showing windbraces.

LA ROCQUE BALAN (1007): Truss with kingpost, upper collar and slot for windbraces.

Below:- LE TERTRE (1026): 16c. bedroom wing. Upper kingpost with slot for windbrace. (Roof much altered.)

LA PORTE (480): Truss above main loft. An upper kingpost and windbrace, leaving plenty of headroom below.

LE CAMPTRÉHARD (656): Purlins and ridge plate run below the truss. Note cleats onto side walls.

WOODWORK

18th century progressed, ideas that first appear in Town architecture are seen more and more in the country. The principal rafters approximated to the 9in. by 3in. size almost universally used in the following century, and purlins began to be notched into them instead of running over them as in earlier times.

When we turn to panelling and doors, we have nothing which we can positively assign to the 15th century. In both cases, our earliest examples probably date from around the close of the 16th century. From this period come the very fine panelling at Les Câches, La Maison de Haut, Les Granges de Beauvoir Manor, and La Rocque Balan, as well as a small piece of linenfold panelling found at La Bellieuse Farm (94), and the door at the top of the stairs at La Ruette (406). This is all very good work in oak. At Les Câches the panelling is divided both laterally and vertically (see Illustration 52), and at Les Granges de Beauvoir Manor the true panels thus formed have a raised ground on one side only (see Chapter XXXV). At La Rocque Balan and La Maison de Haut, the timber partitioning is post-and-panel planking, set into horizontal plates at top and bottom. The in-and-out pattern of this form of partitioning remained common in Guernsey for another 150 years, but this early work differs from the later in that it is in oak, not pine, and that it is nicely moulded at the edges. La Maison de Haut retains its contemporary doors, two-panelled, divided by a cross-ledge. The door at the head of the stairs, giving access to the bedroom extension, at La Ruette, is a type of linenfold.

Both early and late forms of post-and-panel work are side-by-side at 11 Cliff Street (717). Here the 17th-century partitioning on the first floor is a poorer version of that in the houses just discussed, planking of various sizes being used, and none of it with moulding. But upstairs is the much more common, totally regular sort found from about 1675 to about 1750. The planks are 9-in. widths of pine, simply moulded. However, the best examples of this can be found at Les Quertiers (676), Havilland House (685), The Cottage, Hauteville (695), and 3 Salter Street (858). Les Quertiers is known from the fief records to have been built by 1684, and we also have an outside door at Maison d'Aval (241) in similar work, dated 1685 (see Illustration 64). On the other hand, 11 Cliff Street cannot have received its top storey before 1740 at the very earliest, although within the next 20 years, vastly superior Georgian panelling was all the fashion in town and country. We therefore seem to have a progression, with due allowance for an overlap in styles, from the oak panelling of the early houses, up to about 1625, through a transitional period to the post-and-panel partitioning proper, 1675–1750, followed by Georgian, or classical work up to, and beyond, 1787. For more descriptions of panelling, see Chapters XXXV and XXXVIII.

Of other fittings, nothing remains before the 17th century, if then. The larder cupboard, with its vertical slatted doors at Les Adams (328) may be contemporary with the detached kitchen in which it stands, but most kitchen furnishings date at their earliest, from the 18th century. From this period come the settles at Le Chêne Cottage (154), L'Echelle (649) and La Cheminée (551), for example, and an occasional cupboard door elsewhere. Larger doors were also replaced at this time, when the rooms themselves were panelled, and can always be distinguished from later, 19th-century work by the raised ground of their panels. The six-panelled door first became popular here in about 1750.

Moveable furnishings are outside the scope of this book and in any case were few enough in most farms and cottages until after 1700. As they can but rarely have been designed for any one house, they do not concern us here.

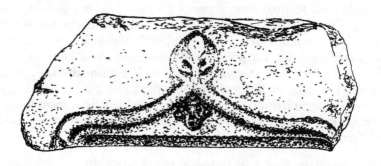

Window head at Casa Seda (896)

Chapter XXV

ARCHES AND DOORWAYS

WHEN WE TURN to the arched doorways we are set an intriguing series of problems. There are at least 193 known in the island. Those which either remain *in situ* or are known to have been in particular houses are listed in the First Schedule; those removed to other sites are in the Fourth Schedule, and are included, whether or not they are complete. The following will show clearly how they are distributed between the types to be explained in this section:

FIRST SCHEDULE

Type	1	2	3	4	5	6	7	Pointed	Plastered over
Total	23	8	20	38	31	5	9	2	2

FOURTH SCHEDULE

Type	1	2	3	4	5	6	7	Pointed	
Total	3	1	6	34	5	1	1	3	
Added together	26	9	26	72	36	6	10	5	2

All arches also divide into two distinct groups: those that are a true semi-circle, turning through 180deg.; and those which are segmental, that is, forming only an arc of a circle whose centre is below the springing, thus forming a definite angle between the head of the arch and the sides. This distinction is of great importance in considering the derivation of our houses. For whereas the semi-circular arch is by far the most popular form in Brittany, the segmental arch is used in the Cotentin area of Normandy almost to the exclusion of any other. Thus, although the longhouse form of our early buildings is Breton, the details may often be Norman in influence, and further study along these lines should not be confined to Brittany. In Guernsey, although the Breton pattern is more popular, some of our finest arches are Norman; and we also find that the Norman type was very often used for back doorways even where the Breton type is at the front.

Fig. 31. NORMAN AND BRETON ARCHES

LA RONDE CHEMINÉE (929) The segmental arch typical of Norman styles.

LES CACHES FARM (112) The semi-circular arch typical of Styles.

If the shape of the arch can help us with derivation, for dating we must look to the actual masonry. And again, useful parallels can be found in the architecture of island churches. The Town Church happens to encapsulate exactly the progression of building techniques to be found in our houses. In the nave, the arches are formed of small stones, set on edge, as one would build an arch in brick: they are only roughly squared, and unchamfered, similar to Type 1. That is 13th-century work and is paralleled at St. Sampson's and the Vale churches, where

Fig. 32. ARCHES: TYPES 1 AND 2

TYPE 1: One order of small stones, unchamfered; The Elms, Pleinheaume (946)

TYPE 2: Two orders of small stones, unchamfered based on Maison de Haut, Pleinheaume (974)

ARCHES AND DOORWAYS

there are also similar arches of two orders as in Type 2. At Castle Cornet and the Vale Castles, too, the same technique occurs in early work. The next development is demonstrated by the chancel at the Town Church, where there is a single order of larger stones, almost square in shape, nicely-worked and with a hollow chamfer; while in the crossing, the arches are the same with the addition of an outer order also of approximately square stones. Both chancel and crossing are 14th century. However, in the imposing arcades of the north and south transepts of 1466, the outer order uses stones almost square, as before, but the stones of the inner order are greatly elongated, just as in Type 3.

This progression is exactly that demonstrated by our domestic arches. Type 1 is made up of small stones, set on edge, roughly squared and with no chamfer. The sides of the doorway are also comparatively small pieces of stone. Type 2 is exactly the same except that there are two orders, or rows, of stones. Almost all arches of these two types are constructed of red Cobo granite: a few exceptions possibly form a transitional stage with Types 3 and 4, since they show a slightly better finish. The arch at The Elms (946) uses contrasting light and dark stone, and the arches at St. Clair (932) are in a light grey stone capable of a very smooth finish. The arches at Le Marais (493) and Le Ménage du Moulin (512), of Cobo granite, also have great base stones at either side of the door and embryonic shoulder stones.

Type 3 arches are vastly superior to the previous types. They consist of an inner order of large, long stones, and an outer order of small ones arranged to resemble a relieving arch, and probably derived from that idea. The inner order is always nicely worked and has a chamfer, sometimes hollow, sometimes straight, carried down the sides of the doorway to end in a chamfer stop. Such chamfer-stops are usually plain, but occasionally have a simple ornament. Some doorways have long, horizontal shoulder stones emphasising the springing of the arch, as at Les Câches Farm (112). Others do not, as at La Petite Câche (959). In other details, these arches vary considerably. For instance that at Les Câches Farm has four stones for its inner order; that at Les Poidevins (661), only two. Most have three. The outer order can consist of as few as nine stones, or as many as twenty-four. At Le Tertre (1026), the two orders are separated by another band of small stones laid horizontally, a decorative technique also used to great effect at La Grande Maison (945). Cobo granite, again, is the most popular stone used, but there is greater variety of material than before.

Type 4 arches consist of one order only, chamfered, with great base and shoulder stones. Both in Types 3 and 4, the sides of the arch are often more or less L-shaped so that they spread themselves on the shoulder-stone below (except that at La Ronde Cheminée [929] which does not quite sit as it should).

Type 5 arches are again of two orders, but now, the outer order is also made up of either five or seven large stones, the shoulder stones being elongated to support the base of this virtually independent arch. Naturally there are one or two examples which bridge the gap between Types 3 and 5, for instance the

Fig. 33. ARCHES: TYPES 3 AND 4

TYPE 3: Two orders, the inner order of large stones, the outer of small stones; chamfered. Les Grands Moulins (520)

TYPE 4: One order of large stones; chamfered. Les Courtils (388)

doorway now at La Couture (310), where the outer order consists of many small stones, but all of them tooled to the same finish as the inner order. Type 5 arches often have ornamental chamfer-stops and are initialled and dated, as at La Pompe (117).

Type 6 includes two sorts of doorway which do not fall into this architectural progression, and can be regarded as parallel forms. The first is the ogival arch, found at La Contrée de Saint (69), La Rocque Balan (1007), and Le Marais Farm 1008). The second is a related form, but more flattened, an accolade or bracket lintel on corbelled and chamfered sides. It is found at Le Villocq (581), rebuilt at St. George (586), and with corbels but no accolade, indoors at Bordeaux House (984).

Type 7 are not arches, but chamfered doorways, not to be confused with the doorways at the bottoms of tourelle staircases which are revetted to take a door, rather than chamfered.

There are also four pointed arches, two at Les Annevilles Manor (948) which have probably been removed from the adjoining chapel, or were intimately connected with it, since they are otherwise like the portals of the Vale and St. Sampson's churches; and two much later arches, chamfered and with hood moulds. One was formerly at La Grande Maison de la Pomare (317) and the other, now bordering Prince Albert's Road, was drawn by F. C. Lukis in 1845 at 'y^e Grand Maison'. But which one?

Finally, there are the entrance gateways and arches, Type 8, of which 11 remain in one form or another. We shall return to them later.

Fig. 34. ARCHES: TYPES 5, 6 AND 7

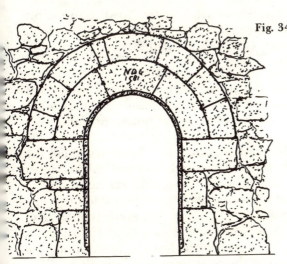

TYPE 5: The 'Guernsey' arch, with two orders of large stones; chamfered. Most have either 5 or 7 stones in the outer order. [...], the earliest dated arch, built by Nicolas de Gerzée at [St.] George (586), has 8.

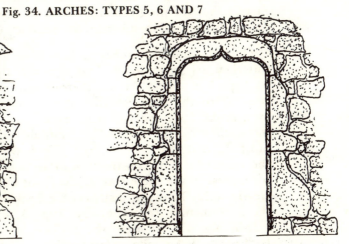

TYPE 6: The ogee arch. A slightly flattened form at Contrée de Saint (69). The ground level has probably been lowered by one stone.

TYPE 6: A flat lintel on corbelled sides; chamfered. [Re]built, possibly from same site, into St. George (586).

TYPE 7: Chamfered doorway, with fleur-de-lys stops; Les Domaines (426).

These, then, are the various forms of arches in Guernsey. It is not suggested that they should be dated exactly as the similar work at the Town Church, but merely that the progression is the same. Types 1 and 2 could not be shown to be 13th-century, and in any case, the nave arcades have pointed arches.

Only the pointed arches at Les Annevilles Manor are possibly 13th-century, but they are exceptional. And although the progression of styles from Type 1 to Type 5 is almost certain, there is another factor to be considered—that is the position of the arch, whether at the front or back of the house, or inside. For even in the 15th and 16th centuries, less expense was lavished on the back of the house than on the front. The front doorway was the most fashionable and the most elaborate the owner could afford, whereas the back doorway might be just the easiest form of construction or an unfashionable design. It was not intended to impress in the same way as the front doorway and doorways inside the house clearly were. Thus, for instance, the back doorway, Type 4, is much simpler than the monumental front doorway, Type 5, at Old Farm, Brock Road (925), and it will be argued that even where a later arch was inserted in the front façade, at La Rocque Balan, the unfashionable ogival doorway was mercifully left at the back. A similar practice has already been been noted in the actual walling of a house (p. 87). Another, much later parallel can be drawn with the fenestration at Les Bordages, 1790. Fashionable guillotine sashes are used at the front of the house, yet the old-fashioned casement sashes are good enough for the back. Similarly, the late 18th-century segmental arch into the farmyard is of granite ashlar in front, but brick behind.

A simple arch of small stones was also often used above window embrasures. The rounded windows of the walling in Le Ville-ès-Pies (992) may well be very early, especially as it is used on the façade itself, but elsewhere, at Bordeaux House, for instance, used on the inner face of the wall only, it is more in the nature of a relieving arch than an ornament, almost certainly intended to be plastered over. The relieving arch of Type 1 design still visible in the garden of one of the demolished houses in Cornet Street is thus not necessarily earlier than the 16th century.

Bearing all this in mind, it is interesting to note that the Type 1 and 2 arches, which can be taken to be more or less contemporary forms, are present in houses where the walling, or the byre windows, the évier or the great thickness of the internal walls all point towards a building of great antiquity: Maison de Haut (974—see Chapter VII); Les Blicqs (610); Le Marais (493); Ménage du Moulin (512); Cobo Farmhouse (596); Retôt Farm (593); or The Elms (946). Both Le Marais and Cobo Farmhouse were listed on the 1471 Livre des Perchages of the Fief Le Comte, and in both these houses this sort of arch forms the back door, the front having been changed. At Les Blicqs, too, the arch is at the back; at the others it is at the front. In the two houses where an arch is plastered over, it is also probably of this type. One of them, Les Paysans (325) has a fine bénitier, similar to that at Ménage du Moulin, but the other, Les Mourants (618), is more difficult to assess. The fireplace here does not look earlier than the 16th century, and the dimensions of the house on such a spacious site (the kitchen only 13ft. wide inside) are curious. It may well be that the simpler Type 1 and 2 arches, needing no dressing, were used as late as 1600 by those who could not afford a better arch. The fireplace at Les Mourants is carved, but is badly assembled. Possibly both the arch and the fireplace were brought from elsewhere. We must therefore always bear in mind the status of a house before determining its date.

In general, however, the evidence all points to Type 1 and Type 2 arches being the earliest forms in Guernsey, already flourishing by 1400 and used until about 1475. But by this time, at least two other forms had become fashionable. The ogee arch (Type 6) was introduced into Spain by the Moors in the early Middle Ages and used extensively in their architecture. It quickly became popular in Christendom, and especially in Venice, where it was almost the exclusive form during the 14th and 15th centuries. In the Gothic architecture of north-western Europe it appears at the end of the 13th century, and is common in churches until 1500. Here in Guernsey, it is found in the staircase doorway at St. Saviour's church, where the surrounding work, notably the piers and the vaulting at the base of the tower, seem to point to a date in the second half of the 14th century, and certainly no later than 1400. Its use in domestic architecture, therefore, could well be before 1450, especially at La Rocque Balan and Le Marais Farm, where the doorways are almost exactly the same as that at St. Saviour's church, even to the detail of the chamfer stops.

During the 15th century, the shape of the ogee arch tended to flatten, until by the 16th century it had arrived at an accolade, or bracket form. The doorway at La Contrée de Saint, existing by 1488, shows this transition. It is of very similar design to the bénitier at La Forge (509), a house built before 1471. The bénitier at La Maison des Pauvres (308), and the stone, either from a bénitier or a window, built into Les Mouilpieds (118), record its further flattening until soon after 1500 it reached the shape seen on the fine doorway at Le Villocq. By the end of that century it had become debased to no more than the indentation of a straight moulding, like the re-used window lintel at La Maison Guignan (92, see Illustration 71).

But by 1475, the Type 3 arch was also being used. This is a form of arch very common in both Brittany and Normandy at the end of the 15th century and beginning of the 16th century. In 1498 it was the design chosen by John Bonamy for his new house, now Les Câches Farm (112). Other particularly fine examples are at Bordeaux House, where the fireplaces and bénitier also point to a fairly early date, and at Les Hêches (225), a house already standing by 1549.

By 1475, too, the Type 4 arch may have been in use. Just as Types 1 and 2 are parallel forms, it is probable that Types 3 and 4 were more or less contemporary. It was already being used in 1365 at Mont St. Michel, where it appears in the fine house, Maison Tiphaine, built by the great Marshal of France, Bertrand du Guesclin, for his wife. In ensuring her safety on the Mount, while he was on campaigns, Du Guesclin was no doubt in a position to afford every latest luxury, and this house, three storeys high, is remarkable for its fine fireplaces, very similar to those at Bordeaux House, and for its bénitier, one of only a very few in that part of France. It is, nevertheless, amazing to find this type of arch, similar in every way to our Type 5 examples, present in a well-documented house in 1365. Mont St. Michel is not far away, and its interests in Guernsey where the abbey held one of the largest fiefs and the livings of several churches, were considerable. Further study of the sophisticated buildings there, some earlier than 1400, might yet lead us to revise our ideas of chronology for island architecture.

At present, however, the most it seems possible to say, is that the Type 5 arch at La Bouvée (25) is in a house standing by 1520, and that this house is of a form exactly similar to Le Marais (493), which was there in 1471. It is therefore probable that, like the Type 4 design, it was known in Guernsey by 1450, at a time when the earliest forms were becoming less popular and being relegated to back doorways, and that both Types 4 and 5 were common for the next 100 years, and occasionally even after 1550.

Further support for this early dating for one form of the Type 5 arch comes again from the Town Church. Here, included in the 1466 work in the south transept, are the arched doorways to the tower staircase, all of them double-chamfered. Only one other complete arch of this type exists in Guernsey, now at the Coach House Gallery, at Les Islets, but formerly at La Maison Bonamy (315), where the fireplace was also an early design. There are remains of similar arches at Saints Farm (83) and La Haye du Puits (582) and another formerly existed at Les Quertiers, illustrated in MacCulloch's *Guernsey Folklore*.

After about 1550, it seems probable that the development in arch types diverged, both directions being variations on Type 4. Either the small stones of the outer order were used in a purely decorative way, as at La Grande Maison (945) and Le Tertre (1026), where the doorways cannot be earlier than the second half of the 16th century, or else the outer order was enlarged until it became as important as the inner one. It will not have escaped the reader's notice that the most common form of arch, in Guernsey, as demonstrated by the Table at the beginning of this section, is Type 4, which is somewhat amusing, as this has become known in the Channel Islands as 'The Typical Jersey Arch.' Type 5, the so-called 'Typical Guernsey Arch', can hardly be said to be our typical arch form at all. Only if all arches of two orders are put together do they dominate the statistics. However, Type 3 arches, as we have seen, are also commonly found in Normandy and Brittany, and are not a specifically Guernsey form. It is probable that many of the Type 4 arches listed in the Fourth Schedule, that is, removed from their houses and preserved elsewhere, were originally Type 3, rather than Type 5, granted that their outer row of stones might not have been kept, since small, unshaped stones are more likely to be destroyed than large, nicely-worked ones.

But at least if Type 5 arches are not typical, they are our distinctive form, for they are not found elsewhere. Their development was in two stages. The first is the reduction of the large number of stones in the outer orders, seen at La Couture and La Maison des Pauvres, first to nine, and then to seven stones. This seems to have taken place between 1550 and 1570. There are examples at La Bellieuse Farm (94); La Forge (221). La Seigneurie (367); Le Gron (433); and St. George (586); and the collection at Pleneuf Court (631) includes three transitional ones with at least nine stones. There are several other examples of these fine arches, which clearly became very fashionable in Elizabethan times. The arch at St. George is dated 1581, significantly, for between 1575 and 1590 the second stage in this evolution of the Guernsey arch took place. The number of stones in the outer order was further reduced to five.

All other dated arches are of this type with five stones. For other details see Chapter XVII. This final stage of arch-building in houses lasted from before 1580, when Le Tourtel (129) was already built, until after 1614, which is the date on La Carrière (208). Undated examples such as Les Granges de Beauvoir Manor (834) and Le Grée (125) are so similar in other respects that they must be contemporary.

There are two particularly massive arches at La Maison de Haut (240) and Old Farm, Brock Road (925), so alike that they must be by the same mason. And there is a very peculiar arch at La Villette (124), unique in that the head of the arch is recessed in line with the side of the doorway, as though to take a door, hung on the outside, or some form of shutters; but there is no mark of any hinge. This arch also stands on a moulded plinth more reminiscent of ecclesiastical work, a feature it has in common with that at Les Queux (555). In other respects, these three arches resemble the best Type 5 examples.

The two pointed arches mentioned, from La Grande Maison de la Pomare and the unlocated Grande Maison (perhaps that at St. Pierre-du-Bois rebuilt last century), are both built of Chausey stone, as are a few of our other arches. The pointed arch was never popular in domestic architecture, even in France, and certainly not after 1500. It is difficult to say precisely how old these two arches are, but they are almost certainly—from the detail of the hood moulding and the end stops of the hood mould, which seem to be heads on the Pomare one—15th century or earlier.

After the Type 5 Guernsey arch had been perfected, by 1600, we might have thought that it would have dominated island architecture for many years. But fashion is a fickle master, and by 1625 at the latest, the straight-headed lintel supplanted it. Whether straight lintels had been used from earliest times, side by side with arched doorways, is debatable. There has been so much re-fronting of island houses that it is quite possible that the accolade lintels already mentioned at Le Villocq and St. George were, in their way, revolutionary. It certainly seems at least likely that all houses before 1550 had arched doorways, and almost all until 1620. The change in fashion, after more than 250 years, must have been dramatic, and signified a real break with much of the established order. It also, as we know, signified in particular, a greater turning to England for architectural ideas. In that country, arched doorways had already been uncommon for 100 years. At first the new doorways in Guernsey were chamfered and properly finished, as the arches had been. The Type 7 doorways thus represent a link between the medieval doorways of La Rocque Balan and the wide, flat-headed ones of the 18th century. They all seem to date between 1600 and 1650.

The arch tradition, however, was not entirely dead. Instead of having them in the house itself, they were now erected at the end of the drive, or on the roadside. Many arches were re-sited in this way when the house itself was re-fronted. We can be relatively certain that the arch outside Les Tilleuls (563) was originally inside the house and was moved to its present position by Pierre Le Roy, the diarist, in the mid-17th century. The same happened at Les Buttes Guest House (453), later on. The origin of this custom did, in fact, date from far earlier times, when houses with courtyards had a large entrance, closed with gates. The oldest example in Guernsey is at Le Tertre (1026), where there are clear remains of an unchamfered entrance arch in Cobo stone alongside a defensive turret, 15th century, if not earlier. La Haye du Puits (582) had a similar arrangement, dating from the second half of that century. Here the fine arch is surmounted by a hood mould which is turned up into a point in the centre, enclosing a head. An almost identical head at La Pouquelaye (574) must have come from a similar arch. Neither of these two wide entrances had a pedestrian arch at the side.

Nor did the segmental arch adjoining La Grange de Beauvoir Manor (834) which, like the other two examples, had some form of porter's lodge attached.

But at Le Groignet (517), the particularly fine entrance gateway, which from its design and its weathering cannot be much later than 1500, has a cart entrance without an arch, and a small, arched entrance for pedestrians alongside. A brief examination will show that the larger entrance was never arched, nor was the similar one at Normanville (883) originally, the present arch being of a different stone hardly yet weathered. However, the ruined entrance to Elizabeth College (819) may have had both a large and a small arch similar to the three remaining complete examples. These are at Les Blancs Bois, in the Castel, where the entrance arch has survived rather better than the house; Les Granges de Beauvoir Manor, and the Town Hospital, where the former entrance to L'Hyvreuse (879) was re-erected in 1742. These three splendid entrances are 17th-century, like almost all such double arches in Brittany. They date from the middle of that century and differ from all earlier arches in having a double or single roll mould. They are the last, and some would say, the most glorious, examples of the arch tradition. There must formerly have been more of them, because two other large arches at Pleneuf Court were probably each once part of a double arch, and at one time the parish churches of St. Pierre-du-Bois and St. Andrew also had double entrance arches. The bottom half of that at St. Pierre-du-Bois

ARCHES AND DOORWAYS

is still in position, with some other stones from it re-used as a mounting block; while the lower half of that from St. Andrew's church has found its way to Monaghan Villa, Route Militaire. Another double arch is noted by Sir Edgar MacCulloch as having stood at the western end of the former rectory garden in St. Peter Port, on the Mill Street side, before the building of the first market in 1771.

It is unnecessary to say much about later doorways, because where they do not date themselves (see Chapter XVII) they are sufficiently similar to those so dated to need little comment. The exceptionally wide doorways (42in.-45in.) of mid-18th-century houses are, strangely, exactly the average width of the earlier arches.

Before we leave the subject of arches, two matters must be mentioned. The first concerns the examples of Type 4 arches to be found giving access to a cellar through the gable end in some houses, for instance, at Duvaux Farm (936) and Les Hougues (956). That there is a cellar under these houses at all is odd, since they are both 16th-century buildings, in essence, of the longhouse pattern, though much altered. In each case the cellar is under the former byre end, and, one suspects, the house has been taken down at that end and rebuilt at a comparatively late date, probably around 1675-1700. Duvaux Farm was again altered in the 19th century. The cellar at Les Hougues was either built, or adapted for use, as a store for cider (*la cave*), the lead piping from the *prinseur* at the other side of the courtyard still running under the house, so that the barrels could be filled in the store itself. The arched doorway differs from all others of the type in being unchamfered, very wide (48ins.), possibly for easy handling of the barrels, and curiously shaped to follow the batter, or slope, of the gable end. They may have been fashioned especially with this in mind, but other earlier arches overcome similar problems by a recessing of the wall at the side of the doorway. These two arches bear an uncanny resemblance to the innermost arch of the entrance gateway to Castle Cornet, and whether this is merely coincidental must await further investigation. Whatever the value of this connection, it is remarkable to find them used at all, and it can only be supposed that the builders did not consider a flat lintel adequate to carry the great weight of the entire gable-end above. The Castle Cornet arch seems, from the accounts attached to the Legge Survey, to have been built *c.* 1680.

The second matter is the discrepancy between late forms of arches, of the Type 5 pattern, and other earlier forms in houses such as La Rocque Balan (1007) and La Bellieuse Farm (94). Each of these houses also has an ogee arch of early type. At La Rocque Balan it is the back doorway, and at La Bellieuse Farm, a window in the back wall of the kitchen. It is almost certain, in fact, that these later arches are insertions, the forerunners of the wholesale re-fronting carried out from 1675 onwards. We shall see in Chapter XXXV that the insertion of the Type 5 arch at Les Granges de Beauvoir Manor (834) was accompanied by an almost complete rebuilding. We have noted that the Forest church and the church of St. Saviour have this type of arch inserted into a 15th-century fabric, in both cases on the north side (perhaps as a Presbyterian riposte to the superstition which regarded the north side of a church as the Devil's side, north doorways being far less common than south or west doors before the Reformation). The walling above the new arch in the Forest church is quite different from the remainder of that wall, and the same is true of the walling above the doorway at La Bellieuse. Both required extensive rebuilding when the arch was inserted. Moreover, the arch itself has been assembled wrongly at La Bellieuse, one shoulder stone being misplaced. Is is also more than possible that at this house, as at Les Granges de Beauvoir Manor, new windows were also inserted at this time (between 1600 and 1650) as Spanish pieces-of-eight of that period were found when renovations to the window sills were carried out this century.

At La Maison des Pauvres (308) too, the surrounding walling looks considerably older than the mid-16th-century arch: either the masonry is simply built in a way more typical of 14th- and 15th-century walling, or the arch—and the bénitier inside—are insertions. We know, then, that arches were inserted in the two churches and at Les Granges de Beauvoir Manor; if it be granted that they were similarly inserted at La Rocque Balan, La Bellieuse Farm and also at Les Raies de Haut (251), the only real difficulty in the dating of these houses is removed. Les Raies de Haut possesses a fine bénitier, though it has been turned inside out so that it now faces outside the house, and the remains of a splendid fireplace which must have been exactly the same as the older ones at Les Câches (237) nearby. Les Câches and La Rocque Balan both possess delightful cusped windows that seem 15th-century; and La Rocque Balan and La Bellieuse have the ogival arches and early éviers not found in any of the other houses with Type 5 arches from 1580 onwards. Finally, Les Câches, La Bellieuse Farm and Les Raies de Haut have all had extra fireplaces inserted *c.* 1600 in the byre end of the house, indicating the creation of an early parlour. At Les Raies de Haut, the added fireplace, which has been recently uncovered, was clearly pushed into an existing wall, and is lop-sided and uneven—a great contrast with the workmanship of the older fireplace at the kitchen end.

The fact that masonry often shows little sign of patching at first sight should not prevent a much closer examination where apparent conflicts of dating suggest these Type 5 arches might have been later additions. Since the whole object was to create an impression and a fashionable façade, it follows that great care would be taken to match the stone, as at the Forest church, where it is only the size of a stone used and not the colour that shows what has happened. Even at La Forge (221), where superb 18th-century re-fronting in ashlar is obviously not original, an effort has been made to match the stone of the Type 5 arch, and it is necessary to look hard to see that, in fact, there are two distinct sorts of granite. And while one does not wish to suggest insertions every time there is a clash of stylistic evidence, it is, to say the least, worth noting that if these few intrusions, all of them Type 5 arches, are allowed, all other elements in pre-1625 houses are compatible.

Chapter XXVI

WINDOWS

WE KNOW THAT the great prosperity of Guernsey in the 14th century must have produced many large and ornate houses. Virtually nothing now remains, for continuing prosperity destroyed what a previous generation had created. In this respect, no parts of our heritage of domestic architecture have fared worse than ancient windows and window frames, for not only are the frames the victims of the high humidity and resultant rot, but the openings themselves have rarely escaped the alterations and enlargings of later times. The relics of window-openings and window-frames remaining from before 1575 are therefore very few. From what we can see, however, and by comparison with similar buildings that have escaped alteration in France, it is clear that the earliest windows were mostly small, often not much larger than the ventilation slit, or 'byre window', and placed wherever it was convenient or necessary to have them without any regard for the symmetry of the façade. Some were more or less square, as at Cobo Farmhouse (see Fig. 6, p. 39), others were much wider than they were high, as at La Mare (928—see Illustration 6), and at Les Grands Moulins (505), where the probable abandonment of this building as a dwelling towards the end of the 16th century and its continued use as a barn, has preserved one of our oldest oak window frames. It forms a sort of rustic arc, and was formerly divided into three lights by two square wooden uprights, or mullions, the mortices for which remain.

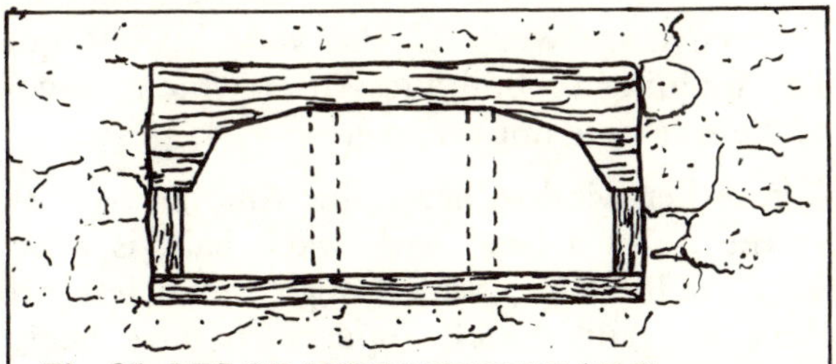

Fig. 35. LES GRANDS MOULINS (505): 15th-century window, 38" wide: 15" high. Mullions missing.

It is interesting that this simple window dating from around 1500 would have lit the loft over the kitchen. The similar opening at La Mare must have had just such a window-frame, long since replaced by other windows. A much more usual place to find the oldest window-frame in a house is at the top of the stairs, in the back wall of the short corridor leading to the main bedroom. Windows in this position frequently remained untouched when alterations enlarged those in the chief rooms of the house, or when the loft was converted into bedrooms. Our finest surviving 15th-century window-frames are in these upstairs passages. They are at Les

Câches (237) and La Rocque Balan (1007), and are unequalled in their delicacy by any later work. Both are oak, that at La Rocque Balan (Fig. 36) having an ogival head, and that at Les Câches, cusped and pointed, being enclosed in an ogival frame (see Illustration 72). The chamfering of this window-head, scarcely more than a quarter of an inch across, is beautifully done. Both windows are of very similar dimension, 15in. wide and 24in. high.

Very different, but of a similar quality is the impressive window now built into Carriaux Cottage, Candie Road, St. Andrew's. (See Illustration 61). It came originally from a house near Les Adams, where it was drawn *in situ* by F. C. Lukis in 1845. The four lights are divided by a stone mullion and transom, and the top two lights are cusped. The stone used appears to be Chausey granite and the entire composition suggests that it was intended for a room of some refinement.

Fig. 36. LA ROCQUE BALAN (1007): Landing window

These are the only early windows to have survived intact. Remains of others, however, show that they were not unusual in their decorative detail. One of the earliest, now over the front door of the cottage at La Haye du Puits, is a lintel, probably of the 14th century, much resembling the carvings at Grosnez Castle in Jersey, and similar to a mutilated window-head on the south nave wall in the Forest church. Enclosed within a semi-circular frame is the top half of a man holding up his hands as though to ward off evil spirits (see Page 135).

At the back of Les Câches, a superb three-cusped window-head of very light granite has been built into the back kitchen in Victorian times (see Illustration 66), and nearby, are the remains of a very fine pillar-type fireplace. Again, both fragments are work of the very highest quality, and date from around 1400. The building or buildings from which they were rescued must once have been of considerable importance.

Another window-head, this time an ogee shape with a roll-moulding enclosing at the point a head with wavy hair, is now underneath a window sill at Casa Seda (896). This, too, though much less provincial in its appearance than the Haye du Puits lintel, appears to have been made about 1400, and is a very handsome piece of work. Dating of these fragments is difficult and not of tremendous importance, since they are dissociated from their original houses. However, it is noteworthy that on stone and brass funeral effigies it was the convention to show men with long, wavy hair throughout the 14th century and up to about 1450, after which time, especially on monumental brasses, the hair is almost always shown as straight. The head on this lintel at Casa Seda is by this criterion the earliest such piece of figure sculpture, from a presumed domestic source, in the island.

A somewhat later window lintel of great magnificence, is now in the garden at St. George (586). It was formerly the top of a mullioned window of 16th-century date, with a double accolade design extended to enclose a coat-of-arms now too worn to distinguish clearly. This was dug up at St. George, and though it may have been part of the chapel, it is more likely to have come from the house demolished in 1824, being a design much more frequently encountered in Renaissance manor houses in Normandy and Brittany. It is the only example in Guernsey (see Illustration 70).

Because the window embrasures of our houses are rarely of dressed stone, some have supposed that the houses themselves were of less importance than those in Jersey, where 'four-piece windows' are common. Although this may be so, it is at least possible that the fashion for this sort of window surround was short-lived in Guernsey. It is also possible that the mania for re-fronting in the 18th and 19th centuries has removed many fine examples of chamfered window-surrounds. Two survive at Le Tertre (1026), in the 16th-century bedroom wing, and there are other small windows with straight chamfered surrounds in many tourelles, for instance at Bordeaux House (984) and formerly at Ville-au-Roi Manor, now demolished. Very unusual windows at the back of Les Quertiers (919) are also chamfered, but are extremely large, and show, with the sumptuous fireplace and early bedroom wing that this was a most important house. Quite how these windows at Les Quertiers were arranged is no longer clear; there is now no sign of mullions or transoms, though they must surely have existed.

The remaining chamfered window surrounds are of a slightly different design, and occur in conjunction with the dated and initialled Type 5 arches. Here, for the first time, the chamfers are slightly hollow, not straight, and they are stopped at the sides. One of the finest unaltered sets of such windows is at Le Tourtel (129) and shows admirably that in the 1570s windows were quite large; but still wider than they were tall. This façade is very similar to that at La Carrière (208) and Les Granges de Beauvoir Manor (834). An alternative, and contemporary way of giving prominence to the windows, either of a complete façade, as at Le Chêne Cottage (154) and formerly at La Pompe (117) and Le Repos au Coin (56) as illustrated by Lukis; or to individual rooms, as at Saints Farm (83), La Forge (509) and Les Tilleuls (563), was to decorate the sill of the window, but not the sides. Some of these sills are relatively plain, and comparable to the sill of a bénitier, but some of the larger windows have cable moulds, sometimes, as at La Pompe, Le Manoir (211) and in the garden at Les Granges de Beauvoir, within a hollow mould, sometimes enclosed in a bolder frame, producing a box-like effect as drawn by Lukis at Le Repos au Coin.

Elsewhere, the sills project but are not ornamented. Indeed, at Le Chêne Cottage, a rough sort of cable mould has been carved without much attempt to work the stone to a smooth finish. In many houses, the bedroom window sill projects, but is only a rough stone. Thus the principal of emphasising the window through the treatment of the sill has been recognised, yet there is no true appreciation of the aesthetic effect. The house at Le Grée (125), for instance, had a fine arch and fireplaces, and could obviously have afforded a window sill to match them. But this was not done. Similarly, next door at La Villette (124), the unique arch already referred to is combined with projecting but rough window sills. Yet another way of showing the importance of the fine new window is employed at Old Farm, Brock Road (925). Here, unusually, huge dripstones project over the windows, but the sides and sills are quite plain.

An examination of Le Grée and Saints Farm will clearly show how the wide, shallow windows have been altered. La Vieille Maison, at La Ville Amphrey (41) also shows where the original windows had surrounds of large, worked stones. Always, it seems, at least one upstairs window in the façade was exceptionally wide, while the remainder might be almost square. These window sizes have been kept at De Bertrands (60) and La Vieille Sous L'Eglise (475), a slightly later house, and they remained the standard size for windows throughout the 17th and early 18th centuries. The window-frame of six lights at La Maison d'Aval (241) is perhaps the earliest example showing how these windows were glazed. They would have been either of four or six lights, divided by a heavy wooden transom and one or two mullions. Between the mullions, vertical iron bars protected the diamond-paned leaded lights, few of which now remain. They can be seen at Le Chêne Cottage, La Forge (221) and Les Quertiers (676), and remained until 1956 at Les Prevosts (463).

The dressed stone jambs of the windows at La Vieille Maison, at La Ville Amphrey and at Saint's Farm had a parallel in some other houses, where there are vertical stones at each side of the windows, somewhat reminiscent of the long-and-short quoins in Anglo-Saxon architecture. They are undoubtedly imitations of the four-part, chamfered windows of the late 16th century. These, however, are all from the 17th century, probably between 1600 and 1660. They occur, for instance, at Le Grée; in the 17th-century renovations and barns at Le Marais (493); and at La Maison d'Aval (975).

Perhaps a final harking-back to the decorated windows and the arched door is to be seen as late as the early 18th century in a few grey lintels of Perelle stone, quarried with wedges and feathers. The grooves of the wedges are used as a decoration along the bottom edge of the window, producing a very distinctive dot-and-dash effect. Sometimes, too, a slightly curved piece of stone will be chosen to serve as a lintel, but will be left undressed. Le Chêne Farm (157), built in 1734, has an example of the former above the window in the back wall of the kitchen, while there is one of the latter over the early 18th-century barn door at La Forge (509).

Fig. 37. LE CHENE FARM (157): Window lintel with simple ornament using wedge marks from quarrying as basis for designs. 1734

Whereas the simpler 15th-century longhouses had unglazed windows, like the upstairs passage window at the back of Les Blicqs (610) where a single strut of oak is placed diagonally in the simple window frame—just like a 'byre window'—by the time that same house was re-fronted in 1720, glass was in common use. The four-light and six-light windows we have been describing would not originally have had any hinged sashes, and maybe no means of opening at all. But usually, the lower lights would have been arranged so that at least one slid sideways. Later on, and certainly by the end of the 17th century, this arrangement was superseded by the hinging of the lower lights, as at Maison d'Aval (241). The 1720 re-fronting at Les Blicqs provided a fine set of square windows, surrounded by grey lintels, quoins and sills, and probably fitted with casement sashes, two opening windows, each with eight small panes divided by glazing bars.

Certainly this pattern was in use by the middle of the century, by which time the guillotine sash had also been introduced into the island, necessitating the lengthwise enlargement of many existing window-openings. At first, both casement and guillotine sashes had very wide glazing bars, often dividing the window into as many as 20 small panes, as at Les Rouvets de Haut (962). Perhaps the chief reason for this was the expense of large panes of glass, for there was almost certainly no glass manufactured in Guernsey until the end of the 18th century. Like bricks, until $c.$ 1780 it had to be imported from Southampton. But the closely-spaced glazing bars also imitated the leaded lights, the commonest form of window-glazing used at the time.

Although these early guillotine sashes have survived at La Grande Maison (945), they do not seem to have been much used outside St. Peter Port. It may be that most of them have had to be replaced, or have been superseded by other fashions in the last 200 years. It is also probable, however, that by the time guillotine sashes became popular in the country parishes, these heavy glazing bars were already being replaced by the elegant, narrow bars used, for instance, at Brockhurst (821) or Choisi (824); in The Grange. Sausmarez Manor (36) must have been the earliest and best set of guillotine sashes in the island. No. 26 Cornet Street (726) retains a few early ones and they have occasionally survived in the staircase dormers of other Town properties. Probably the best example of this sort of fenestration in St. Peter Port is at Moore's Hotel (795); but the Venetian windows and other details of the fashionable Town houses and villas of the gentry at the end of the 18th century need not concern us here. Throughout the second half of that century, in the countryside, the casement sash, with its eight-paned windows opening on L-shaped hinges, was by far the commonest form, still used, as we have noted before, in the back of Les Bordages in 1790, even though the guillotine sash dominated the front.

Chapter XXVII

FIREPLACES

TO DEVELOP A STYLISTIC SEQUENCE for the corbels of carved fireplaces has been one of the subordinate aims of the present survey. As with the arches, our knowledge of Guernsey architecture would be greatly advanced if we could establish such a sequence and also discover more about the making of these fine expressions of taste and craft. If the stone were not local, was a fireplace, like a cider trough in the 18th century, ordered from Normandy, fashioned over there, and fitted in Guernsey? Or was the stone shipped here and shaped on the site? Many questions have yet to be answered.

John Bonamy's notebook ought to help us. At his new house—Les Câches Farm (112)—he decided to have a fireplace of red granite from Cobo, and in 1499 owed Thomas Cluett for providing one. But we do not know if Thomas Cluett merely shipped suitable stone, or was also a mason, expected to carve the 'mantell de cimeyne' *in situ*. If so, he never finished the work; not, we hope, that John Bonamy had not paid his debts when he left for Rome the following year. But whatever happened, the fireplace at Les Câches Farm is the only 15th- or 16th-century fireplace in Guernsey—and we might also say in Normandy and Brittany, too—to be left unfinished. Its rough stone looks forward 150 years to the 17th century, when no fireplaces were carved, but the size of the massive rocks fitted into the gable as great base stones, corbels and shoulders demonstrate that this was intended as a fireplace of the conventional sort. Yet for some reason, it was never completed. Thus, although the notebook does not tell us much, the fireplace itself seems to tell us quite unmistakeably that at any rate when local stone was used, the surface was dressed on the site, after the raw material had been built into the wall.

Other details elsewhere bear this out. At La Cocquerie (408), for instance, the recent raising of the ceiling levels downstairs shows us that the shoulders of the kitchen fireplace had not been dressed at the top because that part was never intended to be seen. If the fireplace had been prepared off the site and then assembled where it was to stand, it is extremely unlikely that the masons would have known the exact ceiling height. The only reason for leaving a mere two inches of shoulder stone unworked must be that the floor of the loft above was already in position when the stonemason was called in to carve the fireplace. Again, when fireplaces are removed to other sites we find the same thing: the stone is only dressed where it showed. The corbels and shoulder stones, often extending the whole thickness of the gable wall, are only shaped at the front. A recent observation at Le Marais (493) might seem to disprove this. When the upstairs fireplace was removed, the pillars which had been fashioned to stand out from the wall were actually fitted in flush with it. However, as will be seen later, a veritable campaign of destruction seems to have been levelled against this particular sort of fireplace, only about four of which seem to have remained *in situ*. The bedroom fireplace at Le Marais might easily, therefore, have been brought from elsewhere and re-used.

What, then, were the characteristics of these fireplaces, which occur from the earliest houses until about 1625? In common with the later arches, the bottom stone at each side of the hearth usually took the form of a great base, often more than two feet high and as much wide and deep. Above this was usually a considerably smaller stone, underneath the two projecting horizontal ones, the corbel and the shoulder. The technique was probably to choose the great base stones, the corbels and the shoulders, none of which would necessarily have been of matching size, and then to insert a small stone between base and corbel so as to adjust the corbel to approximately the right level. The mason would then have been responsible for the final shaping, making the corbel and shoulder stones appear to be identical to their fellows at the other side. However, in some of the most magnificent fireplaces, the base stone and that above it are often of about the same size, probably indicating that the stone was carefully chosen at the quarry, or, in the case of French or Jersey stone, that it was sent across in the right sizes. Sometimes, as at 5 Berthelot Street (808), there were as many as three stones below the corbel.

These stones at the side (*jambs*) were always chamfered, the width of the chamfer varying between two and six inches, and the bottom chamfer stop, especially on the later examples, often ornamented with a cross, a fleur-de-lys, or some other design. The top chamfer stop was treated as the springing of the corbel above, and was often, as in the two examples quoted above, the bottom two of a series of four complicated convolutions.

In the carving of the corbels, the masons used much ingenuity, and we must examine them in greater detail later. Whatever the shape, the edges of the corbel were often themselves chamfered—the chamfer not exceeding one inch across— and this was then carried onto the shoulder stones, which were supported on the corbels and projected beyond them. The function of the huge shoulder stones, often at least six feet in length and projecting two feet into the room, was to support, in their turn, the lintel which spanned the hearth. Until *c.* 1600, the lintel was always stone, fitted into the shoulders with a dog-legged notch. Occasionally, as at Le Gron (433) and in the case of the two displaced lintels now outdoors at Le Varclin (19) and Les Fontaines (357), the lintel was double-notched in this way. Later on, in some fireplaces built between 1550 and 1625, instead of these dog-legged notches, the lintels were made with each end tapered

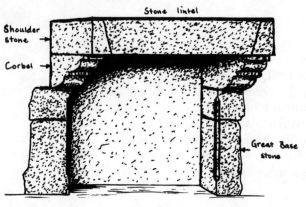

BEDROOM FIREPLACE AT LES VIEILLES SALINES (950)

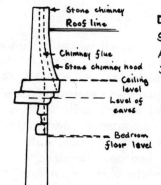

DIAGRAM TO SH[OW] SHOULDER STONE AND CORBEL PR[O]JECTING BEYON[D] GABLE AT LA MAISON DE HAU[T] (418). Usually only shoulder stone proj[ects] in this way.

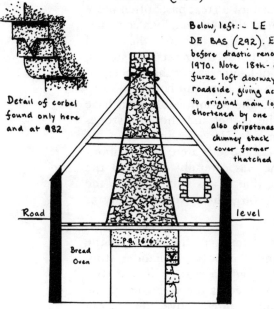

Detail of corbel found only here and at 982.

Below, left:- LE CATILLON DE BAS (292). East gable before drastic renovation c. 1970. Note 18th-century furze loft doorway on roadside, giving access to original main loft, shortened by one bay: also dripstones on chimney stack to cover former thatched roof.

Below:- DOUBLE-NOTCHED LINTEL LYING OUTSIDE LES FONTAINES (357)

Section at side of fireplace to show how lintel tapers, top to bottom.

FLEUR DU JARDIN HOTEL (508) Corbel of downstairs fireplace.

Below:- LA FORGE (924), showing relieving arch and 'secondary' shoulder stones at angle of chimney hood. Doorway from kitchen to adjoining room, later adapted as a forge. Top of stack rebuilt in brick.

LES SAGES VILLA (272): detail of downstairs fireplace.

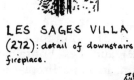

FIREPLACES AT LA MAISON D'AVAL (241) AND CASTLE CORNET: Pillar Type A with Type 3 corbel.

LA MAISON D'AVAL (241): Chamfer stop on 16th-century back kitchen fireplace.

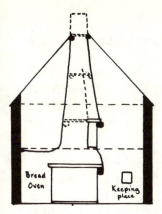

LES PAYSANS FARM (323). North-east gable before renovation, 1978-9, showing kitchen and bedroom fireplaces using same wattle-and-daub chimney hood.

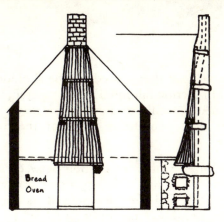

LE PRÉ DES ROMAINS (944). The north-west gable with section through to show construction of wattle-and-daub hoods with hurdling attached to bridging beams supported on subsidiary shoulder stones.

Below:- **ST. CLAIR FARM (933)** Broken lintel lying outside, with snake-like decoration (raised) & faint inscription.

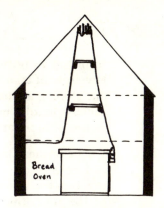

LES BLICQS (610). A 15th-16th century kitchen fireplace altered c.1720 by the insertion of a bread oven, and the replacement of a stone hood by one of wattle and daub. Note hurdling below roofline of former circular chimney stack.

Fig. 38. FIREPLACES AND CHIMNEYS, 1400-1750 (drawings not to scale)

LATE 17th-CENTURY CORBELS. Left: RUE DE L'EGLISE (89); right: LES GRANDS MOULINS ROAD (497).

FIREPLACE TO BE RE-ERECTED AT LE CLOS DE BAS (264). Formerly at Les Caches (111).

Section through jamb

LA CHAUMIÈRE (594): corbel of kitchen fireplace.

LA POUQUELAYE (574): Lintel lying outside, with one shield apparently blank.

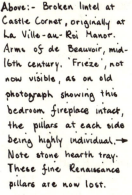

Above:- Broken lintel at Castle Cornet, originally at La Ville-au-Roi Manor. Arms of de Beauvoir, mid-16th century. 'Frieze', not now visible, as on old photograph showing this bedroom fireplace intact, the pillars at each side being highly individual. → Note stone hearth tray. These fine Renaissance pillars are now lost.

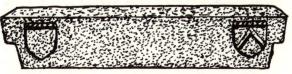

from top to bottom, so that they rested on the shoulders in the same way as the keystone of an arch. In section, all lintels were tapered, being vertical at the front, but sloping at the back to facilitate the flow of air up the chimney. A lintel was usually hardly more than two inches thick at the bottom, widening to nine inches or more at the top.

Above these huge lintels which were often between seven and eight feet long, and resting on them, a tapering chimney hood was constructed in stone, and was bonded into the gable end for the whole of its height. As it neared the ridge of the roof, this chimney hood not only narrowed to about two feet in width, but also ran into the thickness of the wall, so that the granite chimney stack stood on the summit of the gable end.

These massive fireplaces and stone chimneys were descended from the very similar ones first introduced into castles and abbeys during the 11th century. Already, by the 12th century, they were being built into the homes of wealthy merchants, both in France and in England. Some, for instance, still remain in Southampton, with which port so much of our trade was connected. It is thus very probable that the better houses in St. Peter Port were also supplied with this sort of fireplace well before 1400, and that some of our examples in the other parishes may yet turn out to be 14th-century. But until more work has been done on comparison of types, it is safer to assume that those remaining today are from the 15th century onwards, until about 1650, by which time fireplaces were rather differently designed.

The tendency during those 350 years and from then onwards was for the construction and the carving to become simpler. In the average farmhouse it was clearly a matter of great expense to build such a heavy structure, which, moreover, custom demanded should be lavishly decorated. Soon after 1600, it became the fashion to build a much lighter chimney-hood, made of a hurdling of sticks covered with clay plaster. Possibly this idea was imported from those area of Brittany around Rennes where the cob houses (*pisé*), with walls of puddled clay, could not support a stone hood. The advantage of the new form of construction was quickly realised in Guernsey, where it was now no longer necessary to have a stone lintel, since there was no stone hood to hold up. At first a relieving arch of small stones, sometimes with a very narrow, curved piece of wood beneath to form a horizontal line, was used instead of a lintel, to support the wattle-and-daub hood. One survives at King's Mills' Farm (506—see Illustration 48), but a somewhat similar arrangement upstairs at Maison de Haut, Brock Road (927) is probably an older stone hood that formerly served the kitchen below, broken into just under a relieving arch. Such relieving arches, built at intervals of about five feet up the whole height of the stone chimney hood—as, for instance, above the bedroom fireplace of Bordeaux House (984)—had been considered necessary in order to distribute some of the great weight of the hood upon subsidiary shoulder stones inserted right through the gable end in the same way as were the main shoulders of the fireplace below. With the advent of wattle-and-daub hoods, these subsidiary shoulder stones were retained, and bridged across, though not by a relieving arch, but by small beams on to which the vertical sticks of the hurdling were fixed. The wattle-and-daub hood was then carried up in one of two ways. Either the hood was run into the thickness of the gable-end, as before, to terminate in a stone stack, or the hurdling was continued up through the thatch and finished off in the form of a circular, plastered chimney. One of these survives at La Ronde Cheminée (929), and it is interesting that in an old photograph of a house at Le Mont Saint, now demolished, showing a similar cob chimney stack, it is in the centre of the house, and clearly a later insertion between two older stone stacks (see Illustration 76). Indeed, with the exception of La Houguette (528—see p. 51), the rare occurrence of a central chimney stack in a Guernsey house always marks the addition of a later fireplace, usually on a cross-passage wall in order to heat the parlour, newly-converted from a byre. An examination of the chimney-hoods at Les Fontaines (544), for instance, will confirm this, and fireplace types at Les Câches (237) and elsewhere lead to the same conclusion.

No further developments in the construction of chimneys took place in Guernsey until the use of imported brick from England enabled builders to copy the sort of chimney flue already widespread in that country, and different only in dimensions from the modern chimney breast. Now for the first time, a fine surround of classical designs was possible, but only, of course, for rooms other than the kitchen. Until the coming of the Victorian cooking range, food had still to be prepared over an open hearth. The new fireplaces are therefore first found in parlours and bedrooms, except in Town, where by 1750 all the main rooms in new houses had elegant fire surrounds. No doubt the accelerated building of back kitchens in the late 18th and 19th centuries had much to do with the wish to banish the cooking from the main house, so that the chief rooms could all be fitted with those fashionable grates.

In many farmhouses, however, and in all back kitchens, the old pattern persisted well into the 19th century: necessarily, since, as we have just seen, there was no method until then of cooking food other than on an open hearth. And how did you construct an open hearth except in the traditional way? The new house at Les Poidevins still had its back kitchen equipped with such an open fireplace, the lintel supported on two stone corbels, early in the 19th century. Perhaps the latest phase of open fireplace and bread oven is to be seen in the brick constructions at Les Adams (328) and Les Grands Moulins (520), where the stone corbel is dispensed with completely, and the brick hood is supported by a brick wall built out at right-angles on one side of the hearth. Another late development, but in this case perhaps just within the proper range of this book, is the use of wooden shoulders, both instead of stone ones above the hearth, and also at intervals above, carrying part of the weight of the hood as had the stone shoulders previously. The practice was common in Brittany, though there, also, it is probably an innovation of the late 18th century. Exposure of the ends of these shoulder beams to the elements ensured that they did not rot behind damp plaster, and although the practice might seem a fire hazard to those who would substitute any piece of wood in a house for a steel girder, it is clear that it has not been so, any more than the dozens of wattle-and-daub chimney hoods that still remain. A fire of average size on an open hearth would have been at least four feet away from a wooden shoulder of this sort, and proper maintenance of the chimney would have rendered them no more likely to catch fire than many an electrical gadget today. A little cottage at Les Niaux (641), Flambie Cottage (692) and quite a number of valet's quarters all have these wooden shoulders.

After this rather lengthy excursion into the chief characteristics of later styles, it is now necessary to examine the earlier, and finer, fireplaces, in more detail. As we have seen, the enthusiasm for these superb, carved fireplaces, when they first brought the amenities of a castle within the reach of a prosperous merchant or farmer, and ultimately of everyone, began to wane as they became more common. Just as today the popular runabout car has become more stereotyped than the first vehicles, when they were both a novelty and a luxury, so the ornamentation of fireplaces became simpler, the more they were taken for granted and the more people turned to other things to show they were abreast of the times. That is not to say that fine fireplaces were not built throughout the period, any more than to insinuate that fine cars are not manufactured today; but they became the exception. It is necessary to generalise, in order to see the wood for the trees.

Fireplaces built between *c.* 1400 and *c.* 1625 can first of all be divided into two general types: the one already described, where the corbel and shoulder-stones rest on two or three stones, chamfered, and flush with the wall: and a pillar type, where the lower stones are replaced by one, or at the most two, vertical stones forming an attached pillar standing proud of the gable wall at each side of the hearth.

These two groups can be further sub-divided, according to the shaping of the corbel, which is the chief variable part of the design.

Of the sort with chamfered sides, we can distinguish corbels:

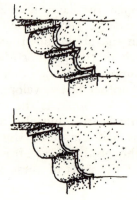

1. With a double convex curve passing through more than 90deg. (*c.* 1400–1475 and 1575–1625);

2. With double convex curve only turning 90deg. (*c.* 1400–1625);

3. Which are double curved, the upper part convex and the lower part concave (c. 1400-1580); 4. With half of an ogee curve (c. 1575-1625); and 5. With a single convex curve (c. 1575-1625). These various types are shown in the Schedules attached and are numbered as above.

The pillared fireplaces divide into: **A.** Those where the pillar or attached shaft is surmounted by a corbel above, usually of Type 3 (c. 1400-1500); **B.** Those where the chamfering either side of the attached pillar is carried up onto the corbel and is stopped just below the shoulder stone (c. 1400-1625); and **C.** Where the pillar takes the form of a flattened, moulded column and finishes below a corbel, usually of the Type 2 design listed above (c. 1550-1625).

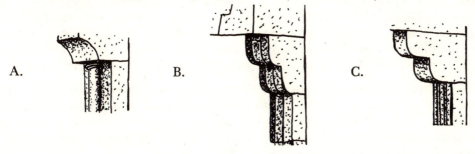

There is some interesting evidence both in Guernsey and from outside the island which suggests that pillar types A and B are the earliest forms. At the Forest church, in the angle where the south aisle of the nave meets the crossing of the tower, a shelf, high up on the wall, is exactly the shape of a corbel from a pillar-type B fireplace. At St. Andrew's church, an attached pillar on the south wall of the chancel supports a corbel, from which springs the internal rib of the vaulted roof. Here it is the shaft which closely resembles a pillar-type A fireplace. In fact, it is highly probable that in these churches the component parts of disused fireplaces have been re-used, and, if so, they must certainly be 14th century as they are in each case integral with the fabric of the church, which itself is not later than 1400.

Other evidence comes from La Maison Tiphaine at Mont St. Michel, already referred to on p. 173 in connection with types of arches. This house, built in 1365, has three main floors where a single room occupies each floor, all three rooms being supplied with a fireplace; on the first floor a Type 3; and on the other two floors a pillar-type A, surmounted by a Type 3 corbel. Two of the fireplaces are provided with a shelf, high up at one side, such as are common in the earliest castle fireplaces.

In the bedroom of La Maison Tiphaine is a window embrasure, whose window splay accommodates a little seat on either side of the window. The only house in Guernsey where such a charming window-seat has survived is the Douit Farm Flats (499) and there, in the bedroom, is also a Type 2 fireplace with a nicely-shaped shelf. Unfortunately, this fireplace is now divided between two rooms, and the entire house had already fallen on evil times before it became flats. Indeed, it seems as though it was turned into a barn early in the 16th century, when the larger house next door was built. It can hardly be coincidence that there is now no sign of a downstairs fireplace here, whereas at Le Douit Farm (498), next door, there is a splendid pillar-type A fireplace, clearly re-used, and, like the re-used fireplace in the parlour at Les Raies de Haut (251), rather badly reassembled. If it did indeed come from next door, as seems highly probable, we have here a house that had many of the ingredients of La Maison Tiphaine—a window-seat, a fireplace with shelf, and a pillar-type A fireplace.

Another feature of the fireplaces at the Mont St. Michel house are the relieving arches built in the gables at the back of the hearths, at the level of the corbel stones. The kitchen also contains a bénitier with a simple, pointed head. At Bordeaux House (984—see Chapter XLI) we have a house with a bénitier of identical shape; a house, moreover, where there are relieving arches at every conceivable point; and where there are two fireplaces with shelves, one of them a pillar-type A with Type 2 corbel, the other, a Type 2 with chamfered sides.

A final comparison from Guernsey must suffice. Le Marais (493) is known to have been standing in 1471. Its fireplaces are almost exact facsimiles of the fireplaces at La Maison Tiphaine, but slightly smaller. The kitchen fireplace has a chamfered side with a Type 3 corbel and shelf; the bedroom fireplace (now removed) was a pillar-type A with Type 3 corbel.

Unfortunately, almost all pillar-type A fireplaces have come to grief, one way and another. At La Bigoterie (812) one is stranded in mid-air, half-way up a gable-end; at Croutes House (827) a similar one has suffered the additional indignity of forming a window frame above a Victorian back kitchen. We have only two examples of pillar-type B, where the chamfer is carried up around the corbel and only stopped underneath the shoulder stone. It was a form very popular in Jersey, and possibly here, too; but if so, virtually all examples of it have gone, one having also been placed safely out of harm's way near the skyline of Les Vardes Farm Hotel (955), and the sole survivor being at Les Granges de Beauvoir Manor (834—see Chapter XXXV).

It is unfortunate that we do not know more about two other outstandingly fine fireplaces, one now inside Pleneuf Court (631) and the other waiting to be reassembled at the Married Quarters (1036) at Castle Cornet. The first was drawn by F. C. Lukis in 1850 at 'La Grande Maison', probably that at St. Pierre-du-Bois, which was totally rebuilt at the end of the last century. If that is so, and the pointed arch in Prince Albert's Road, also drawn by Lukis at a Grande Maison is from the same house, again a very early date is indicated. This batch of Lukis's drawings all seem to have been illustrating houses in St. Pierre-du-Bois, so the inference is probably justified.

The other fireplace also originated from St. Pierre-du-Bois and belonged to a house being demolished in 1870. While he was enjoying a carriage ride one afternoon, General de Sausmarez, of Sausmarez Manor, saw it lying dismembered by the roadside, ready to be broken up for road-metalling. He bought it for 10s. and installed it in part of the old building at the Manor, where it remained until 1979. The old Priest's House, where it originally stood, was almost opposite La Tourelle (238). This splendid fireplace will dominate one part of the museum to be formed at the Married Quarters, just as the other one dominates a room at Pleneuf Court. Both are pillar-type A, with a Type 3 corbel above. They are almost eight feet wide, five feet from the floor level to the underside of the lintels, which are 16in. high, and they stand out from the wall 1ft. 10in. at lintel level (see Illustration 51).

The other fine fireplace of this type is, yet again, in St. Pierre-du-Bois, upstairs at La Maison d'Aval (241). Although partly obscured, it would have been of exactly the same dimensions as the last two mentioned: but its chief interest arises from the fact that it is immediately above a Type 1 fireplace in the kitchen below, and thus shares the same chimney, the flues running side by side. Although this sort of construction is occasionally seen in 18th-century wattle-and-daub fireplaces, for instance at Les Paysans Farm (323), now removed, and was also found in 13th-century castles in Brittany, it is unique in a domestic building of early date in Guernsey. It is clear that this house, owned by the Le Messurier family, must have been of considerable importance, at least from the early 15th century onwards.

A variant form of the pillar-type A fireplaces so far described is the one where the pillar is treated as an engaged shaft. The upstairs fireplace in the Ville-au-Roi-Manor House was of this sort, with the shaft rings, or anulets above the plinth exactly as though copied from the foot of an architectural canopy or pillar. They resemble the detail at the sides of the arches at La Villette (124) and Les Queux (555), or the pillars of the 1466 work at the Town Church. Sir Cyril Fox was of the opinion that the sides of this fireplace were 15th-century, but that the upper part, with astonishing corbels resembling formalised acanthus leaves, and a decorated lintel, with the De Beauvoir arms on the shield, was much later, towards 1600. It is disgraceful that only the lintel of this fireplace remains, lying broken at Castle Cornet.

The Type 3 corbels of a similar fireplace are embedded in the outside gable wall of Les Petites Mielles (568), and another fine, but damaged, fireplace has recently been nicely restored at Huriaux Place (403). Here, none of the stones of the engaged shaft have survived on the left, but on the right-hand side two remain, and are of interest because the masonry is also an integral part of a niche, or keeping-place, to the right of the fireplace. The accolade is taken to be part of the revetting which extends all around the niche for a former door. If this were so, the sides of the accolade would have to be—as they are—flat, rather than an ogee shape, and one could think of the whole design as closer to 1450. The head in low relief on the right-hand corbel is similar to those on the Type 3 chamfered fireplace at Les Sages Villa (272); here the head is larger and the shoulders are shown as well. The matching figure on the left-hand corbel is now too worn to distinguish at all. The shoulder stones are rounded at the outside angles with a fine decoration like a chamfer-stop at the very top, exactly the same as that at Les Quertiers (919) and at many other houses, for instance, La Maison Guignan, on both fireplaces (92). Since the one at Les Quertiers, although really a chamfered Type 2 fireplace, also contrives to include an attached shaft rather like that at the Ville-au-Roi, as well as ogee shapes which Sir Cyril Fox believed to be c. 1475, we might think of the pillar-type one at Huriaux Place as 15th-century, and probably towards the end of this sequence of early fireplaces. Pillar-type A fireplaces seem then to fade out at around 1500.

The juxtaposition of the two fireplaces at Maison d'Aval serves to lead us on to the Type 1 chamfered examples. As can be seen from page 191, these fall into two groups, the early ones seeming to date from c. 1400-1475, and the others from 1580 to 1620. The example at La Maison d'Aval is clearly contemporary with the pillar-type A above, and these 15th-century Type 1 fireplaces differ from later ones in the boldness of their design, the curves of the corbels displaying a tremendous confidence, and running down in unbroken swirls to combine with a double chamfer-stop below, so that there are, altogether, four curves, two on the corbel and two on the chamfer-stop. The chamfer is widened to six inches or more in order to accommodate the lower two curves, and the whole is an immensely impressive design, always carried out in workmanship of the highest quality. There is a perfect specimen at Les Granges de Beauvoir Manor (834) and both fireplaces at Les Câches (237) as well as that at Les Raies de Haut (251) were once of this type. The downstairs one at Les Câches still retains its shelf. A feature of these fireplaces is the particular care taken with the finishing off of the jambs. Those at Les Granges de Beauvoir Manor are carved with a vertical framing that almost forms a pillar, and then continue to the side of a former gable-window. In fact, these Type 1 fireplaces always seem to have had some aperture attached. At Les Câches it was a keeping-place downstairs and a gable-window upstairs: at Les Raies de Haut it was the doorway to the buttery on the left—as indeed it must have been at Les Câches, too. Another similar example with only three curves is at Le Haut Chemin (311), though here a former bread oven was responsible for removing one side (see Illustration 49).

These Type 1 fireplaces all seem to be in houses with other early features, and they are similar but not quite identical to the fireplace in the Royal Court House in Gorey, which is of Caen stone, and traditionally held to be 14th-century. Some of our examples may very well be of Mont Mado granite, since there are no inclusions in them such as are usually present in local stone from Cobo: but this is not proved.

FIREPLACES

Although it occurs at Les Grands Courtils (388) around 1550, a renewed preference for the Type 1 corbel shape seems to have accompanied the building of the later 'Guernsey' arches between 1580 and 1625. But the general effect is of a more contorted design, with the horizontal lines emphasised at the expense of the curves. Nor is there any continuation of the curves into the chamfer-stop, which is a completely separate detail. Two of these later Type 1 corbels also have a curious decoration on the face of the corbel, immediately underneath the shoulder stone, resembling a pair of owl's eyes. They are perhaps more likely to be a reference to the capitals of Ionic columns, and thus evidence of Renaissance influence. The fireplace at La Seigneurie (367) is still in position, though the right-hand side has been rebuilt into a bread oven, and in the wall of an outbuilding there is another piece of corbel with 'owl's eyes', probably from a matching upstairs fireplace of which no other trace remains (see Chapter XL). The other example is behind Le Vauquiédor Manor and here, the entire fireplace, complete with stone lintel, is rebuilt over a garden gate. Its origin is unknown.

The commonest corbel shape of all is the Type 2 corbel. Although it is very similar to Type 1 and probably derived from it, the curves are not undercut, and only turn through 90deg. It is a type used at Bordeaux House, associated with a shelf, but the height of its popularity was during the 16th century, when it was the almost universal type. By far the best example of it, however, is 15th century, at Les Quertiers. This, the most magnificent fireplace in Guernsey, combines a boldness of line with a luxuriance of decoration unmatched elsewhere. The Type 2 corbels are carried into the chamfer stop in the way we have noted at Le Haut Chemin, but which is not typical of this corbel shape, and at the bottom of the chamfer the stopping is also elaborate, on the left perhaps being three bleeding hearts. At the front surface on each side of the chamfers, a slender engaged shaft with shaft-rings rises to the level of the top chamfer stop, to which it is joined by an elongation of the ogee decoration that adorns each of the corbel and chamfer curves. On the outside of the fireplace, the continuation of this feature now produces an effect rather like a bishop's crozier, though originally it was returned down the outside edge. The uppermost curve of the corbel on each side displays a shield bearing the Caretier arms. This curve is separated by a cable-mould from the one below it.

The detailing is slightly different on each side of the fireplace, a feature associated with the Gothic spirit and despised by succeeding generations reared on Renaissance symmetry. The shoulders and lintel have a narrow chamfer around their bottom edge, and the shoulders are rounded with a delicate chamfer-stop returning them to a square angle where they meet the cornice. The lintel is undecorated with any motif, and the plainness of the upper part balances the ornamentaion below to provide a very satisfying composition.

Another Type 2 fireplace with ogee decoration on its corbels is at La Fontaine (422). The ogee is exactly the same shape as Les Quertiers and probably also from around 1475. There are many examples of Type 2 corbels with cable-mould

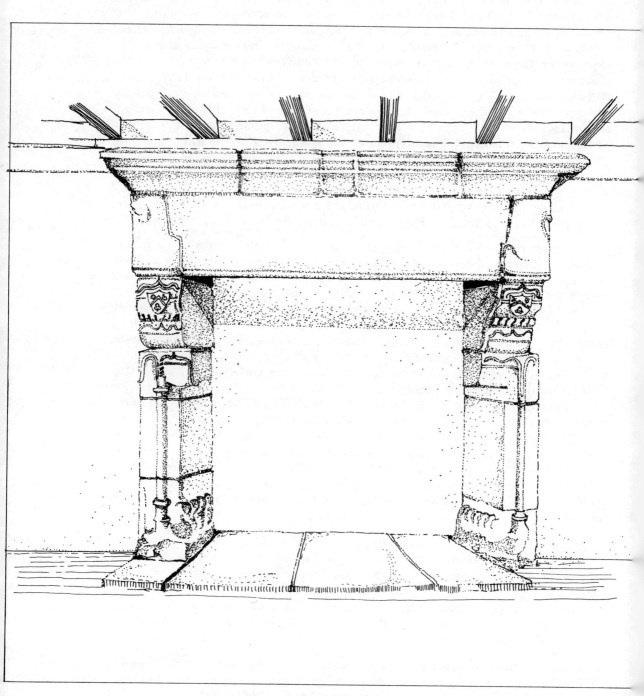

Fig. 39. LES QUERTIERS (919) FIREPLACE

between the curves. Two of unmatched stone and without any chamfering below, re-used in a gable-end at Les Hêches (446) have recently been again removed for use at Les Queux (555). It seems clear that many fireplaces, such as the fine one described at Huriaux Place, were patched up with unchamfered jambs in the 17th century, or, as perhaps here at Les Hêches, brought from elsewhere for use in a new house at that time. There is a complete fireplace with cable-mould at Les Vieilles Salines (950), and one of many undecorated ones at La Bellieuse Farm (94), 15th century.

At Les Câches (111), there was formerly a house much older than the 18th-century building now facing down the drive. It probably stood to the south-west of that house, into which one of its fireplaces was inserted at some time this century. It has now been removed to Le Clos de Bas (264) and is a unique design, the chamfering itself brought forward into a moulding that is almost a shaft, and a further moulding at the edge turned horizontally at top and bottom instead of chamfer stops, to form a framed effect. This most individual of compositions, which again probably shows Renaissance influence, is somewhat disappointingly surmounted by unexciting Type 2 corbels, well-carved, but undecorated. The original lintel has been lost, and may well have boasted a motto or armorial bearing that might have balanced these plain corbels.

However, it they are rather less interesting because they are an almost standard form, the Type 2 fireplaces were usually very fine structures, especially when associated with the other fitments of the medieval kitchen, as for instance, at 5 Berthelot Street (808), where the évier is an arched recess on the right-hand side. A similar arrangement seems to have been followed at La Grande Maison (945), and although the fireplace and évier, if that is what it was, have been much damaged, the other downstairs room here still has a fine mid-16th-century Type 2 example.

Ashbrook House (918) and Les Granges de Beauvoir Manor (834) bring us back again to the pillar type. They are both surmounted by a Type 2 corbel, the one at Les Granges having a cable-mould between the curves (see Illustration 5). The design at Ashbrook House is probably the older of the two, the pillars resembling those at Bordeaux House, but its assymetrical chamfer stops, like those on several of the arches outside Pleneuf Court (631), pointing to the last quarter of the 16th century. The Grange de Beauvoir Manor fireplace is very different. The pillar is monolithic, like that at Ashbrook House, but instead of chamfers and stops, has a moulding somewhat akin to the one from Les Câches (111), producing a design rather like a fluted column. This fireplace belongs to the beginning of the 17th century, when the house came into the possession of the de Beauvoirs and was probably re-designed. Parts of another fireplace of identical design are now in the garden of the house behind, and must either have come from the second-floor bedroom, above the other one, or from the other ruined house across the courtyard. If the former, then it is the first example of three fireplaces, one above the other, using the same chimney. If the latter, it must have been inserted by the de Beauvoirs at about the same time, as the ruins are of a much older building.

By the end of the 16th century, corbel shapes began to be simplified. Some fine, carved fireplaces were still being built, such as that in the early back kitchen at La Maison d'Aval (241) still with a Type 2 corbel and foliated chamfer stop. The fireplace in the new bedroom wing at Le Tertre (1026) is of Type 2 design, but in the similar wing at La Grande Maison, the corbel has only a single curve, of Type 4 shape. This is found, too, at Les Simons (340) and a Type 4 corbel appears in the upstairs fireplace at La Vieille Sous L'Eglise (475), where the wide windows and straight door lintel suggest a date somewhere around 1620. All the two-storey, three-bay houses seem to have had simple corbels of this sort, and although it may be argued that such small houses would not have had such complicated carving, their fireplaces do not lack craftsmanship in other respects. And as we have seen that they are a transitional type of house, they might be expected to exhibit the kind of changing detail which, in fact, we find in them. At Duvaux Farm (936), too, the corbel is a simple Type 5 sort, indicating, in this case, a date for the original main house around 1600.

Another sign of the times was the abandoning of the chamfered sides. Wisteria (502), King's Mills' House (504), and King's Mills' Farm (506) all have fireplaces with unshaped side stones and a variety of late-16th- or early-17th-century corbels. Even later, the cottage at Les Grands Moulins (497), shows a late hankering after shaped corbels in an 18th-century cottage, and La Villiaze (202) possesses a unique fireplace, which seems to be a conscious copying of earlier forms.

The Schedules will show just how many of these carved fireplaces remain. A full description of them and an adequate discussion of their dating could occupy a separate volume. This section has only been a summary, and the following general conclusions are put forward as a basis for further study. Pillar-type A and Type 1 fireplaces are among our earliest forms and seem to die out towards the end of the 15th century. Type 3 corbels, at first associated with pillar-type A fireplaces, are found with decreasing frequency until *c.* 1580—that at Le Tourtel (129) perhaps being the latest instance. Type 2 are the most frequent form, occurring right through the period from 1400–1625, as do the much less common examples of pillar-type B. A variation on the Type 1 shape makes a comeback, *c.* 1580–1625, and is contemporary with pillar-type C, and at the same dates, the simpler Types 4 and 5 corbels are also found. From the beginning of the 17th century onwards, fireplace design underwent a great change. First the chamfered sides were abandoned; then the stone lintels, in favour of relieving arches or wooden beams; and finally the corbel, too, was left unworked.

Chapter XXVIII

STAIRCASES

IT IS NOT SUGGESTED that any sort of close dating can be achieved before about 1600 by examining the form of staircase used in a house. There is little call for ornamentation, even in a tourelle. However, a closer look at them will show some interesting features. As has been explained in Chapter I, the position and way in which a tourelle staircase turns is due to the form of the house, the position of the kitchen, cross-passage and so forth. But how are they related to similar staircases elsewhere and how were they built?

Although there are isolated examples in England and a good many more in Scotland, which was allied to France until 1603, there are so many such staircases in Brittany and Normandy that we shall not look further afield, for it is with those parts of France that our architecture is most closely linked. The great difference between the Breton and the Guernsey tourelle is that in Brittany it does not necessarily open out of the cross-passage as ours do (with the exception here of *les grandes maisons*, Type 3), but is found in a variety of positions, as Fig. 40 will show. There are three main differences between Norman examples and our own.

In Normandy the tourelle was invariably carried up beyond the roof-line: also it is found in manor houses, not ordinary farmhouses, and it is very often octagonal, rather than circular. We have only the octagonal stair-turrets at the Town Church and La Haye du Puits (582) to indicate Norman influence here on staircases in the 15th century; and only the tourelle at Les Granges de Beauvoir Manor (834) later on reaches above roof level, though that one was to prove influential in the 17th-century design of other Guernsey houses.

However, low tourelles like ours are sometimes found in parts of Brittany, particularly around Mur-de-Bretagne, which seems an unlikely area to have had any strong connections with Guernsey, and occasionally on the borders of Normandy near Mont St. Michel, an area which certainly had stronger links with us. In Jersey, where only 20 tourelles are known, the usual shape is the taller, Norman form, although a few like ours occur. It is necessary, therefore, to do much more research before it is possible to suggest a definite origin for our tourelle staircase, of which over 150 exist, or are known to have existed.

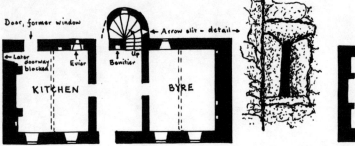
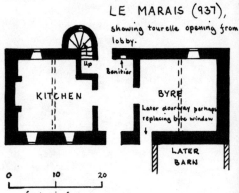

LA FORGE (509), showing back doorway between tourelle and kitchen, with tourelle corbelled over it.

LE MARAIS (937), showing tourelle opening from lobby.

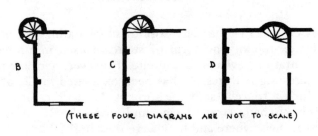
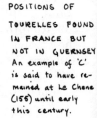

HOUSE AT SORTOSVILLE-EN-BEAUMONT, NORMANDY, the tourelle with access from byre and kitchen

(THESE FOUR DIAGRAMS ARE NOT TO SCALE)

POSITIONS OF TOURELLES FOUND IN FRANCE BUT NOT IN GUERNSEY. An example of 'C' is said to have remained at Le Chene (155) until early this century.

Fig. 40. 15th AND 16th CENTURY TOURELLES

LE HAUT CHEMIN (311)

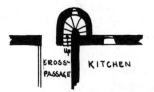

PLAS DYKE FARM (273)

LA HAYE DU PUITS (582)

LA MOYE (999)

THE COTTAGE (5-

KING'S MILLS' FARM (506), showing dog-legged steps

MAISON GALOPIE (284)

LA POMPE (117): tour corbelled over window

A tourelle can also vary considerably in shape, depending upon the position of the newel-post or pillar. If it is placed outside the line of the wall, as often happens in Normandy, then the tourelle will become almost detached and appear to stand away from the house. If the post is placed inside, the tourelle may appear as only a bulge in the outer wall. This is known from several examples in Brittany. If, however, the post is on the line of the wall itself, the tourelle will be roughly semi-circular in shape. This, probably because it is the simplest to build, is the one most usual in Guernsey until about 1600, and frequently afterwards as well. But a few houses, for example La Bouvée Farm (24) and Plas Dyke Farm, Les Sages (273), built their tourelles around huge stones, sometimes four feet high, which project beyond the back of the house. In such cases, the tourelle either stands well back from the house or the steps are narrowed as they pass around the back of the stone. In fact, a considerable variation in shape and proportions gives every tourelle its own character. Les Belles (460) has an extremely wide staircase, 11ft. in diameter outside, while that at Le Haut Chemin (311) is much more compact, scarcely 7ft. across. As for the treads themselves, they may each be of a single, well-finished stone, or of two or more stones, only very roughly shaped. At King's Mills' Farm (506), Maison d'Aval (975) and a few other places, the steps are curiously dog-legged, each one made of two stones set at an angle to each other. Since this arrangement does not make it noticeably easier to negotiate the staircase, the reason for building the steps in this way is a mystery.

By way of contrast, the steps at Bordeaux House (984) are single blocks of stone keyed in, one above the other to form a sort of newel, and the lintels of the doorway at the bottom of the stairs are corbelled and chamfered to give extra headroom. This tourelle is one of half a dozen built square on the outside though rounded in the usual way inside. La Moye (999), a disused house with a round chimney, has a somewhat similar one, and other examples are at 37 Glategny Esplanade (854) and Les Prevosts (463).

It has been suggested that tourelles are later additions to houses which previously had only a ladder or an exterior flight of steps to the upper storey. But although there are a few cases where the present tourelle shows signs of having been rebuilt, it is certain that the majority are contemporary with the earliest parts of the house, for the following reasons. Firstly, from what we know of the layout of the two-storey longhouse and its derivatives in Guernsey, it is inconceivable that access to the bedroom, or *chambre,* which was an innovation, like the fireplaces, only comparatively recently available to the fashionable farmhouse of the 15th century, would have been only by ladder. A man who could afford to employ a mason to make two fireplaces and at least one good arch is not likely to have put up with negotiating a ladder in order to get to his fine bedroom, a feature of which he would have been justly proud. Nor would he have considered using an outside staircase. As we have seen, the earliest outside staircases remaining cannot date from much before 1600, and if there had been more of them, the bottom and top doorways to the tourelles would not have been so exactly placed as we find them. We should, in other words, expect to find signs of blocked doorways from previous outside staircases, built wherever they were convenient, in other parts of the house, and there are none. Indeed, it must be emphasised again that the tourelle is an integral part of the design and the doorway to it was often of dressed stone, revetted to receive a door. The seeming inevitability of the tourelle doorway and back door of the house being side by side is further underlined at Les Merriennes Cottage (98) by the walling between them being fashioned into a pillar, moulded on both sides.

The irregular construction of many tourelles is not, then, due to their being an inferior afterthought, but to the greater difficulty of building a curved wall. We know from John Bonamy's notebook that the building of a house was a communal effort of neighbours and friends, for which they were paid in money or in kind, and that a mason was only called in to finish off the arch and fireplaces. For an unskilled builder, it is much easier to construct a straight wall, where a line can be stretched between two points, or sightings can be made, than to build a vertical circular wall. And it is noticeable, that once a tourelle has been built, the form is often retained even during alterations, just because of the work entailed in altering the positions of the offset doorways at top and bottom. These rebuilt tourelles are noted in the Schedule because they sometimes tell us that a house where virtually every ancient feature has been removed or covered up last century, is nevertheless much older than it now appears. For instance, it is clear enough that Les Hubits de Haut (6) is a very old house, before we notice that its tourelle has been rebuilt square in brick. But should we have been so sure at Les Adams (328)? At La Gaudine (132) there is a staircase altered in this way, projecting in a square Victorian tourelle, and the supposition that it was a far more ancient building than its re-fronting would suggest has recently been vindicated by the discovery of a fine 16th-century fireplace.

Two other tourelles have been rebuilt in a curious way, elongating themselves along the back of the house so as to hold a straight staircase at right-angles to the cross-passage, and arriving upstairs through a newly-pierced doorway. They are La Carrière (1028), which has a truly superb 19th-century facelift, and La Bailloterie (1032). In these two cases, the spacious cross-passage was kept even at the considerable expense of all the new work at the back of the house. The Cottage (543), opposite the Castel church, has a similarly extenuated tourelle, but here it is more difficult to say whether it is original or rebuilt. If the former, it is unique: if the latter, it is very early work in stone with rounded corners, and hardly as elegant as was usual last century.

Another feature of tourelles is the way in which they overlap doorways and windows. At first sight, there seems no reason for this, and again might lead us to think of these staircases as additions, until we notice how frequently these peculiarities occur. At Le Marais (493) it might seem as though a 17th-century rebuilding has partially covered one side of the older back door. But at Les Câches (237), always a wealthy house, the same thing happens; and again, at Old Farm, Brock Road (925). It is a feature also commonly seen in Brittany and Normandy, and can perhaps be explained by the need to have the tourelle doorway and the back door as close as possible together inside the cross-passage. Consequently the thickness of the tourelle wall was bound to overlap the back doorway on the outside.

If the back door seems squeezed in at one side of the tourelle, the back window of the kitchen often seems as though it was purposely built in the way at the other. This perversity is harder to account for. It results in the tourelle being broader at the top than at the bottom, because it has to be corbelled out over the window. Examples are frequent. For instance La Bouvée Farm (24) and La Pompe (117).

At La Forge (509), the tourelle is inexplicably built so as to turn towards the back door, a fine bénitier being placed between the two doorways at the back of the cross-passage. The result is that here, too, it is larger at the top than at the bottom, the massive slabs required to bring the staircase over the back door almost forming a porch.

This last tourelle is one of a number that appear to have an arrow-slit, usually covering the back door. Both the Ville-au-Roi Manor House (demolished 1943) and La Rocque Balan (1007) had proper loopholes, although that at the Ville-au-Roi was in a strange position right at the top of the tourelle. That at La Forge covered the back wall on the side away from the back door and no doubt usually performed the function more of a spy-hole. The examples at Le Grée (125) and Les Queux (555) are rather larger than the one at Le Haut Chemin (311)—about 9in. high and 6in wide. All have a wider splay than the actual window, usually at the back of the tourelle. If, as seems undeniable, these arrow-slits defended the back of the house, what defended the front? Did later re-fronting perhaps remove *eschauguettes* such as can be seen in some French farmhouses (for instance, Le Manoir, Carnet, near Fougères)? This is something we are unlikely ever to know.

All 15th- and 16th-century tourelles have stone steps. It follows that below the steps was more or less solid masonry. But sometimes a square opening was contrived on the outside, probably for the dog. In France there are examples of quite ornate little 'houses' near the farmhouse door for the dog that invariably guarded the farmyard. Here in Guernsey his home was under the tourelle, or sometimes, later on, under the steps to the valet's room. Then, near the top of the tourelle, provision was often made for a pigeonnier—a few square recesses in the wall for doves to nest. Les Queux has some there and along the top of the back wall. La Vieille Sous L'Eglise (475) also has a pigeonnier.

Although the tourelle was the most usual form of staircase in early times, it was not the only one. Many houses must have had straight stone staircases indoors, like the one that survives at Les Poidevins (662—see Chapter XXXII), or else a form of split staircase like that at L'Echelle (649) nearby, a form that was commonplace in the 17th and 18th centuries. Certainly such old houses as La Câche (314) and Les Blicqs (610) seem never to have had tourelles, nor did Le Catillon de Bas (292) before alteration. In that house, the wooden staircase, like the stone one at Les Poidevins, rose towards the front of the house.

In a few houses where the split staircase was used, a hollowing of the back wall at the turn seems to link them with another sort of staircase that must have been introduced here soon after 1600. Just as the wattle-and-daub hoods of the same period allowed a far less weighty fireplace construction, so the introduction of a central wooden post, or newel, enabled builders to discard the stone steps in tourelles.

The French farm just referred to at Carnet has a staircase of this sort, dated 1581, and is a building no larger than our *grandes maisons*; in fact, with considerably less living accommodation. The appearance of the form in Guernsey is associated with early 17th-century panelling and belongs to the time when houses were first being extensively altered. At Les Granges de Beauvoir Manor (834) the great tourelle has wooden treads turning around a newel post that looks like a ship's mast, and the contemporary staircase to the upper loft at Les Câches (237) is made in the same way, with a hollowing of the back wall. Other houses where the staircase is of a similar form and the wall is similarly hollowed are Saints Farm (83) and La Bellieuse Farm (94), where this alteration provides further support for the suggestion that a 'Guernsey' arch was inserted into the much older house at the beginning of the 17th century.

The tourelle at Les Granges de Beauvoir Manor, as has been mentioned before, is the only one in Guernsey where the newel post is placed considerably beyond the line of the back wall. The staircase there is also much more spacious than the usual tourelle allows. A few other houses possessing unusual tourelles, none of them with stone steps, and all possibly dating from this period may perhaps be seen as imitating the wide staircase at Les Granges. At La Villette (123), Maison Galopie (284), Les Queux (555), No. 11 Cliff Street (717), and No. 2 Coupée Lane (723) cannot be earlier than 1600, and both at Maison Galopie and Les Queux there are clear signs that the back wall of the tourelle itself have been partly or entirely rebuilt. La Villette, with its Type 5 fireplace, was probably a new house at this time. The tourelle at 28 Le Pollet (793) is also likely to have been of this type, and it is interesting that here and along Le Pollet, the houses are built into the bank up to first-floor level, an expedient also adopted at Les Granges de Beauvoir Manor.

The building of tourelles seems to have come to an end well before 1650. Following this, the types of staircases in town and country diverged for the first time. There is reason to think that all town houses of the medieval period and in Tudor times would have had a tourelle, either externally, as at 28 Le Pollet and formerly on the old house on the south side of Smith Street, or internally, as

SAINT'S FARM (83)
Quasi-tourelle around newel post with hollowing of back wall: wooden treads.

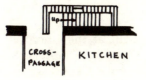

LA CARRIÈRE (1028)
A tourelle rebuilt last century and elongated along back wall.

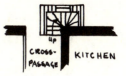

LES LOHIERS (478)
Tourelle rebuilt 1784.

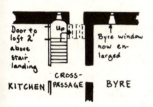

L'ECHELLE (649)
showing hollowing of wall for landing with straight stairs.

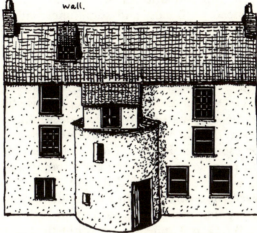

11, CLIFF STREET (717), showing tourelle occupying entire cross-passage and raised by a stair dormer when 3rd storey added in 18th century.

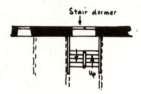

23, MILL STREET (746) Wooden stairs with newel post in central bay of shop, and wall hollowed.

PANDORA, LE POLLET (785)
Stairs with newel post but no hollowing of wall.

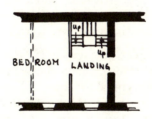

HAVILLAND HOUSE (685)
Staircase with stair well lit from front of house. First floor level: ground floor flight straight in order to leave cross-passage clear and to give headroom for back doorway.

5, ST. GEORGE'S ESPLANADE (860)
Stairs at first floor level in central bay of house.

5 PREVOSTS (?) 17th century stairway with sloping steps

Fig. 41. 17th AND 18th **CENTURY STAIRCASES**

RUE DES VINAIRES (302)
Cross-passage steps to loft inserted into kitchen cross-wall.

in the stairs to the basement at the Guernsey Savings Bank (756) rather like that at Maison de Haut (974—see Chapters VII and XXXIV). After 1650, the usual arrangement was to have a staircase in the middle bay, still around a newel post. These are shown as Type 2 staircases on the Second Schedule. In the country parishes, the design never became popular, and the split staircase was used everywhere. While early examples probably had no handrail, as at Le Bigard (205)—16th century; by 1700 it was usual to have a rather heavy, square post at the top and bottom of the stairs and on the landing, often with thin flat caps instead of finials, and sometimes with a simple moulding at the angles. The handrail was also very heavy, by 19th-century standards, the balustrading square in section and closely spaced.

When the introduction of a stair-well superseded the newel post in Town buildings, around 1700, very similar details are present at first. The advantage of the split staircase in the country was that it was still possible to use the front of the bay over the cross-passage as a separate room, whereas in the houses that adopted the stair-well, such as the three-storey Havilland House (685), this central room had to be sacrificed. Because the stairs now only turned in one direction, the only way to provide access to the bedroom at one side of the house was to make a landing which either extended right over the cross-passage, or else left only enough space for a boxroom in the middle bay. It was not until the middle of the 18th century that this plan, typical of all 19th-century houses, was adopted in the country. By then a much more sophisticated staircase had replaced the earlier, heavy design, such as can be seen at La Porte (526) for instance. From about 1750 onwards, the balusters were more slender, often with classical details of great delicacy, and the banister rail might be returned at the foot of the staircase, as at Plaiderie House (801) or Moore's Hotel (795), a development accompanied by the sophisticated panelling and doorcases we have examined in Chapter XXIV. It is clear that well before the end of the 18th century, all buildings with any pretensions to taste were following the latest English fashions.

Meanwhile, the humbler cottages made do with more utilitarian arrangements. The simple stone steps inserted into the cross-wall at the Rue des Vinaires (302) might well have been typical of internal access to the lofts of many a small cottage in the 17th or early 18th century, though it is now the only one remaining. On the farm, too, it was only the main staircase that kept up with the latest fashion. Other stairs to lofts or valets' rooms were still no more than ladders, wooden steps, or, outside, the stone flights so much associated with the farmyards of the island.

Chapter XXIX

ÉVIERS AND BÉNITIERS

OVER THE YEARS nothing has caused more perplexity in the study of Channel Island houses than the decorated niches called bénitiers. The matter has become further confused by treating éviers and bénitiers as though they were the same thing.

The évier, or medieval equivalent of a kitchen sink, sometimes known in England as a slop-stone, was almost always found in the kitchen of longhouses and early cottages, usually along the back wall; exceptionally in the cross-passage, as at Rocquaine Villa (285) and Les Adams (327). It is common in Brittany in the same positions.

Its purpose was originally to provide the farmhouse kitchen with a way of storing a quantity of water without the constant need to cross the yard to the well; later to provide in addition a means of disposing of dirty water without carrying it to the door; and to fulfil something of the function of the later dresser.

The earliest type seems to have consisted of an arched recess about three feet across and extending into the thickness of the wall about a foot. At The Elms (946) the construction is integral with one side of the arched doorway, and although the door arch is semi-circular, the similar arch of small stones over the évier is segmental. Into this recess, a large trough is inserted, the top of which is at waist height, and one side of the trough forms part of the outside walling. Below it, a very large slab of stone also extends to the outside of the wall, sloping downwards to form a drain, or sluice (see Illustration 63).

At La Rocque Balan, there is reason to think that the recess now pierced by a small window is just half of an arrangement that formerly looked exactly like the superb évier at Le Frie (303), otherwise unique in Guernsey (see Fig. 43). The original cross-passage here was possibly as narrow as at Le Marais Farm (1008) nearby, a very similar house, most likely being increased to its present width when the Guernsey arch was inserted *c.* 1600, thus blocking half the évier; a similar repositioning of a cross-wall has partially obscured the bénitier at Les Grands Courtils (388). If this is so, the arch of the évier would have sprung from the masonry forming one jamb of the ogee back doorway. In other words, it would have been integral with that doorway, as at The Elms. But unlike The Elms, it was almost certainly a semi-circular arch of dressed stone, with provision

Les Grands Courtil (388)   La Forge (509)   La Bellieuse Farm (94)

EVIERS

Pleneuf Court (631)   Les Reveaux (259)   Below St. Andrew's Church

La Tourelle (76)   Les Sages Villa (272)   La Seigneurie (367)

CHAMFER STOPS FROM ARCHES AND FIREPLACES

FIGURE 42

for a wooden shelf, like Le Frie. The trough at La Rocque Balan is a truly enormous boulder, shaped into a trough inside the house, but projecting right through the wall to form a scrubbing stone outside (see Illustration 11). Changed floor levels indoors have obscured the sloping drain below. However, it must be said that if the upper part of this évier were the same as the one at Le Frie, we ought to expect the bottom to be similar as well. It is possible that the trough was moved about two feet to the right when the cross-wall was re-positioned, and that it was always a feature of this structure: or maybe it is an insertion, the original arrangement, as at Le Frie, apparently having no provision for a trough.

Unfortunately, no other examples of éviers complete with troughs remain, but two troughs which might once have been part of éviers still exist and are of very ancient origin indeed.

The trough now at Castle Cornet, the front adorned with two mermaids holding mirrors, and formerly at Les Fontaines (544) was almost certainly an évier, as was the trough with two fine animal heads now outside the Castel church, the carving barbarously damaged at some time by the making of two holes through the outside of the cistern. The fact that each of these troughs is carved on one of the long sides only must indicate that it was formerly exposed only on that side, and in the case of the trough with two animal heads, the rough sides and back strongly suggest that it was let into a wall, the moulding below the heads on the front, if it were in a position equivalent to that at The Elms, then being off the floor level, just above the drain. The front of an évier, in the chief living-room of the house, is an obvious place to expect carving of the standard exhibited by these two fine cisterns (though it would be a good idea to put both of them under cover, or they will be exhibiting very little in two generations' time), and they are remarkable testimonies to the quality of life in the more prosperous 14th-century homes. A good many of the troughs now standing around in farmyards but without any such decoration, although to judge by their weathering, they are of considerable antiquity, may well have been fashioned in medieval times for the éviers of somewhat humbler houses rather than being connected with 16th- and 17th-century cider making.

A few other éviers, now mutilated, may once have contained troughs, notably those at Les Grands Courtils (388), Les Picques (445), and La Grande Maison (945). At any rate they seem to have no provision for a stone shelf such as replaces the trough in other complete examples. The remaining éviers fall into two categories: those in dressed stone, with provision for intermediate wooden shelves, and those simpler ones, either with arched or flat heads and with no provision for extra shelves.

Of the first category, the évier at Le Frie is the outstanding example. The fine proportions and the standard of workmanship displayed here, considered in conjunction with the nice fireplace—now blocked up—must have made this kitchen a very lovely room. In this évier, the stone corbel on either side would have supported a wooden shelf, on which would have been ranged the crockery of the household. Below, on the two stone ledges would have been a large jug of water and a basin, the drain being between them. The implication is that an évier is more for the washing of vessels—perhaps also for keeping milk cool—than for the preparation of food. That would have been done on the large, central

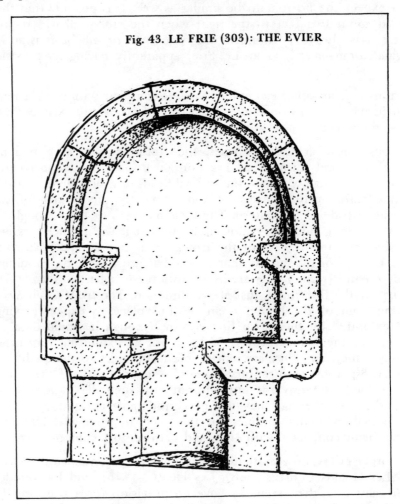

Fig. 43. LE FRIE (303): THE EVIER

table. The évier was the domestic equivalent of the monastic *lavatorium*. Éviers, or *dalles*, like the one at Le Frie, are well known in Brittany, though they usually have a stone slab instead of two ledges. In the 18th and 19th centuries, these Breton examples were often covered over by an ornate wooden front to form a sort of dresser-cum-cupboard, known as a *placard*. There is no evidence that this ever happened in Guernsey—if so all traces of such cupboards have vanished with the introduction of Victorian porcelain sinks into back kitchens. However, the back kitchen at La Vieille Sous L'Eglise (475), with its huge trough at ground level, may preserve a continuation of the évier tradition here in the late 17th and 18th centuries, though no back kitchen seems to have been constructed with an évier of the type we are dealing with. The even later troughs associated with the kitchen pump are probably the last relic of this tradition. In Town, the évier to the left of the first-floor fireplace at 5 Berthelot Street (808), the sides slightly staggered to provide support for two shelves above the vanished stone at waist height, again show that the whole arrangement is part of the original masonry. Many parallels to this and the one at Le Frie remain in the 15th- and 16th-century shops in Dinan, Guincamp and Tréguier.

Rather simpler versions appear in many farmhouses here. They always have, or have had, a slab of stone forming a shelf at about waist height, and can therefore be distinguished from window ledges, which were not formed of a single piece of stone. Some are arched, some have straight lintels. There seems to have been no preference, one way or the other, even in the 15th century. At Maison Bonamy (315), for instance, which we might infer to have been a 15th-century house both from its arch, now at the Coach House Gallery, so similar to the 1466 doorways at the Town Church, as well as from its Type 1 fireplace, the évier has a flat lintel. In the 1581 house at St. George, the évier is arched, with provision for a wooden shelf above the stone one. There is no evidence for the building of any of them after the mid-17th century, but we can say that they were part of every 15th- and 16th-century kitchen.

There remain 45 éviers, of one sort and another, and 16 bénitiers. This does not include the fine piscina from the Le Marchant Chapel at the corner of Lefebvre Street and La Grande Rue (High Street), which was built into the entrance hall at Pleneuf Court (631) by the late Mrs. Huysh and now seems to have dematerialised: or the records of other éviers or bénitiers, such as one seen in a disused house near the Castel Hospital, early this century. Neither does it include church piscinae. Many churches still have their full complement of piscinae. There are five at the Town Church, visible or concealed by screens; one each at the churches of St. Martin, the Forest, St. Andrew, St. Sampson, and the Castel; three at the Vale church, and none at the others.

A church piscina is an ornamented recess almost always on the south wall of the sanctuary, to the right of the altar: or where subsidiary chapels such as used to exist in the south transept of the Town Church had no stone south wall, they might be built into the east wall, but still to the right of the altar. The Vale church has a piscina for a nave altar. They were used to dispose of the water from the ritual washing of the priest's hands, at the beginning of Mass, and for the cleansing of patten and chalice at the end of the service. For this reason they were constructed with a tiny drainage hole, less than an inch across, usually in the middle of a saucer-shaped depression in the bottom of the recess. Above this, a stone shelf held the communion vessels during part of the service. Similarly decorated niches in churches but without any drain and not on the south wall of chancels or chapels are known as *credences* and their function was either to display the patten and chalice if, as in the north chancel chapel at the Town Church, there was no shelf included in the piscina: or else to provide a place for keeping the reserved sacrament. A somewhat smaller niche, but usually with a large bowl and without a drain, was built into the walls of most churches by the doorways, or sometimes was free-standing on a pillar. This was a holy water stoup, in which would be put water blessed by the priest, so that the faithful, on entering the building, could dip their fingers in and cross themselves.

The bénitiers in Guernsey farmhouses possess some characteristics of these three kinds of niches, but not all of them, and they are quite distinct from éviers. The large drainage slab of the évier is entirely absent, and the recess itself is invariably smaller. It is also much more ornate and consequently must have been regarded as more important.

Its position also suggests this. Three of those remaining are not now in their original place, but of the other 13, nine are in the cross-passage and were clearly of some visual importance when entering the house: four are in the kitchen, but three of them so close to the cross-passage that one wonders whether the cross-wall itself is original. A more detailed study would probably clear this point up. The fourth, at Bordeaux House (984), is in a *grande maison* which might once have had a narrow cross-passage like the similar house at Le Marais Farm (1008) and—perhaps—La Rocque Balan (1007).

An alternative way to assess the importance of their positioning is by stylistic comparison, by looking at their shape. As has been mentioned in Chapter XXV, the pointed arch was never so popular in Guernsey or Brittany as in England, especially in domestic architecture, and though it is used more commonly for bénitiers than for front doorways, it is still likely to have fallen out of favour well before 1500. The ogee, too, was more popular in the 15th century than in the 16th century, by which time it had flattened into the accolade. Four examples are not really enough to work on, and it may just be coincidence that those found in the kitchen are all early types—pointed, cusped or ogee. But only one of the nine in the cross-passage has a pointed head, that at Old Marais (1009), in a house so severely altered last century that it is amazing to find it by the side of the front door at all. Its position may well have been changed during re-fronting. All the later, round-headed ones and the accolade example at La Maison de Haut (240) are in the cross-passage—also some with ogee heads. Thus it seems likely that although a bénitier might be built in the kitchen in the 15th century, by 1600 it was always in the cross-passage.

It must also be pointed out that three bénitiers—those at Les Grands Courtils (388), La Forge (509), and St. George (584)—are in houses where there are also éviers. It is inconceivable that such an expensive amenity would have been so needlessly duplicated. In any case, it is quite clear from their other differences that a bénitier could not have been an évier.

Fig. 44. BENITIERS

Nor is there much in the way of hard facts to support the contention that bénitiers all came from the nearest church or chapel. When, in any case, could this have happened? The adherence of most Guernseymen to the Roman Catholic religion, well past the middle of the 16th century, is vividly demonstrated by the letters of Elizabeth College's unfortunate headmaster, Adrian de Saravia, concerning the indignities suffered by the two Protestant ministers when they tried to preach in the rural churches. It is hardly likely that bénitiers could have been extracted from churches until the inhabitants of this island had ceased to harden their hearts against reform, by which time they would have had no use for them anyway. And to place them in the cross-passage, where a visitor could not avoid seeing them, would have been to risk sitting in *la banc des mocqueurs*—the Seat of the Scornful—to be railed against by preachers for ever. Moreover, in the Town Church, the very heart of the Presbyterian organisation here from 1560 to 1660, there are five splendid piscinae and one ornate *credence* —some of them now covered up. Only one of these is even damaged, and that probably by the too-enthusiastic fetching of one of the fire engines kept there last century. So much for the idea of a religious origin.

If this debunking of popular fancy is still not adequate, it must also be said that the farmhouse bénitiers are most clearly contemporary with the houses of which they are a part. They are made from the same stone. At Bordeaux House, one side of the bénitier forms a jamb of the tourelle doorway, while the other side is part of a window splay. At La Forge, too, the bénitier is clearly integral, this time both with the tourelle and the back doorway (see Illustration 75), and this house was here in 1471. It is equally clear at St. George and Les Granges de Beauvoir Manor (834) that the bénitier is part of the fabric of the house. Even in other houses where the masonry is not exposed, its proximity to the front door suggests that the same is true (see Fig. 45). Indeed, where the front door arch is offset to one side of the cross-passage rather than central, it may well be that a bénitier remains to be discovered below modern plaster.

If the bénitier, then, was not an évier, and did not come from a consecrated building, what was it? Clearly it was designed to dispose of small quantities of water, just as a piscina in church. A similar saucer-shaped hollow in the ledge was usually drained by a small runnel leading into the thickness of the wall at the back. We remember that the amount of water being used in an évier was obviously too much to be disposed of in this way, and so the stone slab directed water right through the wall. In the bénitier, however, although it was necessary to avoid water dropping on your feet, or turning the surface of the earth floor into mud, the quantity involved was not considered sufficient to warrant a large-scale drain.

Yet the presence of a drain at all precludes its use as a niche for a statue. So does the post-Reformation date of some bénitiers, for instance, those at La Maison d'Aval, St. George and Les Granges de Beauvoir Manor. Nor is there ever a shelf in a bénitier, as in most piscinae, such as might have provided for a statuette above and something else below.

ÉVIERS AND BÉNITIERS

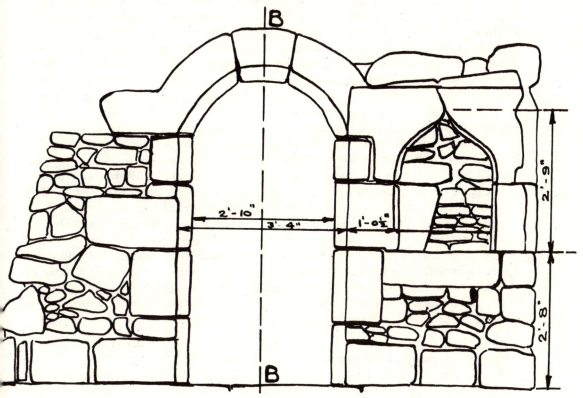

Fig. 45. Arch of Cobo stone and bénitier of Caen stone integral with it, from Les Grandes Maisons, demolished 1949, now at Folk Museum

The drain also precludes its use as a holy water stoup. The essence of a stoup is that water stays in the basin and does not drain away. Nor does the position of the bénitier in the back wall of the house, in the case of eight of those remaining, lend itself to this use. A stoup is always to one side of the chief entrance and would entirely lose its meaning if you had to go to the other side of the house or into the kitchen before you could cross yourself.

Why, then, does a bénitier look so much like a piscina and have the same sort of drain? Surely the answer must be that its function was connected in men's minds with the function of a piscina in church. It seems much the most probable solution to the problem, that the bénitier was in the cross-passage because that was where you welcomed visitors and offered them water for a wash after they had perhaps had a hot and dusty ride along country lanes, or arrived bespattered with mud, depending upon the weather. You might have proffered a bowl of water, with a linen towel over one arm, in much the same way as an altar-boy serves the priest during Mass. By this simple action, you would have indicated that you were at the service of your guest for as long as he stayed in your house. In those bénitiers with a small hollow in the base, the water might perhaps have been held in a basin, suspended by a chain from the top of the niche, where sometimes a hook remains. In other cases, where the ledge is cut away to form a large but shallow tray-like depression with a rim at the front, probably the bowl of water was not hung, but stood inside. Joan Stevens, in *Old Jersey Houses,* Vol. I, in dealing with this problem, illustrates the arched niche shown in the Mérode Triptych, a Flemish altar-piece painted between 1406 and 1444. Here, a laver or bowl, holding water, is suspended by a chain. A towel hangs alongside. It is immediately noticeable that the design of this particular niche is quite remarkably similar to the bénitier at Les Grands Moulins (520), and although the subject of the painting is the Annunciation, the depiction of the Virgin Mary in a domestic context, welcoming the Angel into a typical 15th-century home, is, to say the least, instructive. The ornamentation of our bénitiers may thus be partly a reference to the parallel use of church piscinae, and partly an indication of the great importance attached to hospitality in medieval times. The obligation upon everyone of entertaining travellers and wayfarers so vividly described by Homer in Ancient Greece, is not peculiar to that land or to the Christian tradition, but has been noted by many writers as a characteristic of other races and cultures: and let us hope it is not dead yet in our own.

The term bénitier, then, may be something of a misnomer—the product of 19th-century imagination when any Gothic ornamentation was associated with a church. And we must also consider the bénitier in La Maison Tiphaine, in Mont St. Michel, in this context. If, as seems certain, that house is really the one built by Bertrand du Guesclin in 1365, we might expect that one of the most important figures of his time would make absolutely sure that the amenities of his house were in order. Under the very shadow of the great abbey itself, it is also inconceivable that an object of religious significance could be misplaced. But the bénitier of La Maison Tiphaine (one of the very few bénitiers, in our sense of the word, in northern France) is not by the entry. It is upstairs on the first floor, in the main living room. It is exactly the same shape as that at Bordeaux House, and, like the one there, is integral with the tourelle and with a window-splay.

To summarise, then: a bénitier cannot be an évier, because the two things differ fundamentally; it cannot be filched from a church, because it was part of the structure of the house, built from the same stone; it cannot be a holy water stoup because it is not in the right place, and would not, so to speak, hold water; nor was it intended to hold a statue, or else no drain would have been included. It is most probably a place for washing the hands, especially in connection with the hospitable greeting of strangers, and thus, since it had no religious significance, did not offend the Calvinistic authorities after 1568.

However, just because it was not connected with any Christian ritual is no reason why its design should not have been influenced by those very piscinæ that fulfilled such a similar purpose. Here, if anywhere in the house, perhaps, the Gothic detail might be a little conservative. But with that in mind, it is quite possible to fit the bénitiers into the mainstream of vernacular architectural styles, as we have noted them with the arches of our doorways. So the simple, pointed bénitiers are likely to be hardly any later than 1450—that is, those classed as Type 1 in the Schedule. Those in Type 2 as well, are an early, or mid-15th-century form. The ogee arch merges into the accolade to form Type 3, the earliest ones being at Les Paysans (325); Les Grands Courtils (388); La Forge (509); Ménage du Moulin (512); and the one at the Folk Museum, all between 1450 and 1550. Accolade and round-headed ones (Type 4) are the latest, roughly from the period 1550-1625.

Perhaps the position of these bénitiers also gives us a clue as to the changing pattern of domestic life in the 16th century. We have seen that only the early forms of bénitiers are to be found in the kitchen, the later ones are in the cross-passage. We may be witnessing here a change from the use of the other side of the house from a byre to a store. If cattle were using the cross-passage, the bénitier would have been more suitably placed in the kitchen. Some, at least, of those bénitiers in the cross-passage may therefore be showing us that in these houses the cows had already been put into separate buildings, and that this had now become a more civilised place, fit for welcoming guests. It is also interesting that the majority of the late examples, with their round arch, consciously seem to disclaim all connection with religious niches.

While the building of bénitiers did not continue long into the 17th century, it is likely that a memory of their function continued in the island until recent times. At least in the western parishes it was the practice, as remembered by Mrs. Marie de Garis of Les Reveaux, to provide a basin of water and a towel on a stool inside the back door, so that the farmer or his wife might rinse their hands when they came indoors. The towel—and the water—were changed every day! If this were indeed the practice when bénitiers were in use, it is no wonder that a larger drain was not needed, and that the drips seeping out at the back into the clay mortar of the wall did not in any way disturb the structure of the house.

In concluding this section, we must return briefly to the myth that every piece of carved stone came from the nearest parish church, or (the favourite source) Lihou Island. If it was a conventual priory at all, the monks there must all have been recruited from the ranks of stone-masons! Hopefully, enough has been said in this book to show that many of our medieval and Elizabethan houses were built by people of considerable taste, often by folk who had travelled widely or who made use of the continuous contacts with European craftsmen and merchants brought to Guernsey by the busy trade routes across the Channel. Neither must we forget the influence of craftsmen employed on the parish churches and the castles from time to time, most of them, no doubt, trained elsewhere, and bringing new ideas to the island.

However, having said all that, one of our bénitiers does show signs of including stone from Lihou Island. That is the one at Huriaux Place (403), where the pointed niche is partly made up of 12th-century voussoirs with beakhead ornament. They are carved in Caen stone or a very similar white limestone, and are exactly paralleled by drawings made by F. C. Lukis, *c.* 1850, of several stones from Lihou Island, which were put into the Lukis and Island Museum. The bénitier at Huriaux Place is next to the cross-wall in the kitchen of the house, and in this room there is also the very interesting fireplace with figures on the corbels and the attached keeping-place, discussed on p. 193. All these features are contemporary with the fabric of the house, but in the case of the bénitier, use has been made of much older stone. Assuming from the style and placing of this bénitier, as well as from the fireplace and keeping place, that this house dates between 1450 and 1500, the presence of the limestone beak-heads must indicate a dilapidation or a rebuilding of the priory church well before the Reformation, at which time we know that the Prior, being more in the nature of an official collecting dues than a contemplative monk, lived in Town. Either the priory itself was being used as a source of building material even by 1500, or we have at Les Huriaux Place some evidence for a considerable rebuilding there, perhaps after destruction in one of the French raids, for these stones must have come either from an arch, or from blank arcading such as we can see in the chancel of the Vale church.

It is impossible to say why the bénitier now in the Folk Museum is also in Caen stone. It was rescued from a house demolished at Les Grandes Maisons, next door to the one still standing (922) in 1949, together with the segmental arch adjoining it. Clearly, not all limestone used in the islands was for ecclesiastical buildings. The Royal Court House fireplace in Gorey is in limestone. While the Folk Museum bénitier is unusual in this respect, it is no different from other farmhouse bénitiers in design, and shows no signs at all of having come originally from a chapel. Indeed, the curious construction of its drain, which turns at right-angles and empties itself through the door-jamb seems to suggest, yet again, that it was made specifically for the house at Les Grandes Maisons.

Chapter XXX

MERCHANTS' MARKS AND PELICANS

DURING THE MIDDLE AGES, there grew up among merchants in north-western Europe the custom of devising a mark something akin to our 'trade mark.' Just as the nobility and gentry in medieval times could be recognised by their coats-of-arms, so the merchant stamped his merchandise with his individual device. He also used it to seal his documents. In buildings it shows how much the prosperity of Guernsey depended upon trade, for although it became the practice to issue coats-of-arms to merchants in the late 15th and early 16th centuries, even then the merchant's mark was by no means abandoned in favour of armorial bearings. This is shown, for instance, by the example at Les Granges de Beauvoir Manor (834). For although the de Beauvoirs possessed the coat-of-arms displayed on the keystone of the entrance arch at the end of their drive, James de Beauvoir, the builder of the present house, used his merchant's mark on the lintel now in the garden behind, probably displaced from a fireplace indoors. Major Rybot and Edith Carey, in a joint article 'The Merchants' Marks of the Channel Islands', *Transactions* of La Société Guernesiaise, 1928, show just how wide commercial interests were. James de Beauvoir ran a very profitable wine trade with Spain, and in 1605 had two agents there, John Briard, whose own mark appears on the Guernsey Savings Bank (756), and Thomas Le Marchant, whose brother, at that time, had been a slave for some years in the galleys of Barbary pirates, by whom he had been captured while at sea. De Beauvoir also had trading interests in London and La Hague, and relatives in commercial centres as varied as Vitré, St. Malo and Lyme Regis. Thomas Le Marchant, a little later on, was trading with Newfoundland, and John Briard had his own ship, *The Dove,* which was probably one of the first Guernsey privateers, but also carried valuable cargoes of fish and oil.

Another important island family, the Careys, also had a merchant's mark, having been merchants and shipowners since at least the 15th century, when Laurence Careye was a partner with John Bonamy, whose diary we have referred to, in a ship called *La Pitié*, probably trading from Poole. The mark now over the 19th-century entrance arch at Le Vallon belonged to Peter Careye and dates from 1594. Twenty years earlier he had married the daughter of a prominent merchant of Vitré, then a Huguenot refugee in Guernsey, and his Puritan persuasions made him not only an 'ancien' or churchwarden of the Town Church and a fervent supporter of the Calvinistic régime there, but a friend and

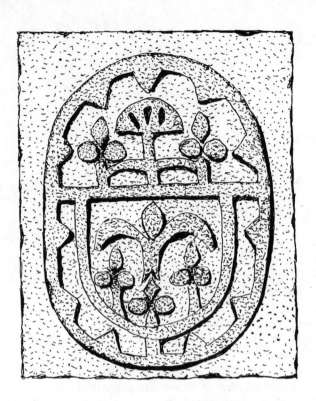

Moulin de Haut (486): Lefebvre merchant's mark.

Le Vallon: Peter Carey merchant's mark, c. 1580.

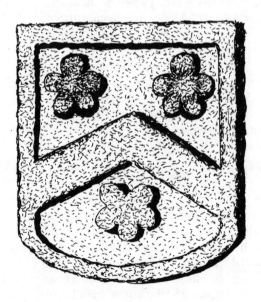

Les Granges de Beauvoir Manor (834): de Beauvoir arms, 17th century.

Les Granges de Beauvoir Manor (834): James de Beauvoir merchant's mark, c. 1603.

ambassador of the Governor, Sir Thomas Leighton. Lady Leighton was first cousin of Queen Elizabeth, and during the Leighton's frequent visits to England, Peter Careye deputised as Lieutenant-Governor. From 1599 onwards, the south arm of the harbour, formerly hardly more than a jetty, was rebuilt on more substantial lines. A stone inscribed 'T.L. 1589', built into one of its steps, remained until last century, and records Leighton's personal interest in the operation. At the end of this southern arm a small house was erected in which prisoners were kept if the weather was too bad for them to be carried over by boat to Castle Cornet. This house must have been built during one of Leighton's absences, for Peter Careye put his merchant's mark over the door, from which place it was removed to the Slaughterhouse when the harbour was again rebuilt, round about 1855. From there it was later moved by General de Vic Carey to Le Vallon. The Slaughterhouse seems a bizarre repository for the various interesting bits and pieces that have been built into it, and one cannot help wondering whether the mounted horseman still on one of the ridge tiles of its roof, possibly 16th-century, and of West Country origin, was also once on Peter Careye's house on the quay.

Peter Careye's youngest brother John married Jacqueline Blondel of Le Groin, or Le Gron (433). Their joint initials appear over the arched doorway to that house, although they seem to have lived chiefly in St. Peter Port, in a house opposite The Guernsey Savings Bank, on the other corner of Berthelot Street and High Street. Similarly, John Briard's initials appear on one of the marks at The Guernsey Savings Bank, while his wife Rachael's appear on the other.

The other merchant's mark over a doorway is on the arch at Le Fainel, rebuilt from an older dwelling belonging, by the 16th century, to the Thoume family. Miss Carey seemed to think that this mark belonged not to Thomas Thoume, who married Laurence Ollivier, heiress of Le Vallon, next door, sometime before 1585, but to their son, another Thomas, in 1616. From the style of the arch and the elaborate chamfering, this is just possible, though a slightly earlier date would seem more likely.

The Careye and Thoume marks carved over doorways clearly belong to the 'Guernsey' Type 5 arches with their dates and initialling, described in Chapter XVII. The merchant's mark did duty for both, for its owner was well-known in the island and his merchandise was identified by it. The Briard marks are equally conspicuous, but the adornment of the outside of the house in this way, as we have seen, is a feature of the late 16th century onwards. Before that time, carving appeared most often on fireplace lintels, such as the very fine one now in the Castel Rectory (556) (see Illustration 83). In Church Square, St. Peter Port (753) two former fireplace lintels, formerly in a house on this site belonging to the de Sausmarez family, now do duty as lintels over upstairs windows (see Illustration 85). The larger one bears a merchant's mark, and the smaller, bedroom one, the de Sausmarez coat-of-arms. They are both in Chausey stone and may belong to the 15th-century Nicholas de Sausmarez who bought the house on 5 January 1445/6 from Lucas Effart, rather than to his great-grandson, Nicholas, in the middle of the next century. As has been mentioned in the introductory chapter, stone from those islands was probably more readily obtainable during the 15th than during the 16th century, although too little is known of the subject to be dogmatic. Another merchant's mark in the same stone, the owner so far unidentified, was found this century at St. George (586), where it is now over an entrance arch (see Illustration 86). It is probably cut down from a fireplace lintel—for where else were straight lintels used in the 15th century?—and also has angel supporters, like the one in Church Square.

All of these merchants' marks are a combination of the owner's initials and 'The Sign of Four', or the sign of the Cross, under whose protection they wished their wares to travel. Some also seem to include a design like two streamers flying from a mast—conventionalised on the Thoume example (see Fig. 46)—possibly being a reference to the pre-heraldic gonfalon of the Lamb of St. John, the patron saint of wool merchants. This is all the more probable, since so much island trade was in the importation of raw wool and the export of finished goods. Of the 24 Channel Islands' merchants' marks known from seals or stones, and of which a complete account is given in the article by Rybot and Carey already referred to, 23 are in Guernsey. Undoubtedly this can only further emphasise how much more important commercially than Jersey this island was at that time.

For dating purposes it is clear that the large amount of information we have about many of these merchants is of great value in confirming our dating of arches and houses in general.

At Le Moulin de Haut (486) there is a curious stone over the front door, said to be a device of the Lefebvre family. Properly speaking it is neither a coat-of-arms nor a merchant's mark, and must belong to the 18th century when that house was re-fronted (see Fig. 46).

Two other houses possess dated stones associated with the legend of a Pelican in her Piety (see Illustration 89). This legend comes from that curious mixture of fact and fiction, the Physiologus, or Bestiary, first mentioned in the fifth century, and much quoted by medieval encyclopaedias, where creatures are classified as beasts, birds, or fishes. The chapters begin with a Biblical mention of the animal, followed by an account of its habits, and then its spiritual significance. It is a curious commentary on the medieval outlook on life that the fantastic mis-statements of the Physiologus were often followed even when they belied facts of nature that could be observed easily enough. Since ostriches were known to run fast, they were portrayed with cloven feet, like deer. The hart pants after cooling streams because of the thirst engendered by the fiery breath of serpents which it eats, having first driven them out of the ground by spewing water down their holes. The 'Pelican in her Piety' portrays the bird restoring her fledglings to life with the blood from her self-wounded breast, after her irritation at their importunities had driven her to kill them. Thus the pelican symbolised the redemption of Man through the blood of Christ after his Fall through sin.

To find two examples of this curious allegory dated 1595 and 1611 demonstrates the amazing influence of the Bestiary 30 or 40 years after the Reformation in Guernsey. The former is built into a later cottage at Les Vallettes (447), but the latter may perhaps be still in its original position above the front doorway at Le Vallon Cottage (37)—it is difficult to say. A great deal of original work, including 17th-century window-frames and beams, remains inside, but the outside of this house has been liberally peppered with the idiosyncracies of Le Vallon Gothick. Bearing in mind the spurious entrance arch to the main house and the merchant's mark inserted in it from Peter Careye's 16th-century building on the harbour, it is not impossible that the Pelican, too, could have been brought from elsewhere. The grey stone out of which it is carved is unusual and almost certainly not local. It is about 20ins. square and shows several pelicans, their wings indorsed, feeding their young from their blood, as well as a lozenge pattern which, like the subject matter, is more reminiscent of the 15th century. However archaic, they are, nevertheless, yet another instance of the passion for dating everything, in the period 1580-1620. As the one at Les Vallettes is not in its original position, and we must also be doubtful of that at Le Vallon, they cannot be relied upon as dating evidence. They are, all the same, quite fascinating in their own right.

Pelicans: Le Vallon Cottage (37)

PART V

DETAILED STUDIES

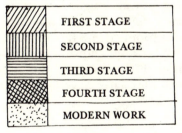

Chapter XXXI

LA GRANDE MAISON (945)

STANDING WELL BACK from the road betweel L'Islet and Pleinheaume is one of the most imposing façades in Guernsey. In 1787, as can be seen from the map, no other houses lay between it and the western end of that tidal inlet of the sea which did indeed make the land to the north almost another islet. By that time, the daily inundation of this reach of the sea had been controlled by sluices and banks so as to form a vast area of salterns, only two fields away. Since then, the area has changed very greatly. In the 19th century, a large quarry encroached almost to the back garden, and after the filling in of The Braye in 1805-6, the salterns also came to an end, and the reclaimed land gradually filled up with other houses and greenhouses.

When it was first built, however, La Grande Maison must have been the most imposing house in these parts: hence its name. It seems to have been constructed in 1586 for the Lainé family, who came to the island from Normandy at about that time. This explains the Norman form of the arch over the back door. Originally, the house consisted of five bays and a cross-passage, and must have been one of the very first in the island to possess two downstairs fireplaces. Whether it originally had fireplaces upstairs as well is impossible now to say, due to later alterations: but although the pattern was derived from the longhouse type, the earliest plan could obviously not have made any provision for a byre in the house itself. The room to the left of the cross-passage seems to have been the kitchen, judging by the later addition of a buttery wing at the end. It contains a fine Type 2 chamfered fireplace, of the standard 16th-century design, and perhaps an *évier*, which may later have been pierced to provide access to the new wing just mentioned.

However, if that was so, the arched recess to the left of the mutilated fireplace in the right-hand room is a mystery. It is formed of small stones exactly like the évier at 5 Berthelot Street (808) and its position vis-à-vis the fireplace is precisely the same as in that Town example. But on the other hand, the siting of an évier in the gable wall of a farmhouse would be unique. Well, never mind, this is an unusual house for its time, and it is possible that this room, not required for cows, was a sort of back kitchen at the side, serving the other rooms across the passage rather as though it were an English hall with screens passage. This is no more than a suggestion. Maybe the arch of the fireplace was only an unusual

DETAILED STUDIES

keeping place. But why then does it appear to have been extended downwards to floor level in such an irregular and apparently inept fashion? Support for this theory exists in an Inventory of Sale in 1646, which lists a room over the kitchen, a room over the sitting room and another over a store. This can only mean that the two original ground-floor rooms were kitchen and sitting-room and that the latter wing was a store, since it was at first unheated. The question is, which was the kitchen and which the sitting-room in 1646?

The original back doorway remains, as usual partially obscured on the outside by the contemporary tourelle. It is a very fine composition indeed, a segmental arch of two orders, with an ornamental layer of small stones between and another above the outer order, exactly the same as the one at Le Tertre (1026), another house that has been re-fronted.

One wonders what the front arches of these houses would have been like. The tourelle turns left, presumably to a loft, depending which end in this house was specifically the kitchen end. Unfortunately, the superb 18th-century work upstairs, together with subsequent removal of all internal partitions in the following century, when the house became barns, has totally erased all signs of the 16th-century room arrangement. The present owners rescued this house from a fearful state of neglect in 1932 and are responsible for a quite outstanding restoration of it to its former glory.

Whatever the truth about the downstairs when it was first built with its two identical fireplaces, it was decided, soon after 1600, to build on a bedroom wing—again, exactly as at Le Tertre. On the ground floor this had an unheated room, presumably with separate external access, though the door and windows on the eastern side have all been altered. Internal access, as already mentioned, was through an opening in the north wall of the original house, perhaps by utilising an existing window-opening or an évier. The gable end of the room was pierced by two small windows, later blocked on the outside by a store and a two-holer lavatory, and on the inside by a Victorian bread-oven.

Upstairs, access was possible by piercing one side of the tourelle. The splendid three-bay bedroom into which this opened, its superb fireplace still intact, may well have been the real reason for the enlargement of the house at this time. It must have been the main bedroom when it was built, and its generous proportions are very satisfying. There were originally two more gable windows, at either side of the fireplace, which is naturally a late, but very fine, design with notched lintel and moulded cornice above. The stone hood rose to a red granite chimney, the earliest of the four at present on the house. The one over the valet's quarters is 18th-century, in grey stone, and the other two were copied from it by the present owners in 1932 and replace the brick stacks then in existence.

La Grande Maison was further extended, during the first half of the 18th century, by a four-bay range. This provided stabling on the ground floor. The first floor was divided into a two-bay loft and a two-bay room for the valet (or

LA GRANDE MAISON

ST. SAMPSON

SOUTH ELEVATION

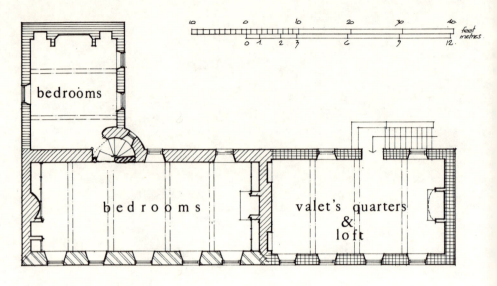

FIRST FLOOR

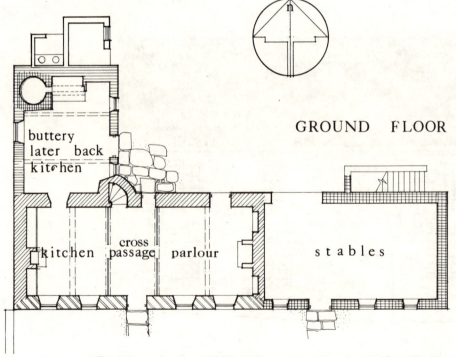

GROUND FLOOR

LA GRANDE MAISON

Sketch from rear garden

17th century fireplace

The tourelle stair

ST. SAMPSON

cowman and chief farm worker). His room was approached by a straight flight of steps along the back of the stabling, the coping stones of the low wall beside these steps being built in exactly the same way as the gable coping of the house. Inside, a Type 8 fireplace with unshaped shoulders and a wattle-and-daub hood heated the room, while above the ceiling was another loft in the roof-space, approached by ladder.

Later on in the same century, probably around 1760, the main house was given a magnificent facelift. The front wall was taken down to the level of the ground-floor window sills. Leaving the bottom of the old wall still in position, the façade was then rebuilt in grey ashlar, contrasting with the Cobo stone in the older parts of the house, and framed guillotine-sash windows and a six-panelled door and fanlight. The glazing-bars of those windows were the thick, heavy sort associated with the first three-quarters of the 18th century, but not common in Guernsey until around 1750. The 24-light upstairs windows were exceptionally large.

Although the front of the house was so completely removed, the 16th-century roof structure was left untouched, an interesting comment on the capabilities of the 18th-century builders. The oak roof is a complete example of the kingpost pattern. There are four trusses, with upper collars and wind-braces, a form of construction almost universal in contemporary Norman houses. With the new façade came improvements indoors. All the rooms were panelled out in the most elegant fashion and although all the woodwork downstairs has vanished, that upstairs has remained intact and is some of the best of its kind in Guernsey. The fireplace in the gable end of the right-hand bedroom has a classical surround with overmantel and fluted pilasters. The coving around the ceiling, and the central beam across the room are heavily moulded with a delicate dentil design below. All the panelling has a raised ground.

While all this later work no doubt destroyed archways, bénitiers, perhaps moulded window sills and so forth, it has provided an example of the best craftsmanship of another era. It was probably fortunate that the disuse of the entire building as living accommodation in the 19th century preserved it from any further modification, so that we can see here a house mostly the product of the 200 years from about 1550 to 1750, but within that time, of four separate stages.

Chapter XXXII

LES POIDEVINS (661-2)

ON THE 1787 MAP, Les Poidevins consists of four buildings at the eastern end of a small bluff, at a point where a stream joins the larger Talbot Valley. Since 1787, one of those four buildings has disappeared and one has given way to the new, 19th-century house. The course of the road has been considerably altered.

Neither of the two remaining houses is occupied. One is a ruin, facing south, and the other is now a barn, facing east. The south-facing house is the older, dating from about the middle of the 16th century perhaps, to judge by the arch, which is somewhere between Type 3 and Type 4, with the peculiarity of having only two voussoirs in the inner order. Although the window-openings are mostly quite large, the upstairs one slightly to the left of the arched door is very strange, being scarcely more than a slit. It would have opened into the main loft over the kitchen and its purpose is a mystery. At any rate, it shows a total disregard for any sort of symmetry in the façade, pointing to a date rather before the sort of house exemplified by Le Tourtel (129) in the 1570s.

In plan, this house is a four-bay cross-passage one of the usual type, with the kitchen on the left and possibly a byre on the right. However, a cart entrance has been made at the byre end, removing the back wall to roof level, so that no sign of a 'pour' or byre window remains: and from the comparatively large size of the front window, it might be that this side of the house consisted of a store rather than a byre, with a bedroom above.

The stone tourelle staircase turns left towards the kitchen end. All internal partitions have been removed, but there is no indication that a stone cross-wall ever existed. If it did, it was not bonded into either the front or the back wall.

In the kitchen, the fireplace has been destroyed, but an inserted bread oven and a wattle-and-daub hood remain. In the bedroom the fireplace seems to be a fairly late type, with a wattle-and-daub hood perhaps replacing a stone one. There are no gable windows. Each gable end still has its red granite chimney, and the entire building is in red gneiss, probably quarried locally, with Cobo granite for quoins, chimneys and the dressed stonework of the arch.

It is now joined to the 19th-century house by a covered way over the old track shown in the map, similar to that at Le Gron Farm (435) whose loft floor

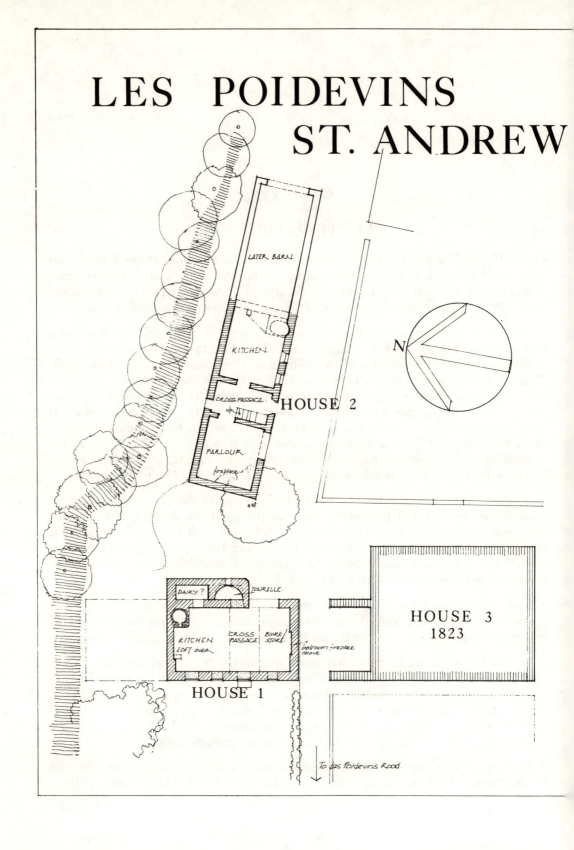

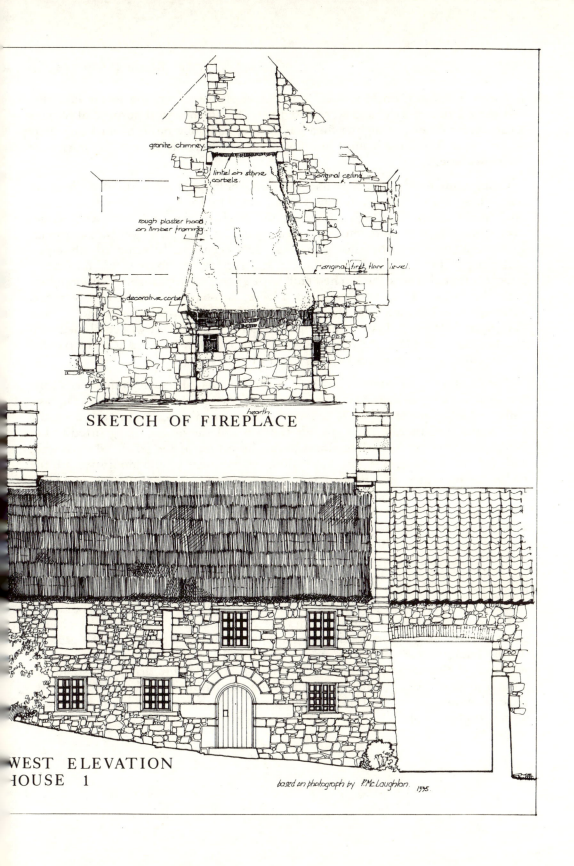

SKETCH OF FIREPLACE

WEST ELEVATION
HOUSE 1

is shown in Illustration 38). Such farm entrances were common in the late 18th and early 19th century, and were often used for the practical purpose of parking a cart under cover overnight, when haymaking had gone on until dusk and there was no time to unload it until morning. This covered way is contemporary with the new house.

Going underneath it, and behind the 16th-century building just described, we reach the other old house, its length emphasised by the low walls front and back, only about eleven feet high. However, the pitch of the roof was steep, rather over 45deg., so that there must have been space for large lofts over the bedrooms. Unfortunately, the right-hand gable wall has been totally removed, though a hollowing of the front wall inside, where the angle of the house would have been, indicates that this was the kitchen end, with a furze-oven probably contemporary with the house. The other end had a large, two-bay parlour with a fireplace. Although this has vanished, the flue shows clearly that the construction would have been wattle-and-daub on unshaped shoulders, and that it was combined with the bedroom fireplace above, using the same chimney-hood. An exact parallel was recently removed at Les Paysans Farm (323).

The chief point of interest, however, is the fact that although so much has gone the two stone cross-walls have survived, and an extremely unusual stone staircase. Only at Le Camptéhard (656), nearby, is there a similar flight. In each case, the solid stone construction rises towards the front of the house, being fitted at Les Poidevins between the parlour doorway in the centre of the left-hand cross-wall, and the front door. On the first floor, consequently, the doorways to the bedrooms on either side (or loft—it is impossible to tell) are at the extreme front rather than at the back, as was the standard pattern. No other houses with this arrangement have come to light, with or without stone stairs, so we must ascribe this peculiarity to the inventiveness of someone living in the Talbot valley in the second half of the 17th century. It is a pity that no more of this interesting building remains, but enough survives to give a good idea of the original arrangement. It is clear, from the two central doorways in the upper loft that it would have been very similar to 17th-century houses elsewhere, for instance at Les Vieilles Galliennes (353) or King's Mills' Villa (510), except that Les Poidevins was a poorer house, its walls on the line of an existing track, and its ground floor stepped down from kitchen to parlour, following the slope of the ground. At the back, it was very close indeed to the valley side, and there is no sign of windows in the back wall. In fact it shows a considerable decline in standards from 100 years before, when the earlier house alongside it was built. Both houses were abandoned last century in favour of the fine new building that now dominates the group.

Chapter XXXIII

LE MARAIS (493)

LE MARAIS, at Le Gélé in the Castel parish, and only 200 yards from the coast at Vazon, is a particularly interesting house because it preserves evidence of many changes of use, of extension and partial rebuilding. Like almost every island settlement it seems to have remained in continuous occupation since it was first built. In Guernsey, at any rate until the 19th century, a house was very rarely pulled down to build larger or more convenient accommodation. Either the family moved elsewhere to a larger house, or the old one was modified and altered to serve changing needs and fashions.

This house measures 42ft. by 15ft. and was a longhouse divided by a cross-passage with doors front and back. The front door arch, if there ever was one, has gone, but the one at the back is a flattened version of the Type 1 arch, with small stones of Cobo granite. Both cross-walls are original, the one on the kitchen side being carried right up to the apex of the roof. The other cross-wall, recessed to take the back door, rises only to the level of the eaves. The ground floor plan is thus the usual one of kitchen, cross-passage and byre, though the cross-passage is unusually wide—over nine feet.

As it was first designed, the two-bay byre at the eastern end housed the cattle and other farm animals and the two ventilation windows, or *pours* as they are known in France, have survived at the back, blocked, but clearly visible to the left of the arched doorway on either side of an inserted window. They are of different sizes and are at different heights. No doubt they would have been unglazed originally, fitted only with a couple of vertical bars like the similar one discovered in a byre wall at La Madeleine de Bas (306). There is now no sign of a drain having been provided: probably this finally disappeared when a skim of cement was given to the floor at the beginning of this century. Alternatively, drainage could have been through the cross-passage, since the site is virtually flat.

At the other end of the house was the kitchen—the chief living area of the family. It was provided with a fine fireplace in Cobo granite, with corbels of Type 3, and a wide chamfer of six inches. At the left is a handsome shelf, but there is now no sign of one the other side. This fireplace, so similar to the one at La Maison Tiphaine at Mont St. Michel (see p. 191), together with the early form of the arch, both point to a date no later than the mid-15th century. This is

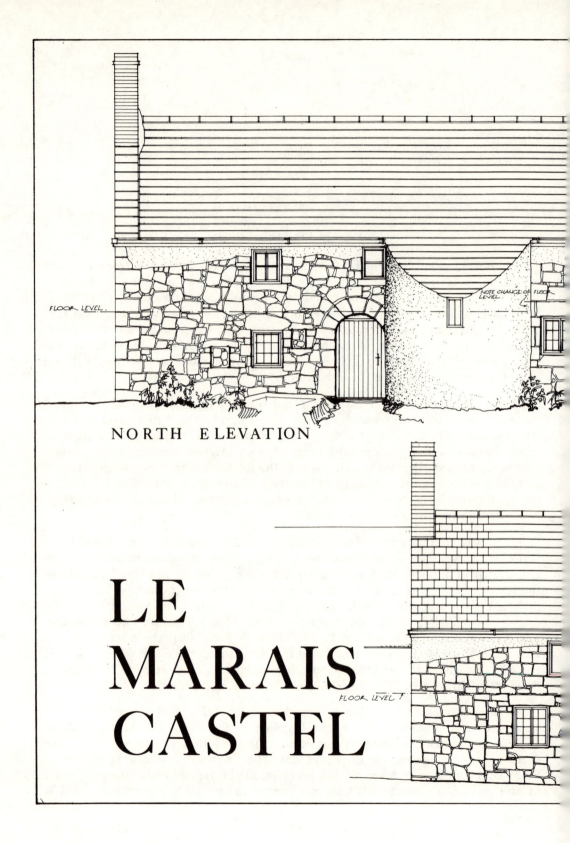

NORTH ELEVATION

LE MARAIS CASTEL

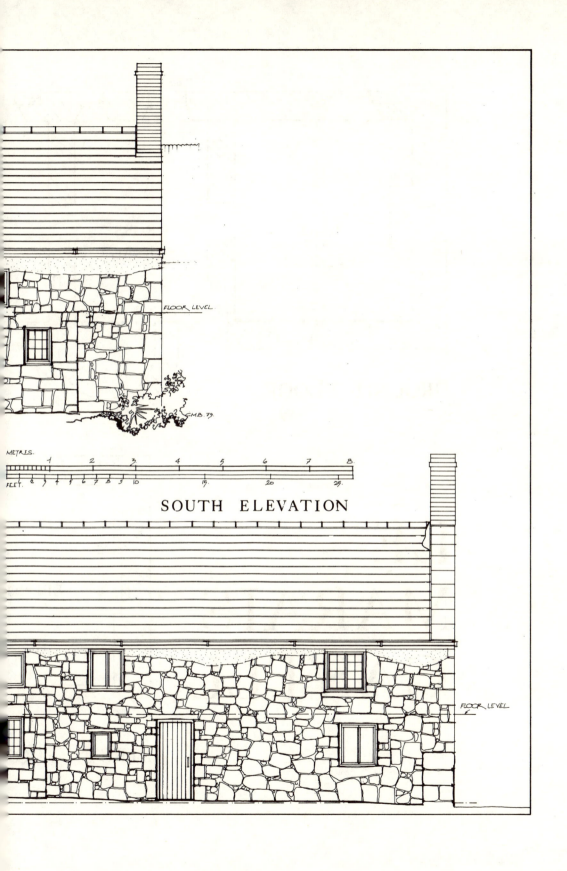

SOUTH ELEVATION

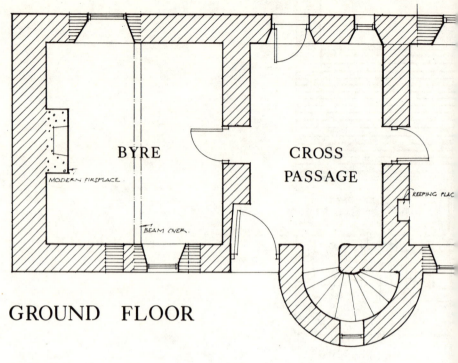

GROUND FLOOR

LE MARAIS CASTEL

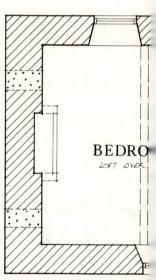

FIRST FLOOR

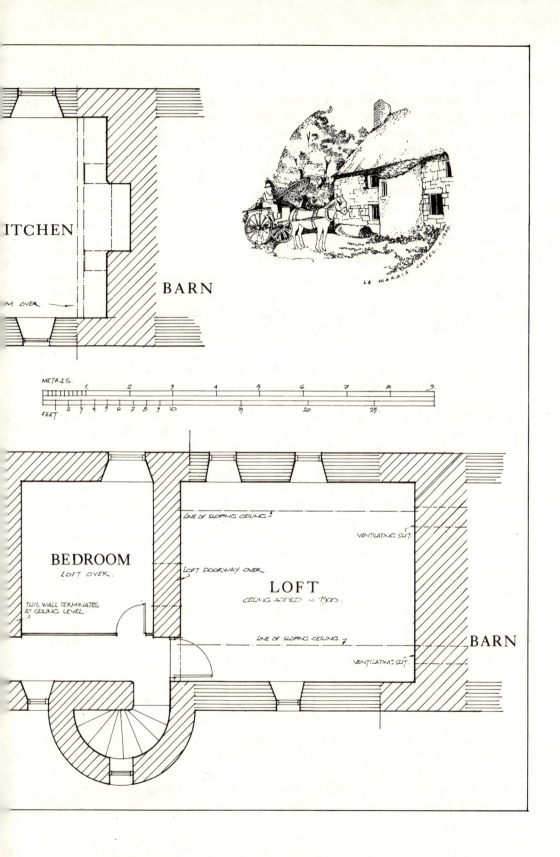

certainly the house mentioned in the earliest surviving Livres des Perchages of the Fief Le Comte, in 1470/71, at which time it belonged to Collas (or Nicholas) Le Beir, a family that held various other property at that time in the Castel parish. It remained in the family until the end of the 18th century.

On the first floor, the house was similarly divided into three compartments by the two cross-walls. The room over the byre was a bedroom of two bays, its pillar-type A fireplace flanked by two gable windows, now blocked. In both front and back walls the bedroom has one window opening, that at the back probably original, though its heavy transom and mullion are more likely to date from the early 17th century, when the front window was made larger as well.

Between the bedroom and loft, the upstairs passage window has also survived without enlargement, though again, the heavy transom lacks the sort of detail we find in 15th-century windows elsewhere, making it more likely that the frame is *c.* 1625. The room in the middle bay may have been an unheated bedroom, or an additional store.

Unusually, the tourelle opens into this upstairs passage and not beyond the cross-wall in the loft as is more common; a peculiarity of the house possible because of the great width of the ground-floor cross-passage. A somewhat similar plan at La Ruette (406) brought the top of the tourelle out opposite the end of the cross-wall: but here there was enough room to have had a door between the head of the stairs and the loft.

This area above the kitchen was the main loft, or *grenier,* as it would have been known in France. There was probably additional direct access from outside by means of a doorway in the back wall, now a window almost at floor level, higher here than at the other end of the house. Here, it was more important to have reasonable headroom in the kitchen below. At the other end the headroom was needed in the bedroom above, rather than the byre.

From the main loft, the upper loft over the two bedrooms was reached by ladder through a square opening in the main cross-wall. At the base of the opening there is a good piece of shale for the ladder to rest against on one side, whereas on the other, towards the upper loft, there are small stones only. Both main loft and upper loft were ventilated by two slits in each gable end, those for the main loft being lower than those for the upper.

Thus Le Marais, in its earliest form, was a typical longhouse—a compact unit where without any other permanent buildings, people, cattle and plenty of storage space could all be accommodated under one roof.

Considerable modification of the original plan seems to have taken place early in the 17th century. By then, a partial rebuilding had become necessary, and provision of more rooms for the family was required, as well as greater space for animals and probably also for other farming activities such as cider-making. So a long range of barns and stabling, about the same length as the house itself, was built against the kitchen end, using red stone very similar to that of the original work but more angular.

At the same time both front and back walls of the kitchen were taken down and rebuilt. It may be that they had developed a bulge, perhaps due to the weight of thatch or perhaps because the roof had deteriorated through lack of proper maintenance. But it is more probable that the opportunity was taken to put in larger and more regular window openings in the kitchen at the same time as putting the cows into the new byre at the side of the house.

Again, the new work is characterised by angular stone, and also by the long-and-short work of the window surrounds both in the house and the stable range. The byre now became an unheated store with proper windows, and no doubt, in the fullness of time, a parlour. The main loft was unchanged. Probably at this time the bénitier, if ever there was one, was discarded and a small window pierced through the front wall to the left of the door to give light to the cross-passage. By the 19th century part of this area had been partitioned off and the window gave light to a dairy.

At some time the front doorway has been altered and a very thin piece of granite used as a lintel. Since the back doorway, from what we know of other houses, was hardly likely to be arched unless the front one was of similar design, it is highly probable that the original arch was discarded and maybe the fireplace lintel was re-used as the head for the more fashionable doorway. The bedroom fireplace has, at any rate, lost its lintel, and the use of such a narrow stone from any other source would be highly unusual.

Later additions have not greatly changed the character of Le Marais. At about the turn of the last century, the main loft, above the kitchen, was lined with matchboarding, ceiled at the height of the original collar of the roof truss (higher at this end as was usual in lofts) and made into a bedroom. Elsewhere, partitions and floors were renewed, though the principal beams of kitchen, byre and original bedrooms are 15th-century. They are about six feet apart and average 12in. square. Projecting stones about a foot below the ceiling in the gable-end of the byre, in the cross-passage, and on the bedroom side of the main cross-wall, show where additional timbers once supported the floor-joists above. All floor joists are now 19th-century, notched into the 15th-century timbers.

A light corrugated-iron roof, supported on modern rafters, now encloses the old trusses, simple trunks of elm, halved and crossed at the top to take the roof tree. These trusses, all in a very poor condition, supported a thatched roof until the 1930s. Elsewhere, although walls have been patched and slightly raised to strengthen up the roof line when the thatch came off, no great changes have been carried out.

Outside, the tourelle, which characteristically completely obscures the jambs of the arch door, has been pebbledashed. The building line between 15th- and

17th-century work is very clear, both on the back and front walls. The great scrubbing stone outside the back door should also be noticed.

Since this was written, Le Marais has been sold and completely renovated. New roof timbers and a slate roof have made it sound for another few generations. In the course of the work, an évier came to light in the back wall of the kitchen, and the upstairs fireplace has been removed, but will be made good use of elsewhere. The large fireplace downstairs has been cleaned and properly exposed, and the gable windows have been opened out in the bedrooms. Le Marais can now confidently be expected ro reach its sixth century of existence.

Chapter XXXIV

THE GUERNSEY SAVINGS BANK (756)

THERE ARE VERY FEW Town properties left which date from before 1650. For although the prosperity of St. Peter Port produced wealth to build many fine houses from at least the 14th century onwards, the improvements of one generation removed what another had considered fashionable. The building we now know as The Guernsey Savings Bank, though much older than 1650, has also seen many changes. Its original layout is partly conjectural, at least until another major alteration with the next 12 months (1980/81) allows us an opportunity to investigate as fully as possible what lies behind panelling and plaster. In this book we show it as it was until the 19th century, and as it will be again when renovations are completed.

As medieval towns became more and more congested, so it became more difficult and at the same time more desirable to have a frontage on a street. The long, narrow burgage strips of the English burghs and the French villes, held in feudal times in connection with socage, produced a pattern of urban development that was to determine the layout of towns until the present day. In Guernsey, socage, or the duty of holding a local court, was probably compounded with other dues and obligations. However, the land in the centre of St. Peter Port was split up in the same way, with long, narrow strips running back from the road. The main Guernsey Savings Bank building combines two of these land-holdings. One fronted La Grande Rue (High Street), the other Berthelot Street. The two are therefore at right-angles to each other, and since the combined holding dates back at least to the 16th century, it is probable that the present building replaces two entirely separate medieval houses. The two holdings are therefore labelled 'House 1' and 'House 2' on the plan.

Both parts of the combined structure have extensive cellarage, extending not only the full depth of the site, but also underneath Berthelot Street as far as the property on the other side of the road. However, the cellars of House 1 are stone-vaulted, while those of House 2 are brick and give the impression of being much later, probably 19th-century. The land rises very steeply, with ground level in High Street for House 1 being basement level in Berthelot Street for House 2. The brick vault in Berthelot Street is consequently two floors below ground level there, which would have been a highly unusual arrangement in medieval or Elizabethan times, though common enough in St. Peter Port from

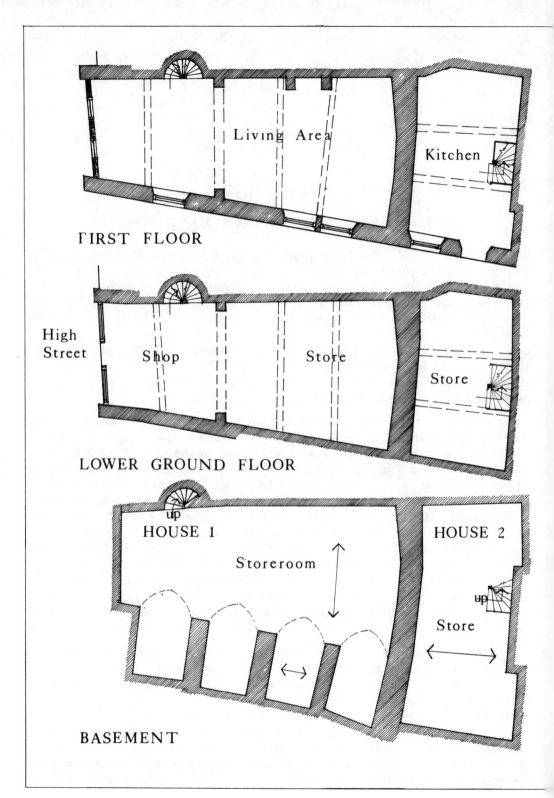

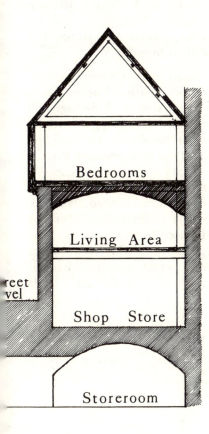

TYPICAL SECTION

Sketch looking down High Street

GUERNSEY SAVINGS BANK
ST PETER PORT

about 1750 onwards, when tier upon tier of vaults, basements, stores and warehouses climbed the cliff from the Harbour to the High Street.

In Southampton, the English port chiefly associated with Channel Islands trade in historical times, it was only in the 13th-and 14th-century houses that a basement or undercroft was sunk at all. Fifteenth-century town buildings had cellarage at ground level. If this was also the practice in Guernsey, the stone-vaulted undercroft of House 1 might be considered as pre-dating the building we see from ground level upwards. But we must also take into account French parallels: and, although most 15th- and 16th-century town properties in Brittany are without basements, there are isolated examples that possess them. However, none of these known to the author is stone-vaulted. We may say tentatively, then, awaiting further evidence, that the undercroft of House 1 could be 14th-century or even earlier, whereas House 2 may have had no basement level at all originally, its foundations, in that case, being two storeys above those of its neighbour. Alternatively, House 2 might also have had an undercroft, at House 1's ground level, destroyed in order to sink the brick vault below it.

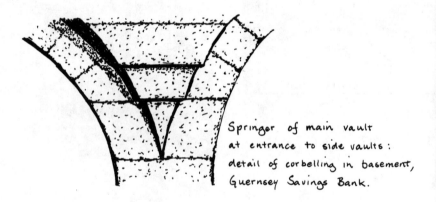

Springer of main vault at entrance to side vaults: detail of corbelling in basement, Guernsey Savings Bank.

As can be seen from the plan, the stone vault of House 1 is a barrel vault, running from front to back, with four subsidiary bays at right angles, under Berthelot Street. These also are barrel-vaulted, and run into the main vault below its apex, and without ribs. Where these smaller vaults spring from the little cross-walls that support them, the corbelling is in dressed stone, the detail very closely resembling 14th-century work in the Forest church, where the ribs of the simple vaulting rise from very similar corbels in the side walls.

From the undercroft of House 1, a newel staircase of stone runs up at least to ground floor level in the thickness of the south side wall. Whether this staircase continues further will not be known until after this book has gone to press. If it does not, and certainly it was not usual in Brittany to have the staircase so positioned in 15th-century houses, this would be additional evidence for an earlier dating of the undercroft.

THE GUERNSEY HOUSE

The newel staircase emerges at ground floor level in what would have been the second bay back from the frontage of a five-bay house. Maybe, if the undercroft is older than the present building, a four-bay house originally existed, in a line with the divisions between the subsidiary vaults. At any rate, thinking of House 1 as five-bay, internal buttresses at each side of the building divide the second bay, with its staircase, from the third. This buttress is carried up the walls for two storeys and then spans the entire house in a wide, segmental arch, the intention presumably being to strengthen and brace the building by this means.

We are dealing with a corner site, where it was easy enough to provide windows for every part of the house. But elsewhere in towns, the great problem was to give adequate light to a building which had to run back from the road a considerable way merely because that road frontage was so narrow. Sometimes an alley, or venelle, between properties allowed light to filter through side windows. At 26 Cornet Street (726), there was not even an alley, only a few inches separating it from the Elizabethan house now demolished (see Illustration 37), yet side windows were put in so that every bit of light could be obtained. Where properties shared a party wall the problem, of course, was even more acute. The solution universally adopted was to built only these side walls of stone, leaving front and back gable ends open, so that a half-timbered construction could include an unbroken range of windows from side to side. Fifteenth-century examples remaining in Rennes, Dinan and Tréguier are numerous enough, and 17th-century prints of St. Peter Port show that it was also the rule here. Although it occupied a corner site, House 1 followed this pattern, as did House 2.

It is difficult to know how old the combined properties are above ground level. If the undercroft of House 1 is early, possibly 14th-century, did the building above it stand until it was re-fashioned in the 16th century, or was it rebuilt, as were so many island houses, in the 15th century? Certainly the moulding of the plinth stepping up the Berthelot Street side bears an uncanny resemblance to the plinth on the west end of the Town Church—late 15th-century work. On the other hand in the Guille-Allès Library there is a *sablière* from the Savings Bank, that is, one of the beams running across the frontage between the side walls to support the overhanging or jettied first floor. This *sablière* bears the inscription 'La Paix de Dieu soit ceans, fait le 18 Octobre 1578 de par André Monamy'. This seems clear enough. But look at the corbelling of those side walls. They are carved with the merchants' marks of John and Rachel Briard who bought the house in 1594 from the young heiress of Gille de St. Germain (see Illustrations 87 and 88). They are raised inscriptions, looking integral with the building, as do both the dates in the walling along Berthelot Street— 1606 and 1616. Yet we know the house was here in 1578, unless the *sablière* was built in from elsewhere, which is unthinkable, for there was no reason to put a spurious inscription on a new house. Another authority says the house was constructed in 1569. If all these later dates were added to an existing building so convincingly that they now look original, it is quite possible that the present side walls are indeed 15th-century; that the timber façade was renewed, possibly to provide larger windows, by André Monamy in 1578; and that it was again altered by Jean Briard at the end of the century.

It seems almost certain, in fact, that it was Briard who merged both houses into one property, carrying the earlier plinth around a new doorway to the enlarged house in the Berthelot Street frontage of the former House 2. A 15th-century plinth would not have framed a square doorway as this does. It would have run into the side of an arched entrance. The very fact that the Berthelot Street doorway is square-headed suggests Renaissance influence and a date not much before 1600. We may infer, then, that Briard undertook extensive alterations soon after he bought the property, probably using the proceeds of his privateering, for he was issued with one of the earliest Letters of Marque, to intercept enemy vessels and capture them for the Queen, in 1598.

He presumably cut back the earliest corbels of the house on the High Street frontage so as to bear his merchant's mark. Also, he probably rebuilt the third floor (taken down in the 19th century and now about to be replaced). The great corbels supporting the jetty, both at the High Street angle and along Berthelot Street, bear some resemblance to the corbels in the Brock chapel of the Town Church formerly supporting the Ecclesiastical Court—another pointer to a 15th-century date for the side walls. It seems as though this third floor, supported on the corbels and above the top of the stone walls with their arch bridging across between them, must always have been completely of timber, for when John Briard rebuilt it, his neighbours in Berthelot Street, the de Beauvoirs, complained that he had built his house so far out that they could no longer see the harbour from their window, no doubt a serious consideration when so much island wealth was tied up in shipping. The result of this complaint was a 'vue de justice' by the court in 1616, when he was made to take the house back six inches. This could only have referred to the jettied top floor, since the position of the main side walls would have been fixed by the thoroughfares of High Street and Berthelot Street. We must therefore imagine that by 1616, the house was three-storeyed, with attics and undercroft, stretching back five bays from the High Street and including the three-bay property in Berthelot Street behind it. The ground floor and first floor would have been stone-built with timber front, and the second floor entirely of timber.

Unfortunately, of the internal arrangements in this house we at present know virtually nothing. Whatever divisions there were between rooms have long been entirely removed, and all staircases altered. From the position of Jean Briard's grand entrance in Berthelot Street, giving access to the house-part at what would be first-floor level on the High Street side, it is possible to deduce that the ground floor, approached from the High Street, and the vaulted undercroft below, were given over to a shop-cum-warehouse. At Southampton, medieval buildings had two entrances in their front gables: one going up a few steps to a small, two-bay shop on the ground floor; and one leading down to a large shop, or a sort of wholesale warehouse in the undercroft. There is no real indication that two such shops ever existed here, or in remaining buildings in Breton towns. It is more likely that the shop consisted either of the whole ground floor and the cellarage below, or at least the front two bays of the ground floor and the cellarage, approached by the newel staircase of the second bay. The position of the internal buttressing might in that case also have marked a division between shop and house part in the three bays behind. But this we shall not find out, if ever we do, until there is a chance to examine the side walls in due course.

At 5 Berthelot Street (808), just round the corner, it is clear that the living quarters were on the first floor, with a shop below, because the évier is upstairs to the left of the fireplace, in the back bay. In the Savings Bank building in House 1, there appears to be a flue of some sort in the middle bay, but until positions of évier and fireplaces are known, we can speculate no further. However, is is probably safe to assume that ground floor and cellarage were in part or whole, a shop; that the first floor, approached separately from Berthelot Street, was the chief living area; and that the jettied upper floor contained bedrooms. It will be particularly interesting to see if it is possible to learn the function of the three bays of House 2, in Jean Briard's combined structure. Upstairs, no doubt, they would have given space for extra bedrooms: but what was below?

Chapter XXXV

LES GRANGES DE BEAUVOIR MANOR (834)

THE LARGE, three-storeyed house at Les Granges de Beauvoir Manor was almost certainly built soon after 1603, when James de Beauvoir bought the estate from Louis de Vic. His home remains our most complete example of early 17th-century architecture, and one of the most impressive houses in the island.

But the estate already possessed at least one dwelling house before James de Beauvoir bought it. From an earlier, 15th-century building came the arch in the walling opposite the front of the later house. It is a Type 1 arch and is probably integral with the wall in which it now stands. There are faint traces of other openings in this wall, but although roofed 100 years ago, it has become so ruinous that it is impossible to make out its original form. It has also probably been reduced in width in order to support the gable-end of a greenhouse. Nearby, another arch now forms a back entrance to the courtyard, and the lintel behind it is from a fireplace, probably once in the main house. Fragments of another arch lie in the grounds, and nearby, two window-sills with cable-mould are built into some walling, together with parts of a fireplace and a lintel with the James de Beauvoir merchant's mark (see Fig. 46). It is possible that some of these bits and pieces came from a third building, closing the courtyard on the western side. But little of this now remains, and what does, seems more closely associated with the new house of James de Beauvoir.

The foundations of his new house and the very bottom of the eastern gable end, now masked by steps, show distinct signs of being older than the rest of the structure, and on the first floor at this end the fireplace, as will be noted in due course, is very different from all the others and dates from the 15th century. It is thus possible that when James de Beauvoir bought the property in 1603, he incorporated into his new house some of the walling and one superb fireplace, from an older building. Certainly the type 1 arch already noted seems unworthy of the de Vics and the de la Courts who owned Les Granges in the 15th and 16th centuries. It might have been merely a barn entrance, while their house stood opposite. For while the walling on the east of the courtyard may have been from another house, the 1787 map marks no building here, and what is left is insufficient to assist us further.

LES GRANGES DE BEAUVOIR MANOR

We can say with a reasonable degree of certainty that the present house dates from just after 1603, because the front arch, a 'Guernsey' Type 5 doorway in grey stone, is one of those we have met elsewhere, from the 1580–1620 period: and the fireplaces, woodwork and most of all the chamfered windows, all belong to the years around the turn of the 16th and 17th centuries. Moreover, there is a considerable similarity between details here and in what we know of other de Beauvoir houses in the 17th century, especially the Ville-au-Roi Manor.

Les Granges de Beauvoir Manor is a remarkable house, the earliest three-storey home to be built in the countryside, as it was then. Indeed, very few three-storey houses appeared afterwards until 1800. The layout is as follows: on the ground floor, 55ft. 6in. long by 23ft. 6in. wide (outside measurements), there is a two-bay kitchen to the left and a two-bay store to the right. The central bay is a cross-passage, 10ft. 6in. across, with a round-headed bénitier in the back wall. To the left of the bénitier a doorway leads into the largest tourelle in the island. The back door of the house did not open out of the cross-passage, but as at a few other houses (see p. 204), from the tourelle itself, in this case, after going up the staircase six steps. This doorway is now blocked. Alongside it, to the left, a peephole 8in. square looks along the back wall of the house to the main gateway.

The tourelle is 10ft. 6in. across, as wide as the cross-passage. After reaching ground level at the back, the stone steps become wooden treads, rising around a great newel post, probably a ship's mast, 9in. in diameter. It was probably the first tourelle staircase in Guernsey to be built in this way, perhaps being inspired by similar turret stairs in Normandy, and as the newel post is positioned well beyond the line of the back wall, it projects behind the house much more than is usual. This expedient allowed the width of each step to be greater, as the staircase could turn through more than 180deg. of a circle between each floor.

The first floor contained the main rooms of the house: a three-bay living-room at the western end, above the kitchen and cross-passage; parlour and service-room, each of one bay, above the store. Each gable end had a large fireplace.

On the next floor, there were three bedrooms, two of them heated. These were the two-bay ones at the gable-ends. Between them was a single-bay room.

The ceiling of this second floor was very curious. The two central trusses of the roof used the ceiling beams as tie-beams in the usual way: one was therefore at each side of the central bedroom, whose ceiling had intermediate joists running between them at the level of the eaves. But in the two larger rooms, the roof-trusses only had collars and upper king-posts: and the bedroom ceilings were at the level of the collar.

This strange arrangement allowed the tourelle staircase to continue above roof level, giving access to another single-bay room in the loft, over the central bedroom. Above the others, there are just shallow lofts. The roof timbers, like all the beams and joists, are 375 years old, and in perfect condition.

LES GRANGES
DE BEAUVOIR MANOR

ST. PETER PORT

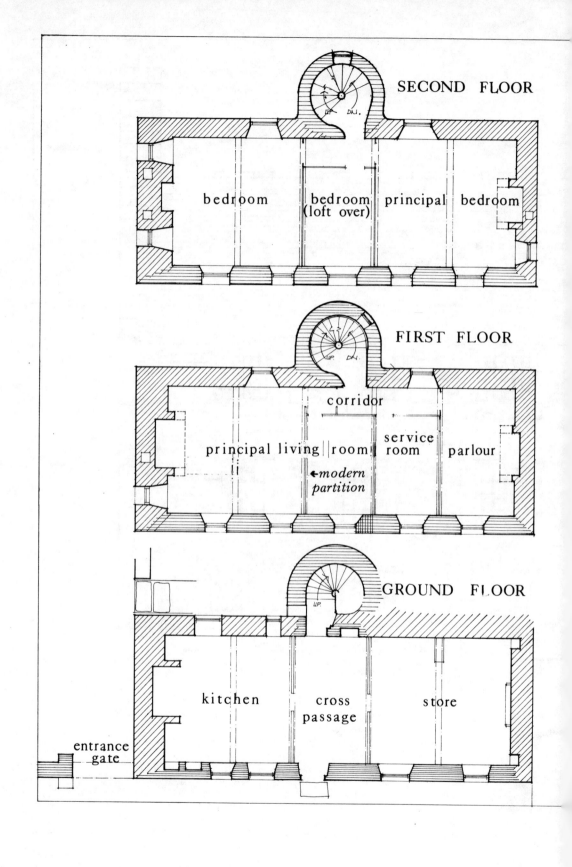

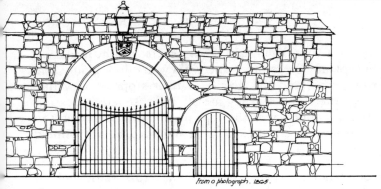

Gateway to the Rohais

LES GRANGES DE BEAUVOIR MANOR

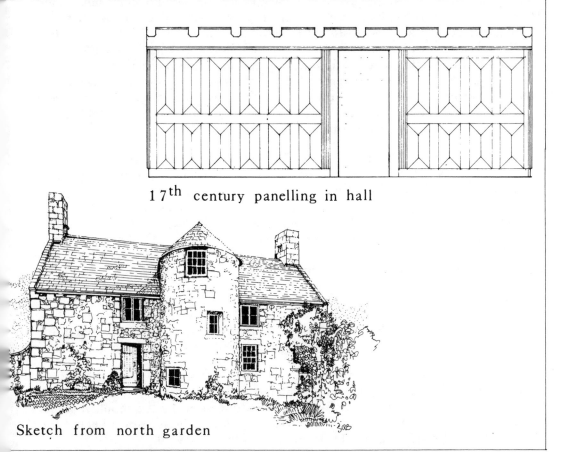

17th century panelling in hall

Sketch from north garden

The woodwork is, in fact, of a very high quality everywhere. All the joists and beams have mouldings, except in the store, where they are left plain. The mouldings of the main cross-beams, and the details of their stops, is very fine indeed, equalled in very few other houses. They are all 10-in. square in section and the joists 5in., the latter running across the tops of the beams, though the space between them seems to have been masked by a moulded board forming a fillet.

The panelling, too, is outstanding. There are no stone cross-walls, and all partitions are therefore of wood, divided horizontally and vertically into panels 34in. deep and 10in. across, all with raised grounds. The horizontal bars are 5in. wide with simple stopped chamfers, whereas the vertical bars are 4in. across, and moulded. All the timber appears to be oak.

The window openings were all designed originally for four-light or six-light frames, none of which remain, except for one four-light window in the living-room gable. All the window openings of the façade had chamfered sides and lintels, with chamfer stops just above the sill. On the ground floor and second floor, the window-openings have remained their original size, but on the first floor they seem to have been altered towards the end of the 18th century, when guillotine sashes, with heavy glazing bars, were inserted. This work necessitated the narrowing of the central window, which had formerly been the same size as the one above it, and the removal of all the sills. It is more than likely that the two cable-moulded sills, now built into a wall behind the house, were originally part of these first-floor windows: they exactly match the cable mould of the *croissettes* at the bottom of the gable coping.

The fireplaces are of great interest. The kitchen one is a Type 6 design with chamfered sides and a cable-mould on the corbel. That in the main living-room, which would no doubt have done duty as sitting- and dining-room, consists of a monolithic pillar with moulded angles, surmounted by a Type 6 corbel exactly the same as in the kitchen below. It cannot be coincidental that the two sides of a similar, though smaller, pillar-type fireplace, now built into the wall behind Les Granges, is almost identical in design, except that the corbels, if they are contemporary, more resemble the capitals of a column.

This fireplace is almost certainly from the bedroom above the living-room. If that is so, the house would be the first in Guernsey to have had three flues inside one chimney-stack. One of these days, perhaps, someone will put his head over the top of the stack and see if there were three flues, or only two.

The bedroom at the eastern end of the house on the top floor was also a pillar-type, but here the pillar is chamfered instead of moulded and the two chamfers are carried round the corbel to be stopped below the shoulder-stone. Probably it is the lintel from this fireplace that is now upside-down behind the head of the arch that forms the back entrance of the courtyard.

All these fireplaces are in a very coarse, grey granite from a quarry somewhere in the north of the island. But although they are very fine, they cannot compare in magnificence with the fireplace in the bedroom over the store. That is a Type 1 design in Chausey stone and must be 15th-century (see p. 194). It is one of the noblest fireplaces in the island, an extra wide chamfer allowing the two curves on each corbel to be joined by two more curves forming a top chamfer stop. The outside edge of the jambs is framed by the unusual device of bringing the front surface forward to form a sort of shallow pilaster. What is this fireplace doing in a 17th-century house? Either it must have been saved or moved from an older building, or else this gable end must itself be older. However, although it could be argued that the store below and the heated room above are the remains of an earlier house of longhouse type, this fireplace is larger than the usual bedroom fireplace. If it has been in an older house on the site, it must have been removed from the other end and rebuilt upstairs, while the gable end of the byre or store below was left untouched.

There is no way of proving this theory. It is interesting to note, however, that although the fireplace was preserved, it was obviously considered somewhat unfashionable and banished to a single-bay room, whereas the new ones were all put into two-bay rooms.

Modifications of the house have been very few. The insertion of 18th-century window sashes has been mentioned. It may be that the presence of a little post-and-panel partitioning of about 1700, and even later tongued and grooved woodwork along the first-floor corridor may indicate that there was originally no passage. The door from the tourelle would then have opened immediately into the end of the living-room, and access to the other two rooms would have been only by passing from room to room. However, in view of the fact that La Rocque Balan (1007) and La Maison de Haut (240) have early 17th-century panelling along the bedroom passage, it is unlikely that this house was without such an amenity.

Les Granges de Beauvoir Manor was, in addition to being the splendid residence of one of the leading families during Stuart times, a semi-fortified house, similar in that respect to La Haye du Puits (582) and Le Tertre (1026). A great gate at the western gable closed the paved courtyard. This arched gateway still exists, with a pigeonnier above it, and the remains of a porter's room alongside, as at La Haye du Puits. A peephole, 24in. across and 19in. deep, narrowing to a slit, 4in. across and 14in. deep, allowed him to challenge any visitors before opening the gates. At Le Tertre, the slit was in a tower that covered the entrance as well as the road at right-angles (see Illustration 22). Whether an equivalent tower ever existed here is doubtful.

Towards the end of the 17th century, the entrance to the long driveway to the house was also dignified by the addition of the handsome double arch. Its proportions have been somewhat spoilt by raising the road level outside by one foot (the sketch shows it last century, before this happened). Guernsey seems to have very few of these arches, unlike Jersey and parts of Normandy and Brittany, where they are very popular. This one is adorned with a hollow chamfer, a roll-mould around its inner and outer edges, and is probably a little earlier than the arch now at the entrance to the Town Hospital. On the keystone over the larger arch are the de Beauvoir arms. Although the estate has long been split up, this double arch is still at the top of the wide drive shown on the Duke of Richmond's map. The broad tree-lined way leads down to the house itself, which now on the very edge of Town, miraculously preserves both its great dignity and its rural aspect.

Chapter XXXVI

LE GREE (125)

ONE OF NEARLY A SCORE of old buildings at La Villette in 1787, Le Grée dates from around 1600. It is one of the houses to have a 'Guernsey' Type 5 arch at the front, with provision for initials and date inside a raised shield on its keystone: which in this case were not added, unless weathering has since obliterated them. However, it was not unusual for shields to be left blank. The fireplace behind Le Vauquiédor Manor has two blank shields on its lintel, and the similar one outside Le Pouquelaye (574) also has one of its two shields empty. The general form of this arch closely resembles the one at La Falaise (144) with the inscription 'PLP 16(?)0', known to have come from another house at La Villette, burnt down in the 1930s. Unlike La Pompe (117) or La Seigneurie (367), Le Grée only has simple chamfer stops, but must clearly be of the same sort of period.

In plan, the house is five bays long, the byre or store being to the left of the cross-passage and the kitchen to the right. Other houses built at about this time show no signs of having been longhouses, and we can probably assume that by 1600 most new houses did not accommodate cattle. That would explain why the kitchen is at the lower end of the house and the store at the upper. A longhouse might be expected to put the kitchen at the upper end, if the site sloped, so that drainage from the byre did not run past it. The storeroom at Le Grée is not so wide as the kitchen, although it is spanned by a cross-beam, and it may be that the shorter bays here also indicate a transition from the house with a single-bay byre. In other respects, the longhouse plan is adhered to. The tourelle stairs, complete with arrowslit recently uncovered overlooking the back doorway, turn right towards the kitchen, and the main bedroom is over the store.

The kitchen fireplace has a carved corbel, but it is a fairly simple pattern with single curve—again typical of the period around 1600. It has been altered by the insertion of an 18th-century bread oven. At that time its stone lintel and stone hood were destroyed. The upstairs fireplace, though damaged, still keeps a stone hood.

Although the window openings were not treated with the same magnificence as La Pompe or even Le Chêne Cottage (154), the projecting sill, now broken, of

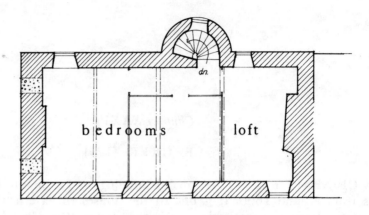

FIRST FLOOR

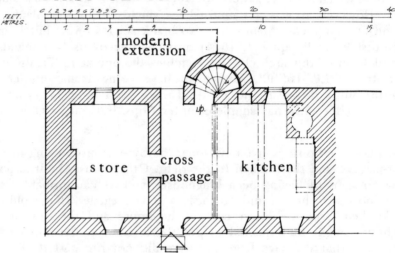

GROUND FLOOR

LE GRÉE

LA VILLETTE   ST. MARTIN

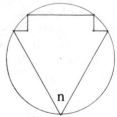

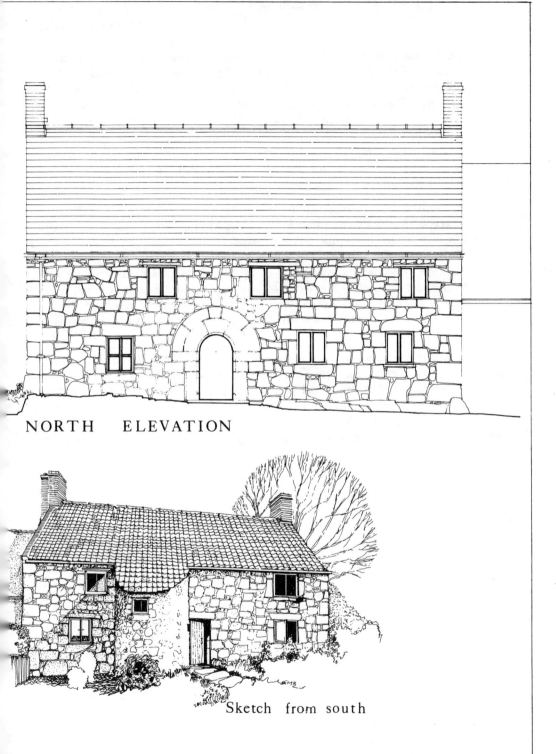

NORTH ELEVATION

Sketch from south

the bedroom window in the back wall of the house showed that this was a most important room. Next door, at La Villette (124), there are several unshaped window sills projecting in this way. Elsewhere in Le Grée, the long-and-short work, using vertically-placed stones as window jambs, is probably a reflection of the fine window-surrounds at Le Tourtel (129), just along the road—a house built slightly before 1580. All the window frames themselves have been changed, but fortunately the original façade remains unaltered. Le Grée escaped re-fronting, and so preserves rather more of the atmosphere of Elizabethan times than do some of its more well-to-do neighbours.

The roof timbers, too, are original: all of them collared trusses with upper kingposts, except that over the main loft, at the kitchen end of the house, where the truss has only a heavier collar lower down. This is a peculiarity of houses in which the loft above the kitchen was open to the roof, and where greater headroom and storage space was achieved by using the different sort of truss. It might also have been used to hoist heavy weights. It is rare to find a complete set of roof timbers, as we have here, and we can very easily imagine the thatch on the roof, because the steep pitch has been retained. The proportions of walls to roof is also still correct.

In fact, except for changed window-sashes, new floors, and timber partitions making extra bedrooms from the former loft, Le Grée remains very much as it was when built. The red stone, local Icart gneiss, with occasional lintels and arch of grey granite, has been pointed so that the exterior surface is fairly smooth, whereas originally the stonework would have looked rather more like that on the old photograph of Le Rocque Balan (see Illustration 11); but otherwise little else has changed.

Chapter XXXVII

LE CHENE COTTAGE (154)

THE 1787 MAP SHOWS this house as one of a small group of buildings at the head of a little valley going down to Petit Bôt Bay. Like almost every farm in Guernsey it was surrounded by cider apple orchards, the detached barn by the road probably being the *prinseur*.

Le Chêne Cottage probably dates from the last years of the 16th century, and is a five-bay, cross-passage house, on the longhouse plan, but without any indication of a byre. The two-bay room on the left, on the ground floor, was probably a store: the kitchen, another two-bay room on the right. The tourelle staircase led from the cross-passage, alongside the back door, and turned towards the kitchen, and as this house had two stone cross-walls, it leads to the three-bay loft above the kitchen. From this loft, a door in the cross-wall opens into a large, two-bay bedroom over the store. Basically, therefore, the plan was very similar to that of Le Marais (493).

However, this house was built more than 100 years after Le Marais, and is different in various details. It is constructed mostly in ashlars of various sizes, with more attention, as usual, paid to the front than to the back. There has been no re-fronting, so that all the window-openings of the façade are probably the original sizes, those upstairs having projecting sills. An attempt has been made to produce a cable-mould on these rough stones, but the decoration really amounts to no more than diagonal lines. From this detail, and others, it is probably fair to suggest that Le Chêne Cottage pre-dates Les Granges de Beauvoir Manor (834), with its properly-chamfered windows and cable-moulded sills, as well as Le Repos au Coin (56) and La Pompe (117), both from the first decade of the 17th century. Here only the six-light bedroom window has chamfered jambs.

The front arch, very nicely dressed, is a Type 4 one, with a very wide single order. The choice of this design rather than that of the 'Guernsey' arch which had become common by 1580, also suggests a 16th-century rather than a 17th-century date.

At the back of the house, too, the window sizes are original, except for a large window in the former store. Above, there is a small pigeonnier, two holes

LE CHÊNE COTTAGE FOREST

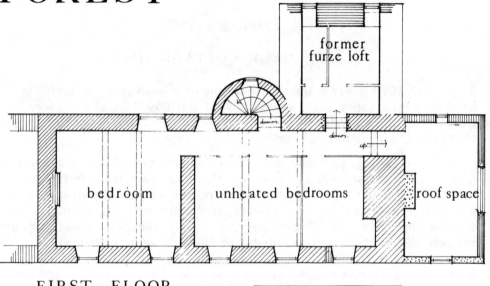

FIRST FLOOR

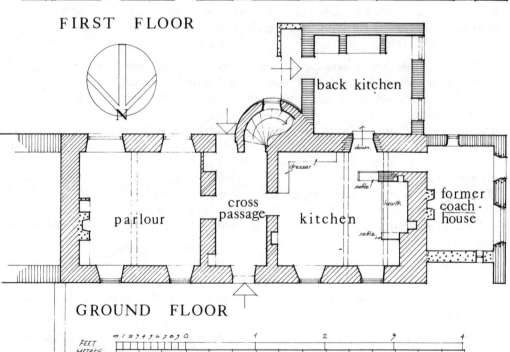

GROUND FLOOR

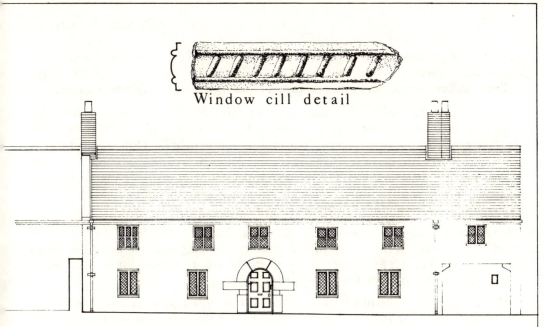

Window cill detail

North elevation

Kitchen fireplace

sharing a single flat stone as a perch. Many of the original window frames with leaded lights have survived, both at the back and the front, divided by heavy mullions and transoms: and indoors, too, a great deal of early woodwork remains.

The kitchen fireplace is a fine example of the Type 2 design with wide chamfers, the two chamfer stops continuing the curves of the corbels. This fireplace is all the more impressive because of the delightful 18th-century settles at either side, with quaintly curving ends. An old pork rack hangs from the ceiling joists in front of the hearth, and the kitchen—now a dining-room— has kept its original proportions. Throughout the house, the beams and joists are 16th-century, with simple mouldings and chamfers.

Particularly unusual, however, is the pillar between the back door and the tourelle doorway. It is monolithic and resembles the one at Les Merriennes Cottage (98). The stone steps of the staircase are also particularly well made from single blocks of stone forming a proper newel stair.

There have been singularly few alterations at this house. A furze oven has disturbed one side of the downstairs fireplace, and the bedroom one has vanished, but there seem to have been no other changes. This is the more remarkable in that the front yard was separated from the road in 1744 by a gateway topped by a flat lintel that may be from a fireplace. But in spite of this gesture towards gentility, the house remained otherwise untouched. In recent times, too, only the most necessary replacements and improvements have been put in hand with great care, so that we have a comparative rarity in Guernsey, a house dating in all essential features entirely from one period.

Chapter XXXVIII

LES CÂCHES (237)

THIS HOUSE is one of three *grandes maisons* surviving very close to each other. La Mare (239) and Les Raies de Haut (251) have features which show that they were once very similar to Les Câches, but have been altered far more drastically over the centuries. Les Câches, too, has seen several changes.

When it was built, it must have been one of the largest houses in the island, being eight bays long. Not only was it equipped with a pantry or buttery behind the kitchen, but the cross-passage, though perhaps not quite as wide as it might appear on the plan, which shows partitions repositioned after re-fronting, must have been more than 10ft. across. The original arched doorway remains at the back, its left jamb obscured by the tourelle, but in common with most houses of this pattern (see p. 52), this staircase opened out of the kitchen. With the back doorway in the extreme corner of the cross-passage, and the tourelle turning towards it, the tourelle doorway could not be alongside, but was in about the middle of the kitchen wall.

The kitchen fireplace was originally a really bold design, with Type 1 corbels of the early sort. Both this and the upstairs fireplace show 15th-century workmanship of the highest quality, and it is a pity that succeeding generations saw fit to destroy all but the jambs of the bedroom one. The jambs of both fireplaces were fashioned in ashlar about one foot high, again absolutely typical of the best 15th-century work on the island. In the kitchen, they were squared off on the left to form one side of a way through into the pantry. At Les Raies de Haut, this way through was lit by a window-opening almost exactly opposite the end of the fireplace cross-wall—a most unusual position. The placing of the doorway into the Victorian back-kitchen at Les Câches may well indicate that this house once had an identical window.

The two-bay pantry or buttery was unheated, as was the bedroom above it, whereas at La Houguette (528), a somewhat later house, that bedroom also had a fireplace. The byre, if that is what it was, at the other end of the house, was also unheated when it was first built, but the main bedroom was above it, its fireplace having a gable window on the right.

As for the arrangement of the rest of the first floor, it is impossible to determine, due to major alterations round about 1600. It may be that most of it

LES CACHES

RUE DES CACHES

ST. PIERRE DU BOIS

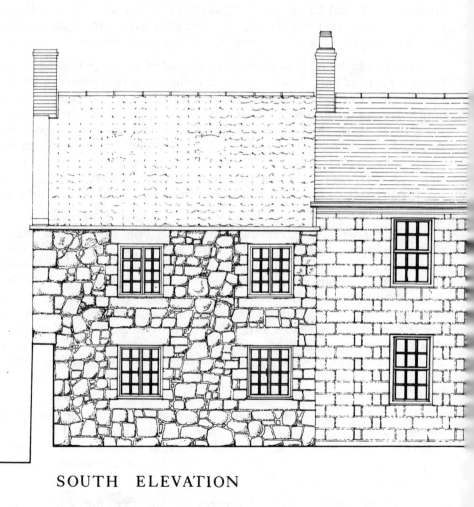

SOUTH ELEVATION

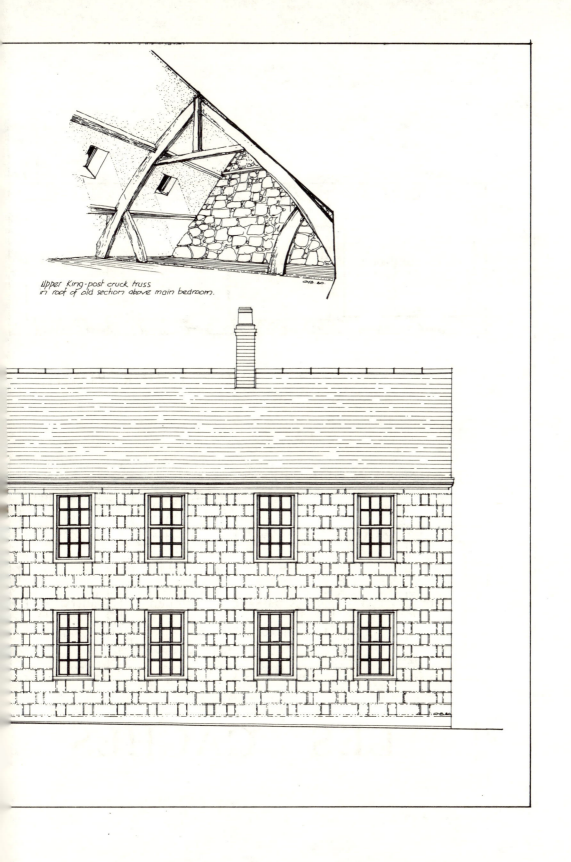

Upper King-post cruck truss in roof of old section above main bedroom.

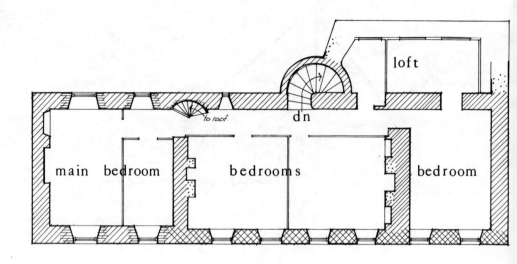

FIRST FLOOR PLAN

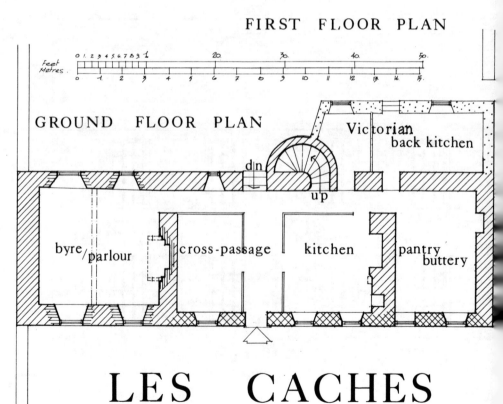

GROUND FLOOR PLAN

LES CACHES

sketch from garden

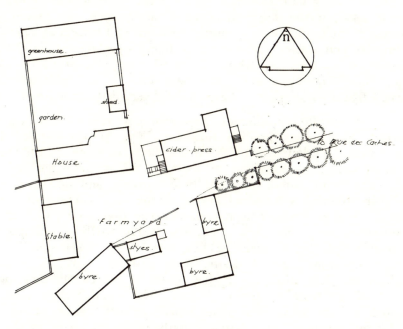

layout of farm buildings

RUE DES CACHES   ST. PIERRE DU BOIS

was a loft or *grenier,* a plan which was quite common in *petits manoirs* in Normandy and Brittany in the 15th and 16th centuries, in which case there would probably have been access to yet another loft over the bedroom by way of a ladder to a central opening in the cross-wall: a larger version of Le Marais (see Chapter XXXIII).

Two window-openings seem to have survived from this earliest phase: the one at the back of the original cross-passage, next to the back door; and the one in the back wall upstairs. The latter has also retained its original window frame, which is of such high quality that it is, in fact, difficult to think of this area as a *grenier.* At least it seems highly probable that there has always been partitioning to form a passage from the bedroom doorway to the top of the tourelle. This delightful window frame is of oak, its head a delicate cusped ogee (see Illustration 72). There is a similar one at La Rocque Balan (1007), a roughly contemporary house: but this is the finer of the two.

The form of these early fireplaces, the arch and the little window just described, suggests a date around 1425–1475 for the first building of Les Câches. We might also put the detached stable at about the same period, or shortly afterwards. In fact, the entire complex of barns and houses at Les Câches is of great interest and shows perhaps better than anywhere else in Guernsey, the appearance of a farmstead when the 1787 map was produced. All of the buildings shown then are still there, and apart from replacement of thatch everywhere by tiles or slates, they have changed very little since (see Illustration 1).

Round about 1600, considerable improvements were carried out, perhaps in two stages. In the first, another fireplace (Type 3) was inserted downstairs, making a heated parlour out of the former byre or store. In the second stage, larger windows, either four-light or six-light with mullions and transom, were put into the front and back walls both upstairs and downstairs. An early 17th-century frame has remained in one of the back windows of the bedroom, but elsewhere they have all been replaced. The first floor panelling also dates from this time: very fine work again, and similar to the contemporary woodwork with which Les Granges de Beauvoir Manor (834) was fitted out. In particular, the nine-panelled doors, with patterned grounds derived from earlier linenfold decoration, are the best in the island. One of these doors opens onto a small staircase to the roof-space. The wooden steps turn around a newel-post, and the outside wall of the house has been hollowed to accommodate them. By this ingenious use of space, vastly improved access to the lofts over the bedrooms became possible. Moreover, the construction is interesting, because it shows a type of staircase that was to be widely used in the island until about 1700.

The roof trusses themselves are older than this 17th-century facelift and are upper crucks springing from the inner faces of the walls, where they are slotted and pegged into the ceiling-beams below. They are also braced at the level of the lower purlins. There is a collar with kingpost, but with no sign of windbraces.

Greater use of the loft is possible with this arrangement, because the centre of the space is unencumbered with the large kingpost used in most roofs in Guernsey.

Apart from the replacement of some sashes, and the construction of various outbuildings, including a barn for cider-making (*le prinseur*) little seems to have been done at Les Câches for about 200 years. During that time it passed into the ownership of the Le Messurier family after a long occupation by the de Lisles. But in the 19th century a back kitchen was added, and part of the house was re-fronted. The resulting façade, though very handsome, obscures the true plan of the house because it left the parlour end untouched, so that it looks as though it had not been an original part of the building. On the other side, however, the pantry bays have been included in the face-lift, again rather giving the impression of a Victorian establishment with dower wing. The expedient of heightening front and back walls and slightly lessening the pitch of the roof also helps to create confusion. So many Guernsey houses which display little more than 19th-century propriety on the outside, are in fact much older structures brought up-to-date at that time. This partial re-fronting was not only practised at Les Câches, either. Another *grande maison* treated in exactly the same way is Le Tertre (1026), and Illustration 31 of Le Colombier (336) shows one of the innumerable homesteads where the house has been re-fronted but the barns left.

The impressive fragments of early masonry built into this house or standing behind it were almost certainly collected by a previous owner. There is no indication that they were once part of Les Câches itself, though all memory of their previous positions has been lost.

Chapter XXXIX

LES PREVOSTS (463)

THE SETTLEMENT of Les Prevosts, about a quarter of a mile east of St. Saviour's church, is an unusual group of houses in that it is sited on high ground, protected from the winds only by belts of trees, and not by the topography. It is also unusual because almost all of the buildings shown in the map 200 years ago are still there, and, moreover, few other houses have been built since. As a result, much of the 18th-century atmosphere has been kept. Even 19th-century improvements to the houses have not materially altered this.

From such a group of houses it is difficult to select one for special study. However, this one has some unusual features. In essence it is a five-bay, cross-passage house of the 15th century, probably then having a two-bay byre. There is one stone cross-wall on the kitchen side, from top to bottom of the house, and the tourelle stairs are arranged in the usual way, so that they turn towards the kitchen to emerge in the former loft beyond the cross-wall.

In the kitchen, the fireplace is a good example of a Type 3 design with chamfered sides, in red Cobo stone. It has been mutilated to the right by insertion of a furze oven, probably in the very early 18th century when the façade was re-fronted. The chamfered jambs of the old fireplace have been taken out and rebuilt as the bread oven's front angle.

Many of the original joists seem to have remained, both here and in other rooms, but they are all notched into the main beams, suggesting perhaps a re-flooring and reorganisation of the timbers during the 18th-century alterations.

The tourelle is extraordinary, neither semi-circular nor properly square. Inside, the stone steps are also arranged in a very odd way. At the top and bottom of the staircase they are only three feet wide, but half-way up, that is from front to back of the tourelle, they are 5ft. 4in. across. This irregularity produces a very rustic, though charming effect.

The first-floor arrangement probably consisted originally of a three-bay bedroom and a two-bay loft, as has remained in a neighbouring house, Les Belles (460). Like Le Marais (493—see Chapter XXXIII), the upper loft, over the bedroom, would then have been entered by ladder from the main loft. In fact, this house at Les Prevosts is very similar to Le Marais, its downstairs fireplace having been almost identical.

Here, too, as at Le Marais, there were several changes made at the beginning of the 17th century. At Les Prevosts, two extra bedrooms were created by partitioning off one bay on either side of the cross-wall, this being carried out in post-and-panel work with moulded edges, very similar to the door at Saint's Farm (83, see Illustration 82).

At the same time, a second downstairs fireplace was put into the former byre, to create a heated parlour. This is a very interesting piece of work, not that it is nearly such a good fireplace as the kitchen one, but that it is a transitional type very similar to those still to be seen at Wisteria (502), King's Mills' House (504) and King's Mills' Farm (506). The jambs are made up of a number of small stones, with a narrow chamfer, none too well carried out, and the corbels are omitted completely. The shoulders are comparatively insignificant, designed either to support an arch, as at King's Mills' Farm (see Illustration 48), or for a wooden lintel. The upstairs fireplace was altered at the same time, and closely resembles the one just described. Both fireplaces used the same chimney hood, presumably of wattle-and-daub, though now replaced by brick.

To the left of the house, a two-bay, two-storeyed byre may also date from this time, though subsequent alterations have made it difficult to date accurately and it may be later. Certainly the whole complex of outbuildings towards the road on the other side were present by 1787: they included a valet's quarters with fireplace, and post-and-panel partitioning of the early 18th century.

Soon after 1700, the front of the house was taken down and completely rebuilt in very attractive red Cobo granite, used more or less as ashlar. Grey granite quoins, lintels and sills were used for windows and door, but the older red ones were left at each gable end. The elevation clearly shows how much larger these older quoins are than the coursings of 18th-century stone in the new façade.

It is the use of the good red granite from Cobo for the walling, rather than local Icart gneiss, that makes this façade one of the most delightful in the island. As usual, only the house was re-fronted: the barns to left and right were not altered.

Indoors, a few improvements probably accompanied the changes outside. The partitioning along the upstairs passage seems to have been renewed at this time, since it is the later sort of post-and-panel work with pine planking of regular widths. Possibly the cross-beam in the main bedroom, and the ceiling joists were also replaced, the joists having a simple moulding at the edges. Downstairs, the bread oven was inserted, and the area above, one bay at that end of the first floor, became a furze loft, remaining open to the roof timbers above. The present curious ceiling there is very recent.

Until 1956 the façade retained its early 18th-century window-frames, four leaded lights separated by heavy mullion and transom, the lower two lights

LES PREVOSTS

ST. SAVIOUR

SOUTH ELEVATION

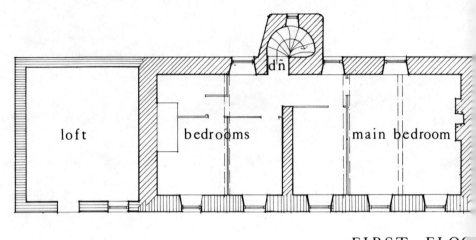

FIRST FLOOR

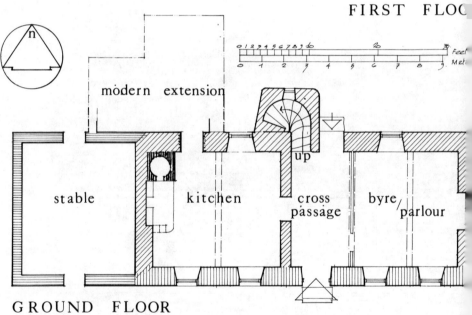

GROUND FLOOR

LES PREVOSTS

ST. SAVIOUR

Sketch from north
prior to modern extension

Tourelle stair

opening. Two vertical iron bars protected the window on the inside, these having all been replaced by six-light casement sashes. The older front door has survived.

We show the roof with thatch, as it was until early this century. Unfortunately, when it was removed, the old timbers also seem to have been taken down, and the present roof is a very lightweight structure of corrugated-iron sheeting on modern trusses. It is always difficult to know what materials should be chosen when a house is re-roofed, and when the present sheeting wears out, it is to be hoped that bright red modern pantiles will not be used as a replacement. They too often transform a pleasant country farmhouse into a rather ungainly extension of suburbia.

Chapter XL

LA SEIGNEURIE (367)

ON THE 1787 MAP, this house is almost the furthest west in the island, sheltered from the prevailing winds by its position under the western slope of a little valley that runs down to Rocquaine Bay. The only other houses of ancient origin nearby are the two at the head of this valley, at Pleinmont, and apart from a few fields around them, large unenclosed areas of common lands, or *camps,* stretch right up to the edge of the cliffs themselves.

The house faces south and is built with the right-hand or eastern gable on the roadside and the left-hand end, where it has been lengthened by the addition of a later store or stable, dug into the hillside. This is characteristic of many of the farmhouses and farm buildings of the period, especially in most of the steep-sided valleys leading down to Rocquaine Bay.

Although there seem to have been alterations carried out at least twice before the end of the 18th century, the house was originally designed on the five-bay, cross-passage pattern, somewhere around 1580–1600. The 'Guernsey' arch, a Type 5 one, with seven stones in the outer order, must just pre-date the final evolution of such arches to a form where there were only five stones. However, the extremely fine chamfer stops, and the matching ones indoors on the fireplace are almost identical to those at La Pompe (117), 1606; Le Fainel, near Le Vallon; and Les Mielles (1003); the last two arches being undated.

There seems to have been a stone cross-wall only on the kitchen side of the house. Here the fireplace is one of the small group of later Type 1 corbels, where the curves are not carried down to the top stopping of the chamfer. The fireplace at Les Grands Courtils (388) is similar to it, but this one is most closely connected with another one, now behind Le Vauquiédor Manor, where it forms an arch over a garden entrance. It is a pity that we do not know from whence it came, because like the one here in Torteval, the upper part of the corbel is carved with a design not found elsewhere. Either it is an imitation of the scrollwork of an Ionic column, which is possible at this date, showing Renaissance influence on traditional forms, though the chamfer stops below are derived from Gothic cusping: or else it is intended to be a pair of eyes with a beak between, in which case the reference may be rather to a defence against witchcraft, as are the acorns on other chamfer stops. Slight differences of detail are noticeable between this

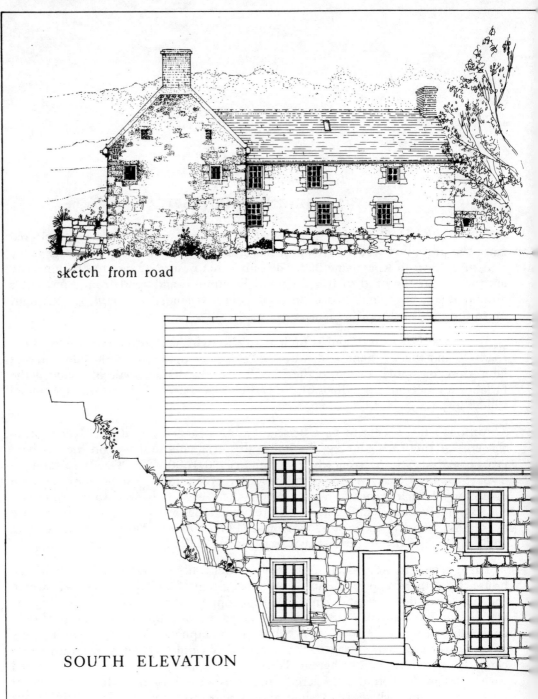

sketch from road

SOUTH ELEVATION

LA SEIGNEURIE

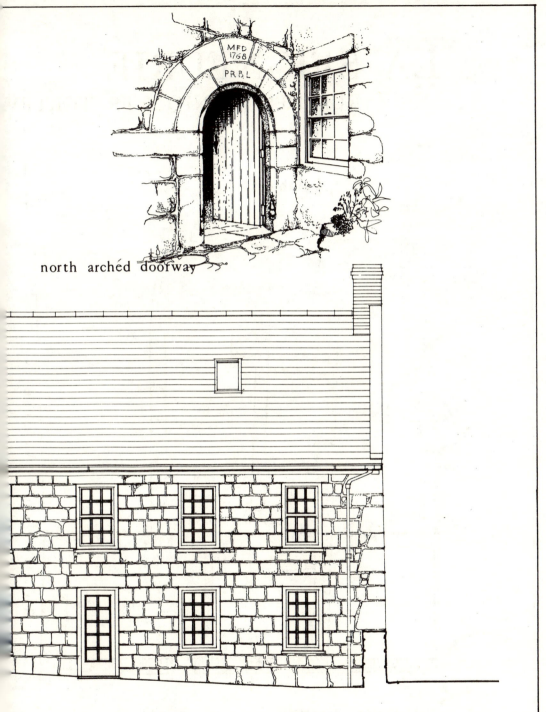

north arched doorway

RUE DES VALNIQUETS TORTEVAL

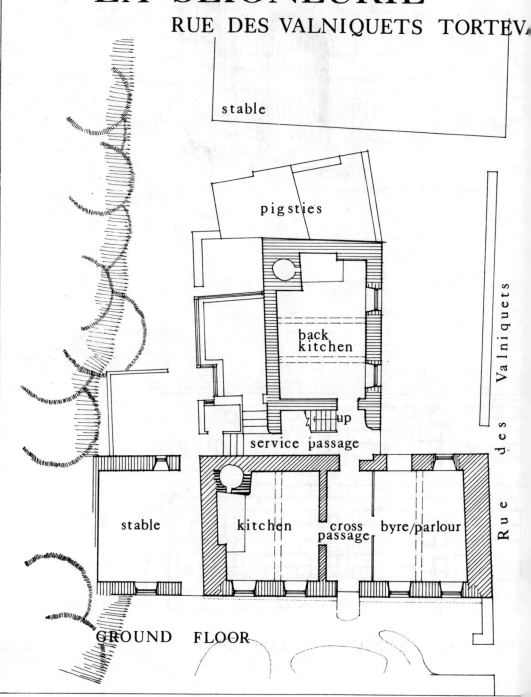

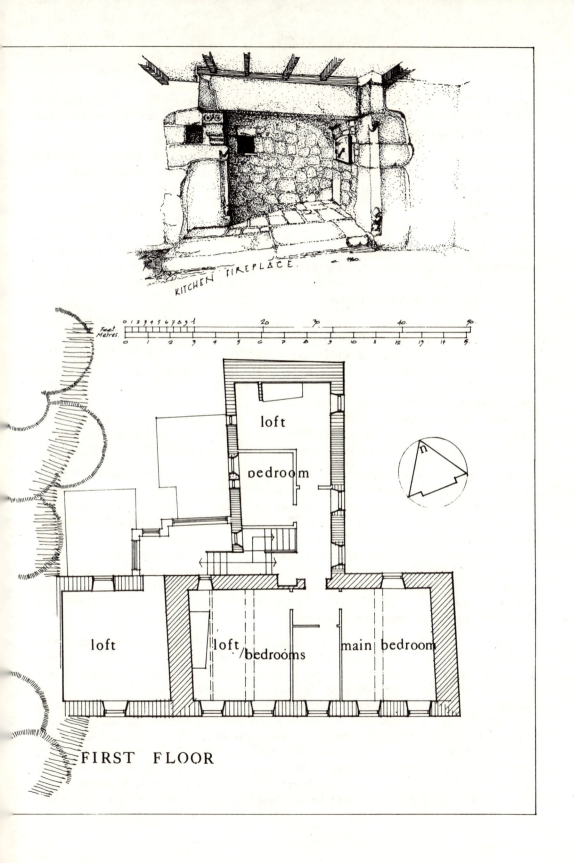

KITCHEN FIREPLACE

FIRST FLOOR

and the Vauquiédor fireplace, but in general they are so similar, with an identical corbel shape, that they must be by the same mason. Whoever he was, he seems to have been working in Guernsey between 1590 and 1620.

One of the corbels was removed during the building of the bread oven in the early 18th century and has been put into a low wall at the back of the house, with just the two 'eyes' showing. Whether the bedroom fireplace also had this design is impossible to say, because it has completely vanished, perhaps to Le Vauquiédor! Detailed measurement might establish if that one could have been an upstairs fireplace made for La Seigneurie. Originally both upstairs and downstairs fireplaces had stone chimney hoods. The one at the kitchen end is still complete, and it is easy to see where the bedroom one was bonded into the gable end. The two gable windows of the bedroom and the two ventilation slits of the loft above, remain unaltered.

By the 18th century La Seigneurie was in the possession of the Robilliard family, and it appears to have been Pierre Robilliard who greatly enlarged his home in 1768. The syllabic initialling 'PRBL' cut into the earlier arched door records this. He was seigneur of four small fiefs that date back to the 14th century, being formerly part of the Fief Canelly, forfeited at the political separation of Guernsey and Normandy in 1205. They were the Fiefs Thomas Blondel, Guillot Justise, Bouvée Duquemin and Cour Ricard. La Seigneurie therefore takes its name from the possession of these fiefs by this family from the 18th century until recent times. (*Transactions,* Société Guernesiaise 1960, p. 59.)

Pierre Robilliard's enlargement of his house is unusual in a number of ways. To begin with, the wing he built on is twice as long as usual—four bays instead of two. Moreover, it has its own cross-passage, a feature sometimes found in other houses, for instance, at St. Briocq (277), but here, separated from the three-bay back kitchen by a stone wall. The staircase is accommodated inside it, a highly unusual expedient if it had originally been in the cross-passage of the main house. We may suppose that it had not, and that La Seigneurie used to have a tourelle, with stairs turning to the left towards the kitchen. The alcove shown on the plan halfway along the old back wall upstairs is the sole reminder of this, being the tourelle's upper opening, now blocked.

Leaving the old gable wall standing, including all its quoin stones, Pierre Robilliard built a new façade of grey ashlar, almost certainly with windows nearly square. It is probable that these were again altered, the lintels raised and the sills removed, about 100 years later, perhaps when the thatch came off. But whereas in the course of most re-frontings the arched doorway was thrown out completely, at La Seigneurie it was retained and put round the back. Perhaps the old back doorway had been much simpler than the front one, as it had in the contemporary house (1608), now demolished, at Les Beaucamps de Bas. The front doorway from that house, since built into Le Pré de Merlin, near La Seigneurie, is a 'Guernsey' Type 5 pattern, whereas the back doorway was a Type 2. However that may have been, the old front doorway here now became the back door, opening not into the old cross-passage, but into the new parlour. Some adjustment on this side of the house must have been necessary while converting the old byre into a parlour, for the parlour is wider than the byre would have been, and the cross-passage in this older part of the house is consequently narrowed. So the arch is not exactly where the original back doorway would have been, but a little more towards the parlour gable.

Presumably the bread oven in the old kitchen was already in existence in 1762. It was then abandoned in favour of another one built into the new back kitchen, where a typical unshaped corbel supports a timber lintel on a skew, its other end inserted above the bread oven itself. It is likely that the small window, which the sketch shows on the right upstairs, indicates a furze loft above the last bay of the back kitchen remaining until recent times.

The 1762 work seems not to have been responsible for the two-bay stable, or store, built to the left of the original house into the bedrock of the valley side. This was probably added in the 19th century. But it is difficult to sort out exactly how old it is, and in view of the fact that the masonry is uncoursed, it may well be pre-1800.

The barn at right-angles to the road, below the house, is on the 1787 map, and probably dates back to the beginning of that century.

Chapter XLI

BORDEAUX HOUSE (984)

IN 1787, THE SETTLEMENT at Bordeaux Harbour consisted of a small group of houses on the southern side of marshy land stretching inland from the coast. Three of the houses still remain, as well as a few pieces of walling from a fourth building. Bordeaux Haven (982) probably dates from around 1600 and like Bordeaux House (984) is a *grande maison*. Armorel (983), which is between them, is interesting because its square tourelle and arched windows are so similar to those next door, in Bordeaux House, which is currently being renovated and extended. During this conversion, a number of very interesting features have come to light. The typical *grande maison* plan consists downstairs of a store on the left of the cross-passage, a kitchen on the right, and a buttery alongside, now forming part of a separate cottage. Upstairs the heated bedroom is over the store, with lofts over the kitchen and buttery and an upper loft over the bedroom.

The house seems to possess so many early features that it is a little surprising to find a store instead of a byre, especially when the neighbouring Bordeaux Haven retains its byre window. But the back window of this room in Bordeaux House is large, and spanned by a shallow segmental arch of small stones inside, as were all the other windows in the building. There is, therefore, no question of its being an insertion.

The cross-passage was comparatively narrow, entered at the front through a fine arch of local grey granite. It is a segmental arch, with the voussoirs incised to imitate the small rows of decorative stones found in other arches, as at La Grande Maison (945) or Le Tertre (1026). However, a flat stone lintel spans the back doorway, outside which is a stone seat, integral with the walling of the tourelle.

Although the tourelle is next to the back doorway, as in the usual longhouses, here, as in almost all of the other *grandes maisons,* it opens out of the kitchen. It is particularly well-built, being square on the outside and curved on the inside. Each step is a single block of stone, keyed in to form a newel, and the stone lintels above both top and bottom entrances to the staircase are nicely finished and chamfered, to give extra headroom. The small central window is also chamfered and rebated on the inside to hold either leaded lights or a shutter, probably the former.

The masonry of the tourelle entrance in the kitchen is particularly instructive, because the right-hand jamb also forms one side of a handsome bénitier, pointed and in the same sort of position as the one at La Maison Tiphaine at Mont St. Michel. The other side of the bénitier is similarly part of the splayed side of an arched window. It is therefore quite clear that all this must be an integral part of the original design and not an insertion from elsewhere. The stone chosen is the same as that of the front door arch.

Just as the bénitier is integral with the tourelle doorway and window, so the évier on the other side of the room is integral with one side of the front doorway. The arrangement is very similar to the one at The Elms (946, see Illustration 63), though this évier shows no signs of having a trough. Possibly there would have been the more usual shelf. Unfortunately, the left-hand side was destroyed by the insertion of a 19th-century window, which was presumably an enlargement of an older one, for both the évier and the window are spanned by a great relieving arch above, with its centre about two feet above loft floor level. No other similar relieving arch has yet come to light, and its presence underlines the superb construction of this house, where every detail shows a solidity and a degree of finish far above average.

This is true of the kitchen fireplace, even though it has been partly taken down in order to put in a bread oven on the left-hand side, where the old stone has been re-used for the front angle. But the right-hand side is complete and also forms an integral part of the corbelled doorway to the buttery. There is little doubt that this fireplace would once have looked very similar to that at La Maison Tiphaine (see p. 191), with a shelf on either side. One has vanished with the insertion of the oven, but the other survives, and has a head carved sideways where it meets the back wall. The embellishment of this shelf and that of the bedroom fireplace is without any parallel elsewhere in Guernsey and the fact that the head is shown on its side is interesting, suggesting that it was meant to be symbolic rather than decorative. It is clearly not intended to be appreciated as part of the design in the same way as the heads at Les Sages Villa (272) or Huriaux Place (403), where they are carved on the corbel and face the room.

The bedroom fireplace has both shelves intact. This time it is the one on the left which is carved in low relief in a truly surprising fashion, for the whole of its underside forms a phallus (see Illustration 9). In this case the symbolism is obvious. Is there, then, a similar sort of reference on the other fireplace? If so, it is certainly not as explicit. If the bedroom was connected with fertility, the kitchen was concerned with eating. We might suppose, therefore, that the downstairs carving was perhaps intended to emphasise not so much a head as a mouth. It would certainly be interesting to know whether parallels for these carvings exist elsewhere, and if some other explanation for them is more likely.

Almost every wall of the main rooms seems to have been designed as a single composition from end to end, the masonry being continuous. Thus the back wall in the kitchen, from left to right, contained tourelle doorway, bénitier and

LA MAISON BORDEAUX VALE

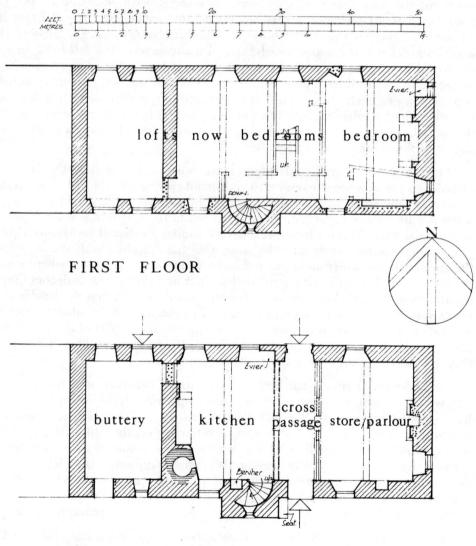

WEST WALL ground floor kitchen

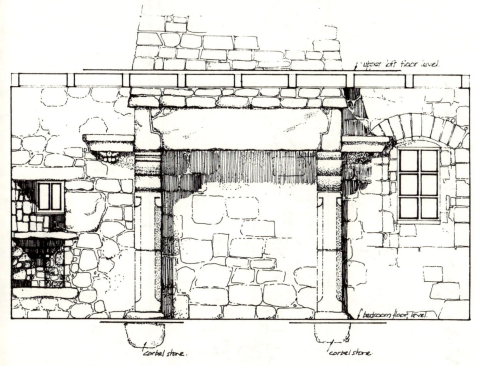

EAST WALL first floor bedroom

LA MAISON BORDEAUX
VALE

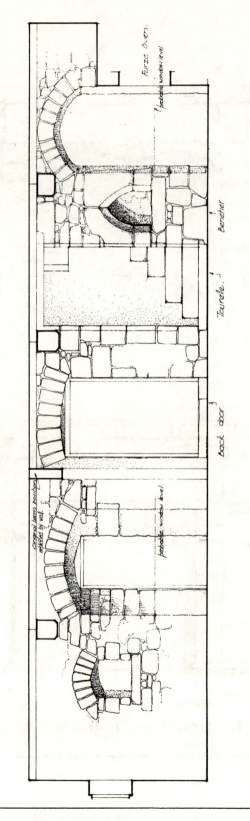

SOUTH WALL   ground floor

window; the gable wall probably had a keeping-place (now obscured by the bread oven), fireplace and buttery doorway; the front wall had a window and the *évier*. In the bedroom the gable wall was treated in the same way: the fine fireplace was flanked by an arched gable window to the right and a balancing évier to the left. This bedroom évier is a unique feature, and the design is also unique in having the upper compartment pierced to form a tiny window with a central bar. Why this should have been done is perplexing. No other évier in Guernsey, upstairs or downstairs, is lit in this way. It was not necessary to have a spy-hole to look towards the harbour, since the gable window on the other side of the fireplace fulfilled that function: and the room was very adequately lit at front and back with more arched windows. Indeed, the first-floor accommodation of this house was particularly well-lit and the ceilings uncommonly high. During renovation, the opportunity has been taken to raise the upstairs floor levels by six inches in order to gain more headroom below, and whereas such an adjustment is often ruinous to the proportions of a house, in this case the bedrooms still seem very high. Originally, the measurement from floor to ceiling was 8ft. 3in.

A more unfortunate alteration is the removal of the fine chimney hood over the kitchen fireplace. This was completely of stone and identical to the bedroom one which remains. Like the one at La Forge (924), it did not taper continuously to the apex of the gable, but sloped quickly back, so that the flue was in the thickness of the wall for almost all its length, and there was thus no chimney-breast, the walling of the flue being flush with the gable. The points where both chimney hoods met the gable were marked by yet more relieving arches.

The house was re-roofed *c.* 1900, and all the old timbers were removed, but elsewhere beams and ceiling joists are original and of black oak, except for the beam inserted to ceil the main loft, formerly open to the roof. That one is of greenheart and is almost as massive as the older ones, which are 12in. square, with a simple chamfer. All the joists are laid flat, resting on the beams rather than being notched in. It seems probable that the insertion of the bread oven with the granite surrounds to its doorway and the sub-division of the old two-bay loft into an extra bedroom and one-bay furze loft, was carried out well before 1700, thus accounting for the continuity of style between the original ceilings and the later work. As for the date of the house itself, the early fireplaces and bénitier taken together with the superb masonry and simple chamfering of the main arch, suggest that it is between 1450 and 1500—certainly no later. If that is right, the design of the arch shows that this form was popular for at least 100 years, since the similar one at Le Tertre cannot have been put into the early bedroom wing there much before 1600. But the fact of having a store rather than a byre is unusual in a 15th-century house and more detailed work needs to be done before a satisfactory dating is possible. Unfortunately, the buttery and loft above it do not help us, as they now form a cottage that retains no original features. However, on balance, the date is likely to be closer to 1450 than 1500.

PART SIX

THE DUKE OF RICHMOND MAP

MUCH OF THE FOLLOWING INFORMATION is taken from an article in the 1958 issue of the *Transactions* of La Société Guernesiaise, written by L. F. de Vic Carey, the first Guernseyman to be Director-General of the Ordnance Survey. He states that after the Battle of Culloden, in 1745, the need was felt for a systematic survey of the whole of the British Isles, and although the Ordnance Survey was not officially constituted until 1791, a considerable amount of work was put in hand before that date, those areas most difficult to defend or most vulnerable to attack being surveyed first. By the time Charles Lennox, 3rd Duke of Richmond, was appointed Master General of His Majesty's Ordnance in 1783, much of Scotland and the south coast of England had been completed, mostly under the supervision of General Roy, who was a pioneer in this field. He was appointed to the Board under the duke and was involved in the decision to survey the Channel Islands, after the unsuccessful French attack on Jersey in 1781.

Five men were sent over, under the leadership of William Gardner, a surveyor draughtsman, who later became chief draughtsman in the offices of the Board of Ordnance at the Tower of London. The scale chosen was six inches to one mile, and the engraving was made on copper plates by John Warner. The two Guernsey sheets were completed in 1787 and the four Jersey ones in 1795, and were housed at the Tower of London until 1841, when the Ordnance Survey moved to Southampton.

The 1787 survey was the first official map of Guernsey since the Legge Survey of 1680 and was vastly more accurate and complete than the latter. Whereas the Legge Survey had only shown the houses of St. Peter Port in detail, the Duke of Richmond map was intended to show every building in the island, every track and field boundary as it was in 1787. In fact, a handful of buildings were omitted or wrongly drawn, but in the vast majority of cases, the siting as well as the orientation are correct, as far as can be made out from existing buildings. Some houses are shown with gardens, some as having only a short space between them and the road. At Les Martins, for instance (132–136), the track turns into a sort of continuous farmyard, the various houses grouped around it in no particular order. The large number of fields around almost every farm given up to apple orchards for cider-making show up well, and poor pasture and rough land on the cliffs is also indicated.

THE DUKE OF RICHMOND MAP

Since the 1787 map is so essential to the present survey, we reproduce it in full in this book, and at the original size, except that the cartouche has been re-arranged and those pages which would only have shown part of the coastline without any houses have been omitted. Those houses which wholly or in part date from before 1787 are inked in and numbered and the numbers refer to the Schedules which follow. Because of the practical difficulty of putting three or four figure numbers next to the houses in parts of St. Martin's parish where the apple orchards are most dense, it was decided to number those sheets first and the Clos du Valle last. The numbering, while following a logical pattern from sheet to sheet as far as possible, is also in parish order, in the following sequence: St. Martin; Forest; St. Pierre-du-Bois; Torteval; St. Saviour; Castel; St. Andrew; St. Peter Port; St. Sampson and Vale.

It would have been confusing, if not impossible, to number the centre of St. Peter Port, and consequently, no attempt has been made to do so. Numbers from 700 to 818 inclusive are therefore omitted.

Almost all the houses which are numbered will be found listed in the First Schedule. Any that are not may be regarded either as gentlemen's residences or town houses of the period 1750–1787. They do not have any of the features itemised in the First Schedule and will be found in the Third Schedule. The numbering is also used, where appropriate, to refer to stones listed in the Fourth Schedule.

Where houses seem to have been omitted in error on the original map, they have been inserted and numbered in the same way as the others—for instance, Les Lohiers (478), where the space for the house had been left blank, but the re-fronting, dated 1784, clearly shows that it should have been included. The parish boundaries have also been added, but otherwise the map has not been altered.

AN *Accurate* SURVEY

and Measurement of the

ISLAND of GUERNSEY

Surveyed by ORDER of

His Grace the Duke of Richmond &c.

Master General of the Ordnance

By WILLIAM GARDNER,

1787.

Scale of 2100 Yards.

Scale of 80 Chains or One Mile.

Grand Rogue Point

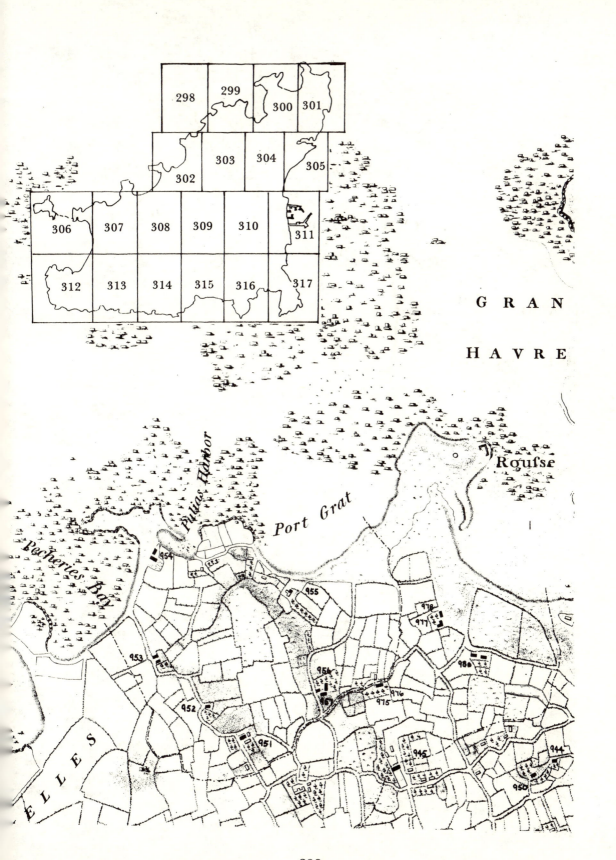

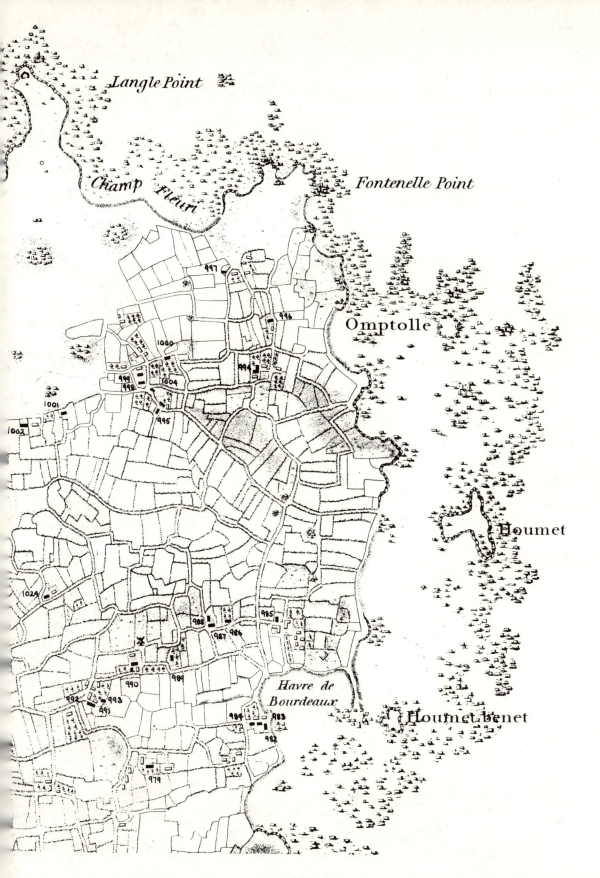

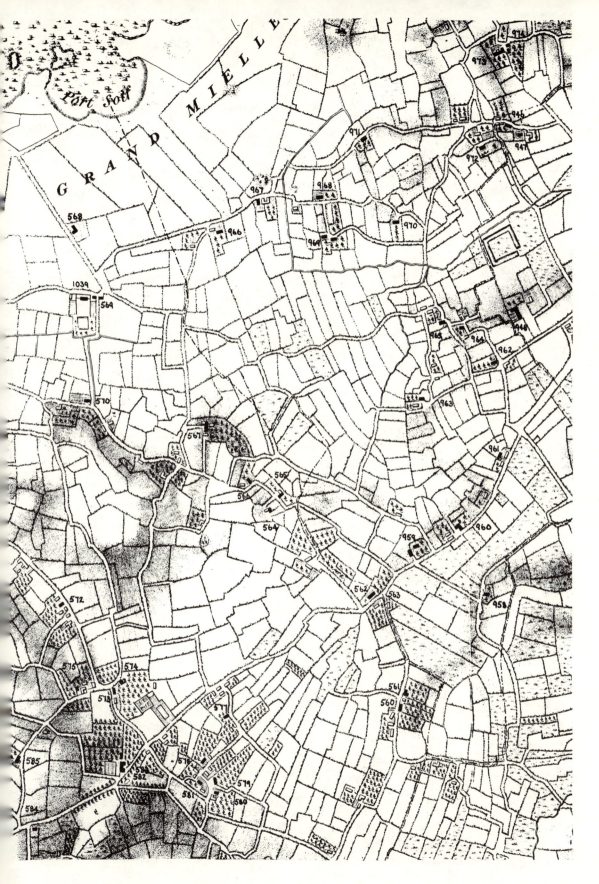

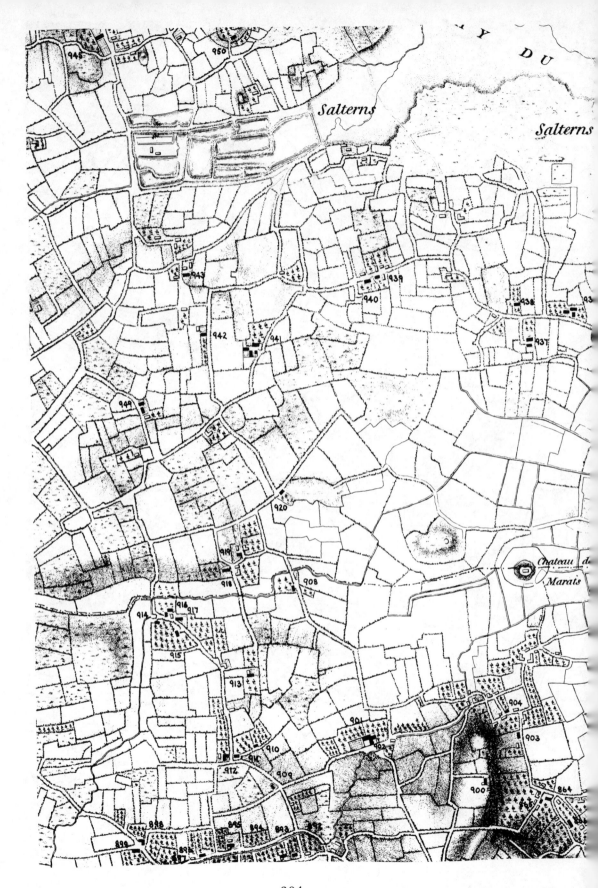

LIHOU
ISLAND

Lerée Point

R O Q U A I N E

B A Y

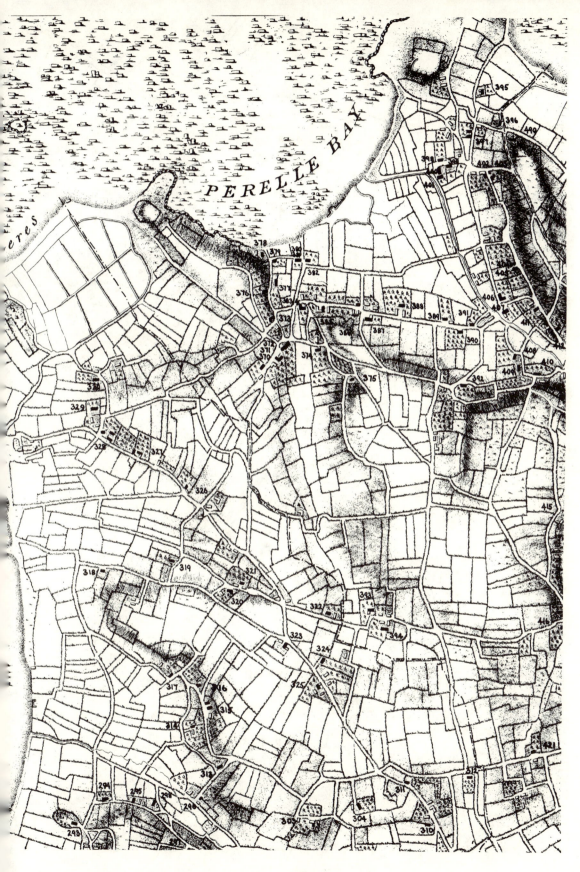

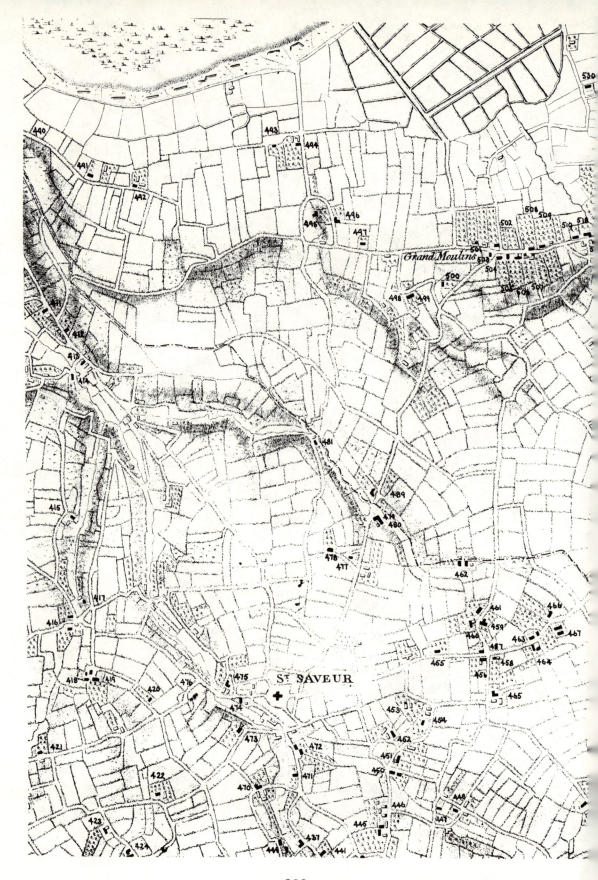

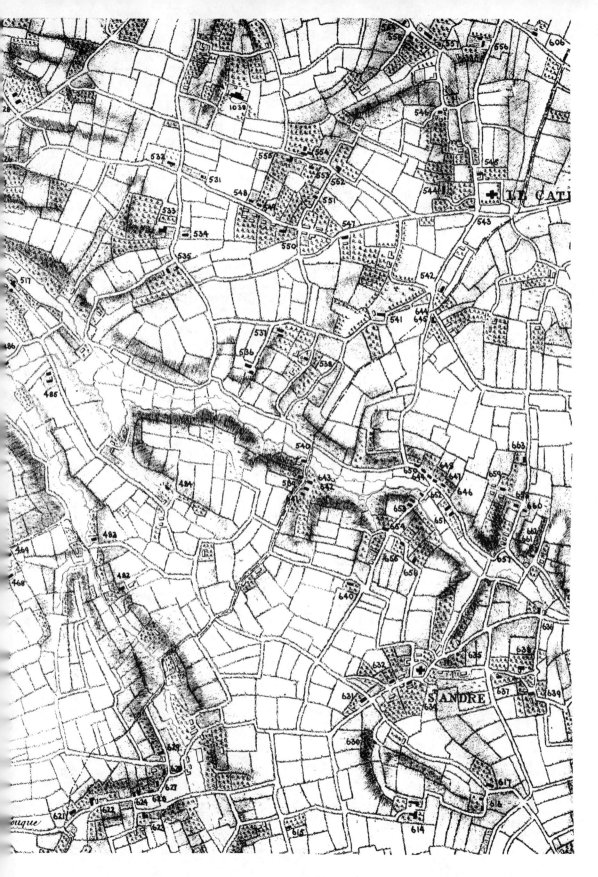

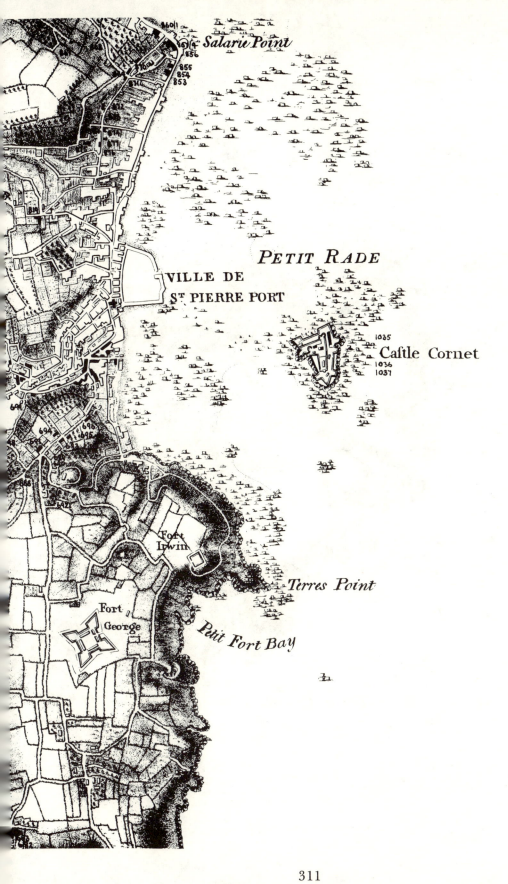

A La Fosse Equerre (622)

B Le Grand Douit (384)

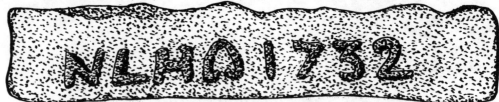

C Somerset House, Les Prevosts (466)

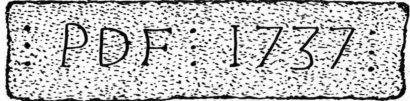

D Le Bourg de Bas (164)

E Les Prevosts (465)

F Les Eperons (614)

G La Maison Guignan (92)

DATED LINTELS

PART SEVEN

THE SCHEDULES

THE SCHEDULES

The four Schedules which follow comprise:

The First Schedule, listing all the types of houses (Types 1–11) described in Parts I and II of this book: that is, almost every house and cottage which seems to be older than 1787 in all the parishes except for the centre of St. Peter Port;

The Second Schedule, listing almost all pre-1787 shops and houses in St. Peter Port not included in the First Schedule;

The Third Schedule, listing the remaining pre-1787 houses not found in the first two Schedules, these being gentlemen's residences and town houses outside the vernacular tradition, most built *c.* 1750–1787;

The Fourth Schedule, listing all pieces of carved stone thrown out during renovations and demolitions, as well as those which have been re-used in other places.

Brackets indicate that a feature is known (or in the case of wooden panelling, presumed) to have existed, but has since been removed.

THE FIRST SCHEDULE

It is convenient to explain the Schedule column by column.

Stars. The stars against some houses are meant to indicate those, in the author's view, which are most important or interesting architecturally. It must be emphasised that this is necessarily a personal selection and that the criteria used have not been the same for every house. For instance, it is not possible to weigh up a house like Les Granges de Beauvoir (834) against the derelict cottage at Le Campréhard (656), but each deserves three stars because it is the best example of its type. Moreover, in some cases the star denotes that the entire house is of some interest: in others that a particular feature, not necessarily visible from outside, is of special note. Perhaps it should be said that in no case have stars

THE SCHEDULES

been awarded on the basis of how the house is kept. They are intended purely to indicate architectural merit. Neither does the absence of stars imply that a house has no interest.

Numbering. The numbering is done parish by parish, beginning with St. Martin, and continuing with the Forest, St. Pierre-du-Bois, Torteval, St. Saviour, Castel, St. Andrew, St. Peter Port, St. Sampson and the Vale. Where there are gaps, the houses omitted will be found listed either in the Second or the Third Schedule.

Address. Wherever possible, the address given is that in current use, even where it conflicts with the traditional name of the house. If it has proved impossible to find out the correct address, an attempt has been made to provide an adequate indication of its whereabouts and to locate it, the Duke of Richmond map should be used in conjunction with the Schedule. For this purpose, a reference has been included at the head of the column to the page on the map where the houses will be found.

Type. The house types are listed in Parts I and II of this book, viz.:

1.—Two-storey longhouse
2.—One-storey longhouse
3.—Les Grandes Maisons
4.—The three-bay house
5.—Two-storey house with cross-passage
6.—One-storey house with cross-passage
7.—House with byre but outside access
8.—The low-loft house
9.—The split-level house
10.—Other one-storey 18th-century cottages
11.—Other two-storey 18th-century cottages

A question mark before a Type 1 or a Type 2 house indicates that it is pre-1625 and might be presumed to have been built as a longhouse, but that definite proof is lacking. Elsewhere a question mark indicates that the house has been so altered that its original form is debatable. Where the column is left blank, it is because the house has been rebuilt or demolished, but farm buildings remain from the 18th century or earlier.

Bays. For the purpose of this work a bay is defined as the distance between one cross-beam or cross-wall and another, or between them and the gable-ends. A question mark denotes that alterations have removed cross-beams or cross-walls so that the internal arrangements are no longer clear.

Facade. An attempt has been made to indicate whether a house has been re-fronted. However, there are a good many cases where so many windows have been inserted or enlarged that the character of the original walling has been largely lost, though the house has not technically been refronted. Thus, although all houses that have been completely refronted are listed as 'R', so have those which have been drastically altered. Those left as 'O' may also have some inserted or enlarged windows, but preserve their original character.

Arch. The types are as explained in Chapter XXV, viz:

1. One order of small stones, unchamfered.

2. Two orders of small stones, unchamfered.

3. Two orders, the inner one of large stones, chamfered, the outer of small stones.

4. One order of large stones, chamfered.

5. Two orders, all large stones, chamfered.

6. Ogee, accolade and corbelled lintels.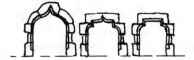

7. Flat-headed, chamfered.

R indicates red and G grey. This is a rough guide only to the colour. It can be assumed that Chausey and Cobo granites are listed as red, and most others as grey.

Stone Chimneys. The figure indicates the number of chimneys, the letter, either R or G, describes the colour. A few are a mixture of colours. Where only the base of a granite stack remains, it is nevertheless included in this listing.

THE SCHEDULES   323

Fireplace downstairs. The types are explained in Chapter XXVII, viz.:

1. Corbels with a double convex curve passing through more than 90deg.

2. Corbels with double convex curve only turning 90deg.

3. Corbels double curved, with upper part convex and the lower part concave.

4. Corbels with half an ogee curve.

5. Corbels with a single convex curve.

6. Other carved corbels.

7. Shaped corbels covered up: or lost—in brackets.

8. Unshaped corbels.

9. Wooden corbels.

N.B.—Brackets have been carefully placed to indicate whether the bread oven, the fireplace, or both bread oven and fireplace have been removed.

P indicates a pillar-type fireplace, but for more details of these please see Chapter XXVII, p. 191 onwards.

Some houses have two fireplaces downstairs.

Fireplace upstairs. The same symbols are used as for the previous column. Where a later valet's room over an adjoining stable has been fitted with a fireplace, this has been noted in the final column rather than here, so that the typology of the house itself will not be confused.

Chimney hoods. The figure denotes the number of hoods remaining. The letters indicate either stone ('S'); or wattle-and-daub ('W').

It must be remembered that many wattle-and-daub hoods, constructed when later fireplaces or furze ovens were inserted, cover indications of earlier stone ones.

This is not a complete list, for it was obviously not possible to penetrate the loft in every house. The information given here should not, therefore, be used except as supportive evidence in any work based on this Schedule.

Gable windows. The figure denotes the number of gable windows. The letters indicate their positions:

    K—kitchen.
    P—parlour.
    B—bedroom.
    L—loft.

It has been assumed that no longhouse would have gable windows in the byre, and that where they exist at that end of the house, the room must therefore always have been a parlour or store.

A question mark between a number and a letter indicates that alterations have made it difficult to determine which end of the house is which, and hence whether the window was in a kitchen or in a parlour.

A question mark before a number or a letter indicates some doubt, for instance, as to whether a recess was originally a keeping-place or a window.

Back kitchen. Y=yes.

Back kitchen fireplace. Symbols as for other fireplace columns.

THE SCHEDULES

Tourelles. R or L denotes the direction in which the stairs rise, that is, whether they turn to the right or the left as you go up.

→ K or ← K indicates whether they turn towards the kitchen end of the house or away from it.

'r' shows that the tourelle has been rebuilt, usually in the 19th century.

Cross walls. The figure denotes the number of stone cross-walls.

K indicates that the stone wall is on the kitchen side of the house; B, that it is on the byre side.

Where only one stone cross-wall exists, the other division may be assumed to be of planking or panelling.

P Indicates that both divisions are wooden. (P) usually indicates that these wooden partitions have been replaced by brick walls, studwork or other partitioning, and is intended to show that no stone wall ever existed.

Bénitiers/Eviers. Types 1 to 4 inclusive are bénitiers:

    1.—Pointed.

    2.—Cusped or trefoil.

    3.—Ogee or accolade.

    4.—Round.

Types 5 comprise éviers: SQ = squareheaded.
                                    R = round-headed.

Byre window. The figure denotes the number of byre windows.

Panelling. 16th-century includes both panelling proper and early forms of post-and-panel partitioning, mostly in oak;

    17th-century, regular post-and panel partitioning, mostly in pine;

    18th-century, classical panelling.

The dating of panelling is only very approximate: 16th-century more properly extends *c.* 1500–*c.* 1650; 17th-century spans the period *c.* 1650–*c.* 1750; and 18th-century is between *c.* 1720–1787, and mostly towards the end of that period.

Farm buildings. Unfortunately, this section is incomplete. Pressure of time has prevented a complete survey of all farm buildings. The figures show the number of barns, where they have been noted, and whether they are attached to the main house (att.) or separate structures (det.).

Final column. This is an attempt to provide a date for the origin of the present house. It may or may not apply to the entire building, and frequently may be at odds with the date displayed, if the house has been re-fronted (see Chapter XVII).

Although every effort has been taken not to be misleading, clearly there are many buildings where, for one reason or another, it is difficult to arrive at a date. In particular, some houses in the general grouping, *c.* 1400-1550, may, in fact, be somewhat later, *c.* 1550-1625; and vice versa. Similarly, some houses placed *c.* 1625-1700 may, in fact, be *c.* 1700-1750; and vice versa. There is less doubt about pre-1625 and post-1625 houses, but of course all dates in these general groupings are approximate only. There is nothing magical about the years 1625 or 1700, for instance.

All dates appearing on the house itself as inscriptions have been quoted in inverted commas. Where a dated doorway seems to convey the age of the whole house reliably, no other date has been put forward.

In cases where it has been possible to trace a house on the Livres des Perchages (see Chapter XX), the date is given in one of two ways. If the house appears on the earliest records, it is given as 'before 1523' or whenever that earliest record was made. If, however, a house appears on a book of 1642 but not on the previous one of 1607, it is given as 'between 1607 and 1642'.

The other information given here is necessarily incomplete, and intended only to highlight the most interesting or unusual features not already covered by the rest of the Schedule.

THE SECOND SCHEDULE

The notes on the First Schedule apply here, except in the following columns:

Type
    1.—A house or shop built gable-end to the street.
    2.—A house or shop with gable-ends at the sides.
    W.—A warehouse or store gable-end to the street.
    3.—Other houses and cottages.

Storeys. The figure denotes the number of storeys, excluding attics.

THE SCHEDULES

A indicates the storeys above ground-level at the front of the building; B shows the storeys below ground level at the front of the building.

Fireplaces. The types are as for the First Schedule, except that the elegant fire-surrounds from the second half of the 18th century associated with the fine panelling of that period, are noted as '18th-century'.

Staircases
 1.—Tourelle staircase.
 2.—Internal staircase with wooden newel post.
 3.—Staircase with stair-well; *c.* 1675–1750.
 4.—Staircase with stair-well; *c.* 1750–1787.

Vaults
 S = Stone-vaulted.
 B = Brick-vaulted.

THE THIRD SCHEDULE

Although many of these houses contain very fine examples of the woodwork noted in the other Schedules, they are really outside the scope of this book and are listed here for the sake of completeness only.

THE FOURTH SCHEDULE

Where a house is numbered, it will also be marked on the Duke of Richmond map and listed on one of the other three Schedules. Where a house is not numbered, it is post-1787 and is the address where an older piece of carved stone is now to be found. For types of arches and fireplaces listed, please see the notes for the First Schedule.

SCHEDULE ONE

	No.	Address Map Page 310, 316, 317	Type	Bays	Facade: Original/ refaced	Arch: Type, colour	Stone Chimneys: Colour	Fireplace Downstairs	Fireplace Upstairs	Chimney Hoods	Gable Window
	1	Les Hubits de Haut	6	4	R		1R				
	2	Les Hubits de Haut	5	5	R						
	3	Mare Mado, Hubits de Haut	?1	5	O		(2R)	(8f)		(2W)	
	4	Imphal Lodge, Hubits de Haut	5	5	R						
*	5	Les Hubits de Haut	5	5	O						
*	6	Les Hubits de Haut	?1	4	O			8f			
	7	Centuries, Hubits de Bas		?4							
	8	Norton House, Hubits de Bas	5	5							
	9	Wylfa, Hubits de Bas	1	5	O	7R					
	10	The Holderness, Hubits de Bas	5	5	R						
	11	Goldways, Sausmarez Road	5	5	R			?8			
	12	Le Friquet Cottage, Sausmarez Rd.	10	3	R						
	13	Rose Cottage, Le Varclin	6	5	O			8(f)			
	14	Bon Air Cottage, Les Maindonnaux	6	5	O			8	8	1S	
*	15	Les Maindonnaux	?1	5	O	5G		4s;8		1S	
	16	Varclin Cottage									
	17	Le Varclin	?1	5	O			f			
	18	La Grange, Le Varclin	?1	5	O			(8)			
	19	Le Varclin	5	5	R						
	20	Fernbank, Calais Road									
	21	Calais Road	10	?3	O						
	22	La Ronde Porte, Calais Road	6	5	O	5R					1?K
	23	Calais Farmhouse	?1	5	O			7	7		
*	24	La Bouvée Farm	?1	5	O	4R		4f	5	2W	
	25	La Bouvée	5	5	R			7			
	26	Le Mont Durand	?1	4	O			7			
	27	Le Vier Mont Durand	6	5	R						
	28	The Cottage, Les Salines	6	5			1R	8			
	29	Les Courtes Fallaizes	5	5	R						
	30	Cottage at Courtes Fallaizes	6	5	O			8		1W	
*	31	Les Blanches	?1	5	R			7f			
	32	Les Blanches	5	5	R			(8f)			
*	33	Les Blanches	5	5	R	?4R		5(f)	(5)	1W	1P;?1P
*	34	Les Blanches	1	5	O	5G		7	7		
*	35	Sausmarez Manor: Old house	?5	6	R						
	37	Le Vallon Cottage	1	4	O			7f			2B
	38	Ville Amphrey	5	5	O			8f			
	39	Old Byre, Ville Amphrey	6	5	O						

Back Kitchen	Back Kitchen Fireplace	Tourelle	Cross Walls	Bénetier/ Evier	Byre Window	Panelling	Farm Buildings	Fief: Earliest recorded date; additional information **PARISH OF ST. MARTIN**
			P				1 ATT	c.1700-1750
			(P)				2 DET	Built 1726
			(P)					c.1625-1700
			2					c.1550-1625
			2				1 DET	c.1725-1775. Barn c.1650
		R→K r	P			17c.		c.1550-1625 '1639' added to front lintel
								'1724 PMCI'. House much altered
			(P)					c.1700-1750
Y			(P)		1			c.1625-1650
			(P)					c.1700-1780
Y			1B			18c.		c.1700-1750
			(P)					c.1750-1780
			(P)					c.1650-1700
			(P)					c.1650-1700
			1B					c.1580-1625
Y	8							c.1700-1750. House rebuilt 19c.
Y		L→K	(P)					c.1550-1625 Stable below byre end c.18c.
			2					c.1700-1750
								c.1750-1780 Stable converted into house
			(P)					c.1750-1780
			(P)					c.1550-1625
		R→K	(P)					c.1400-1550
		L←K	1K					Fief de Sausmarez. Before 1523. 'Id P' on upstairs fireplace: perhaps Jehannet des Perques
		R→K r	(P)					c.1550-1625
			1K					Fief de Sausmarez. Before 1498
			(P)					Fief de Sausmarez. c.1750-1780 on site of 15c house
			2					c.1625-1700
			(P)					c.1700-1750
			(P)					c.1700-1750
		L→K	(P)					Fief de Sausmarez. Built 1603? 17c. window
			(P)					c.1700-1750. Survey incomplete—no access
Y 1820		L→K	1K					c.1550-1625. 'NT 1789' refronting. Arch damaged
		R→K	(P)		1			c.1550-1625
			P					c.1460. '1585 IA' on beam. 'M.D.S. 1777' and 'I.D.S. 1789' on back facade of 18c.
			1K					c.1400-1550. Gothick work applied 19c. Plaque of pelican feeding young '161?' over front door
			1K					c.1625-1700
			1K					c.1625-1700

No.	Address Map Page 316	Type	Bays	Facade: Original/ refaced	Arch: Type, colour	Stone Chimneys: Colour	Fireplace Downstairs	Fireplace Upstairs	Chimney Hoods	Gable Windows
40	Ville Amphrey	6	5	R						
** 41	La Vieille Maison, Ville Amphrey	1	5	O	5G		7	(7)	(W)	1B
42	La Petite Maison, Ville Amphrey	6	5	O						
43	Le Hamel, Ville Amphrey	5	5	R						
** 44	Le Ville Amphrey	?1	5	O			7			
45	Renate, Ville Amphrey	5	5	R						
46	Waterlanes Cottage	5	5							
* 47	La Vieux Port, Le Rocher	9	5	O			4:8			
48	La Fosse	?1		O						
49	Beverley Cottage, La Fosse	6	5	O			(8)			
50	La Fosse	5	4	R			(8)			
* 51	La Fosse de Bas	?1	5	O			6f		1W	
** 52	La Ruette	?1	5	O			6f	3		2P
53	The White Cottage, La Fosse	6	5	O						
* 54	Fay Dell, La Fosse	?1	5	O			7f			
55	Bella Luce, Fosse de Bas	?1	5	R		1R				1P
56	Le Repos au Coin	?1	5	R	5G					1?B
57	Le Hurel Farm	5	5	R						
58	Les Profonds Camps	5	5	O			8			
59	Bon Secours, La Fosse	5	5	O			(8f)			
** 60	De Bertrands, La Fosse	?1	5	O			2(f)			
* 61	The Old Farmhouse, La Fosse	?1	5	O			7:8f		1W	
62	Adjoining The Old Farmhouse	?1	4	O						
* 63	La Fosse	5	5	O			?8			
64	La Fosse Cottage	6	5	R						
* 65	Le Reculé, Saints Road	?1	5	R			8			
* 66	Saints Road	?1	5	O	1R					
* 67	Saints Bay Villa	?1	5	O		2R				
68	St. Cergue, Saints Bay Road	?1	5	R						
** 69	La Contrée de Saint	1	4	R	6R		7	7		
70	Simla, Saints Bay Road	5	5	R			(8)			
* 71	La Boiselée, Icart Road	6	5	O			(8)			
** 72	Galliot Cottage, Icart Road	4	3	O			8		1W	
73	La Motte Cottages	?2	5	R			(8f)			
74	Ma Normandie, Saints Bay Road	6	5	R						
75	Saints, Saints Bay Road	5	5	R			8 (f)			
** 76	La Tourelle, Icart Road	?1	4	R		1R	2(f)			1B
77	Llandaff Lodge, Icart Road	?1	5	R		1R	2(f)			

Back Kitchen	Back Kitchen Fireplace	Tourelle	Cross Walls	Bénetier/ Evier	Byre Window	Panelling	Farm Buildings	Fief: Earliest recorded date; additional information PARISH OF ST. MARTIN
			(P)					c.1750-1780
		R→K	(P)	5 sq	1			c.1550-1625
			(P)					c.1625-1700
			(P)				1 ATT	c.1625-1700
			P	5 sq		17c.	1 ATT	c.1550-1625 33 ft. purlins in 18c. barn roof
Y			(P)					c.1750-1780
			(P)					c.1700-1750
			1K	?1				c.1625-1700
								c.1625-1700 Survey incomplete: no access
			2	1				c.1625-1700
			(P)					c.1700-1750
			1B					Before 1550 '1617'—lintel
		R→K	1K					c.1500-1550 '1586' added to lintel
			2					c.1700-1750
			2					c.1450-1550 2 orig. window frames in kitchen
			1K					c.1550-1625 3-bay wing 18c.
			(P)					c.1580-1625 'IDM 1604' on arch
Y	8f		1K					c.1625-1700
			2					c.1700-1750
			2					c.1700-1780 'IDP 1753' on lintel
		L→K	1B		17c.			c.1400-1550 'BD 1732' on lintel
			2					c.1550-1625 Fireplace lintel re-used as hearthstone
			?P					c.1550-1625 'DDMP–M–1789': date of galleting?
			2					c.1770-1750 '1733' lintel. Fine galleting. Omitted from map
			2					c.1700-1750 'DDP RB' partly obscured
Y		R→K	2					c.1550-1625 'IMG 1745' lintel
Y			1K					c.1400-1550
			2					c.1400-1550
			(P)					c.1400-1550
			1B	?5 sq	1			c.1400-1450 Existed in 1488: Fief Blanchelande
			(P)					c.1750-1780
			1K					Between 1581 and 1666: Fief Blanchelande. 17c. 4-light windows. 2-bay wing's fireplace has wooden shoulders
Y			1B					Between 1581 and 1666: Fief Blanchelande
			1	5 sq				Between 1488 and 1580: Fief Blanchelande. ?'WRB' lintel
			(P)					1649: rebuilt from ruins of Blanchelande Priory. Fief Court Seat
			(P)				1 DET	c.1700-1750 on site of 15c. house. '1728' barn
		R→K	(1K)					Before 1488: Fief Blanchelande. Tourelle doorway partly rebuilt. Chamfered window stones re-used
Y			(P)					c.1400-1550

No.	Address Map Page 316, 310	Type	Bays	Facade: Original/refaced	Arch: Type, colour	Stone Chimneys: Colour	Fireplace Downstairs	Fireplace Upstairs	Chimney Hoods	Gable Windows
78	La Heaumerie, La Ruette du Navet	9	?5	R					?1W	?2
* 79	Saints Cottage, Icart Road	6	5	O			8			
80	Rose Farm, Icart Road									
81	Orlenda, Icart Road	9	5	O						
82	Fisherman's Cottage, Icart Road	6	5	O			(8f)		1W	
** 83	Saints Farm, Icart Road	?1	6	O		2R	2f		2S	
* 84	Maze Hollow, Rue Maze	5	5	O			8f			
85	Horbury House, Rue de l'Eglise	?1	5	R			(f)			1B
86	Rue de l'Eglise	5	5	O			8			
87	Grande Rue	?1	5	R			?7f			
* 88	Rue de l'Eglise	?1	5	R			6f	6	(2W)	
* 89	Rue de l'Eglise	11	3	O			8f			
90	Rue de l'Eglise	?1	5	O						
91	Le Bordage, Rue de l'Eglise	?1	5	R	1R					
** 92	La Maison Guignan	?1	5	R		2R	2	2		
93	Rue de l'Eglise	5	5	O						
*** 94	La Bellieuse Farm	?1	6	R	5G		2f:6	2	(S)	1K:2L
95	Blanche Pierre Lane	5	5	R						
96	Le Douit	5	5	R			8			
97	Paschendale, Le Douit	5	5	R			(8)			
** 98	Les Merriennes Cottage	1	5	R				(7)		
99	Rose Cottage, Rue de l'Eglise	6	5	O						
100	Ronnie Ronalde's Hotel	5	5	R						
101	La Vieille Maison, Grande Rue	5	5	?R			(8f)			
102	Merriennes Cottage	11	2	O			8			
103	Les Pastorelles, Les Merriennes	?5	?5	O			?8			
104	Westbury, Les Merriennes	5	5	O					(1W)	
105	Les Hamelins, Les Merriennes	5	5	R						
106	Mill Hill, Rue Poudreuse	5	5	R			8f			
107	Hedgeleigh, Rue Poudreuse	5	5	O						
* 108	Les Quatre Vents	7	5	O					1W	
109	Les Huriaux	?1	5	O	1R					
110	Les Varioufs	?1	5	R						
111	Les Câches	5	5	O			8f			
** 112	Les Câches Farm	?1	5	O	3R	6†			(2W)	2B

Back Kitchen	Back Kitchen Fireplace	Tourelle	Cross Walls	Bénetier/ Evier	Byre Window	Panelling	Farm Buildings	Fief: Earliest recorded date; additional information **PARISH OF ST. MARTIN**
			1					Between 1726 and 1781: Fief Blanchelande; earlier house existed 1666. No access: survey incomplete
Y			2					Built 1680 (owner)
							1 DET	House mostly rebuilt
			(P)					c.1700-1750
			2					c.1700-1750
Y			2			17c.		c.1400-1550 Heavily moulded window sill in bedroom. New stairs (quasi-tourelle) inserted 17c.
			1K			17c.	1 ATT	c.1625-1700 'IGN 1738' lintel. 17c. deeds
			(P)					c.1550-1625 Refurbished after fire in 1799
			1K					c.1700-1750 Many knuckle bones built into gable end of loft
			?1K					c.1550-1625
		R→K	(P)					c.1550-1625 'CNV:SGN:1729' lintel
			P					c.1700-1750 Earth floor
			(P)					c.1550-1625
			(P)					c.1400-1550
		(R→K)	(P)					c.1400-1550 'PGN 1725' lintel
			(P)					c.1700-1750
			P	5R;5		16c.	1 DET	c.1400-1450 Existed in 1488: Fief Blanchelande. '1707' facade. Quasi-tourelle stairs. Linenfold panelling
			(P)					c.1700-1750
			(P)					c.1700-1750 Originally 1-storey. Downstairs beam had been roof-truss
			2					c.1700-1750
		R→K	P		1	17c.		c.1400-1550 Pillar between back doorway and tourelle doorway. 17c. window frame
			(P)					c.1700-1750
			(P)					c.1700-1750
			(P)					c.1700-1750 '1728' on bricks
								c.1750-1780
			1K					c.1700-1750 3 bays only of old house now forming wing of 19c. building
			(P)					c.1750-1780
Y	8f		(P)				1 ATT	c.1700-1750 Furze oven external—though now covered—to back kitchen
			(P)					c.1700-1750
			1K					c.1700-1750
Y	8		1K					c.1625-1700
Y	(?f)		2					c.1550-1625
Y	8f		(P)					c.1450-1550 Stone from 16c. fireplace re-used in back kitchen. 'T:DMP&M:BD1810' lintel-refronting
			(P)				2 DET	c.1750-1780 Some 16c. work in present outbuildings perhaps part of previous house
		L→K	2	5 sq			1 ATT	Built 1492 by Jean Bonamy. †15c. fireplace with unshaped stones

No.	Address Map Page 316, 315	Type	Bays	Facade: Original/ refaced	Arch: Type, colour	Stone Chimneys: Colour	Fireplace Downstairs	Fireplace Upstairs	Chimney Hoods	Gable Windows
*113	Balderstone, Cornus Road	?1	4	O				7		
114	Le Repaire, La Planque Road	6	5	R			8f		1W	
115	Les Cornus Farm	5	5	O						
116	Les Cornus	5	5	R			(8)	(8)		
*117	La Pompe, Les Mouilpieds	?1		O	5G		5f			
118	Les Mouilpieds	5	5	R						
**119	Les Mouilpieds	?1	5	O	2R		6f	(6)		2B
120	Les Gachères, Les Mouilpieds	5	5	R			7f			
121	Clos au Barbier, La Villette	5	5	R			(8f)			
122	La Marcherie, La Villette			O						
*123	La Villette	?1	5	R			5f			2K
*124	La Villette	?1	5	R	5G†					
***125	Le Grée, La Villette	?1	5	O	5G	(2)	6f		1S	2B
126	Le Morel, La Villette			O						
127	La Villette									
128	Simtora, La Villette	?1	5	R			8f			1L
***129	Le Tourtel, La Villette	1	5	O	5G		3f			1B
*130	La Ruette	?1	4	R	2G					
131	La Maison Godaine,	?1	5	O	5G					
*132	La Gaudine, Les Martins	?1	5	?R		2G	2:8		1W	
*133	Les Martins	1	4	O			7f			
134	Les Martins	5	5	R						
*135	Les Martins	?1	5	O						
*136	Les Martins House	?1	5	O						
137	La Croute, Les Martins	?1	5	R						
*138	Meadowview, Les Pages	?1	5	R			7f			1B
139	Les Pages	5	5	O						
*140	Les Pages	?1	5	O			8f			
141	Les Pages	2	5	O	X		5		1W	
142	L'Ormette, Les Pages	6	5	O	4G		(8f)			
143	The Chalet, Les Pages	10	3	O						
*144	La Falaise	5	4	R			8f			
145	Les Rebouquets	5	5	R			?8			
146	Petit Bot: Upper Mill									

Back Kitchen	Back Kitchen Fireplace	Tourelle	Cross Walls	Bénetier/Evier	Byre Window	Panelling	Farm Buildings	Fief: Earliest recorded date; additional information PARISH OF ST. MARTIN 113-143 PARISH OF THE FOREST 144-146
		R→K	2					*c.*1400-1550 'NMD 1715' lintel
			(P)					*c.*1700-1750 Formerly 'Le Bouchez': earliest contract is of 1638: house rebuilt 18c?
Y	8f		(P)					*c.*1625-1700
			(P)					*c.*1700-1750
		R→K	1K				1 ATT	*c.*1606 'TTLT 1606' arch with date also of new house: '1863 JMD MG'. 3 bays only of old house remain
			(P)				1 DET	*c.*1625-1700 'NT 1698' and 'JRB ELDN 1848' lintel. House virtually rebuilt 19c. Valet's quarters and remains of cider press—'NT 1782'—in barn
		R→Kr	1K				1 ATT	*c.*1400-1550
			(P)					*c.*1625-1700
			1K					Between 1666 and 1726 '1754 IFL' lintel. Re-used fireplace lintel may indicate house is 16c.
								*c.*1700-1750. 2-bay wing only remains
		L→K	(P)					*c.*1400-1550 House much altered. Tourelle occupies entire width of (narrow) cross-passage
			(P)					*c.*1400-1550 Unshaped projecting window lintels at back. †Unique arch
		R→K	1B					*c.*1550-1625
Y								*c.*1700-1750 Back wing only remains: house rebuilt
								Gable end of house only
		L→K	1K					*c.*1550-1625 Galleting. Carved head over doorway
		L→K	(P)		1		1 ATT	*c.*1550-1600 1581- la 'neuve maison'—Fief Blanchelande. Chamfered windows. 16c. mullioned window
		R→K	1K					*c.*1400-1550 'NMT TLLG 1731' lintel: refronting
			(P)					*c.*1400-1500 Before 1488—Fief Blanchelande
		L←Kr	1K				1 ATT	*c.*1400-1550 Type 8 fireplace in valet's room: 18c.
		L→K	P		1		1 ATT	*c.*1400-1550 Earth floors
			(P)					*c.*1625-1700 'PMG 1819' lintel: refronting
		R→K	(P)					*c.*1550-1625 Before 1488—Fief Blanchelande
Y	(8)f	R→K	1K					*c.*1400-1550 Upstairs fireplace lintel re-used above front door. Drainage channel in cross-passage
		L→Kr	1K					*c.*1550-1625 ?before 1581—Fief Blanchelande
		R→K	(P)					*c.*1550-1625 'PRB 1713' lintel: refronting
Y	(8)f		2					*c.*1625-1700 'TMT 1706' lintel: refronting
			2					*c.*1550-1625 Chamfered window and good chamfer stop to front door
			1K					*c.*1550-1625
			(P)					*c.*1625-1700 Arch from La Couture House, 893
								*c.*1700-1750
			1K				1 ATT	*c.*1625-1700
			(P)					*c.*1625-1700 'G H 1853' date of refronting
								Only a little old walling remains; demolished, 2nd World War

No.	Address Map Page 315	Type	Bays	Facade: Original/refaced	Arch: Type, colour	Stone Chimneys: Colour	Fireplace Downstairs	Fireplace Upstairs	Chimney Hoods	Gable Windows
147	Petit Bot: Lower Mill									
*148	Les Nicolles	?1	5	R			2f		(1W)	
*149	Les Nicolles Farm	?1	5	R			7f			2W
*150	Les Pièces	8	5	O		1G	8f:8			2W
151	Les Pièces Farm	5	5	R						
152	Banavie, Les Pièces	5	?5	R			(8f):?8			
153	Le Russel Farm	?1	5	R		(2)	5(f)		?1W	
***154	Le Chêne Cottage	5	5	O	4R		2			
155	Le Chêne	?1	5	R						
156	Le Chêne	5	5	O						
*157	Le Chêne Farm	5	5	R			8		1W	
**158	Les Messuriers	?1	6	R					(1W)	
159	Les Messuriers	6	5	O			(8)			
160	Shipley Glen	10	3	R			(8)			
161	Oak Lodge, Les Messuriers	5	5	R			(8)			
*162	Le Bourg de Bas	5	5	R			8	(8)	(1W)	
163	Le Bourg de Bas	5	5	R						2B
*164	Le Bourg de Bas	?1	5	R	1R					
**165	Le Bourg	5	5	R			8f			
166	Le Bourg	5	5	R						
167	Le Bourg	5	5	O						
168	Le Bourg	5	5	R			8f:8		(2W)	
**169	Le Bourg	?1	5	R	?		8f			
170	Rue des Landes	5	5	R			8f			
171	Le Bourg de Haut	6	5	O			(8f)			
172	La Croisée, Petit Bot	?		R						
173	Les Houards de Bas									
174	Les Houards	5	5	R					(2W)	
175	Occupation Museum, Les Houards	10	2	R			(8)			
176	La Fontaine, Le Variouf	6	5	R			8f		(1W)	1B
177	Le Jardin des Fleurs	?1	4	R			5			1B:1P
**178	Le Petit Jardin, Le Variouf	?2	4	O	4R		2		1W	1K
*179	The Cottage, Le Variouf	?2	?4				5f			

Back Kitchen	Back Kitchen Fireplace	Tourelle	Cross Walls	Bénetier/ Evier	Byre Window	Panelling	Farm Buildings	Fief: Earliest recorded date; additional information PARISH OF THE FOREST
								Much altered during 2nd World War: shell only remains
		R→K	1K				1 DET	c.1400-1550 Earth floor until 1960
Y	8f		(P)					c.1400-1550
			1K					c.1700-1750
			2					c.1700-1750
			?				1 ATT	c.1625-1700 Much altered 19c.
			1B				1 DET	c.1550-1625 '18th February 1812' on beam before plastering
		R→K	2				1 DET	c.1550-1625 Ornamented window sills: chamfered jambs. Fireplace lintel over roadside gate, PRG·IAD·1744'
Y	8f	(YES)	(P)				1 ATT	c.1550-1625 Tourelle apparently was near gable end of kitchen
			(P)					c.1700-1750 Rebuilt c.1880 except E. end of back wall and E gable
			2					c.1625-1700 'GLP MDG 1734' refronting. Earth floor.
Y	8		1K				1 DET: 1 ATT	c.1400-1550 Strange bulge for height of house near gable end at back of kitchen: not large enough for a tourelle
			1K					c.1700-1750
			(P)					c.1700-1750
			(P)					c.1700-1750
			1B					c.1700-1750 2-bay kitchen detached, with date on beam '(I)RP 1770'
Y	8f		2					c.1550-1625 Ships' timbers in roof
		L→K	2					c.1400-1550 ':PDF:1737:' refronted
			2					c.1625-1700 17c. window with leaded lights. Furze oven door in back of fireplace
			(P)					c.1700-1750 '1727' said to have been at hearth
			(P)					c.1700-1750
			(P)					c.1625-1700
		L→K	(P)		1			c.1400-1550 'EP 1727' over kitchen doorway. Arch plastered over
			2				2 DET	c.1625-1700 'IVDM 1680 ♡ M ♡' on barn
			(2)					c.1700-1750 Earth floor until c.1948
								c.1700-1750 A little old walling only remains
								House rebuilt. Barns possibly early 18c, but '1788' on beam
Y	8f						1ATT	c.1625-1700 Contemporary doorway through gable end into stables
								c.1700-1750
			1B					1603 (owner). '1706' on window-sill
			1K					c.1550-1625
			1B					c.1400-1550
			1K					c.1400-1550 Niches in all window-splays

No.	Address Map Page 315, 316	Type	Bays	Facade: Original/ refaced	Arch: Type, colour	Stone Chimneys: Colour	Fireplace Downstairs	Fireplace Upstairs	Chimney Hoods	Gable Windows
**180	Le Variouf de Haut	5	5	R		2G	5f		(2W)	
*181	Hillview, Le Variouf	8	5	O			8f			
*182	Le Variouf	?1	4	O			7f		(1W)	
*183	Le Variouf	9	4	R			8f		1W	
*184	Le Variouf	10	3	O			8f		(1W)	
*185	Le Variouf	10	2	O			8		(1W)	
*186	Le Variouf	10	2	O					1W	
187	Les Fontenelles Cottage	6	4	O			8f			
188	Les Fontenelles Farm									
*189	Les Villets Farm	?3	6	R						
*190	Les Câches	?1	5	O	2R		2(?f)			
191	Les Villets									
192	Les Villets									
193	Les Villets	5	5	R						
**194	Les Villets	?1	5	R			6(f)			
**195	Les Villets	1	5	O			2f			1B
**196	Les Villets	?1	4	R	?4R		2f	2	(2S)	
197	La Vrangue	?6		O		1R	8f		1W	
198	L'Epinel	8	5	R			8f			
199	Epinel Farm	5	5	R			?8			
200	La Chaumette Farm	5	5	R			7f			
*201	Nantucket, Torteval Road	?1	5	R		1R;1G	8(f)			
**202	La Villiaze	5	5	O		(2)	6f		(2W)	
*203	Cambrai, Le Bigard	?1	5	R		1R	6f			
204	Les Merriennes	?1	4	R	?					
***205	Le Bigard	?1	4	O		1R	3f	7	2W	
*206	Gracias Cottage	5	5	O			7f			
207	Le Bigard	6	4	R			(8f)			1B
*208	La Carrière	5	5	O	5G				2S	
209	La Chaumine	9	5	R						
*210	Le Cas Rouge	5	5	R			3(f)			1K
211	Le Manoir				4G					
212	The Cottage, Le Bigard	6	6	O			(8f)			
213	La Corbière	?1	5	R		1G				

Back Kitchen	Back Kitchen Fireplace	Tourelle	Cross Walls	Bénetier/ Evier	Byre Window	Panelling	Farm Buildings	Fief: Earliest recorded date; additional information **PARISH OF THE FOREST 180-211** **PARISH OF ST. PIERRE-DU-BOIS 212-213**
			2					*c.*1550-1625 '1642'—back of house; 'ILP 1729'—refronting. Well-head, shelf and troughs now enclosed. Group of keeping-places in kitchen gable
			1B					*c.*1625-1700
Y	8f	R→K	1K					*c.*1400-1550
			1B					*c.*1700-1750
			1					*c.*1700-1750 Cross-wall between side-passage and kitchen. Wooden shoulders originally for fireplace
								*c.*1700-1750 Wooden shoulder—right of fireplace
								*c.*1700-1750
			2					*c.*1700-1750
							1 DET	House rebuilt. 'DLR (1)775' on barn: De la Rue
Y	8f	R→K	2					*c.*1400-1550
			?1B					*c.*1400-1550 'IDF 1775' on arch
Y	8f							*c.*1700-1750 wing only. Main house rebuilt 19c.
								*c.*1700-1750 Barn with valet's quarters only: ruinous
Y	8f							*c.*1625-1700, but main house rebuilt except gable end
Y	8f	L→K	1K					*c.*1550-1625
		L→K	2		1			*c.*1400-1550 Tourelle doorway re-used as front doorway
			1B					*c.*1400-1550 Sides only remain of door arch
Y			1B				1 ATT	*c.*1625-1700 19c. house built between barn and wing
			1K					*c.*1700-1750
			2					*c.*1700-1750
Y	8f		(P)					*c.*1625-1700
		L→K	2					*c.*1550-1625 '1705' lintel
Y			2					*c.*1625-1700 'SAL:SIL:SAL CAL:VA?:AL IAL:DIA:?/1659'—back kitchen. Furze oven door is in back wall of kitchen under lean-to
		L→K	1K					*c.*1550-1625
Y	8f		(P)					*c.*1400-1550 Arch plastered over
			1B					*c.*1400-1550 Loft still open to roof: loft door in back wall
			1B					*c.*1550-1625 '17——' on beam. Very low house
			2					*c.*1625-1700
Y	8f		2					'1614'—doorway. Window surrounds chamfered with stops
			(P)					*c.*1750-1780
Y	8f		1K					*c.*1550-1625 '16th Dec. 1727'—Allez crest
		YES						*c.*1550-1625 'MAL/1611/ILP'—shield on arch. 2 windows with moulded sills. House much altered
			(P)					*c.*1625-1700
Y	8f		1B					*c.*1500-1625 Joists cut for use of pork rack

No.	Address Map Page 314, 313	Type	Bays	Facade: Original/refaced	Arch: Type, colour	Stone Chimneys: Colour	Fireplace Downstairs	Fireplace Upstairs	Chimney Hoods	Gable Windows
* 214	Coin de Terre	1	4	O		1R	2(?f)			2B
** 215	La Corbière	?2	5	O			2f		1S	
216	Les Reines	5	5	R			?8			
217	Les Reines	5	5	R						
218	Les Marchez									
219	La Croix, Croix des Marchez	5	5	O					1W	
* 220	La Croix des Marchez	?1	4	O						
*** 221	La Forge, La Croix des Marchez	1	4	R	5G		7		2S	
* 222	Le Belle, Rue du Vidcocq	5	5	R						
* 223	Pont Renier, Les Hêches	?1	4	R					2W	
224	Le Pont, Les Hêches	5	4	R					(1W)	
* 225	Les Hêches	?1	5	R	3R				(1W)	
226	Les Ménages						8f			
227	La Croute	5	5	R			(8f)			
228	Les Bruliaux, New Road	5	5	R						
229	La Pailloterie									
230	Le Pré, Rue des Prés	5	5	R						
** 231	Les Taudevins, Rue des Prés	4	3	R			7		1W	
232	La Fosse	5	5	R	1G					
** 233	Les Paas, Rue des Prés	?1	4	R					(2W)	
234	Le Marinel, Rue des Prés									
235	Les Landes Farm	5	5	R			8f		(1W)	
* 236	Les Rondiaux	?1	5	R			8f			
*** 237	Les Câches	3	8	R	4G		1s:3	?1	1S	2B
* 238	La Tourelle	5	5	R						
** 239	La Mare	3	7	R			3			
*** 240	La Maison de Haut	5	5	O	5G	1G;2R	3	3	2S	1K;2B
*** 241	La Maison d'Aval	?1		O	1R		1	3P		1K;1B
* 242	La Vieille Corderie	?1	5	O			3(f)			
243	Les Brehauts	5	5	R						
244	Les Brehauts	5	5	O			8f			1P;2B
245	Le Truchon	5	5	O					(2W)	

Back Kitchen	Back Kitchen Fireplace	Tourelle	Cross Walls	Bénetier/ Evier	Byre Window	Panelling	Farm Buildings	Fief: Earliest recorded date; additional information PARISH OF ST. PIERRE-DU-BOIS
		L→K	?	1				c.1400-1550 Tourelle doorway rebated
			(P)					c.1400-1550
Y	8f		1B					c.1625-1700
Y	8f		2				1 DET	c.1700-1750 Standing stone built into barn entrance
								c.1462—Greffe. House rebuilt at right-angles, but back wall of original incorporated with 1 oak window, leaded lights—now lost
Y	(8)		?					c.1625-1700 Valet's quarters with fireplace (Type 8)
		R→K	1K					c.1400-1550
Y	8f		1K	1			2 ATT	c.1400-1550 17c. window at back complete with original glazed leaded lights. Forge with equipment for shoeing oxen. Prinseux with later equipment—1848
Y	(8f)		(P)					c.1625-1700. Before 1685—Fief Corbinez
			(P)					c.1400-1550
Y	f		1K					c.1625-1700 Original roof trusses. Bread oven external: door from back kitchen
			(P)					c.1400-1550 Owner has records of 1549 and 1575. Refurbished 1824 Langlois
								c.1700-1750 Half only of house remains
Y			1B					c.1700-1750
Y	8f		1K					c.1700-1750
Y	8f						1 ATT	c.1700-1750 House rebuilt except back kitchen. Barn 18c.
Y	8		1?K					c.1700-1750—back kitchen. Some older walling in 19c. house
Y	8f		(P)					c.1550-1625 Additional 2-bay extension with 8f
			1K					c.1625-1700
Y	8f	R→K	2					c.1400-1550
								c.1550-1625 House rebuilt except for gable end
			1K					c.1700-1750
Y	?8		2				1 ATT	c.1400-1550 Bases of arched doorway remain
		L←K	1B		?1	16c.	3 DET	c.1400-1550 For full description, see Ch. XXXVIII
			(P)					c.1700-1750
Y	8f	L←K	1K					c.1400-1550 Before 1671—Fief St. Michel
Y	8f	R→K	P	3		16c.	1 DET	c.1400-1550 Earth floors until 1960s. 17c. window. Pigeonniers in gable end of barn
Y	2f		1K				1 DET; 1 ATT	c.1400-1550 17c. windows. 7c. cross forming one quoin of back kitchen. 'ILM:M:1685' in wood on barn door. 'S/TLM/1707' on back of barn. Kitchen and bedroom fireplaces use the same chimney. Half of house remains: new house 1866
			2					c.1400-1550
Y	8f		1?K				1 ATT	c.1700-1750 Valet's quarters with wooden shoulders to fireplace
			(P)					c.1625-1700
Y	8f		(P)					c.1625-1700 Bread oven in kitchen, but door in back kitchen

No.	Address Map Page 313	Type	Bays	Facade: Original/ refaced	Arch: Type, colour	Stone Chimneys: Colour	Fireplace Downstairs	Fireplace Upstairs	Chimney Hoods	Gable Windows
246	Le Truchon	5	5	R			8			
*247	Le Morpaye, Les Martins	5	4	R						
248	La Gallie, Les Hêches	5	5	R						
249	Les Hêches	5	5	R						
250	La Vallée	6	5	R			8(?f)			
**251	Les Raies de Haut	3	7	R	5R	2R	?3:6			
*252	Les Buttes, Les Raies	5	5	R						
253	Buttes View	5	5	R						
254	Les Buttes, Rue de l'Eglise	5	5	R						
255	Rue de l'Eglise	6	5	O						
256	Longfrie Hotel	5	5	R		2G			1W	
257	Les Reveaux	5	5	R						
**258	Les Reveaux	?1	5	R			2f:8		1W(1W)	
***259	Les Reveaux	?1	5	O	5G		1	7	2W	1B
260	Le Douit Farm	5	5	R						
*261	Les Prés, Les Reveaux	1	4	R						2B
262	Le Douit d'Israel	9	5	R			8f		(1W)	
263	Le Vidcocq, Rue des Fontenils	6	5	R			8f		1W	
**264	Le Clos de Bas	1	4	O			3f			
265	Les Falles, Rue des Fontenils	9	5	R			8f			
266	The Cottage, Rue des Fontenils	9	5	O						
267	Le Douit Beuval	5	5	R						
268	Les Graies	?1	5	R	(4G)					
269	Les Sages	5	5	R			8f			
*270	Les Sages	?1	?5	R			5			
*271	Les Sages	5	5	R						
***272	Les Sages Villa	1	5	R	4R	3	3		1W	1B
*273	Plas Dyke Farm, Les Sages	?1	4	O						1B
*274	Les Vallettes, Route du Coudré	1	4	O			7f			1B
275	La Cité, Rue de Quanteraine	6	5	O			(?8)			
276	Les Hures, Rue des Clercs	5	5	O			8f		2W	
**277	St. Briocq, Contrée des Clercs	?1	5	R		2G	2		1W	
278	Les Clercs du Campère	5	5	O			(8f)			

Back Kitchen	Back Kitchen Fireplace	Tourelle	Cross Walls	Bénetier/ Evier	Byre Window	Panelling	Farm Buildings	Fief: Earliest recorded date; additional information PARISH OF ST. PIERRE-DU-BOIS
Y	8f		(P)					c.1700-1750 Bread oven in kitchen, but door in back kitchen
Y	8f		1K					c.1625-1700
			(P)				1 DET	c.1700-1750 A little old walling at base and at back of house
Y			1K					c.1625-1700
			1B					c.1625-1700 Upper cruck trusses removed
			(P)	1				c.1400-1550 Fireplace inserted in 'byre' end. House greatly altered 19-20c.
Y	8f		(P)				2 DET	c.1625-1700
			(P)					c.1700-1750 Completely altered 19c. except gable end
Y	8f		2					c.1700-1750
Y			(P)					c.1700-1750
Y	8f		2					c.1625-1700
Y			2					c.1550-1625
			2					c.1400-1550 'PBH:ABH:1751' on lintel of 2f fireplace. 17c. windows
Y	8f	R→K	1K					c.1400-1550 Back kitchen of 3 bays. Before 1560— fief records
Y	8f		2					c.1700-1750
Y	8f	R→Kr	1K		1			c.1400-1550 'LDB 1814' refronting. Upstairs passage window unglazed until 1968—bars only
			1B					c.1750-1780 Considerably rebuilt 19c.
Y			(P)					c.1700-1750
Y	8		1K					c.1550-1625 Byre used as stable with inserted doorway until recently
Y			1K					c.1700-1750
			(P)					c.1700-1750
Y	8(f)		(P)				1 ATT	c.1700-1750 One oven at side of terpied, one at back, projecting into stable: destroyed 1979
Y	8	R→Kr	1B					c.1400-1550 Arch removed c.19c. and stone built into pig sty and used in roadside entrance opposite
			1K					c.1625-1700
		R→K	1K					c.1550-1625 Fief Beuval seat in front of house
Y	8f		1B					c.1550-1625 Bread oven projects outside back kitchen
Y		R→K	1K		1			c.1400-1550 Downstairs fireplace with a head on each corbel and later shield incised, dated '1747'
Y		R→K	1K					c.1550-1625
Y			2	1				c.1550-1625
			(P)					c.1700-1750
			2					c.1625-1700
2Y	8f:8		1B	5				c.1400-1550 Base of évier in 1st floor of roadside wing, above stable
			2					c.1700-1750 Main house added 19c. with stone from demolished house below (not 279)

No.	Address Map Page 313, 307	Type	Bays	Facade: Original/refaced	Arch: Type, colour	Stone Chimneys: Colour	Fireplace Downstairs	Fireplace Upstairs	Chimney Hoods	Gable Windows
279	Les Clercs									
280	La Campère	5	5	R			(8f)			
281	Les Clercs	5	5	R						
282	Le Ménage, Rue des Clercs	5	5	R					1W	
283	Le Coudré	5	5	R		1G				
**284	Maison Galopie	?1	4	O	3R		7			1B
*285	Rocquaine Villa, Le Coudré	?1	4	R			5f			
286	La Fontaine, Le Coudré	6	5	R						
*287	La Neuve Maison, Le Coudré	?1	5	R			7			1B
*288	Le Coudré de Bas	?1	5	O		1G			1W	1B
289	Les Cambrées									
290	Les Cambrées	5	5	R			?8			
291	Rue du Catillon	6	5	O			8f:8		(1W)	
*292	Le Catillon de Bas	?1	5	R	(2R)		2		(1S)	
293	Le Catillon de Haut	5	5	R			(?8)			
**294	Les Hamelins	?1	5	R		2G	8f	8	(1W)	
295	Les Arquets	9	5	R			(8)		(1W)	
296	Les Arquets	10	3	R			8		2W	
297	La Fontenelle, Rue du Bordage	6	5	R			(8f)			
298	Le Douit	5	5	R				8	1W	1P:1B
299	Rue des Vinaires									
**300	La Fosse, Rue de Quanteraine	9	5	O			8f		1W	
*301	Moulin de Canteraine	?1	5	R			7		1W	
**302	Rue des Vinaires	6	5	R			8f:8		1W(1W)	
**303	Le Frie	?1		O			3f			1K
*304	La Vieille Maison, Rue des Juliennes	1	5	R		1G	2f		1S	
305	Below Les Vinaires									
**306	La Madeleine de Bas	1	4	O		2R	6	?6		
**307	Brouard House, Les Islets	1	4	O	2R		1sf	4		
*308	Maison des Pauvres	1	4	O	3R				(1W)	
309	Les Islets	?1	5	R	1R		?2			
310	La Couture	5	5	R			6(f)			
**311	Le Haut Chemin	?1	5	O			2(f)			
312	L'Eclet	5	5	R						

Back Kitchen	Back Kitchen Fireplace	Tourelle	Cross Walls	Bénetier/ Evier	Byre Window	Panelling	Farm Buildings	Fief: Earliest recorded date; additional information **PARISH OF ST. PIERRE-DU-BOIS**
								c.1625-1700 Ruins: back wall and well remain
			2					c.1700-1750
Y			2					c.1625-1700 Majority of house rebuilt 1832
Y	8f		(P)					c.1625-1700 Many ships' timbers re-used. Main house mostly rebuilt 19c.
			1B					c.1625-1700
		L→K	1K					c.1400-1550 Back door opens out of tourelle. 17c. window
			1K	5R				c.1400-1550
			(P)					c.1700-1750 Much rebuilt
Y	8f		1K				1 ATT	c.1400-1550 'GCLM/ADI/1816' refronting
		R→K	2					c.1400-1550
							1 DET	House rebuilt 19c. Barn prob. 17c.
			1B				1 ATT	c.1625-1700 19c. house may include part of tourelle from earlier dwelling
			1K					c.1700-1750 Derelict
Y	(8f)		(P)					c.1400-1550 'PB 1616' incised on earlier fireplace
			1B					c.1625-1700
		L→Kr	2					c.1550-1625 'ILF/MB/1743' refronting. Clay insulation above bedrooms
			2					c.1700-1750
								c.1700-1750
Y	8(f)		1K					1745. Earth floor until 1940s
Y	8f		2					c.1700-1750
							1 DET	Barn 18c.
			1B					c.1625-1700 Bread oven still in use
Y	8	R→Kr	2					c.1550-1625 Farm here in 15c.
			2					c.1625-1700 Unique stone staircase from cross-passage to loft. Earth floor in part until 1974
				5R				c.1550-1625 Half of house only retained as back kitchen to 19c. main house. Bread oven projects into barn. Superb évier
			1B		1			c.1400-1550 Earth floor in byre until 1978
								Ruins of barn by roadside
			1K		1		1 ATT	c.1400-1550 Outside bread oven remained until 1970s
		(L→K)	2	5R	1			c.1400-1550 Byre intact with drain and tethering rings
			1K	3				c.1400-1550 Huge dripstones on gable below later roof-line towards 307. Poor-house 1627-1798
			2			18c.	1 DET; 1 ATT	c.1400-1550 Panelling in valet's apartment. 'NNT MLP 1740' lintel in barn
			2					c.1625-1700
Y	8f	R→K	2					c.1400-1550 Slit window in tourelle
Y			2					Between 1718 and 1754—fief records

No.	Address Map Page 307, 313	Type	Bays	Facade: Original/ refaced	Arch: Type, colour	Stone Chimneys: Colour	Fireplace Downstairs	Fireplace Upstairs	Chimney Hoods	Gable Windows
313	Le Vallet	6	5	R						
**314	La Câche, Rue du Douit de la Pomare	1	4	O	5G	1G	2	?2		
315	Maison Bonamy, Rue de l'Ardaine	?1	?4	O	(4)		(1f)		(1S)	
*316	La Pomare	?1	5	R			2f:?2			
317	La Grande Maison de la Pomare	?1	?4	O						
318	Les Marais, Rue du Val	6	5	R			(8f)			
319	Le Val de Haut	5	5	R		2G	8f		1W	
*320	La Houguette	5	4	O			8f		(1W)	2B
*321	La Houguette	?5		R						
322	Le Lorier	5	5	R		1R				1B
323	Les Paysans Farm	5	5	O			8f		1W	
*324	Les Paysans	?1	4	R		2G				
*325	Les Paysans	?1	5	R	?1R		8f			
*326	Les Adams de Haut	?1	5	R			2			1K:2B
**327	Les Adams	?1	5	R	4G		8f	2		2B
***328	Les Adams	5	5	R		2G:1R			1W:(2W)	
329	Rue des Claires Mares	?1	?5	O	4R		?3			
330	Les Claires Mares	6	?5	O			8f		1W	1K
331	La Fosse, Les Jehans	5	4	R			8f		(2W)	
*332	Les Jehans Farm	?1	?4	O				7		
333	Les Jehans	6	4	R			?8f			
334	Les Champs, Les Jehans	5	5	R						
335	Les Jehans									
*336	Le Colombier	?1	5	R			8f		1S	
337	Colombier House	5	5	R					2W	
338	Le Clos	5	5	R						
339	Le Croisée, Route de Pleinmont	5	4	R			8f		(1W)	
**340	Les Simons	4	3	O	7		4f	4		1B;1L
341	Les Simons									
342	Les Simons	5	5	R			(8f)			
343	Rockfield, Rue des Rocques	6	5	R			8			
344	Le Sauchet	5	5	R			8f			
345	La Forge, Rue de la Bellée									
**346	Maison d'Aval, Rue de la Bellée	?1	5	R			?7		2W	
347	Laleur	5	5	R						

Back Kitchen	Back Kitchen Fireplace	Tourelle	Cross Walls	Bénetier/ Evier	Byre Window	Panelling	Farm Buildings	Fief: Earliest recorded date; additional information **PARISH OF ST. PIERRE-DU-BOIS 313-331 PARISH OF TORTEVAL 332-347**
			(P)					*c.*1700-1750
			2	5R			1 ATT	*c.*1400-1550
		R→K	1K	5sq				*c.*1400-1550
			1B					*c.*1400-1550 '1822' lintel—refronting. Base stones of unchamfered front arch remain
			?1					*c.*1400-1550 Early extension of 2 bays (*c.*16c.) to W; and also to E by 1 bay (*c.*17c.). Partly ruinous, partly one-storey stables at present
			1B					*c.*1700-1750
			2					*c.*1700-1750 Stable below parlour
Y			1K					*c.*1625-1700
		R?→K	?2	5sq				*c.*1550-1600 2 bays of original house refronted; tourelle with évier in cross passage. Remainder of house rebuilt 19c.
Y	8f		(P)					*c.*1625-1700
			1K				1 ATT	*c.*1723-1750
		R→K	(P)					*c.*1550-1625
		L→Kr	2	3				*c.*1400-1550
Y			2					*c.*1400-1550
		R→K	1B	5R				*c.*1400-1550
Y	8f	R→Kr	2				2 DET	*c.*1550-1625 Very early barns. 17c. bakehouse with well inside, originally detached, 8f
			1K					*c.*1550-1625 Ruins
			2	5sq				*c.*1625-1700 Ruins
			2					*c.*1625-1700
Y	8f		1B					*c.*1400-1550 2 bays of old house demolished for construction of new house 19c.
Y			(P)				1 ATT	*c.*1700-1750
Y	8f		2					*c.*1700-1750 Green bed and pork rack still in use. Bread oven projects into barn
								Barn only remains ?18c.
			1K					*c.*1550-1625 Fief seat to left of house
Y	8f		2					*c.*1625-1700
Y	8f		2					*c.*1700-1750
Y			1K					*c.*1625-1700
			1B					*c.*1550-1625 Before 1592—Fief Blondel. Corbel displaced by bread oven re-used as seat by fire
Y	8f							*c.*1700-1750 Back kitchen only remains; house rebuilt 19c. Fief seat against gable end
			2					*c.*1625-1700
			1K					*c.*1700-1750
								*c.*1700-1750
								Barn only remains *c.*18c.
		L→Kr	2					*c.*1400-1550
			2					*c.*1700-1750 '1729' lintel now plastered over

No.	Address Map Page 313, 312, 307	Type	Bays	Facade: Original/ refaced	Arch: Type, colour	Stone Chimneys: Colour	Fireplace Downstairs	Fireplace Upstairs	Chimney Hoods	Gable Windows
348	La Ferme du Pignon, Les Sages									
349	Les Cambrées	5	5	R			(8f)			
350	La Hure, Rue des Cambrées									
351	Le Douit, Les Buttes	5	5	R			8f		(1W)	
* 352	Les Buttes	6	5	O			8f			
353	Les Vieilles Galliennes	5	5	O						
354	Les Galliennes	9	5	O			10f:(10)		1W	
* 355	Les Portelettes	5	5	R			8		1W	
356	Rue de Rougeval	6	5	O		1G	8f:8		1S	
357	Les Fontaines	5	5	R			(8)		(2W)	
358	Le Rocher	5	4	R			8f		2W	2B
359	Le Hurel	5	4	R			(8f)		(1W)	
360	Le Grenier, Rue du Hurel	?1	4	R					(1W)	1B
361	La Mouranderie	?1	5	R			6	?6	2W	2B
* 362	Caw Chapin, Rue de la Vallée	9	5	R			8f		(2W)	
363	Le Petit Viltole	6	5	O			8f		1W	
** 364	Les Houets, Rue de la Viltole	?1	4	O			8f			
365	La Maison d'Aval, Rue des Vilaines	5	5	R			(8f)			
366	Pleinmont House	5	5	R						
** 367	La Seigneurie	?1	5	R	5G		1f		1S;(1S)	2B
368	Rocque à l'Or, Pleinmont	5	4	R			8			
369	Pleinmont	5	5	R						
370	Les Rouvets de Haut	6	5	R			8f			
* 371	Les Rouvets	?1	5	R	2R		2			
* 372	Les Rouvets Farm	?1	5	R	3R					
* 373	Lower Rouvets	?1	6	R			8f	?8	1W	
* 374	Le Vieux Rouvets	?1	5	O						
375	Les Hêches	5	5	R						
376	La Hougue	5	4	O			8f			
* 377	Hougue Bachelet	5	5	O		2G	8f		1W	
378	La Vallée	9	5	O		2G	8f			
379	La Tablette	6	5	R			8f			
380	Perelle Cottage	6	4	O			8f		1W	
381	La Maison de Douit	6	4	R		1G				
382	Les Ménages	6	4	R			8		1W	
* 383	Le Grand Douit	?4	3	R	3G			7	1S	2B
* 384	Le Grand Douit	5	5	R		2G	(8f)			1P
385	Grande Rue	?					1			
386	Ste. Appoline	5	5	R						

Back Kitchen	Back Kitchen Fireplace	Tourelle	Cross Walls	Bénetier/ Evier	Byre Window	Panelling	Farm Buildings	Fief: Earliest recorded date; additional information PARISH OF TORTEVAL 348-369 PARISH OF ST. SAVIOUR 370-386
Y	8						1 ATT	c.1750-1780 Much rebuilt 19c. Contracts 1769
			2					c.1700-1750
								House rebuilt 19c.; barns c.17c.
		YES	1K				1 DET	c.1700-1750
			2					c.1625-1700
			2					c.1700-1750
			2					c.1700-1750 Derelict
Y	8f		1K				1 ATT	c.1700-1750 Bread oven in kitchen, but fired from back kitchen. Valet's quarters, wooden shoulders to Type 8 fireplace
			(P)					c.1700-1750
Y	(8f)		2				1 ATT: 2 DET	c.1700-1750 Valet's quarters with Type 8 fireplace
Y			1K					c.1625-1700
Y	8							c.1700-1750
Y	8f		1K					c.1550-1625
Y	8f		1K					c.1400-1550
Y			2					c.1700-1750
			1K					c.1700-1750
Y		R→K	2					c.1550-1625
								c.1700-1750 Almost completely rebuilt 20c.
Y	8f		2				1 ATT	c.1700-1750 but mostly rebuilt 19c.
Y	8f	(L→K)	1K					c.1550-1625
			(P)					c.1700-1750
Y	8f		(P)					c.1700-1750
			1K					c.1700-1750
Y	8	R→K	1K				2 DET	c.1400-1550 'NDG 1732'—refronting. Large cellar under one barn
Y	8	R→K	(P)					c.1400-1550
		L→K	2					c.1550-1625
Y	8f	L→K	2					c.1400-1550
			(P)				1 ATT	c.1700-1750 Valet's quarters with Type 8 fireplace
								c.1625-1700
			1K					c.1625-1700
			2					c.1700-1750
			1B					c.1700-1750
			1K					c.1625-1700
			(P)					c.1700-1750
Y	8f		1K					c.1700-1750
								c.1400-1550
			2					?1778 'EDMR ♡ IDMR 1778' lintel
			?					c.1400-1550 Ruined
			2					c.1625-1700

No.	Address Map Page 307, 308	Type	Bays	Facade: Original/ refaced	Arch: Type, colour	Stone Chimneys: Colour	Fireplace Downstairs	Fireplace Upstairs	Chimney Hoods	Gable Windows
* 387	La Grande Rue House	?1	5	R						
*** 388	Les Grands Courtils	?1	5	O	4R	2R	1			1K,2B,2L
389	Primrose Farm, La Grande Rue	?1	?5	R		1G	?6		1S	
* 390	La Grande Rue	1	5	R						
391	La Grande Rue Farm	?1	5	R						1B
392	Near Le Hurel	6	4	O			8		1W	
393	Le Lorier Farm	5	5	R						
394	The Coppice, Rue du Lorier									
395	Rue Mahaut	6	5	R						
396	Le Hamel	5	5	R						
* 397	Les Jenemies	?1	5	R			7f:8			1B
398	Narrabri, Les Jenemies	6	3	R			(8f)			
399	Les Jenemies	?1	?5	O						
* 400	No. 2, Les Jenemies	6	3	O						
401	Les Jenemies	(?1)	(4)		(4G)	(2G)				
402	Les Huriaux	?5	?5	O				(10)	(1W)	
** 403	Huriaux Place	?1	6	R			2			
* 404	Homelea, Rue du Mont Saint	9	5	O			8f		1W	
405	The Cottage, Rue du Mont Saint	10	2	O						
** 406	La Ruette	?1	5	R			(8)		(2W)	
* 407	Maison du Douit	1	5	R	3R		2			
** 408	La Coquerie, Rue de la Terre Norgiot	2	5	O			6		(1W)	
409	La Terre Norgiot	5	5	R					(2W)	
410	Terre Norgiot Cottage	6	4	R			8f			
411	Le Mont Saint									
412	Le Mont Saint	11	2	O						
* 413	St. Michel	1	5	R					1W	
* 414	Le Vieux Moulin	5	5	R			8f			
415	Les Annevilles	5	5	O		1R				
* 416	Les Padins	?1	5	R	7R	1G			1W	
417	Les Padins	5	5	R			8		1W	
** 418	La Maison de Haut	1	5	O	4R		6	?2	(2W)	2B
* 419	La Maison de Haut	?1	5	R		2R				
420	Les Trepieds	6	5	R		1				

Back Kitchen	Back Kitchen Fireplace	Tourelle	Cross Walls	Bénetier/Evier	Byre Window	Panelling	Farm Buildings	Fief: Earliest recorded date; additional information PARISH OF ST. SAVIOUR
Y	8f	R→K	2					c.1400-1550
Y		L→K	(P)	3;5R				c.1400-1550
			?					c.1550-1625 Partial access; survey incomplete
			2		1			c.1400-1550 '178?'—partial refronting
Y	6f		(P)					c.1550-1625 Furze oven with chamfered stone probably re-used from main house
			1B				1 ATT	c.1625-1700 Stable with separate access behind kitchen. Well-head integral. Derelict—used as barn
Y	8f		2					c.1700-1750
			?1					House almost completely rebuilt c.1970. Gable end c.18c.
			(P)					c.1700-1750 Derelict. Tiny window in back wall
			?1					c.1625-1700
		R→K	2					c.1550-1625
			?2					c.1750-1780
			?					c.1550-1625 Ruined
			(P)					c.1750-1780
			?				2 ATT	c.1550-1625 Rebuilt 1928, but gable ends remain with barns attached
							1 ATT	c.1700-1750 Ruined. Barn 16c.–17c.
Y	8f	R→K	1K	1				c.1400-1550 Benitier constructed partly from c.12c. beak-heads in limestone. Niche to right of fireplace has accolade lintel
			2					c.1700-1750
								c.1750-1780
Y	8f	L→K	2				1 ATT	c.1400-1550 Early wing of 3 bays. Original door at top of tourelle. '♡:NDMP ⚭ ИBD~/MDMP RCB 1782'—refronting. Clay insulation over bedroom ceiling
		R→K	(P)	5R	2			c.1400-1550 Tourelle doorway. House mostly reconstructed
			1K		1			c.1400-1550
			(P)					c.1625-1700 'DDM EDM 1769' refronting
			(P)					c.1700-1750
							1 DET	House rebuilt 19c., incorporating fireplace lintel over side door. Barns c.17c.
								c.1700-1750 Present house probably stables to older ruined house adjoining
Y	8		(P)		1			c.1550-1625
			1K			17c.		c.1625-1700
			(P)					c.1625-1700
Y	8f	R→K	2					c.1550-1625
			2					c.1700-1750
		R→K	1K		1			c.1400-1550
Y	8	R→K	1K					c.1550-1625
			1K					c.1700-1750

No.	Address Map Page 308, 314	Type	Bays	Facade: Original/refaced	Arch: Type, colour	Stone Chimneys: Colour	Fireplace Downstairs	Fireplace Upstairs	Chimney Hoods	Gable Windows
421	Les Massies	?1	5	R	1R		(2)			
**422	La Fontaine	?1	5	R		2G	2:3f			
423	Le Haut, Rue du Douit Manchot	?1	5	R	3R					
**424	Les Domaines	?1	5	R		2(f)			1S;(1S)	
425	Les Domaines									
*426	Les Domaines	?1	5	R	7R		8			
427	Les Frances	5	6	R						1K
428	Les Frances	?1	5	R			7f		1S;(1W)	
429	Les Frances	?1	5	O		1R;1B				
430	Le Belial	6	5	R			8f		1W	
*431	Les Ruettes	?1	5	R	7R					
*432	Le Petit Vallon	?1	5	R			5			1K
***433	Le Gron	?1	4	O	5R		?7	2	1S	
434	Mon Abri, Le Gron	5	5	O						
*435	Le Gron Farm	5	5	R						
**436	Le Grée, le Gron	2	5	O			2f			1K
437	Maison d'Aval, les Issues	9	6	O			(8f)			
438	Les Issues	5	5	R			8f		(1W)	
439	Les Ruettes Cottage	9	7	R			7;8		1W;(1S)	
440	Les Issues	5	5	O					(1W)	
441	La Cour de Longue	5	5	R						
*442	La Cour de Longue	7	5	O			8f		1W	
*443	La Bonne Vie, Rue des Issues	9	5	R			7f		1S;(1W)	
444	La Longue Maison									
**445	Les Piques	1	5	R	5R		2		1S	2L
446	Les Hêches						2			1K
447	Les Vallettes	9	5	O			(8f)			
*448	Les Vallettes	6	5	O			8f			
449	La Hougue Fouque	5	5	R						
*450	Les Raies Farm	5	6	O		1	8f;8		2W	
451	Les Raies House									
***452	Les Bordages	3	7	R			6s(?f)		(1W)	1B
453	Les Buttes Guest House									

Back Kitchen	Back Kitchen Fireplace	Tourelle	Cross Walls	Bénetier/Evier	Byre Window	Panelling	Farm Buildings	Fief: Earliest recorded date; additional information PARISH OF ST. SAVIOUR
Y			1K					Between 1555 and 1583—fief records
		R→K	2					c.1400-1550 Tourelle doorway. Loft survived until 1970
Y	8f		2					c.1400-1550
Y		L→K	1K					c.1400-1550 Early door (c.16c.) bottom of tourelle
Y	8f							House rebuilt 19c., back kitchen probably 18c.
Y	8f		1K					c.1550-1625 Fleur-de-lys stop on front doorway. 2 stones from older fireplace incorporated in back kitchen fireplace
Y	8f		2					c.1625-1700
			1K					c.1550-1625
		R→K	2					c.1550-1625 Demolished 1979
			(P)					c.1700-1750
Y	8f	R→K	2					c.1400-1550 Before 1535—fief records
Y		L→K	2					c.1550-1625
Y	8f	L→Kr	1K					c.1580-1590 Mason's mark on arch 'JC and JB'— John Carey and Jacqueline Blondel. Fireplace lintel double-notched—bedroom
			(P)					Between 1622 and 1663—fief records
			(P)				1 ATT: 1 DET	House perhaps 19c. Barns 17-18c. Plaited reed 'thatching' to underside of cart entrance
Y	8		2	1				c.1550-1625 'IDL 1739' kitchen beam
			(P)					c.1700-1750
Y			2					c.1700-1750 '1723' lintel
Y	8f		(P)					c.1550-1625
Y	8f		1K					Between 1662 and 1708 'PLH:1764' lintel. Clay insulation over bedroom ceilings
Y			(1K)	?5R				c.1700-1750
			(P)					Between 1622 and 1663—fief records
			2					c.1550-1625 Before 1586—fief records. 'Byre' side fitted with additional fireplace and leaded-light windows c.17c.
								Barn only remains: house rebuilt 19c.
Y	8f	L→K	(1K)	5R	(1)	18c.		c.1400-1550
								c.1400-1550 Ruined. Fireplace removed to Les Queux (555) 1980
			1K					Between 1664 and 1708—fief records
			2					Between 1622 and 1664—fief records
Y	8f							
			1K				2 ATT	c.1625-1700 on site of older house. 1 barn now cottage
								House rebuilt 19c. but older walling in barn and out-buildings
		R→K	(1K)				1 ATT	c.1400-1550 Many alterations made in 1790 when 'new' house was built. Earliest document 1550
							1 ATT	House rebuilt 19c. Barn possibly 18c.

No.	Address Map Page 308, 309	Type	Bays	Facade: Original/refaced	Arch: Type, colour	Stone Chimneys: Colour	Fireplace Downstairs	Fireplace Upstairs	Chimney Hoods	Gable Windows
454	Les Buttes Cottage									
455	Le Clos Hoguet, Les Prevosts									
456	Le Bricquet Cottage, Les Prevosts	?6					8f			
**457	Le Carrefour	?1	5	O			2		(2S)	
458	Le Bricquet, Les Prevosts									
*459	Les Prevosts Farm	5	5	R					(1W)	
**460	Les Belles	?1	5	R			8f	8	2W	1K
**461	Maison d'Aval, Rue des Câches	?1	5	O	2R					1B
462	Les Câches	5	4	O				7	(?1W)	
**463	Les Prevosts	?1	5	R			3f;7	?3		
*464	Les Prevosts	?1	5	O			6			
*465	Les Prevosts	?1	5	R	1R;1B					
*466	Somerset House, Les Prevosts	?1	5	R			8f			
*467	Les Prevosts	5	5	R			6;(8)			
468	Les Jaonnets	5	5	O		2G	8f			
*469	Les Jaonnets	?1		O	2R		8		(1W)	
*470	La Neuve Volante, Frie au Four	?1	5	O		2G	7		2S	
471	La Fevresse Cottage	9	5	O			(8f)			
*472	Le Douit, Rue Fevresse	?1	5	R	2G					
*473	Sous l'Eglise	?1	6	R			7		(1W)	
474	Sous l'Eglise	5	5	R					(1W)	
**475	La Vieille Sous l'Eglise	?1	5	O	7R	(1 round)		3	2W	
476	Les Comptes Farm	5	4	O	?7					
477	Les Lohiers									
*478	Les Lohiers	?1	5	R						
*479	La Porte, Rue du Hechet	5	5	R			?8			2K
*480	La Porte, Rue du Hechet	?1	4	R			6		1W	1K;2L
481	Les Choffins	5	5	R						
482	Les Fauxquets Farm	3	7	R			(8f)	8		
483	Fauxquets de Bas	5	4	R					(1W)	

Back Kitchen	Back Kitchen Fireplace	Tourelle	Cross Walls	Bénetier/ Evier	Byre Window	Panelling	Farm Buildings	Fief: Earliest recorded date; additional information PARISH OF ST. SAVIOUR 454-481 PARISH OF THE CASTEL 482-483
							2 DET	House rebuilt 19c. Barns and well-head 17-18c.
							1 ATT	House rebuilt 19c. Barns 18c.
			1K					c. 1625-1700 Half of house demolished
Y	(8f)		1K				1 ATT	c. 1400-1550 Valet's quarters with Type 8 fireplace over barn. Upper cruck with collar, upper kingpost and wind braces (lost) on main roof. Oven from back kitchen projected into kitchen
								House rebuilt c. 1840. Barns 18c.
Y	8f		2					c. 1700-1750
Y	8f	L→K	2					c. 1400-1550 Before 1597—fief records. Tourelle 11 ft. diameter
Y		R→K	1K					c. 1400-1550 Before 1597—fief records. 17c. windows
			(P)					c. 1625-1700 Main house rebuilt 19c. Possibly the 17c. building was always barn with valet's quarters over
Y		L→K	(P)			17c.	2 ATT	c. 1400-1550 17c. panelling in valet's quarters; Type 8 fireplace
Y	8f		1K	5sq				c. 1550-1625
		R→K	2					c. 1550-1625 'PNT:SLP:1700' window lintel. Blue granite chimney is 19c.
		L→K	1K					c. 1550-1625 'NLH ♡1732' refronting
Y			1K				1 ATT: 1 DET	c. 1625-1700 '♡ I·LH ♡1740♡' refronting
			2					c. 1625-1700
			1					c. 1400-1550 Half of house demolished when 'new' house built c. 1824. Original byre end refurbished as back kitchen re-using earlier fireplace stones
Y	(8f)	L→K	2					c. 1550-1625 'WLM·MDLM 1748' lintel: Helier Le Mesurier and Marie de la Mare
			1K					c. 1700-1750
		R→K	1K					c. 1400-1550
Y	8f	L→K	2				1 DET	c. 1400-1550 Clay insulation on top of bedroom ceilings. Valet's apartment with Type 8 fireplace over barn
			1K					1662—Fief records
2	10f;10f	R→K	(P)				2 ATT	c. 1550-1625 Pigeonniers front of house and along back kitchens. Furze oven from back kitchen on L. projected into barn. R. back kitchen covers well
Y			(P)				1 DET	c. 1625-1700
								House rebuilt 19c. Barns probably 18c.
Y	(8f)	R→Kr	1K				1 DET	c. 1550-1625 'INT:♡ LES LOHIERS 1784' refronting. Possible valet's quarters with Type 8 fireplace with simple corbel downstairs in barn
Y			1K				1 ATT	c. 1625-1700 Shield over front doorway—Blondel arms
		R→K	(1K)					c. 1400-1550 Dripstones over windows
Y	8f		(P)					c. 1700-1750
Y	(8)		1B	1			1 ATT	c. 1550-1625 Gable end rebuilt 19c.
Y	(8f)		(P)				1 ATT	c. 1625-1700

No.	Address Map Page 309, 308	Type	Bays	Facade: Original/ refaced	Arch: Type, colour	Stone Chimneys: Colour	Fireplace Downstairs	Fireplace Upstairs	Chimney Hoods	Gable Windows
* 484	Candie	?1	4	O			?8f		(1S)	
485	Candie Road	5	4	O			8f			
** 486	Moulin de Haut	?1	5	R					(1W)	1B
487	Cottage, Moulin de Haut	11	3	O				8	1W	
488	L'Etiennerie	5	4	R			8f			
489	Le Hêchet	?1	5	R						
490	La Hougue au Lierre	6	4	O			8f		(1W)	
* 491	Le Marais Cottage	6	5	O			8f		(1W)	
492	Le Marais	?1	5	R			7		(1W)	
*** 493	Le Marais	1	5	O	1R		3s	3P	(2W)	2B
494	Le Gélé	5	5	O			(8f)		(2W)	
495	Le Rocher	9	5	O						
496	La Cherverie	5	5	R			8(f);8		(1W)	
497	Les Grands Moulins Road	6	5	O			8f		(1W)	
** 498	Le Douit Farm	?1	5	O			2p		1W	
** 499	Le Douit Farm Flats	?1	5	R				2S		
500	La Hurette Cottage	6	5	O			8f;8		2W	
501	Courtil Jardin									
* 502	Wisteria, King's Mills	5	4	R			2	8	1W	2B
503	La Pointe, King's Mills	6	4	O			8f			
* 504	King's Mills' House	?1	6	O			7f	?8		
* 505	Les Grands Moulins	?1	?6	O						2K
** 506	King's Mills' Farm	3	8	O	3R		6f:8(f)	6	2S	2B;1
507	La Bohème/Millmount									
* 508	Fleur du Jardin Hotel	?1	5	O			4	(7)		2B
*** 509	La Forge	?1	5	R	3R		2(f)	?2		2B;1L
510	King's Mills' Villa	5	5	R						
511	Les Grands Moulins									
*** 512	Ménage du Moulin	1	5	R	1R		8f	2	1S	2B
513	Maison de Haut	5	5	R			(8f)			
* 514	La Sauvarinerie	?1	4	R				2		1B
* 515	Moulin de Milieu		3	O			8		(1W)	1B

Back Kitchen	Back Kitchen Fireplace	Tourelle	Cross Walls	Bénetier/Evier	Byre Window	Panelling	Farm Buildings	Fief: Earliest recorded date; additional information PARISH OF THE CASTEL
			(P)					c.1550-1625 Much altered when 'new' house built 1874
			(P)					c.1625-1700
Y		L→Kr	2			18c.	Mill c.18c.	c.1550-1625 Refashioned in 18c. with galleting; sundial; arms of Lefebvre over front door
			1					c.1700-1750 Ruined
Y	(8f)		2					c.1625-1700 Galleting
Y	(8f)		2					c.1400-1550 Valet's apartment with Type 8f fireplace and wattle and daub hood
			1K					c.1700-1750
			2					c.1700-1750
Y	8(f)		1K					c.1550-1625 '⁀NAR✠PALR·RLM/1783' refronting
		L→K	2	5	2			Before 1470—Fief records
Y	8f		1K					c.1700-1750
Y	8f		2				1 ATT	Between 1583 and 1634. Attached barn probably an early house
Y	(8f)		2					c.1625-1700 'IDR:SDBC:1788'—lintel of coursed barn. Earth floor in back kitchen until 1950
			(1K)					c.1700-1750
Y	8(f)		2					c.1550-1625 Kitchen fireplace perhaps inserted with later shoulders. Back kitchen oven projected outside
	? removed		1B					c.1400-1550 Window seats at side of bedroom window
			(P)				1 ATT	c.1625-1700
								Barn only remains
			2				1 ATT	Between 1584 and 1634. Galleting
			(P)					c.1625-1700 House shortened for road widening
		R→K	1K					c.1550-1625
		L→K	1B					c.1400-1550 House possibly lengthened at kitchen end by 1 bay, removing fireplace. Byre end widened. 15c. window. House possibly here in 1380
		L→K	1K	5R			1 ATT	c.1400-1550 Contract 1590
								House rebuilt 19c. 2 barns—possibly 18c.—now houses
Y		R→K	1K					c.1400-1550 Cross on fireplace corbel
		L→K	1K	3;5R			1 ATT	Before 1470—Fief records. Tourelle doorway: arrow slit. Stairs turn towards back door
			1B		?1			c.1625-1700, but possibly 16c. if small 'byre' window indicates longhouse
								Gable end of house only; c.18c.
		L→K	1B	3				c.1400-1550 'RLP 1620'; 'TML'; 'NM' on jambs of arch. Byre used as stable until recently. Furze oven opening at back of fireplace. No back door
			(P)					c.1700-1750 1724—Fief records
		R→K	1K					c.1400-1550 House much altered 19c. Top of tourelle rebuilt square
Y								c.1625-1700

No.	Address Map Page 308, 309	Type	Bays	Facade: Original/refaced	Arch: Type, colour	Stone Chimneys: Colour	Fireplace Downstairs	Fireplace Upstairs	Chimney Hoods	Gable Windows
516	Moulin de Milieu									
*517	Le Groignet	5	?4	R	8	2R		5	(1W)	1B
*518	Les Grands Moulins	?1	5	O	(4R)		6(f)	6		1B;1L
*519	King's Mills' Lodge	?1	5	R			8;?7	?7	(1S)	
***520	Les Grands Moulins	?1	5	O	3R		1			2K
521	Les Grands Moulins	6	5	R	?4		(8)f			
*522	Coutances, King's Mills	?1	5	O			6;8		2W	
*523	Le Pavé	1	?6	R			(8)		(1W)	
524	St. Anne, King's Mills	6	5	O			8f			
525	Beaumont, Rue de la Porte	6	5	O			8f			
526	La Porte, King's Mills	5	5	R						
527	Les Granges	6	5	O		2	?8		2S	
***528	La Houguette	3	7	O	(?5)	5R	7f;5	2	2W	1B
529	La Houguette	?2	5	R			2f		(1W)	
530	La Mare	6	?5	R			(8:8)		(1W)	
531	Bon Accord, Les Eturs									
532	Les Eturs Cottages	6	5	R			8f		1W	
**533	Woodlands	?1	5	O		2R	7	7	1W	2B
534	Vau des Vallées	5	4	R						
*535	La Vallée	?5		O			8		1W	
**536	Les Roussiaux	5	5	?O			8(f)		2W	
537	Les Pelleys									
*538	Les Pelleys de Bas	?1	5	R			3			
539	Les Niaux	8	5	O			8f		1W	
540	Les Niaux Mill	5	5	O			(8f)			
541	Le Ponchez Farm									
542	Helena Villa	5	?5	R						
**543	The Cottage	?1	4	O		2	7f		1W	1B
**544	Les Fontaines	?1	5	O		1 round 2R	2		1S;(2W)	
545	Castel Hill	1	?4	O	(?5)		5(f)		(1S)	1B
546	La Bernauderie		?5				?2f	6		
547	Route de l'Eglise	6	?5	O						
548	Queux Manor Vinery	5	5	R			?8			

Back Kitchen	Back Kitchen Fireplace	Tourelle	Cross Walls	Bénetier/Evier	Byre Window	Panelling	Farm Buildings	Fief: Earliest recorded date; additional information — PARISH OF THE CASTEL
								Mill house altered and heightened 19c. 'IBD 1763' by window
Y			(P)				1 DET	c. 1625-1700 Double entrance at end of drive c.15c. Basin of benitier re-used as quoin. Stable under back kitchen
			1B				1 ATT	c.1550-1625 Valet's quarters with Type 8 fireplace in barn. Chamfered windows
Y	8f	R→K	2					Between 1584 and 1636—fief records
Y	8f		1K	2				c.1400-1550 '1623' arch. Butter-making machine in back kitchen
			2					c.1700-1750 incorporating a little older walling
Y			1K				1 ATT	c.1550-1625 Before 1624—Fief records. Galleting
			1K	1				c.1550-1625 Before 1624—Fief records. Cross-passage subdivided with plank wall and long seat
			(P)					c.1700-1750 Wooden shoulders to fireplace
			1				1 ATT	Between 1690 and 1705. Attached stabling now cottage. House raised 1 storey 19c.
Y			1K			18c.		c.1700-1750
			1K					c.1625-1700 Chimneys painted
		L→K	2			16c.; 18c.	1 DET	c.1550-1625 Valet's quarters with barn below. Type 5 fireplace. Galleting on house
			1K					c.1550-1625 Cross-wall perhaps rebuilt when altered into stable
			(1K)					c.1700-1750 Additional Type 8 fireplace in later wing, now removed
								House rebuilt. Barn c.18c.
			(?P)					c.1700-1750 Now divided into 2 cottages
Y		L→K	1K			18c.		c.1400-1550 'CM 1769' on rain-water head
Y	8f		(P)					c.1625-1700
			1B					c.1625-1700 Half of house demolished when 19c. house built. 18c. settle
			1B			17c.		Between 1602 and 1653 '♡IRS RRS♡/1767' lintel
							1 ATT	House rebuilt 19c. Barns with 17c. window
Y	8f		1K				1 DET	c.1550-1625 Before 1555—Fief records
			1B					c.1625-1700 Bread oven projects beyond gable. Rebuilt 1980
			1B					c.1700-1750
								House rebuilt. 'NM' upstairs window of barn 1692
			(P)					c.1700-1750 Completely modernised
		L→K	2	?5sq				c.1400-1550 Tourelle flattened against back wall. Possible évier to R. of fireplace
			2					c.1400-1550 Second fireplace inserted c.17c. upstairs
			(P)	1				c.1550-1625 House reduced in height: now a store
								c.1400-1550 Ruined
								c.1625-1700 Ruined
			2					1740

No.	Address Map Page 309, 303	Type	Bays	Facade: Original/ refaced	Arch: Type, colour	Stone Chimneys: Colour	Fireplace Downstairs	Fireplace Upstairs	Chimney Hoods	Gable Windows
* 549	Le Préel House	5	5	R					(1W)	
* 550	La Tanière	5	5	O					(2W)	1P;1B
* 551	La Cheminée, Ruette de St. Briocq	?1	4	O			8f		1W	
* 552	Les Effards	?1	5	R	3R					
553	1 and 2, Ruette des Effards	6	5	R			(8f)			
** 554	Le Manoir, Les Effards	?1	5	R	2R		7f			
*** 555	Les Queux	?1	4	R	3R		7f	7	(2W)	1B
556	Castel Rectory	5	5	O						
* 557	Les Girards	?1	5	O	2R		2f	7		
558	Les Covins	5	5	R	2R					1B
559	La Croix, Rue des Covins	5	5	R						
560	Le Friquet Cottage	6	5	R			8f:8		2W	
561	Le Friquet	5	5	R			8		(1W)	
*** 562	Les Tilleuls	?1	5	O			2			1K
** 563	Les Tilleuls	3	6	O			7f;2	7s;7		
564	Soucique, La Charuée									
* 565	Charuée Lodge	?1	5	R	?4	1	7f	7		2B
* 566	Grand Clos	?1	5	R			7	(7)	1S;(1S)	
567	Hotel Hougue du Pommier	5	5	R						
568	Les Petites Mielles	11	?3	O						1
569	La Mare de Carteret	11	3	O						
570	La Maison Fontaines	6	5	R						
571	Les Petits Cherfs	6	5	O		1				
572	Les Houmets									
573	Folk Museum	5	5	R						
574	La Pouquelaye	5	5	R						
* 575	Les Mourains									
576	Les Blancs Bois				8					
** 577	Maison Villocq	1	5	O		2R			1S	
578	Le Ménage	5	5	R					(1W)	
579	Le Villocq Farmhouse	5	5	R			8f		(2W)	
** 580	La Vieille Maison, Le Villocq	4	3	O			5f	5	1W	2B
*** 581	Le Villocq	?1	?5	O	6R				?1S	1L

Back Kitchen	Back Kitchen Fireplace	Tourelle	Cross Walls	Bénetier/ Evier	Byre Window	Panelling	Farm Buildings	Fief: Earliest recorded date; additional information **PARISH OF THE CASTEL**
Y	(8f)		1					*c.*1700-1750 Deeds of 1731
Y	8f		2					Between 1602 and 1634. Unique galleting edge on
			(P)			17c.		Before 1555—Fief records, but present house possibly 17c.
			2	2				Before 1470—Fief records. 'DDB 1745' on attached wing with valet's quarters above
			2					Between 1602 and 1634—Fief records
			1K					*c.*1400-1550 'IH 1750'—barn
		R→K	1K	5				Before 1470—Fief records. Arched window openings. Base of arched doorway as at 123
			2					1785 2-bay building behind originally with wattle and daub chimney hood. Present rectory two rooms deep front to back 'NDD:RP(?)1785'—facade
			1K	5sq.				*c.*1400-1550 Chamfered lintel over gable window of loft. Back door lintel rebated
			1					*c.*1625-1700
			1B					*c.*1625-1700
Y								*c.*1700-1750
Y	(8f)		1K			18c.		*c.*1700-1750
		(?R→K)	?					*c.*1400-1550 Now used as barns
Y	8f		1B					*c.*1400-1550 Perhaps a little later than 562. 17c. window and nicely ornamented sill to bedroom window *c.*16c.
								House rebuilt 19c. Barn adjoining *c.*18c.
			2					*c.*1400-1550 Arch and stone chimney painted
Y			2					*c.*1550-1625
			2					*c.*1700-1750
								*c.*1700-1750
								*c.*1700-1750
								*c.*1700-1750
			2					*c.*1625-1700 Loft opening (now window) over front door
								House rebuilt 19c. Barn *c.*18c.
			1					*c.*1700-1750 'TCH: ♡ :1786' lintel—refronting
Y			1K				1 ATT	*c.*1700-1750
							2 DET	House rebuilt 1818 'IOZ 1722' John Ozanne—beam in cider-press barn; 'IOZ 1735'—cider press; 'IOZ 1745'—gate in lane; 'IOZ 1765'—pump
								House rebuilt
			1K	1				*c.*1400-1550
			2					*c.*1625-1700
			1B			17c.		*c.*1625-1700
			P			17c.	(1 ATT)	*c.*1550-1625 Panelling mostly renewed 19c. Blocked doorways downstairs front R. and upstairs back R. to barn since demolished.
		L→K	2					*c.*1400-1550 No access: survey incomplete

No.	Address Map Page 303, 302, 315	Type	Bays	Facade: Original/ refaced	Arch: Type, colour	Stone Chimneys: Colour	Fireplace Downstairs	Fireplace Upstairs	Chimney Hoods	Gable Windows
**582	La Haye du Puits	3	7	R			7			
583	La Haye du Puits	11	3	O						
*584	La Maison du Mont Val	6	5	O			8f;(8)		1W	
585	Mont Plaisant	6	?4	O			(8)	(8)	(1W)	
**586	St. George	?1	5	O	5G		(7)			
587	Behind St. George	6	?4	O			8f			
588	Rue de la Hougue									
589	La Fosse, Les Queritez	6	5	O			8f			
590	Le Camp, Rue des Hougues	?1	5	R			(8f)		(2W)	
591	Rue des Goddards									
592	Le Bourg	5	5	R						
*593	Retôt Farm	?1	5	O	?4	1	(7f)			
594	La Chaumière, Retôt Road	?2	5	O		1	2f			
***595	Old Cobo Farmhouse	1	5	R			5f:2	(7)	(1S)	
***596	Cobo Farmhouse	1	5	O	1R	1R	5f			1K
*597	Le Guet	6	4	R			8f			
**598	La Rocré	8	4	O		1R	8f	(8)	1W;(1S)	1B
599	Rozel, Ruette des Marottes	6	5	O			(8f)			
600	Les Landes	5	5	R						
*601	Le Tertre	6	5	O		1R	5(f)		(1S;1W)	
602	Les Blanches Roches	6	5	O			8f;(8)		(2W)	
603	Le Gardinet	5	5	R			8f		(1W)	
*604	Les Fries	5	5	R		2R	8f		(2W)	
*605	Les Fries	?1	5	O			(7)			
606	Maison Varendes	5	5	R			8f;8f			
607	Border Farm, Les Blicqs	?1		R	4G		8f			
608	Sunnyside Cottage	?1	5	O			6f			
*609	Les Blicqs	?1	5	R			6	6	(2W)	
***610	Les Blicqs	1	5	R	1R;7		2(f)	2	1S;1W	2B
*611	Les Blicqs	?1					5f			
612	The Meadows	5	5	O			8			

Back Kitchen	Back Kitchen Fireplace	Tourelle	Cross Walls	Bénetier/ Evier	Byre Window	Panelling	Farm Buildings	Fief: Earliest recorded date; additional information PARISH OF THE CASTEL 582-598 PARISH OF ST. ANDREW 599-612
		Turret L→K	?					c.1400-1550 Entry originally by fine carriage arch with porter's room—blocked by 18c. alterations. 2 corner turrets added c.1750
								c.1700-1750
			2					c.1625-1700 Access to loft originally by ladder only
			1B					c.1700-1750 Loft fitted with fireplace, possibly 18c.
		(?)	?	5R;4				c.1550-1625 '1581' arch. House reduced in height with entrances made in both gables 19c. Tourelle possibly removed to form cart entrance
			(P)					c.1700-1750 Derelict
								c.18c. barn with valet's quarters only
			2					c.1700-1750
Y	8f		2					c.1550-1625 2-storeyed bread oven projects on angle of back kitchen
								Gable ends only remain in sheds
			?					c.1625-1700 House almost completely rebuilt. Gable end may be 16c.
		L→K	1B	?5R				c.1400-1550 Arch and chimney painted
Y			2					c.1400-1550
		L→K	1K; (1B)		1			Before 1470—Fief records. Arched window at back now door. Oak roof trusses—collar and upper king-post; windbraces lost
			2	5R	2		1 ATT; 1 DET	Before 1470—Fief records
			(P)					Between 1588 and 1634—Fief records
Y			2					c.1550-1625 1-bay kitchen
			(P)					c.1625-1700
Y	8f		2					c.1625-1700
			1K				1 DET; 1 ATT	c.1550-1625 Bread oven formerly projected beyond kitchen gable. Clay insulation on loft floor
			2					Between 1750 and 1798—Fief records
			2					c.1625-1700
			1K					c.1625-1700
			1K					c.1400-1550
			1K			17c.; 18c.		c.1625-1700 One tiny window downstairs in back wall of both rooms
			1K					c.1550-1625 Half of house demolished for 19c. house; kitchen retained as back kitchen
			(P)				1 ATT	c.1550-1625 House narrowed for road widening
Y	8f		(P)					c.1550-1625 Chamfered sides of bedroom fireplace appear to be same stone as lintel
			½K	?5sq.	1		1 ATT; 1 DET	c.1400-1550 Valet's quarters with Type 8 fireplace with rough corbel; '1720 PLSV' refronting. Upstairs passage window never glazed. Drain in byre and central gable window. Monolithic side to barn entrance
								c.1550-1625 Half of house demolished for 19c. house which retained kitchen as new back kitchen
Y	8f		(P)					'ILLC 1775' lintel: date of construction

No.	Address Map Page 315, 309	Type	Bays	Facade: Original/ refaced	Arch: Type, colour	Stone Chimneys: Colour	Fireplace Downstairs	Fireplace Upstairs	Chimney Hoods	Gable Windows
613	Les Buttes	5	5	R			(8f)			
614	Les Eperons	?1	?5							
615	Les Hunguets	?1	5	O			7f;8f			
616	Les Gouies	5	5	R						
617	Les Gouies Farm	5	5	R			8f			
*618	Les Mourants	?1	5	R	1?R		3f			
619	Maison des Trésors									
620	La Villaize	5	5	R			8f			
621	La Mézière									
*622	La Fosse Equerre	?1	?5	R			(7)	?2	(1W)	1B
623	Le Bouillon	5	5	R			(8f)			
624	Le Hurel	?1	5	R						2B
625	Les Norgiots	5	5	R						
626	La Jaonnière	6	5	O			8f		1W	
627	La Carrière	6	5	R			8f			
628	View Vauxbelets	6	3	R			8f			
*629	Les Grands Guillaumes	?1	5	R	5G		6:(7f)			
*630	La Vassalerie	?1	4	R	5G/R		2f			
**631	Pleneuf Court	5	5	R						
*632	La Contrée de l'Eglise	?1	5	R						
**634	La Pelleyrie	?1	5	R	1R		3f			
**635	Hillside	?1	5	R			2f		1W;(1W)	
636	Les Près	5	5	O			8f			
637	Courtillet de l'Eveque	5	5	O			(8f)		(1W)	
***638	Les Bailleuls Cottage	?1	5	O			8f	7	(1S)	1B
639	Les Bailleuls	?1	5	R						1B
640	Les Friquets	?1	4	O			6f			
*641	Les Niaux	10	2	O			(8)		(1W)	
642	Les Niaux	6	5	O			8f		1W	
*643	Les Niaux	6	4	O						
644	Les Bourgs	5	5	R			(8f)		1S	
645	Les Bourgs	5	5	R						
*646	La Vieille Maison de l'Echelle	?1	?5	R			6f		1S	

Back Kitchen	Back Kitchen Fireplace	Tourelle	Cross Walls	Bénetier/ Evier	Byre Window	Panelling	Farm Buildings	Fief: Earliest recorded date; additional information PARISH OF ST. ANDREW
			(P)					*c.*1700-1750
			(P)					*c.*1550-1625 'IR:IS 1760'—lintel of van shed: John Rougier and Juliette Sarre
			1K					*c.*1400-1550
			(P)					*c.*1700-1750 House much altered
			1B					*c.*1700-1750 Now part of conservatory
Y			(P)					*c.*1400-1550 Arch painted. Inside width of house only 13 ft.
Y	8f							Main house 19c.
			(P)					*c.*1625-1700
								Main house rebuilt 1816. Barns 18c.
			?				1 ATT	*c.*1550-1625 House rebuilt from ruins. Cider barn now part of house. '1730' and 'IGV:1776' on barn. '?PG 1722' stone at angle of barn and house
Y	8		1K				1 ATT	*c.*1700-1750 Cider press remains
			1K					*c.*1550-1625
			(P)				1 ATT	*c.*1625-1700 Valet's quarters with Type 8 fireplace over barn
			1K					*c.*1750-1780
			(P)					*c.*1700-1750 Rebuilt 19c. except gable ends and foundations
			(P)					*c.*1750-1780
			1B		1			*c.*1550-1625 Possibly a single-storey cottage originally: otherwise gable rebuilt in part, 19c. Byre window inserted into larger opening
			(P)					*c.*1550-1625
Y	(8)f		(P)					*c.*1625-1700
		L→K	(P)					*c.*1550-1625 'PLLC 1746' refronting: Pierre Le Lacheur
		R→K	(P)					*c.*1550-1625 Tourelle doorway
			(P)					*c.*1400-1550 'GR♡MLLC♡1776' refronting
			2					'HRB 1731' lintel—date of construction?
			1K					*c.*1625-1700 Possibly 16c. if information about an arch previously at back of house is correct
			2	5				*c.*1400-1550 Stone with indecipherable inscription L. of front doorway. House slopes 3 ft. R.—L.: kitchen—byre
Y	8f		(P)					*c.*1550-1625 Central window in byre gable
			(P)					*c.*1400-1550
								*c.*1750-1780 Wooden shoulders for fireplace project into later barn. Single-roomed dwelling with stable but no internal access
			?					*c.*1700-1750 Ruined
			1B					*c.*1625-1700
			(P)					*c.*1700-1750
			(P)				1 ATT	*c.*1700-1750
			(P)					*c.*1400-1550 Bread oven projected beyond gable

No.	Address Map Page 309, 310	Type	Bays	Facade: Original/ refaced	Arch: Type, colour	Stone Chimneys: Colour	Fireplace Downstairs	Fireplace Upstairs	Chimney Hoods	Gable Windows
647	La Neuve Maison de l'Echelle	5	5	O						
648	L'Echelle	6	3	R			8f		1W	
**649	L'Echelle	1	5	R			8f		(1W)	1K
650	Talbot Valley	6	5	R						
651	Talbot Valley	?1	5	R						
*652	Moulin de l'Echelle	5	5	O			(8f)			
**653	Beaucoin, le Camptréhard	4	3	O			7	(7)	1W	
654	Le Camptréhard de Bas	5	5	R						
655	Le Camptréhard									
***656	Le Camptréhard	7	5	O			(8f)	(8)	(2W)	
657	La Petite Bernarderie	?5					(8)			
658	Le Monnaie	5	5	R					(2W)	
659	Le Monnaie	5	5	R						
660	La Petite Maison, Le Monnaie	4	3						1W	
**661	Les Poidevins	?1	4	O	3R	2R	f	6	2W	
*662	Les Poidevins	5	5	O			(8f:8)	(8)	(1W)	
663	Newlands, Le Monnaie	6	5	R						
664	Meadowview, La Rue Marquand	?					5(f)			1K
*665	Les Naftiaux	3	7	O			7f			
666	Naftiaux House	5	5	R						
**667	Les Mauxmarquis Cottages	?1	5	R			(7)	(?7)	1S	
668	1, Mauxmarquis Cottages	11	3	O			8f			
**669	Les Mauxmarquis	?1	5	R	5G		7			
670	La Brigade Farm Guest House									
671	Le Vauquiédor	5	5	O			(8f)			
672	La Maison de Bas, Les Truchots	?1	5	R						
673	Clos du Fauconnaires	5	5	R						
*674	Les Fauconnaires	5	5	R		1R				
675	Les Fauconnaires	5	5	R						
***676	Les Quertiers	5	5	R			6f		2W	
677	Vaux Douit	9	5	R			8f			
678	Les Ruettes	10	3+2	O			(?8)		(1W)	
679	Les Ruettes Lane	6	?5	R			8		(1W)	

Back Kitchen	Back Kitchen Fireplace	Tourelle	Cross Walls	Bénetier/ Evier	Byre Window	Panelling	Farm Buildings	Fief: Earliest recorded date; additional information PARISH OF ST. ANDREW
			(P)					c.1700-1750
			(P)					c.1700-1750
			1B		1	17c.		c.1550-1625 Byre window 6 ins. x 9 ins. now enlarged. Internal access to loft over kitchen by iron steps let down onto stairs
								c.1700-1750 Probably only gable end 18c.
		L→K	(P)					c.1400-1550
			(P)				Mill ATT	c.1700-1750 Bread oven projected into mill
			(P)				1 ATT	c.1550-1625 Doorway to L. of fireplace giving access to barn
Y			1K					c.1625-1700 Earth floor until 1950s
							1 DET	House rebuilt 19c. Barn c.17c.
			1B					c.1625-1700 Stone stairs down to byre and up to bedroom above byre
								c.1700-1750 Gable end only remains as part of shed
Y	?8		(P)					c.1700-1750
			1					'NRN FDG 1759'—lintel: date of construction
			(P)					c.1700-1750
		L→K	(P)					c.1400-1550 Derelict
			2					c.1625-1700 Straight stone staircase in cross-passage. House now used as barn
Y	8f		(P)				1 ATT	c.1700-1750 Small store or stable attached now cottage to R.
								c.1550-1625 Ruined
			2					c.1550-1625 Doorway R. of kitchen fireplace gave access to 'buttery'
Y	8f		(P)					c.1700-1750
		L→K	1K					c.1400-1550 '1720' lintel: refronting. Earth floor until 1967
								c.1700-1750
Y	8f	L→K	(P)					1610
Y	8f						1 ATT	House rebuilt 19c. Wing to R. of house c.1700
			2					c.1700-1750
Y	6f		1K				1 ATT	c.1550-1750 Building at right turned into back kitchen c.19c. and corbel and shoulder stones inserted possibly when main house redesigned
			?1					c.1700-1750 Remodelled 20c.
Y			(P)					c.1625-1700 House remodelled 19c. 17c. wing and barn
			(P)				1 ATT	c.1625-1700
			P			17c.		c.1625-1700 Before 1684—Fief records. 17c. windows at back
			1B					c.1700-1750
			1					c.1625-1700 Single room dwelling with byre built slightly later
								c.1700-1750 Gable end by road rebuilt 19c. Remainder demolished for rebuilding 1980

No.	Address Map Page 310, 311	Type	Bays	Facade: Original/ refaced	Arch: Type, colour	Stone Chimneys: Colour	Fireplace Downstairs	Fireplace Upstairs	Chimney Hoods	Gable Windows
680	Rohais Manor									
681	Ashburton									
682	St. Kilda, Les Hubits									
683	Huntspill, Les Hubits	5	5	R						
684	Les Damouettes	9	5	R			8(f)			
***685	Havilland House	5	5	O			8;?8		(1W)	1B
*686	Havilland Mead	?1	5	O			2/3(f)			1K;1L
687	La Panache	5	5	R			6f		1S;(1W)	
688	83, Hauteville	5	4	R						
692	Flambie Cottage, 11, Havelet	1	4	O			8f	?7	1W	1K
693	Le Beuna Vista, Hauteville	5	5	R						
694	Hauteville	5	5	O						
***695	The Cottage, Hauteville	5	5	R			8(f);?8		(1S)	
*697	Chateau de la Montagne	5	5	R			8;(8f)			
699	46, Pedvin Street	5	4	R						1P;1B
701	6, Pedvin Street	11	4	R						
702	8A, Pedvin Street	11	3	R						
703	4, Pedvin Street									
**717	11, Cliff Street	?1	5	R			7			1B
721	Tour Beauregard, Cliff Street	5	5	R						
*723	2, Coupée Lane	5	3	O			8			2Bs
727	Le Guet, 3, Coupée Lane	5	4	O						1K
728	6A, Lower Vauvert	5	5	R						1B
729	Lower Vauvert	5	5	O						
730	Antique Shop, Victoria Road	5	5	R						
732	Back Street, Burnt Lane									
**733	3, Back Street	5	5	R				(8)		2Bs
735	Stamp Shop, Contrée Mansell	5	4	R						
736	D.M.W. Enterprises, Contrée Mansell	5	5	R					1S	2B
*737	Milnes, Contrée Mansell	11	3	R						
738	Sam's Salon, Contrée Mansell									
795	1, Forest Lodge, Forest Lane	5	5	O						
797	La Plaiderie	?	?							
809	9, Berthelot Street	5	5	R			1;8			

Back Kitchen	Back Kitchen Fireplace	Tourelle	Cross Walls	Bénetier/ Evier	Byre Window	Panelling	Farm Buildings	Fief: Earliest recorded date; additional information PARISH OF ST. ANDREW 680-681 PARISH OF ST. PETER PORT 682-809
								*c.*1700-1750 Entirely remodelled. Some old walling only
								House rebuilt 19c. Barns *c.*18c.
								House rebuilt 1816, except for gable end
			(P)					*c.*1700-1750
			1B					*c.*1700-1750 House raised by 1 storey
Y			1K			17c;18c.		*c.*1625-1700 3-storeys
			(P)	5sq.				*c.*1550-1625 Small limestone pillar built into gable window. Downstairs fireplace corbels do not match
			(P)					*c.*1625-1700
			(P)					*c.*1700-1750 No access. Survey incomplete
Y			1K		1			*c.*1550-1625 Wooden shoulders for wattle and daub hood
			1B					*c.*1625-1700
			(P)					*c.*1750-1780
Y			P			17c;18c.		*c.*1625-1700 Earth floor to 2-bay annexe until 1945: annexe has wooden shoulders to fireplace
			P					*c.*1625-1700 3-storey
			(P)					*c.*1625-1700
			(P)					*c.*1750-1780
			(P)					*c.*1750-1780
								*c.*1750-1780 Some old walling in lower part of 19c. house
		R→K	2			16c;17c.		*c.*1400-1550 Heightened by 1 storey 18c. Tourelle occupies entire width of cross-passage
			(P)					*c.*1550-1625 16c. bases at side doorway: modernised 18c.
		L→K	P			17c.		*c.*1625-1700 3-storey. Very late tourelle with wooden newel. 1 gable window each bedroom
			(P)					*c.*1750-1780
			(P)					*c.*1750-1780 Brick-fronted. Drip-stone over gable window
			(P)					*c.*1750-1780
			(P)					*c.*1750-1780
								Ruined—*c.*18c.?
			P			17c.		*c.*1625-1700 Stairs on newel. 'DNT—MNT 1747' lintel. 3 storeys. Gable windows 1st and 2nd floor
			1					*c.*1625-1700 Raised by 1 storey 19c.
			P			17c.		*c.*1625-1700 Bases to doorway. Stairs on newel
								*c.*1625-1700 Stairs on newel at back R. angle of shop. 1st floor rebuilt in brick at back *c.*19c.
								Gable wall of *c.*18c. 3-storeyed building only
								*c.*1700-1750 3-storeys
								Gable end only survives *c.*1700-1750
			P			18c.		*c.*1400-1550 Modernised 18c. 'William Henry 1723' rain-water head

No.	Address Map Page 311, 310	Type	Bays	Facade: Original/ refaced	Arch: Type, colour	Stone Chimneys: Colour	Fireplace Downstairs	Fireplace Upstairs	Chimney Hoods	Gable Windows
811	Below La Bigoterie	5	?5	O			2			
812	Below La Bigoterie	?	?		1G			3P	(1S)	
815	Above La Bigoterie	5	5	R			8			2B
817	Coin Cottage, Le Truchot									
819	Elizabeth College	?	?		8					2B
**820	The Grange	?1	5	R			2	2		2B
822	1 and 2, St. Thomas' Village	?1	5	O						
**823	Vieille L'Hyvreuse	?1	5	O	4R	2R	5;7			1K
*827	Croutes House	?1	5	R			8f			
828	Les Gravées	5	5	O						
829	Tangela, Les Croutes	6	4	R			8;(8f)		(2W)	1B
830	Belmont Cottages, Les Croutes	6	5	R					(1W)	
831	La Collette, Les Croutes	6	5	R			(8f)			
833	Foulon Farm	5	5	R						
***834	Les Granges de Beauvoir Manor	5	6	O	8;4G	2G	1;6	2;6	2S	1K;1;1B
835	Les Granges de Beauvoir Manor	?1	?		1G					
836	Les Granges de Beauvoir Manor	?	?		5G					
837	Havilland Hall Farm	5	5	R						
840	2 and 3, Mount Row	?	?							
841	Courtil Rozel, Mount Durand									
843	68-72, Mount Durand	5	5	R						
844	99, Mount Durand	10	2	O						
845	Below Mount Durand									
846	Ivymount, 51, Mount Durand	5	5	O			(8)			
*847	Grove Hill House, Mount Durand	4	3	O						
848	10, Mount Durand	5	5	R						
849	La Vignette, 13, Mount Durand									
853	Le Courtillon, 36, Glategny Espl.	5	4	R						
*854	37, Glategny Esplanade	5	3	O						
855	39 and 39a Glategny Espl.	5	4	R						
856	1, Salter Street	5	5	O						
857	2, Salter Street	5	5	R						
**858	3, Salter Street	5	5	R						
859	4, Salter Street	?								

Back Kitchen	Back Kitchen Fireplace	Tourelle	Cross Walls	Bénetier/ Evier	Byre Window	Panelling	Farm Buildings	Fief: Earliest recorded date; additional information PARISH OF ST. PETER PORT
			?					c.1400-1550 Ruined
			?					c.1400-1550 Ruined
		R→Kr	1K			(18c.)		c.1550-1625 Gable window with wooden transom and diagonal wooden bars—for leaded lights. Panelling now at 111
								Some old walling. Altered 19c.
								c.1550-1625 Lower building now classrooms. Remains of entrance arch attached: mostly demolished 1829.
Y		(YES)	(P)				1 DET	c.1400-1550
			1K					c.1550-1625
Y		L→K	1B	5sq				c.1400-1550
Y			1K					c.1400-1550 Altered 18c. with wide window at front
			(P)					c.1700-1750
			(P)					c.1700-1750 Omitted from map
			1B				1 DET	c.1625-1700 Barn now cottages
			2					c.1700-1750
Y	8f		(P)					c.1625-1700
		R←K	P	4		17c.		c.1400-1550 For full description, see Chapter XXXV
								c.1400-1550 Some walling only
								c.1550-1625 Some walling only
Y			2				1 DET	c.1700-1750 Barn adjoins 19c. house opposite
								c.1400-1550 Gable end walls encased in 19c. houses
								c.17c. barn, now part of 19c. complex
			(P)					c.1700-1750 2-bay extension at each side
								c.1750-1780
								House rebuilt 19c., but some old walling on ground floor
			(P)					c.1750-1780
			P			17c.	1 ATT	c.1625-1700 Stairs on newel. Barn now part of house. Back door out of kitchen; narrow cross-passage
			(P)					c.1625-1700
							1 ATT?	19c. house encloses older building: 'IMG MGL 1766' lintel. c.16c. walls adjoining
			(P)					c.1625-1700 Newel staircase. Refurbished 19c.
		L→K	(P)					c.1625-1700 Square tourelle opens out of recess at back of narrow cross-passage
		L→Kr	P			17c.		c.1625-1700 (Nos. 853-5 could well be late 16c. houses)
			(P)					'DW ERN 1782' lintel—construction of house? Wide windows at front
			(P)					c.1700-1750 Back wall only old. Refurbished 19c.
Y			P			17c.		c.1625-1700 Well at back built into cliff
								c.1625-1700 Back wall original. Most of house rebuilt 19c.

No.	Address Map Page 311, 305, 304, 310	Type	Bays	Facade: Original/ refaced	Arch: Type, colour	Stone Chimneys: Colour	Fireplace Downstairs	Fireplace Upstairs	Chimney Hoods	Gable Windows
860	5, St. George's Esplanade	5	5	R						
861	Penryn, St. George's Espl.	11	2	O						
862	La Piette Hotel	5	5	R						2B
863	The Absolute End	5	5	R			8f			
865	Byways, Rouge Rue	?1	?5	R						
867	Rope Walk Cottage	11	3	O						
870	1, New Paris Road	5	5	R						
872	Psycho, Les Canichers	5	6	O						
874	Hilltop, Les Canichers	11	1	O						
875	La Frégate	5	5	R						
881	La Fosse André	?5	6	R						
882	La Gibauderie									
883	Normanville	?1	?5	R	8		(7)			
884	Les Sauterelles, St. Jacques	?5	5	R						
885	De Quetteville, St. Jacques	5	5	R			8			
886	Monamy, St. Jacques	?1	5	R			2f		1W	
* 887	Shrubwood, St. Jacques	4	3	R						
888	La Colline, St. Jacques	?1	5	R						
889	The Old Farm, St. Jacques	?1	5	O						
890	Jardin Rozel, Rozel Road	5	5	R						
891	Mon Plaisir House	5	5	R		2G				
** 892	Malator Cottage, Collings Road	1	5	O			8f	(7)		1B
* 893	La Couture House	?1	4	O	?4	1				
894	La Bruyère, off Water Lanes	5	5	R			8			1B
895	Hamilton House, Water Lanes									
896	Casa Seda, Water Lanes									
* 897	La Planque Farm	5	5	R			?8f		(2W)	
* 898	Les Ozouets	5	5	R						
899	La Ville Herode, Les Ozouets	6	4	O						
900	Arculon Cottage, off Mont Arrivé	?1	5	R			?8f		(1S;1W)	
** 901	Vrangue Manor	?1	7	R						
902	Vrangue Manor	4	3	R						2B

Back Kitchen	Back Kitchen Fireplace	Tourelle	Cross Walls	Bénetier/Evier	Byre Window	Panelling	Farm Buildings	Fief: Earliest recorded date; additional information PARISH OF ST. PETER PORT
Y	(8)		(P)					c.1625-1700 17c. doors in attics. Inscription on door lintel covered by porch
								c.1625-1700 or possibly 18c. extension to 860
			(P)					c.1625-1700
			(P)					c.1625-1700
			1					c.1550-1625 No access: survey incomplete. Possibly walls lowered when mansard roof built c.20c.
								c.1700-1750
			1B			18c.		c.1700-1750
			(P)					c.1700-1750 3-storeys
						18c.		'1750' on 1 of 4 sandstone and limestone arches. Possibly gazebo to Le Grand Bosq
			(P)					c.1700-1750 On site of 16c. house. Arms of Dobrée, 1720; 'ED 1720'—lintel; 'ED—1721'—back rainwater head; 'PDR 1752'—rainwater head. House much altered and extended 19-20c.
			(P)			18c.		c.1700-1750 3-bay cottage adjoining. All much altered 19c.
								17c. barn with valet's quarters over: type 8 fire. Now house. Main house adjoining rebuilt c.1900 using old gable end
								c.1400-1550 Ruined. Much stone built into new house, whose lintel records '1478-1717-1969': original construction, refronting, rebuilding
			1					c.1700-1750 Now 2 houses
			(R)					c.1625-1700
			(P)			17c.		c.1400-1550
			(P)					c.1625-1700
			1?K			17c.		c.1550-1625
			1B					c.1550-1625 Moulded oak joists in kitchen
			(P)					c.1625-1700
			(P)					c.1625-1700 Valet's quarters adjoining, now house
			(P)	1				c.1400-1550
		L→K	1B					c.1400-1550 Arch plastered
			?2					c.1700-1750
								Gable end of old building in garden
								Part of walls and windows of La Jaspellerie, c.15c.
			P			17c.	1 ATT	c.1625-1700 Stair hollow in back wall. Galleting. Ruined wall of barn
			P			17c;18c.		c.1625-1700 'PP 1763' refronting
			(P)					c.1700-1750
		R→K	1B					c.1550-1625 Tourelle built into bank—no back door downstairs
		L→K	(P)					c.1550-1625 'DDB ANNO DM 1674' and arms of De Beauvoir & Carey: over front door. 17c. window surrounds altered 19c.
			(P)				1 DET	c.1625-1700 Square stair projections on this and 901. 19c. additions. Barn c.16c.

No.	Address Map Page 304, 305	Type	Bays	Facade: Original/refaced	Arch: Type, colour	Stone Chimneys: Colour	Fireplace Downstairs	Fireplace Upstairs	Chimney Hoods	Gable Windows
903	Newbourne, Petit Bouet	5	5	R						
*904	New Place, Petit Bouet	?1	5	O		1G	6f		(1S)	1K
905	Bon Air, Grand Bouet	6	5	O			(?8f)			
906	Wulfpuna, Grand Bouet	?1	4	R	5G		7			
907	Homelea, Les Banques	6	5	O					(2W)	
*908	Coutanchez	?1	4	O	4G				1S	
909	Roseville, La Ramée	6	5	R						
910	Le Bordage, off La Ramée	6	5	O		1G	8f		1W	
911	Oatland Place, La Ramée	6	5	R			8f			
912	La Rousaillerie, La Ramée	5	5	R						
913	St. Catherine's, La Ramée									
914	La Ramée	5	5	R						
*915	La Ramée	5	5	R		1	(7f)		2W	1K;1L
916	La Ramée	?1	5	R						
917	La Ramée	?1	?5	O						
**918	Ashbrook House, Les Quertiers	?1	5	R			1	2P		
***919	Les Quertiers	?1	6	O	3R;3R		2			
920	Les Osmonds Farm	?5		R			8f			
921	Pieds des Monts, Delancey	11	?3	O			(8f)			
*922	Les Grandes Maisons	4	?3	R			2			
923	Belscote, Church Lane	6	5	R			(8)			
*924	La Forge	?2	5	R			5		1S	
**925	Old Farm, Brock Road	?1	5	O	5G;4	1R;1G	7(f)		2S	2B
*926	Maison de Bas, Brock Road	?1	4	R						
*927	Maison de Haut, Brock Road	?1	4	R				6	1S	1K;1L
***928	The Old Farmhouse, La Mare	1	4	O	1;1		7f			2B
***929	La Ronde Cheminée and Pixie Cottage	3	7	O	4R	1 Round	7f			
930	Fulwood, Ronde Cheminée Road	5	5	R						
931	Myrtle Cottage, La Robergerie	6	5	O			8		(2W)	
*932	St. Clair	?	?3	O	1G;2G					
933	St. Clair Farm	5	5	R			8			
934	Le Murier Cottage	6	5	R						
935	Les Marais Farm	?1		R	7G					
**936	Duvaux Farm, Baubigny	?1	5	R	?4G		4			

Back Kitchen	Back Kitchen Fireplace	Tourelle	Cross Walls	Bénetier/Evier	Byre Window	Panelling	Farm Buildings	Fief: Earliest recorded date; additional information PARISH OF ST. PETER PORT 903-904 PARISH OF ST. SAMPSON 905-936
			P			17c.		*c.*1625-1700
			(P)					*c.*1550-1625
			(P)					*c.*1700-1750
			(P)					*c.*1550-1625
			(P)					*c.*1700-1750
			(P)					*c.*1400-1550
Y			(P)					*c.*1700-1750 'TBT:ELP:1786' lintel—refronting
			2					*c.*1700-1750 Annexe to L. dated 'TGL 1787'
			2					*c.*1700-1750
Y	8f		(P)				1 ATT	*c.*1700-1750 Bread oven in attached barn
								House rebuilt 19c. Wing at back *c.*18c.
Y			2					*c.*1700-1750
			2					*c.*1625-1700 'DLP MDG 1778' refronting
Y			(P)					*c.*1400-1550
		YES						*c.*1550-1625 Ground floor remains as shed
			1B					*c.*1400-1550 Bedroom fireplace now removed downstairs
Y		L→K	1K	?5R				*c.*1400-1550 Very large chamfered windows
			1K					*c.*1700-1750 Half of house demolished for building of 19c. house
Y			(P)					*c.*1700-1750
			(P)					*c.*1550-1625 '1676' lintel and crest of Le Marchant arms
Y			1B					*c.*1700-1750
			(P)				1 ATT	*c.*1550-1625 17c. wing used as forge with access by door to L. of kitchen fireplace (now blocked)
		R→K	(P)				1 ATT	*c.*1550-1625 'IML 1740' on arch. Dripstones over windows
		R→Kr	(P)					*c.*1550-1625 House shortened for road widening
			(P)					*c.*1550-1625 Valet's quarters now part of house
			(P)		1		1 ATT	*c.*1400-1550 Small and irregular windows. Barn continuous. Thatched until 1950 with hand-threshed corn from Sark. 3 gable windows in barn
			(P)					*c.*1400-1550 Access limited: survey incomplete
			1?B					*c.*1700-1750 Virtually rebuilt by 'J.L.G. 1799'—lintel—but some older walling incorporated
Y			(P)					*c.*1700-1750
								*c.*1400-1550 Cottage incorporating part of medieval chapel. 3rd arch removed when road widened, 1920s
Y			1K					*c.*1700-1750 'I:M 1726' lintel
			1K					*c.*1700-1750
			?1					*c.*1550-1625 Half of house only—now stables. 19c. house alongside
Y	8f		(P)					*c.*1550-1625 Extensively remodelled. ? 'ID 1604' cellar arch in gable

No.	Address Map Page 304, 303	Type	Bays	Facade: Original/ refaced	Arch: Type, colour	Stone Chimneys: Colour	Fireplace Downstairs	Fireplace Upstairs	Chimney Hoods	Gable Windows
***937	Le Marais	1	5	O			7f	4	(1S)	1B
938	Baubigny Stables	5	5	R			8f			
939	Penrose, Les Effards	5	5	R			8		(1W)	
940	Maison des Effards									
941	Les Grandes Capelles	5	5	R	4R				(2W)	
942	La Pièce Cottage, Coutanchez	5	5	R			8f		(2W)	
943	Capelles Handy Stores	6	4	R			8f			
**944	Les Romains	5	5	O		2R	8f		1W	
***945	La Grande Maison, L'Islet	5	5	R	3R	1R;1G	2;?2	5	1W;1S	2B;4wing
**946	The Elms, Pleinheaume	?2	4	O	1R/G		5		(1S)	
947	The Old Farm, Pleinheaume Lane	?6		O			(8f)		(1W)	
948	Les Annevilles Manor	?1	5	O	1R;1R					
949	Les Abreveurs	5	5	R					(2W)	
*950	Les Vieilles Salines	1	?4	O				2	(1S)	
***951	Les Cottes	7	3	O		2R/G	8f	5	1S	2B
952	La Cailloterie									
**953	The Old Farm, Rue de la Passée	?1	5	R			6f		(1W)	
*954	Luarca, Pulias	?5		R			8f		1W	
955	Les Vardes Farm Hotel							3P		
*956	Les Hougues	?1	5	R	4G;4R;4					
957	Les Hougues	?6	?5	O			8			2
958	Chez Nous, Rue du Pont Vaillant	6	5	O			(8f)		(1W)	
959	La Petit Câche	?1	4	R	3R;4		7			
960	Landes du Marché	6	4	R			(8f)			
961	La Chaumière, Landes du Marché	5	5	R						
962	Les Rouvets de Haut	1	5	O			5f	5	2W	
963	Les Sommeilleuses, Arguilliers Lane	5	5	R			8f			

Back Kitchen	Back Kitchen Fireplace	Tourelle	Cross Walls	Bénetier/ Evier	Byre Window	Panelling	Farm Buildings	Fief: Earliest recorded date; additional information PARISH OF ST. SAMPSON 937-957 PARISH OF THE VALE 938-963
		L→K	1B	4				c.1400-1550 Oak timbers everywhere. Joists in cross passage ornamented with rosettes. Loft arrangement original. Tourelle opens from recess at back of cross passage
			1K					c.1625-1700
			P			17c.		c.1625-1700
								House rebuilt 'J.F.B. 1798'. One barn c.18c.
			(P)				1 ATT	c.1550-1625 'ERB:OMH 1772' refronting. 'ERB 1769' lintel
			2					c.1625-1700
			2					c.1700-1750
			2					c.1625-1700 Fireplace has rough corbel under shoulder stone. Bulge in outside wall for bread oven carried up to roof level
Y	8f	L→K	(P)	?5R		18c.		c.1400-1550
			1B	5R				c.1400-1550 évier consists of stone trough the thickness of front wall. Elaborate keeping places in cross wall
								c.1625-1700 Half of house removed 19c. for new house. Thatched until 1950s
			(P)					c.1550-1625 On site of much earlier house at right-angles and 4 ft. lower. Arches pointed. Chapel adjoining. Fief seat in house porch
			(2)					c.1700-1750
Y			(P)		1			c.1550-1625
			1					c.1550-1625 No cross-passage. Front door opens into kitchen near gable end; back door into byre next to cross-wall
								House rebuilt 19c. Some older walling in outbuildings
Y			1K	5R				c.1400-1550 Forked timber used in kitchen ceiling
			P			17c.		c.1625-1700 Bedroom fireplace uses same flue as kitchen fireplace. Half of house removed when 19c. house built
								House rebuilt 1792 but perhaps incorporating bedroom gable end of 16c. building, whose upstairs fireplace is now in mid-air
			(P)				1 ATT; 1 DET	c.1400-1550 'ALN 1735' arch at back of house. Unchamfered arch in gable end of cellar under 'byre'
			(P)					c.1700-1750 Possibly ground floor valet's room and stabling with loft above
			(P)					c.1700-1750
			(P)					c.1550-1625 'ICH 1758' on arch. Valet's room with Type 8 fireplace
			1K				1 DET	c.1625-1700 Possibly 16c. stabling behind
Y	(8f)		2					c.1700-1750 House mostly rebuilt (possibly incorporating some old walling), but stabling 18c.
Y			1K		1			c.1550-1625 Earth floor until 1939
			1B					c.1700-1750

No.	Address Map Page 303, 301	Type	Bays	Facade: Original/ refaced	Arch: Type, colour	Stone Chimneys: Colour	Fireplace Downstairs	Fireplace Upstairs	Chimney Hoods	Gable Windows
964	Côte ès Ouets, Les Rouvets Road	5	5	R			8			1K
965	La Parchonnerie									
*966	Les Grandes Mielles	5	5	O		(2)				
967	Les Grandes Mielles Lane									
968	Cruchebrée, L'Etonellerie	4	3	R			6(f)		1S	
**969	Les Mainguys	?1	5	R				6		2 wing
970	L'Etonellerie	5	5	R			8f			
971	Les Barras	?1	5	O			7f		1W	
972	Rue de la Câche	5	5	R						
973	Maison de Bas, Grandes Maisons Road	5	5	R						
***974	Maison de Haut, Grandes Maisons Road	?	4	O	1R;2R			8f	(W)	2
*975	Maison d'Aval	?3	6	O			5;8f;8f			
976	Maison d'Aval	5	5	R						
*977	Houmets Lane	1	?4	O	1R		6f	(7)	1S	
978	Houmets Lane									
*979	Les Juqueurs	?1	4	R						
980	The Elms, Houmets Lane	6	5	R			8f		1S	
981	Les Monmains	5	5	R			(8f)	(8)	2W	
**982	Bordeaux Haven	3	6	O			6f	6	1S	
**983	Armorel, Bordeaux	?1	5	O			6f		(2W)	1B
***984	Bordeaux House	3	7	O	3G		2sf	2Ps	1S;(1S)	2B
985	Millstone, Cocagne Lane	?			1G				(1S)	
986	Les Grippios	5	5	R			8f			
987	Les Grippios	6	5	R			8f			
988	Les Grippios	10	3	O						
989	Rue des Petites Hougues	?5		R						
990	Les Petites Hougues	5	5	R					(1W)	
991	Dalgary Cottage, Ville-ès-Pies	5	4	O			8f		(1W)	
992	Next to Dalgary Cottage	?2	?	O	1G					
993	Belle Vue, Ville-ès-Pies	4	3	R			6f	(6)	(2W)	1B
*994	Paradis	?1		R		1				
995	Luchen Vian	10	2	R						
*996	Saint Magloire	3	7	O	1G		6			
*997	Les Landes	1	?5	O						

378

Back Kitchen	Back Kitchen Fireplace	Tourelle	Cross Walls	Bénetier/Evier	Byre Window	Panelling	Farm Buildings	Fief: Earliest recorded date; additional information PARISH OF THE VALE
Y	8f		1B					c.1625-1700 Valet's quarters over barn adjoining
								House rebuilt 19c. Barn c.18c.
			2					c.1700-1750
								Rebuilt 'MPV 1812': barn c.18c.
			(P)					c.1550-1625
Y			2					c.1400-1550 '1·7·2·3/S·L·N' lintel—refronting. 16c. wing with bedroom fireplace
			2	?1				c.1625-1700 Possible byre window
			1B					c.1550-1625 Blocked loft doorway in front facade at floor level. Tradition of animals using 'byre' end
Y			1K					c.1700-1750
Y			1K					c.1700-1750 Valet's quarters adjoining
		YES	1K					c.1400-1550 Internal stone tourelle. Huge foundation stones. Upper storey adapted as 18c. cottage
		R→K	2					c.1550-1625 Positions of fireplaces altered 18-19c. Bulge in back wall to accommodate bread oven carried up to roof level
			1K					c.1700-1750
Y	(8)	L→K	1K		1			c.1400-1550
								Barn only, c.18c. now house
		L→K	(1K)					c.1550-1625
			2					c.1625-1700
Y			2					c.1700-1750
			(P)	?5sq	1			c.1400-1550 Stone seat along gable end inside byre
		R→K	1B	5R				c.1400-1550 Square tourelle
		R→K	1K	1;5R				c.1400-1550 Square tourelle with stone seat outside
								Only gable end remains at side of modern house
			1K				1 ATT	c.1750-1780 Barn and foundations of older house c.17c.
			(P)					c.1625-1700
			(P)					c.1700-1750
			1					c.1700-1750 Barn and half of house only
2	8;8f		(P)					c.1625-1700 Refronted c.1845. Back kitchen and bakehouse
			(P)					c.1700-1750
								c.1400-1550 Ruined: 2 arched windows blocked
Y			(P)					c.1550-1625 ?'1743' under roughcast
Y	(8f)			5sq				c.1400-1550 Half of original house demolished for 19c. house. 19c. valet's room in original loft. Back kitchen 18c.
								c.1700-1750
		R→K	(1K)	5sq	1			c.1400-1550 Shortened for road widening. Now workshop
		R→K	(1K)		1			c.1400-1550 Square tourelle opening out of kitchen or cross-passage recess. Tiny loft window

No.	Address Map Page 301, 300	Type	Bays	Facade: Original/refaced	Arch: Type, colour	Stone Chimneys: Colour	Fireplace Downstairs	Fireplace Upstairs	Chimney Hoods	Gable Windows
998	La Moye House	5	5	O					(1W)	
999	La Moye	?1	?5	O		1 round		6	1S	2B
1000	Rue de la Moye	5	5	R						
*1001	Les Mielles	5	5	O		2G	8f			
1002	Les Mielles									
*1003	Les Mielles	?1	5	R	5G		(8f)			
1004	La Maison de Garis	6	5	O			8f		1S	
*1005	The Old Cottage, L'Ancresse	3	7	O	4G	2G	2f	(?7)	(2W)	1 central
1006	La Cloture	5	5	R						
***1007	La Rocque Balan	3	7	R	6G;6G;5G	1G	3f		1S	1 central
***1008	Le Marais Farm	3	5	O	1G;6		7f		(1W)	
1009	Old Marais	?1	5	R						
1010	Two Wells	6	5	O			(8)			
1011	Le Douit Lane									
1012	La Grève	?1	5	R					1S	
1013	Le Hurel									
*1014	Le Hurel	?1	5	R	2G			2s	(1S)	
1015	Le Hurel	5	5				8f			
1016	La Grève, Rue du Closel	5	5	R			8f		1W	
1017	Retour au Nord	5	5	O						
1018	Retour au Nord	?1	5	R	(1R)		8f		(1W)	
1019	La Corvée Lane				(4)					
1020	La Canurie	5	5	O		1	8f			
1021	Maison de Haut Cottage	?1	4	R				6	(2W)	
1022	Maison de Bas	?5		R			8		(1S)	
1023	Ville Baudu	?1	5	R	(1)		8			
1024	Houmtel Lane									
*1025	Tertre Farm, Rue de L'Essart	?1	5	O	3G	3G	7(f)			
***1026	Le Tertre	3	8	R	8;3G;4G	1G	6	2	1S;1W	1B
1027	La Vieille Ecole, Carrière Lane	6	4	O						
**1028	La Carrière	3	7	R	4;?4					
1029	St. Mary Anthony	1	5	O			(?8f)		(1W)	
*1030	Braye Farm, Carrière Lane	6	5	O			8f		(2W)	

Back Kitchen	Back Kitchen Fireplace	Tourelle	Cross Walls	Bénetier/ Evier	Byre Window	Panelling	Farm Buildings	Fief: Earliest recorded date; additional information PARISH OF THE VALE
Y			2					'NFL 1744' date of construction
		L→K	(?1K)					c.1400-1550 Square tourelle. Now barn
			1K					c.1625-1700
Y			1K					1727
								House demolished: barn c.17c.
			1B					c.1550-1625
			(P)					c.1700-1750
			(P)					c.1400-1550
			(P)					c.1700-1750
		R→K	1B	5R	1	16c.	1 ATT; 1 DET	c.1400-1550 Earth floor in byre until 1945; small ogee window, upstairs passage. Central gable window over byre and central slit in gable over bedroom
Y		R→K	1B		1		2 ATT	c.1400-1550 'MCL 1777' in plaster over arch— possibly date of back kitchen and window enlarging
			(P)	1			1 ATT	c.1400-1550 Greatly altered c.1800
Y			1K		?1			c.1625-1700 Deeds of 1642. Possible byre window
								House rebuilt; barn c.18c.
			2				1 ATT	c.1550-1625 1598—Greffe records. 1 gable end rebuilt 19c.
								Cottage once farm buildings: farm opposite has vanished
–		–	1B					c.1400-1550 'MDM 1799' refronting. Raised by one storey 19c. Ruined.
			1K					c.1625-1700
			1K					c.1700-1750
Y	8f		1K					c.1750-1780 Possibly post-1787, rebuilt on site of older house
		R→K	1K				1 ATT	c.1400-1550 Ruined barn with long inscription 1787. Arch removed when facade repaired 1960s
								House rebuilt and arch at back destroyed c.1965. Barn c.17c.
			(P)					c.1625-1700
Y	(8f)		1K					c.1400-1550
			2					c.1625-1700 Half of house removed when 19c. house built
Y	8f		1K					c.1400-1550 Print of 1784 shows house at time of John Wesley's visit, with arch and before refronting
								Barn only remains c.18c.
Y	(8f)		1K				1 DET	c.1400-1550 Arch rebuilt in barn; perhaps stones of inner order wrongly reassembled
Y	8f	L→K	2			17c.		c.1400-1550
			(P)					c.1700-1750
		R→Kr					1 DET	c.1400-1550 Very fine 19c. refronting and refurbishing inside. Arch partly covered in upstairs passage. Second arch perhaps included in refronting
			(P)		1			c.1550-1625
			2					c.1625-1700 In 1936 still thatched with 'eyebrow' window in front

No.	Address Map Page 300	Type	Bays	Facade: Original/ refaced	Arch: Type, colour	Stone Chimneys: Colour	Fireplace Downstairs	Fireplace Upstairs	Chimney Hoods	Gable Windows
1031	Grange, Sohier Road	5	5	R						
1032	La Bailotterie	?1	4	R			(7)		(1W)	
1033	Earlswood Nurseries, Ville Baudu	6	4	O			8;8		(2W)	
1034	Vale House, Ville Baudu	?1	4	R			6			2B
1035	Sohier	5	5	R						

382

Back Kitchen	Back Kitchen Fireplace	Tourelle	Cross Walls	Bénetier/ Evier	Byre Window	Panelling	Farm Buildings	Fief: Earliest recorded date; additional information **PARISH OF THE VALE**
			1K				1 ATT	c.1700-1750 Coach house, now cottage, probably 17c.
		R→K					1 ATT	c.1400-1550 'DMH 1792' refronting. Tourelle square and elongated along back wall to form straight staircase
			(P)					c.1700-1750
Y			(P)					c.1550-1625
Y			2					c.1700-1750

SCHEDULE TWO

No.	Address Map Page 311	Type	Storeys A: above ground B: below	Bays	Facade: Original/ refaced	Fireplace first floor	Staircase	Bénetier/ Evier
700	Coal Stores, Pedvin Street	W	2A	?	O			
704	1, Pedvin Street	2	3A;1B	3	O		4	
705	3, Pedvin Street	2	3A;1B	3	O		4	
706	11 Hauteville	2	2A;1B	5	R			
707	7, Hauteville	2	3A;1B	3	R	18c.	2	
*708	5, Hauteville	2	3A;2B	2	O		2	
709	3, Hauteville	2	3A;1B	3	O		2	
710	1, Hauteville	2	3A;1B	3	O		2	
713	14, Hauteville	2	3A	3	O			
714	12, Hauteville	2	3A	3	O			
715	10, Hauteville	2	3A	3	O			
716	Whistlers, Cliff Street	2	3A	5	O			
724	30, Cornet Street	1	3A;1B	5	O		3	
*725	28, Cornet Street	1	3A;1B	4	O		2	
***726	26, Cornet Street	1	3A;1B	5	O	18c.	3	
731	13, Back Street	1	3A	3	O			
734	10, Back Street	2	2A	3	O			
739	20, Contrée Mansell	2	3A	5	R			
*740	23A, Mansell Street	2	3A	2	R			
741	Miller, Clements, Mill Street							
742	Next to Minimates, Mill Street	2	3A	5	R			
743	20, Mill Street	2	3A	5	R		2	
744	29, Mill Street	1	3A	4	R		3	
*745	25, Mill Street	1	3A;1B	4	O		2	
*746	23, Mill Street	1	3A;1B	3	O		2	
747	21, Mill Street	1	4A	?5				
748	15, Mill Street	1	3A	5			4	
749	13, Mill Street	1	2A	3				
*750	4, Mill Street	1	3A;1B	5			3	
751	1, Mill Street	1	3A	5			4	
752	Kosy Korner, Church Square	3	4A					
753	Sound Track, Church Square	1	3A	?5	R			
*754	Maison Mohair, High Street	1	3A	?5	O			
*755	The Old Gatehouse, High Street	2	3A;1B	3	O			
***756	Guernsey Saving Bank, High Street	1	3A;1B	5	O			
*757	Creaseys, High Street	1	3A	5			4	
*758	Creaseys, High Street	1	3A	5			4	
*759	Creaseys, High Street	1	3A	5			4	
*760	Creaseys, High Street	1	3A;2B	6			4	

Panelling	Vaults	Fief: Earliest recorded date; additional information
		c.1700-1750
		c.1700-1750 Door on R.
		c.1700-1750 Door central
(17c.)		c.1625-1700 Panelling plastered over
17c.		c.1625-1700 Door on left
17c.		c.1625-1700 Stairs at front left
17c.		c.1625-1700
		c.1625-1700
		c.1625-1700
		c.1625-1700
		c.1625-1700 Raised one storey in brick—'1765'—rainwater head
		c.1700-1750
(17c.)		c.1625-1700 Panelling plastered over. 2-bay basement different shape from house—c.15c.
17c.		c.1625-1700 Cellar different shape and on different line from house—c.15c.
17c.; 18c.		c.1625-1700 Front bay raised 18c. 6-bay cellar. 18c. lean-to shop towards Coupée Lane
		c.1700-1750
		c.1700-1750
		c.1700-1750
17c.		c.1625-1700
		Rebuilt, perhaps enclosing older walling:'PPR/SLF/1746' on front
		c.1700-1750
17c.		c.1625-1700
		c.1700-1750
		c.1625-1700 Stair hollow in wall
		c.1625-1700 Stair hollow in wall
		c.1625-1700 Patching with small, yellow bricks
		c.1700-1750
		c.1700-1750
17c.		c.1625-1700
		c.1625-1700 Front bay raised 18c.
		c.1700-1750
		Rebuilt c.1608 on site of house built 1444-5
		c.1400-1550 Corbelling of side walls for jetty in Arcade and High Street
		c.1400-1550
	S	c.1400-1550 Corbelling for jetty on High Street and Berthelot Street. 3-bay vault below. Altered 1578—beam with inscription—and in 1616. Merchant's marks of Briand family. Includes 5-bay shop on Berthelot Street and rebuilt Maison des Pauvres, Berthelot Street
		c.1700-1750 Ashlar gables. Staggered stairwells. Heavy glazing bars 18c.
		c.1700-1750 Ashlar gables. Staggered stairwells. Heavy glazing bars 18c.
		c.1700-1750 Ashlar gables. Staggered stairwells. Heavy glazing bars 18c.
18c.	1B	c.1700-1750 Heavy glazing bars. 'Judith Beauvoir' scratched on glass of stair well—?18c.

No.	Address Map Page 311	Type	Storeys A: above ground B: below	Bays	Facade: Original/ refaced	Fireplace first floor	Staircase	Bénetier/ Evier
761	Lipton's, High Street							
*762	Burton's, High Street	3	3A					
763	Steak and Stilton	W	2A					
764	Bucktrouts	W	3A;2B	5			4	
765	Behind Pioneer, High Street	W	2A	5				
766	Behind Pioneer, High Street	W	2A	5				
767	Samuel Pepys, High Street	1	3A;1B	5	R			
**768	Marquand's (Maison du Quay)	W	4A;1B		O			
**769	Boots, High Street	3	3A;1B	5	O	18c.	4	
770	Royal Channel Islands Yacht Club		3A;1B		R			
771	Kimbers, Le Pollet	1	3A;2B	4			4	
772	Gruts, Le Pollet	1	3A;3B	5				
*773	Wyatts, Le Pollet	1	3A	5	O		2P	
774	Parfums de Paris, Le Pollet	1	3A	5			3	
775	Kimbers, 7, Le Pollet	1	3A;3B	5			4	
776	Dorothy Perkins, 11, Le Pollet	1	3A	5		18c.	4	
777	Curry's, 15, Le Pollet	1	3A;3B	5			4	
778	Purdy's, 17, Le Pollet	1	3A;2B	5				
779	19, Le Pollet	1	4A;2B	5				
780	Besants', 21, Le Pollet	1	3A;2B	5				
781	Lexicon, 23-25, Le Pollet	1	3A;2B	5				
782	Lexicon, 23-25, Le Pollet	1	3A;2B	5				
783	Samuel Pepys, 31, Le Pollet		4A;2B	5				
784	Pandora, 33, Le Pollet	1	4A;1B	2				
*785	Pandora, Le Pollet	1	3A;2B				2	
786	16, Le Pollet	1	3A;1B	3				
787	Strumbles, 18, Le Pollet	1	3A	2				
*788	20, Le Pollet	1	4A	5			4	
789	22, Le Pollet	1	4A	?5				
790	Warry's, 24, Le Pollet	1	4A	5				
791	Monsieur Margot, 26, Le Pollet	1	4A	4				
792	Paints, Le Pollet	1	4A;1B	4				
**793	Robilliard, 28, Le Pollet	1	4A	3			1	
794	The Samaritans, Forest Lane	1	3A					
**798.	Lloyd's Le Pollet	1	3A;2B	5				
**799	Baker's Bazaar, Le Pollet	1	3A;1B	5			4	
*800	Walter Keyho, Le Pollet	2	3A;1B	3			2P	
802	Sheppard's, Le Pollet	W	2A					
803	Dario's, Le Pollet	1	3A	5	R			
**804	Warehouse, Le Truchot	W	3A					

Panelling	Vaults	Fief: Earliest recorded date; additional information
		c.1700-1750 '1726' rainwater head at back
		c.1700-1750 Double shop frontage in ashlar and wing behind
	1B	c.1700-1750 Front part not vaulted: 'warehouse' beams closely spaced
18c.	2B	c.1700-1750
		c.1625-1700 Much altered inside
		c.1625-1700
		c.1625-1700
	2B	c.1625-1700 Much altered 18c. Double width warehouses, basement and ground floor vaults; 'warehouse' beams elsewhere
18c.		c.1700-1750 2 houses wide; 2 staircases originally
17c.		c.1625-1700
		c.1700-1750
		c.1700-1750
		c.1625-1700
		c.1625-1700
	B	c.1700-1750 3 brick arches under Le Pollet
18c.		c.1700-1750 Venetian window in dormer for stair well
		c.1700-1750 Fine rainwater head
		c.1700-1750 'Warehouse' beams on bottom floor
		c.1700-1750
		c.1750-1780 or possibly 19c.
		c.1700-1750
		c.1700-1750
		c.1700-1750
		c.1700-1750
17c.	2B	c.1625-1700 '1750' rainwater head
		c.1625-1700
		c.1625-1700
18c.		c.1700-1750 End wall corbelled for earlier jetty: now plastered
		c.1700-1750
		c.1700-1750
		c.1700-1750
		c.1700-1750 Side wall corbelled for earlier jetty
		c.1625-1700 Tourelle now not used as staircase. Inside refashioned early 20c. Shop not served by tourelle
		c.1625-1700 Side walls old: remainder rebuilt
	2S	c.1625-1700
18c.		c.1750-1780
		c.1625-1700
		c.1750-1780 or perhaps later. Ashlar. 28 huge beams span each floor at 2ft. centres. Original capstan and block and tackle
		c.1700-1750 Fireplaces front and back bays, ground floor
	2B	c.1700-1750 5 aisles of brick vaults, 2 storeys. Open square above

No.	Address Map Page 311	Type	Storeys A: above ground B: below	Bays	Facade: Original/ refaced	Fireplace first floor	Staircase	Bénetier/ Evier
806	Nino's, Lefebvre Street	W	2A					
807	Le Riche's, Lefebvre Street	3	2A;1B	3				
***808	Hume Corporation, 5, Berthelot Street	1	2A	5		2		5R
*810	United Club, Berthelot Street	1	3A	5			4	
**813	La Bigoterie, Berthelot Street	1	3A	5			3	
817	Langlois Auction Rooms	W	2	6				
1035	Sutler's House, Castle Cornet	1	2A	3	O	(7f)		

Panelling	Vaults	Fief: Earliest recorded date; additional information
	1B	*c.*1700-1750
		*c.*1700-1750 Some 18c. walling around Le Riche's top entrance in Lefebvre Street
		*c.*1400-1550 Fireplace and évier, back 2 bays, 1st floor, on right. Originally, another fireplace on ground floor, front bay, right
18c.		*c.*1625-1700 Front and back bays raised 1 storey 18c., when interior refurbished
17c.		*c.*1625-1700 Front bay raised 1 storey 18c.; back 2 bays demolished for 19c. building
		*c.*1700-1750 Double width stores. No 'warehouse' beams
		*c.*1550-1625 Double width house

SCHEDULE THREE

No.	Address	Type*	Additional Information
36	Sausmarez Manor, St. Martin	G	
689	74, Hauteville	T	
690	76, Hauteville	T	
691	78, Hauteville	T	
696	36, Hauteville	T	
698	2, Charroterie	T	'IML 1786'
711	16, Hauteville	T	
712	18, Hauteville	T	
718	1, Cliff Terrace	T	
719	2, Cliff Terrace	T	
720	8, Cliff Terrace	T	
722	14, Cornet Street	T	
795	Moore's Hotel, Le Pollet	G	
801	Plaiderie House	T	'1763' rainwater head
805	Constables' Office, Lefebvre Street	G	1787
814	La Bigoterie	T	'PLM 1774'
816	Le Marchant House	T	
818	Old Government House Hotel	G	
821	Brockhurst, The Grange	G	
824	Choisi, The Grange	G	
825	Melrose, Les Gravées	G	
826	Rocquettes Hotel, Les Gravées	G	
832	Belmont House, The Queen's Road	G	
838	Pierre Percée, Prince Albert's Road	G	
839	Ville-au-Roi Manor, Prince Albert's Road	G	
842	Government House, The Queen's Road	G	
850	1, Park Street	T	
851	Royal Hotel, Glategny Esplanade	G	
852	29, Glategny Esplanade	T	
864	Trafalgar House, Petit Bouet	T	
866	9, St. John's Road	T	
868	Lynn Place and Wren Cottage, Les Amballes	T	
869	La Maison, Paris Street	T	
871	44, Les Canichers	T	
873	The Myrtles, Les Canichers	T	
876	Gympie, Les Canichers	T	
877	21, Les Canichers	T	
878	Les Canichers	T	Derelict
879	L'Hyvreuse, Cambridge Park	G	
880	Maison du Guet Hotel, La Butte	G	
1036	Married Quarters, Castle Cornet	M	1745 '1750'—rainwater head
1037	Main Guard, Castle Cornet	M	1750
1038	Beaucamp de Haut	G	
1039	La Mare de Carteret	G	
1040	Guille-Allès Library		Assembly Rooms 1780

*G=Gentleman's Residence; T=Town House; M=Military

SCHEDULE FOUR

No.	Present Address	Description
	**PARISH OF ST. MARTIN**	
17	Le Varclin	Type 4R arch; in garden
22	La Ronde Porte, Calais Road	Chamfered stone; at entrance
22	La Ronde Porte, Calais Road	Part of fireplace lintel; now doorstep
	Valley Cottage, Moulin Huet	'1769' datestone; built into side of later door
	Le Vallon	Shield of Peter Careye (1550-1629); over roadside arch. From guard-house on S. arm of Old Harbour, c.1594, demolished 1853
	Le Fainel	Thoume merchant's mark ?c.1616; over arch Type 4R; both rebuilt from house once in front of present house
	La Fosse	Fireplace corbel, Type 5R; in roadside wall as quoin
38	Ville Amphrey	Primitive head; built into gate pillar behind house
	Les Douvres	Arch, top 3 stones Type 4G; part of fireplace re-used as sides
75	Saints, Saints Bay Road	Type 2 fireplace corbel; on outside of barn
76	La Tourelle, Icart Road	Fireplace made up of 4 grey chamfered stones, 2 with chamfer stop of leaf. 2 of these are probably window jambs; 2 (with chamfer stops) more probably from fireplace. All found in garden
76	La Tourelle, Icart Road	Type 1 fireplace; from Maison Bonamy, Rue de l'Ardaine (315)
80	Rose Farm, Icart Road	Red stone with chamfer R. and L.; in yard (1979). Either a window mullion or (more probably) part of a pillar type fireplace
83	Saints Farm, Icart Road	1 voussoir of Type 4G arch with double chamfer; in mounting block
92	La Maison Guignan, Rue de L'Eglise	1 voussoir and 1 chamfered stone with stop, from Type 4 arch; in gable
92	La Maison Guignan, Rue de L'Eglise	17c. grey window lintel (broken) with shield, upside down; over front window. Re-used in refronting, c.1725
110	Les Varioufs	Type 5R arch; in garden
117	La Pompe	4 window sills with cable mould repositioned in 1863 house. Shown by F. C. Lukis (c.1850) in situ in old house
117	La Pompe	Type 5G arch; rebuilt in 19c. house; shield inscribed 'TLT 1600'
118	Les Mouilpieds	Accolade lintel of window; re-used as quoin in 1698 house: 16c.
118	Les Mouilpieds	Bedroom fireplace lintel; re-used as front door lintel upside-down
118	Les Mouilpieds	1 corbel or croissette: re-used in side of front doorway
123	La Villette	Fireplace base with chamfer; in pig-sty
	Blanchelande	2 Type 3 fireplace corbels; in front wall
	Blanchelande	2 jambs from very elaborate fireplace; in courtyard
128	Simtora, La Villette	1 jamb of fireplace, wide chamfer, in garden. Primitive head over door
144	La Falaise	Type 3R arch; in garden
144	La Falaise	Type 4R arch
144	La Falaise	Type 5G arch 'PLP 16?0' in shield. From demolished house, La Villette
144	La Falaise	Female head, possibly from fireplace corbel; as finial on porch
144	La Falaise	Small trough possibly made from cross base; in garden
	**PARISH OF THE FOREST**	
158	Les Messuriers	1 stone with chamfer stop from fireplace; in stable doorway
188	Les Fontenelles Farm	Re-used chamfered stones built into barn c.1775
208	La Carrière	1 chamfered window jamb; as doorstep at middle gate
210	Le Cas Rouge	Fireplace lintel; over side entrance

No.	Present Address	Description
211	Le Manoir	Base stone with chamfer stop; back gable
211	Le Manoir	Red fireplace lintel; at back of house
214	Coin de Terre, La Corbière	One voussoir from Type 4R arch; front wall

PARISH OF ST. PIERRE DU BOIS

No.	Present Address	Description
225	Lês Heches	Doorway with rebate from bottom of tourelle; in gable end of barn
237	Les Câches	Cusped window lintel *c*.14c.; over back kitchen doorway
237	Les Câches	Both sides of pillar type fireplace; in garden
238	La Tourelle	Type 2 fireplace corbels; built into porch
238	La Tourelle	Type 2 fireplace corbels; at side door
238	La Tourelle	Type 4R arch; at side
238	La Tourelle	Type 4G arch; in barn
238	La Tourelle	Fireplace lintel; over barn door
238	La Tourelle	Broken fireplace lintel; top of outside stairs to barn
238	La Tourelle	Chamfered stones; in barn attached to house
241	Maison d'Aval	Part of fireplace with chamfer stop made into 'trough'; at back of house
257	Les Reveaux	Lintel of fireplace; upside down as step in garden
259	Les Reveaux	Lintel of fireplace, broken; hearth stone in back kitchen
264	Le Clos de Bas	Type 1 fireplace; from house demolished at Les Câches, *c*.19c., then built into 111
268	Le Grée	Type 4G arch; top 3 stones in roadside entrance opposite house: 2 bases with fleur-de-lys and 2 other stones in pig-sty
292	Le Catillon de Bas	Type 4G arch; in barn opposite—now house
	Le Couteur's stoneyard	1 jamb of grey arch. No stop
	Le Couteur's stoneyard	3 sections of Type 4G arch and 2 stones of side: 'IM(?T)/PLR'
	Le Couteur's stoneyard	1 curved stone of Type 4G arch and 2 stones from side
310	La Couture	Type 3R arch in house; brought from house demolished 1872—other side of road
	Opposite La Couture	Type 4G arch; in roadside wall
	Les Islets	Type 4G arch double chamfered; from Maison Bonamy, Rue de l'Ardaine (315); at side of Coach House Gallery
307	Brouard House, Les Islets	Bedroom fireplace lintel; on ground in 'back kitchen' adjoining Maison des Pauvres
309	Les Islets	Sides of fireplace; built into barn doorway
316	La Pomare	1 voussoir of Type 4R arch lying by front door
316	La Pomare	Fireplace corbel; re-used at back of gable
316	La Pomare	Chamfered window lintel; in steps to barn
	Les Marais, Rue des Vicheries	Pointed arch with hood mould; from La Grande Maison de la Pomare (317)

PARISH OF TORTEVAL

No.	Present Address	Description
	Les Jehans	Type 2 fireplace; in hedge by garden steps; above chapel
355	Les Portelettes	Fireplace lintel (type as at Le Gron, 433) and 2 Type 2 fireplace corbels—in garden
	Le Pré du Merlin	Type 5G arch; from demolished house Les Beaucamps de Bas: 'PDBC 1608'
366	Pleinmont House	Type 2 fireplace corbel; inserted back kitchen

PARISH OF ST. SAVIOUR

No.	Present Address	Description
384	Le Grand Douit	Upstairs fireplace lintel; in back garden
394	The Coppice, Rue du Lorier	Shoulder stone from fireplace; in garden

No.	Present Address	Description
411	Le Mont Saint	Fireplace lintel with shield enclosed in circle; upside down over side door
430	Le Belial	Base stone of fireplace; in hedge
433	Le Gron	Grey shoulder stone from fireplace; forms gatepost
449	La Hougue Fouque	1 shoulder stone of fireplace; in field gateway opposite entrance
458	Le Bricquet	Stones from Type 4 arch; built into steps to barn
458	Le Bricquet	1 stone from side of fireplace; in pig-sty
460	Les Belles	1 stone from side of fireplace; at back of house
461	Maison d'Aval, Rue des Câches	Type 4G arch; on roadside
462	Les Câches	Type 4G arch; on roadside
462	Les Câches	Type 4R arch; in back yard, on ground
464	Les Prevosts	Type 4G arch; rebuilt from Le Bricquet (458)
472	Le Douit, Rue Fevresse	Top of Type 1R arch; rebuilt at roadside
	St. Saviour's Rectory	Type 4G arch; in roadside wall
476	Les Comptes Farm	Chamfered door lintel re-used
484	Candie	Type 4R arch; side entrance
484	Candie	Type 3R arch; side entrance
	La Jaonière, Mont Saint	Type 2R arch; in 19c. house. Inner order only of front door arch from house with round chimney
	PARISH OF THE CASTEL	
	Les Eturs	Type 3 fireplace; by side of vinery; from Les Massies (421)
506	King's Mills' Farm	Part of Type 5 fireplace built into house; from Les Grands Moulins (511)
509	La Forge	Parts of pillar type fireplace inserted: kitchen; from Le Couteur's, Rocquaine
517	Le Groignet	'HDI·E·MR/1748' Datestone rebuilt in gable of 19c. house
517	Le Groignet	Base of bénitier; used as quoin at back of 18c. house
518	Les Grands Moulins	Side of Type 4G arch; in garden; top rebuilt at King's Mills' Lodge (519)
555	Les Queux	Type 2 fireplace; corbels built into house, 1980; from Les Hêches, (446)
	Castel Church	Stone finial; on top of wall beside steps to north of church
	Castel Church	Trough with two animal heads and moulding below; possibly an évier
	La Remise, Rue de la Câche	Type 1R arch; in roadside wall
556	Castel Rectory	15c. fireplace lintel, with initials and design inside lozenge, and inscription 'Orate pro m̄', in 18c. house
	Les Beaucamps de Bas	Type 4R arch; built into back of house
563	Les Tilleuls	Type 4R arch; in roadside wall. 'P. le R'—Pierre Le Roy—diarist
568	Les Petites Mielles	Corbels of pillar type fireplace: built into outer gable wall of 18c. cottage
572	Les Houmets	Type 4R arch; built into side of 19c. house
	Folk Museum	Bénitier Type 1 in Caen stone
	Folk Museum	Type 4R arch, integral with bénitier
	Folk Museum	Type 2 fireplace with bread oven
574	Le Pouquelaye	Fireplace lintel with 2 shields, one blank; in garden
574	Le Pouquelaye	Type 3R arch—outer order missing; in boundary wall
574	Le Pouquelaye	Stone head—finial of arch; in garden
582	La Haye du Puits	1 voussoir of Type 4G arch double chamfered; inside house

No.	Present Address	Description
582	La Haye du Puits	Base of bénitier; re-used as window lintel
582	La Haye du Puits	?13c. window lintel with head inside arc; above doorway in 18c. cottage
586	St. George	Doorway as at 581, Le Villocq; inserted in gable end
586	St. George	Type 2 fireplace corbels; in garden near pond: probably from previous house at St. George, demolished 1824
586	St. George	Lintel of ornamented and mullioned window *c.*1500; in garden: matching mullion in house. Found in grounds, probably from house demolished 1824
586	St. George	Head of cow; above arch in back courtyard
586	St. George	Rounded arch with hood mould; in roadside wall. Brought from Les Quertiers (919) in 1840
586	St. George	Fireplace lintel cut square with shield (Guille, previously Caretier, arms) and date '1625', above roadside arch; from Les Quertiers
586	St. George	Shield in lozenge; over courtyard entrance: found in grounds: De Sausmarez arms
586	St. George	Two angels supporting merchant's mark; over side entrance: found in grounds
586	St. George	Guille arms and angel supporters; over main entrance of 1821 house; from old Guille house in Le Pollet
586	St. George	6 large pieces of attached columns; almost certainly from chapel: now in old house: found in grounds
586	St. George	Large red sill with moulding; used as seat by pond: found in grounds
602	Les Blanches Roches	Type 4G arch; in wall nearby
606	Maison Varendes	Re-used piece of grey granite with two parallel lines; front facade
	PARISH OF ST. ANDREW	
608	Sunnyside Cottage	Part of pillar type fireplace; used as doorstep
614	Les Eperons	Type 4G arch; rebuilt in 19c. house; inscribed 'HDG 1619' and 'IR:IS 1760'
	Le Chouet de Roche	Fireplace corbel with female head and 15c. head-dress; in garden; previously on top of wall opposite Les Vauxbelets
617	Les Gouies Farm	Red lintel with two faces: brought from Rose Farm (80) 1980
618	Les Mourants	Red fireplace lintel, broken; re-used as hearth stone: from Les Gouies Farm (617)
630	La Vassalerie	Fireplace lintel; used as footbridge over stream
631	Pleneuf Court	Magnificent pillar type fireplace complete; re-assembled in house: drawn by F. C. Lukis (1850) at La Grande Maison
631	Pleneuf Court	Type 3R arch; in garden
631	Pleneuf Court	Type 3G arch; in garden
631	Pleneuf Court	Type 3G arch; in garden
631	Pleneuf Court	Carriage entrance of double arch *c.*1600; in garden
631	Pleneuf Court	Carriage entrance of double arch, early 17c.; in garden
	Below Church	Type 4R arch in freestanding wall
	Carriaux Cottage	Fine 15c. 2-light window, cusped, with transom and mullion; in gable-end; from 'Sarre' house near Les Adams (F. C. Lukis 1845). Removed before 1927
639	Les Bailleuls	Bedroom fireplace lintel; doorstep
	PARISH OF ST. PETER PORT	
686	Havilland Mead	Type 4G arch; in roadside wall
684	Les Damouettes	1 red chamfered stone; in garden; from Les Granges de Beauvoir Manor (834)

No.	Present Address	Description
717	11, Cliff Street	Base stone for fireplace; step in back garden
733	3, Back Street	Chamfered stone re-used in 18c. front doorway
	Brennan's, Bordage	'EM 1721' datestone at entrance to yard
	Brennan's, Bordage	Doorcase made for Burton's (762), a Brock House
	Between Back Street and Burnt Lane	1 shoulder stone from fireplace built in as end of wall
752	Kosy Korner	1 Type 5 fireplace corbel; projecting into Cow Lane. (But perhaps this is jettying support)
753	Sound Track, Church Square	1 fireplace lintel; over window; c.16c., De Sausmarez merchants' mark, rebuilt c.1608 or perhaps later
753	Sound Track, Church Square	1 bedroom fireplace lintel; over window; 2 angels supporting de Sausmarez arms, c.16c., rebuilt c.1608
763	Steak and Stilton	2 Type 1 fireplace corbels; inserted high up in venelle
	Slaughterhouse	'·H·B·1716/SHPETVIST' (?); built into west side
	Slaughterhouse	'TV/SVP/1764'; built into east side
	Town Hospital	Type 8 arch; from L'Hyvreuse (879)
762	Burton's, High Street	1 window lintel with shield; on ground in venelle at side. Arms of De Beauvoir—before 1660
	Berthelot St./Arcade	Base stone of fireplace; in steps to tiny yard
	Town Hospital	Double entrance arch; from L'Hyvreuse (879). Dated 1742, when moved to Hospital; but early 17c.
819	Elizabeth College	By Upland Road entrance; arms of Elizabeth I and underneath, arms of Adrian de Saravia, c.1561; much worn; originally over arch of main entrance
820	The Grange	Type 7 doorway; in roadside wall
827	Croutes House	Pillar type fireplace; as window surround above back kitchen
	Prince Albert's Road	Pointed arch with hood mould; in roadside wall; in front of La Grande Maison house, 1845
	Prince Albert's Road	Type 4G arch; in roadside wall
	Prince Albert's Road	Type 1R arch; in roadside wall
	Courtil Rozel, Mount Durand	Red sandstone (?) or Chausey granite rood built into house above lintel
	St. Barnabas	2 moulded pieces of grey granite; base and finial of attached pillar?
836	Les Granges de Beauvoir	Pillar type fireplace; built into wall behind house
836	Les Granges de Beauvoir	2 window sills with cable moulds; built into wall behind house
836	Les Granges de Beauvoir	Merchant's mark of James de Beauvoir; on fireplace lintel cut square built into gateway behind house
836	Les Granges de Beauvoir	One small piece of red stone with moulding; built into wall behind house
845	Off Mount Durand	Type 2 fireplace corbel; used as step in garden
	Cottage behind Savoy Hotel	2 Type 3 fireplace corbels; used as croissettes
	Candie Gardens	1 piece of chamfered stone; angle of wall by top entrance of Lower Gardens
896	Casa Seda, Water Lanes	Ogee arched window lintel with finial and head—c.14c.; below window
916	La Ramée	Fireplace lintel; behind house
920	Les Osmonds Farm	'PLG 1773'; inserted on 18c. barn, now garage
	2, Union Place, Mt. Row	Type 4R arch incomplete; in summer house
	PARISH OF ST. SAMPSON	
931	Myrtle Cottage	Chamfered stone; as gatepost, opposite side of road
933	St. Clair Farm	Fireplace lintel with ornament and faint inscription: in garden

No.	Present Address	Description
	Monaghan Villa, Route Militaire	Gateposts; at front entrance; from St. Andrew's Church
	Le Cognon, Hougue Jehannet	Type 5G doorway; inserted into 19c. house; from demolished house at La Grève. Arms of Jean Henry in shield 'IH 1596 CH' and fleur-de-lys above
	PARISH OF THE VALE	
	Figtree Farm, Landes du Marché	Fireplace lintel; on ground behind house
	Les Mielles, L'Ancresse	Type 4G arch; in wall near 'bus terminus
1029	St. Mary Anthony	Type 3G arch; re-used as doorway in later part of house
1029	St. Mary Anthony	1 shoulder stone from fireplace; used as gatepost to field opposite
	Vale Church	Stone incised with grisaille work and cross; as step to south of church. Perhaps a mandylion (Veronica's cloth)
	Rectory Garden, Vale Church	6 pieces of worked stone; re-assembled in shape of font, and one of them as base to later font. One is perhaps base of cross
	Castle Cornet	Fireplace lintel with De Beauvoir arms; from Ville-au-Roi Manor
	Castle Cornet	Cross-base (octagonal) made into trough, and shaft; all in grey stone; from Les Padins
	Castle Cornet	Trough with 2 mermaids in low relief on front, within border with cusping at top angles; from Les Fontaines (544); ?13c.
	Castle Cornet	Cross-base, originally octagonal on square, but 3 angles removed and made into trough; red stone
	Castle Cornet	Pillar-type fireplace; originally from priest's house, demolished 1870, St. Pierre-du-Bois

INDEX

Les Adams, district 35
Les Adams (328) 207
Les Adams (327) 79, 154, 165, 189, 202
Les Adams de Haut 35
Alan Barbetorte 8
Albecq 144, 157
Alderney sandstone 5
L'Amichet 78
L'Ancresse granodiorite 4
Angevin Empire 14, 17
Anglo-Saxons 7, 151, 182
Anjou 112
Les Annevilles Manor 61, 170, 172
Aquitaine 14, 68, 112, 151
Arcade Steps 115
Armada 113
Armorel 11, 290
Armorica 7
Ashbrook House 197
Atlantic Coast 6
Avranches 7

Back kitchens 84
Back Street 123
3, Back Street 82, 128
Les Bailleuls Cottage 24, 30, 39
La Bailloterie 202
Baker's Bazaar 124
Balderstone 26
The Baltic 6
La Banc des Moqueurs 214
Bara brith 77
Barbary pirates 220
Barfleur 14
Barley, M. W. 37, 68
Les Barrières de la Ville 18, 114-5, 119, 121, 123, 131
Bastide towns 16, 68
Bayeux Tapestry 68
Bayonne 16, 114
Les Beaucamps de Bas 137-8, 288
Beauchamp, Henry 17
Beaucoin 54, 56

De Beauvoir family 116
Le Beir, Nicholas 242
Bellegrève Bay 4
Les Belles 24-5, 201, 276
Belle Vue 54
La Bellieuse Farm 35, 83, 123, 165, 175, 177-8, 197, 204
Berthelot Street 115-9, 221, 245-51
5, Berthelot Street 34, 117, 161, 185, 197, 211, 226, 251
Bessin, Vicomte du 8, 10, 148
The Bestiary 222-3
Beuval, Fief de 146
Biele, Vital de 16
Le Bigard 26, 38, 206
La Bigoterie (812) 192
La Bigoterie (813) 124
La Bigoterie (815) 36
Les Blancs Bois 90, 176
Les Blanches (33) 136
Blanchelande, Fief de 41, 148-9
Blanchelande, France 104
Les Blicqs 28-9, 35, 37, 40, 52, 172, 182-3, 204
Blondel, Jacqueline 222-3
Bonamy family 130
Bonamy, John 17, 31, 144, 157, 173, 184, 202
La Bonne Vie 103
Boots' 124
Bordeaux diorite 4
Bordeaux, France 15, 114
Bordeaux Haven 11, 47, 50-1, 290
Bordeaux House 11, 34, 36, 38, 46-7, 50-1, 76, 161-2, 170, 172-4, 181, 188, 192, 195, 197, 201, 212, 214, 216
Le Bordage 119, 130
Les Bordages 46-7, 51-2, 65
Les Bordages, new house 75, 86, 127, 157, 172, 183
Bosham 68

Le Bosq 131
Botoner 144
Boulangeries 79, 154
Le Bourg 86-7, 89
Le Bourg de Bas 79, 81, 154
La Bouvée 39, 174, 201, 203
Bower 73
Les Brehauts 107
Brennan's 130
Breton, Rachael 146
Briard, Jean 116, 220-1, 249-51
Briard, Rachael 221, 249
Brick, use of 127
Bristol 16, 113
Britons 7, 151
Brockhurst 183
Bronze Age 6
Bucktrout's 124
Bull of Neutrality 17, 72, 118
Burgage strips 245
Burton's 32, 106
Les Buttes Guest House 176

La Câche (314) 26, 204
Les Câches (111) 197
Les Câches (190) 30
Les Câches (237) 6, 27, 37, 41, 46-7, 50-3, 58, 63, 84, 163, 165, 178, 180, 189, 194, 203-4
Les Câches Farm (112) 31, 144, 169, 173, 184
Caen 7
Caen stone 194, 218
Calvinism 58, 119, 216, 220
Les Camps 10
Le Camptréhard 84, 98-9, 236
Candie Museum 13
Cap de la Hague 7
Cardiff 32
Carentan, Vicomte de 114
Caretier arms 195
Carey arms 89
Carey family 130, 220

Carey, Edith, 112, 131, 144, 220-2
Carey, General de Vic 221
Carey, L. F. de Vic 296
Carey, Thomas 17
Careye, John 221
Careye, Lawrence 220
Careye, Peter 220-1, 223
Caritey, John 148
Carnet, Le Manoir 52, 61
Le Carrefour 163
Carriaux Cottage 33, 180
La Carrière (208) 47, 50-1, 88, 138, 175, 181
La Carrière (1028) 202
Carteret 7
Casa Seda 33, 180
Le Cas Rouge 90
Castel Church 9, 209, 211
Castel Hospital 211
Castel Rectory 118, 221
Castle Cornet 19, 76, 86, 113-5, 127, 169, 177, 192-3
Le Catillon de Bas 36, 38, 50, 204
La Cave 177
Caw Chapin 104
Celtic settlements 9
Chamber 73
Charlemagne 7
Charles the Bald 7
Charles the Simple 151
Château de la Montagne 82, 128
Le Château du Marais 113
Chaucer 31, 73
La Chaumière 44
Chausey 5-8, 36, 114, 118, 152, 157, 160, 175, 221, 259
La Cheminée 165
Le Chêne Cottage 36, 88, 90, 165, 181-2, 261
Le Chêne Farm 182
Cheshunt 108
Chichester 68
Childe, V. G. 12, 20
Choisi 183
Choucan-en-Paimpont 31, 57, 67
Chouet granodiorite 4
Chroniques de Coutances 6
Church Square 118, 130, 221

Circular chimneys 40
Civil War 120
Clay insulation 37
Cliff Street 114, 128-9
11, Cliff Street 81, 116, 123, 127, 165, 204
Climate 1
Le Clos de Bas 30, 197
Clos du Valle 11, 297
Cluett, Thomas 184
Coach House Gallery 174, 211
Coal Quay 121
Cob 156, 188
Cobo Farmhouse 35, 39, 148, 156, 172, 179
Cobo longhouse 13
Cobo stone 4-5, 63, 85, 106, 153, 157, 160, 169, 176, 184, 194, 232, 237, 276-7
Le Cocquerie 44, 184
Le Cognon 137
Cohu family 148
Le Colombier 59, 275
Colombiers 59
The Colonies 72
Constables' Office 73, 106, 115
Le Conte, Fief 41, 146, 148-9, 156, 172, 242
La Contrée de Glategny 119, 136
Contrée Mansell 123, 126-8
La Contrée de Saint 41, 50, 148, 170, 173
Conwy 115
La Corbière, district 77
La Corbière 44
Cornet Street 114, 116, 118, 130, 172
26, Cornet Street 123-7, 183, 249
Cornwall 7, 9, 13-4, 78
Côte ès Ouets 75
Cotentin peninsula 7-8, 10, 112, 118, 151, 167
Cotentin, Vicomte de 146
The Cottage (179) 44-5
The Cottage (212) 92
The Cottage (543) 26, 202
The Cottage (695) 82, 165
Les Cottes, St. Peter Port 115
Les Cottes 44-5, 96, 98-100
Couesnon, River 8
Coupée Lane 125

2, Coupée Lane 83, 121, 127, 204
La Cour de Longue 98, 104
Coutances 8, 16, 151
Le Couteur's stoneyard 118
La Couture 170, 175
La Couture House 26
Cow Lane 129-30
Le Crasset 78
Creasey's 124
Cresset lamp 78
Croissettes 89-90
Cross, 7th-century 58
Cross-walls 24 *et seq.*
Croutes House 192
Cruchbrée 54
Crucks 163, 274
Culloden, Battle of 296
Cumbria 9, 13
Curry's 128

Dalgary Cottage (992) 44, 172
Les Dalles 210
Les Damouettes 104
Dartmoor 68
De Beauvoir arms 89, 193, 260
De Beauvoir family 130, 197
De Beauvoir, James 220, 252
De Bertrands 24, 26, 36, 182
De Calverley, Sir Hugh 113
De Chesney, Sir William 31, 113
De Garie, Mrs. Marie 217
De Grandisson, Otto 113
De Guérin 146
De Havilland, Thomas 17
De la Court 252
De Lucy, Geoffrey 114
De Saravia, Adrian 211
De Sausmarez arms 221
De Sausmarez family 118, 193, 221
De Sausmarez, Nicholas 221-2
De Vic family 252
Devon 9
Dieppe 115
Dinan 117, 211, 249
Dobrée family 128, 130
Dog kennels 203
Dol-de-Bretagne 17, 116
Les Domaines 90
Dordogne 12, 16, 68
Dorset 79

INDEX

Le Douit Beuval 75
Le Douit Farm, 87, 192
Le Douit Farm Flats 36, 192
Dover 14
Dry-stone walling 156
Du Guesclin, Bertrand 113, 173-4, 216
Du Port, Michel 152
Dur Ecu, Manoir de 86
Duvaux Farm 40, 76, 78, 177, 198

Earth floors 108
L'Echelle 27, 29, 38, 78, 123, 165, 204
Ecole, La Petite 119
Edward I 17, 61
Edward III 18
Les Effards (552) 148
Effart, Lucas 118, 222
Elizabeth, Queen 221
Elizabethan house 116
Elizabeth College, 119, 176, 214
The Elms (946) 33, 44, 96, 157, 169, 172, 207, 209, 291
England 7
L'Epinel 100-1
L'Erée 10
Eschaugettes 203
L'Etables-sur-Mer 61
L'Etiennerie 26
Eye-brow windows 39, 93
Les Eyzies 12

Le Fainel 221, 283
La Falaise 138, 261
Les Fauxconnaires 77
Les Fauxquets Farm 46-7, 50-1
Fay Dell 24, 30
Fenêtre à meneaux 88
Feudal dues 146-7
Fief Blanchelande 41, 148-9
    Bouvée Duquemin 288
    Beuval 146
    Canelly 288
    Le Comte 41, 146, 148-9, 156, 172, 242
    Cour Ricard 288
    De la Cour 147
    Guillot Justice 288
    Le Roi 146
    Thomas Blondel 288

Figeac 68
Fireplaces, stone 14
Flambie Cottage 107, 190
Le Fleur du Jardin 163
Folk Museum 217-8
Les Fontaines (422) 35, 68, 189, 209
Les Fontaines (544) 41, 189, 209
Forest Church 9, 134, 178, 180, 211
Forest Lane 115, 121
La Forge (221) 28, 36, 87, 175, 178, 182
La Forge (509) 36, 148, 181-2, 203, 212, 214, 217
La Forge (924) 38, 44, 295
Fortified farmhouses 60 *et seq.*
La Fosse district 36
La Fosse (63) 88, 137
La Fosse (300) 78, 105, 159
La Fosse (331) 26
Les Fosses (61-2) 10
Fougères 61, 203
Fountain Street 114-6, 118, 123
Four, Sign of 222
Fox, Sir Cyril 193-4
Frankish law 8
La Frégate 128
French châteaux 29
    flooring 34
    Revolution 72
Le Frie (303) 152, 207, 209, 210
Les Fries (604-5) 10

Gabbro 4, 85
Galleting 88
Gallia Lugdunensis 7
Les Galliennes 104
Galliot Cottage 54, 56
Gardner, William 76, 296
La Garenne 61
Gascony 15-16, 68, 113, 151
La Gaudine 202
Gazebo 106
Genoese galleys 113
Geoffrey of Anjou 14, 112, 146
Geology 216
Georgian architecture 72, 86
Le Get, Nicholas 146

Girard, Jean 145
Glategny, Contrée de 119
37, Glategny Esplanade 201
Gonfalon 222
Gorey 112, 194, 218
Governors of the Isles 113
Les Grais 90
Le Grand Bosq 106
Les Grands Courtils 34-5, 195, 207, 209, 212, 217, 283
Le Grand Douit 54, 56
La Grande Brière 11, 41, 85
La Grande Maison (?) 175, 192
La Grande Maison (945) 34, 54, 56, 60-1, 63-4, 87, 125, 163, 169, 174, 183, 197-8, 209, 290
La Grande Maison de la Pomare 170, 175
Les Grandes Maisons 210
Les Grandes Mielles 90
Les Grands Moulins (505) 35, 39, 59, 179
Les Grands Moulins (520) 141, 148, 189, 216
Les Granges de Beauvoir Manor 27, 32, 40, 60-1, 83, 88, 150, 162-3, 165, 175-8, 181, 192, 194, 197, 199, 204, 214, 220, 265, 274
The Great Fire of London 120
The Great Schism 16
Le Grée (125) 36, 38, 175, 181-2, 203
Le Grée, Le Gron 42, 95, 103, 140
Green Bed 33, 77
La Grève district 137-8
La Grève (1012) 11, 159
Le Groignet 176
Le Gron 175, 185, 221
Le Gron Farm 29, 233
Grosnez Castle 180
Grove Hill House 54, 56
Guernsey range 126
Guernsey safe 68
Guernsey Savings Bank 56, 116-8, 130, 152, 161, 206, 220-1
Le Guet 93
Guingamp 116, 211
Guyenne 112

Hagioscope 68
La Hague 220
Les Hamelins 37
Harold, King 68
Le Haut Chemin 84, 159, 194-5, 201, 203
Hauteville 106, 120, 126, 128, 131
1,3,7,11, Hauteville 126-7
16,18, Hauteville 129
Havilland House 36, 82, 128, 165, 206
La Haye du Puits (582) 47, 50, 61, 63, 174, 176, 199, 259
La Haye du Puits (583) 33, 108, 180
La Haye du Puits, France 61
Les Hêches (225) 173
Les Hêches (375) 85, 107
Les Hêches (446) 36, 197
Hengistbury Head 6
Henry II 14, 146
Henry III 17, 114
Henry IV 17
Henry V 146
Henry, Hémon 114
Herm 7
High Street 115, 117, 130-1, 161, 211, 221
Hilltop 106
Hillview 100-1
Holland 120
Homer 211
Horn window 88
Les Houets 26
Hougue Jehannet 137
Les Hougues 177
La Houguette (321) 34
La Houguette (528) 4, 35-6, 40-1, 47, 51-2, 64-5, 81, 85, 189, 269
La Houguette (529) 44, 50
Les Hubits de Haut (6) 137, 202
Huguenots 98, 152, 220
Humphrey, Duke of Gloucester 17
Hundred Years' War 5, 16, 118
Le Hurel 95
Huriaux Place 193, 218, 291
Hut circles 11
Huysh, Mrs. 211

L'Hyvreuse 176

Icart gneiss 277
Ionic columns 195
Ireland 7, 11, 22, 42, 57, 151, 153
Iron Age 6, 11, 12
Isle of Wight 113
Les Islets 26, 28-30, 38, 87
L'Islet 226
Les Issues 30, 37, 73

Jaon 77
La Jaonière 40
Jehan, Colas 145
Les Jehans 10
Les Jenemies 95
Jerbourg 5
Le Jersiez, Jean 148
Jerzual, la Rue 117
Jibbes de Jaon 77
John, King 14-15, 112
La Jonctierre 77-8
Jewellers' and Silversmiths' 126

Keyho's 121
King's Mills district 149
King's Mills' Farm 39, 46-7, 50-1, 188, 198, 201, 277
King's Mills' House 198, 277
King's Mills' Lodge 74
King's Mills' Villa 236
Kitchens, detached 79
Knuckle bones 29

Le Lacheur, Pierre 87, 136
Les Landes 10
Lefebvre family 222
Lefebvre Street 115, 211
Legge Survey 19, 121, 126, 129-30, 143, 177, 296
Leighton, Sir Thomas 221
Lennox, Charles 296
Lihou Island 59, 217-18
Limestone paving 78
Lincoln 17
Lipton's 128
Le Lit Clos 33
Lloyd's 130
La Logis Tiphaine 36
Les Lohiers 118, 297
Le Loire 7
Lombardic script 118

London 220
London, Tower of 292
Long-and-short work 189
Lukis and Island Museum 218
Lukis, F. C. 33, 36, 170, 192-3, 218
Lyme Regis 16, 220

MacCulloch, Sir Edgar 161, 174, 177
La Madeleine de Bas 29, 237
Mahy family 148
Main Guard 127
Les Mainguys 60, 64
La Maison Bonamy 174, 211
La Maison d'Aval (241) 27, 35, 51, 58, 60, 75, 87, 140, 165, 182-3, 193-4, 198, 214
La Maison d'Aval (975) 40, 47, 182, 201
Maison de Bas 78
La Maison de Haut (240) 27, 58-9, 161-3, 165, 175, 212, 259
La Maison de Haut (418) 160
La Maison de Haut (927) 188
La Maison de Haut (974) 66-69, 154, 161, 172, 206
La Maison des Pauvres (308) 40, 159-60, 173, 175, 178
La Maison des Pauvres, St. Peter Port 118, 161
La Maison du Mont Val 93, 95, 98
La Maison du Quay 143
Maison Galopie 204
La Maison Godaine 148
La Maison Tiphaine 36, 173, 191-2, 216, 237, 291
Malator 29
Le Manoir 181
Le Manoir, Carnet 52, 61, 203-4
Le Manoir de Dur Ecu 86
Le Manoir de Haut 115
Manoir ès Marchants 72, 130
23a, Mansell Street 128
Manston 68
Manuscript Girard 145
Maples' 126
Le Marais (493) 4, 24, 26-8, 38-9, 41, 148, 159, 169,

INDEX

Le Marais (493) contd.
172, 174, 182, 185, 192,
202, 265, 274, 276-7
Le Marais (937) 27, 38, 78,
163
Le Marais Farm 46-8, 51, 170,
173, 207, 212
Le Marchant arms 56
Le Marchant family 106, 115,
130
Le Marchant, Denis 114
Le Marchant, Fort 4
Le Marchant House 128-30
Le Marchant, Thomas 220
Les Marchez 36, 88
La Mare 47, 50, 52, 61, 179,
269
La Mare de Carteret 108
La Marie 114
Market Halls 115
Market Square 115
Markets 130
Marmoutiers 8, 146, 151
Marquand's 129, 143
Marquy, Hélier 148
Married Quarters 86, 127,
192-3
Les Martins, district 10, 148,
296
Les Martins (135) 148
Martinvast 104
Les Massies 85
Les Mauxmarquis 89
1, Mauxmarquis Cottage 108
Mediterranean 6-7, 16, 112
Meirion-Jones, Gwyn I. 12,
153
Memorial brasses 20
Le Ménage du Moulins 169,
172, 217
Les Merriennes Cottage (98)
202, 268
Merriennes Cottage (102) 108
Mérode, Triptych 216
Le Messurier family 58, 193,
275
Les Messuriers (158) 78
Michael, Chapel of the
Blessed 115, 211
Les Mielles, district 10
Les Mielles (1001) 11, 75,
283
Mill Street 106, 116, 120,
127-8, 131, 177

l, Mill Street 124
21,23,25, Mill Street 83, 121,
123
Milne's 106, 127
Monaghan Villa 177
Monamy, André 161, 249-50
Monmouthshire 13
Le Mont Durand 148
Mont Mado 4-5, 152, 194
Le Mont Saint 40, 189
Le Mont Saint (412) 108
Mont St. Michel 5, 7-8, 20,
36, 114, 116, 146, 151,
173-4, 191-2, 199, 216,
237
Montpazier 16
Moore's Hotel 86, 123, 130,
183, 206
The Moors 173
Morbihan 153
Les Mottes Cottages 45
Les Mouilpieds (118) 173
Le Moulin de Haut (486) 81,
88, 222
Le Moulin de Haut (487) 108
Moulin Huet 145, 157
Moullin, Abraham 146
99, Mount Durand 106
Mount Pleasant 95
Les Mourains 85
Les Mourants 172-3
La Moye, district 68
La Moye (999) 40, 201
Mur-de-Bretagne 199

Les Naftiaux 39, 47, 50-1
Nantes 16
Napoleonic Wars 72
Neadon 68
Neustria 151
Newlands 95
New Place 35
Les Niaux (539) 75, 96, 100-1
Les Niaux (641) 107, 190
Nicholas, Pierre 114
Normandy 8, 86, 98
Norman Empire 14
Normanville 89, 176
Norsemen 8
Nucleated villages 9

Old Cobo Farmhouse 148-9,
156
Old Cottage (1005) 11, 47, 50

Old Farm, Brock Road 38, 58,
172, 175, 182, 203
Old Farmhouse (928) 39
Old Marais 212
Ollivier, Laurence 221
Open fields 10
Orientation 10
Oxford 68
Ozanne, Denis 145

Les Paas 26
Les Pages 10
La Palette 77
Pandora (785) 124
Panelling 27
Papal Bull 17, 72, 118
Paqueteau, Francois 156
Paradis, France 12
Partage 28
Paston Letters 144
Le Patourel, J. 8, 14
Le Patourel, Mrs. 13
Les Paysans 172, 217
Les Paysans Farm 193, 236
Peate, Iorwerth C. 11, 67
Pedvin Street 126
Les Pelleys 146
Pembrokeshire 9
Perelle 3, 85, 182
Petit Bôr Bay 265
La Petite Câche 138, 169
La Petite Ecole 119
La Petite Maison 54
Les Petites Mielles 108, 193
Le Petit Jardin 44-5
Les Petits Cherfs 93
Philip Augustus 14, 112
Physiologus 222
Les Picques 89, 209
Les Pièces 100-1
Pieds des Monts 108
Pigsties 11, 66, 90
La Pitié 17, 114
Pisé 188
Placard 210
La Plaiderie 115, 130
Plaiderie House 114, 123, 128,
206
La Planque Farm 83
Plantagenets 16, 113
Plas Dyke Farm 201
Pleinheaume 226
Pleinmont 283

Pleneuf Court 138, 175-6, 192-3, 197, 211
Les Poids de la Reine 115
Les Poidevins (662) 84, 169, 184, 204
Le Poitevin, Philipin 145
Poitou 112, 151
Le Pollet 115-6, 120, 123, 129-30
11, Le Pollet 124
15, Le Pollet 128
18, Le Pollet 126
20, Le Pollet 124
28, Le Pollet 83, 121, 204
30, Le Pollet 121
La Pompe 36, 170, 181, 203, 261, 265, 283
Poole 16
Population figures 18
Pork rack 78
La Porte (480) 35, 38
La Porte (526) 81, 206
Les Portelettes 85
Portland stone 5
La Pouquelaye 176, 261
Le Pré du Merlin 137, 288
Presbyterianism 178, 214
Les Prevosts, district 10-11
Les Prevosts (463) 88, 182, 201
Les Prevosts (465) 136
Les Prevosts (467) 65
Priaulx family 130
Priest's House 193
Prince Albert's Road 170, 192
Le Prinseur 79, 85, 177
Les Profonds Camps 75

Quarrying 2
Les Quatre Vents 84, 99
Quay Street 130
Les Quertiers (676) 27, 82, 165, 182
Les Quertiers (919) 174, 181, 194-5
Les Queux 28, 30, 32, 36, 148, 175, 193, 197, 203-4

Les Raies de Haut 6, 47-8, 63, 178, 192, 194, 269
Rainwater heads 127
Raleigh, Sir Walter 113
The Reformation 104, 214, 223

Refronting 86-7
Regency architecture 72, 86
Regneville 6
The Renaissance 33, 72, 181, 195, 197, 250, 283
Rennes 161, 188, 249
Le Repos au Coin 181, 265
The Restoration 120, 218
Retôt Farm 172
Retour au Nord 137
Les Reveaux (258) 138, 140
Les Reveaux (259) 58, 84, 161-2
Richard I 16
Richmond, Duke of 129, 147
Robert I, Duke 8
Robilliard, Pierre 288
La Rochelle 15, 114
Le Rocher 104
Rocquaine 3, 283
Rocquaine Villa 207
La Rocque Balan 11, 27, 33, 37-8, 47, 50-2, 77, 81, 163, 165, 170, 172-3, 176-8, 180, 203, 207, 209, 212, 259, 264, 274
La Rocré 100
Rollo 8, 151
Les Romains 78
Roman conquest 6
  houses 12
  times 112
  vessel 6
Rome 145
La Ronde Cheminée 35, 40, 47, 50, 169, 189
Roof structures 11, 38, 58, 94, 163, 232, 253
Rope Walk Cottage 106
Rosemary Lane 115
La Rotarre 77
Rouen 8
Les Rouvets de Haut 183
Roy, General 296
Le Roy, Pierre 176
Royal Hotel 106
Rue de L'Eglise 108
Rue des Landes 140
Rue des Vinaires 93, 206
La Ruette (52) 137
La Ruette (406) 37, 60, 64, 165, 242
Les Ruettes (678) 106
Les Ruettes Cottage 103

Rybot, Major 220, 222

Les Sages (270) 146
Les Sages Villa 60, 64, 138, 194, 291
St. Andrew, church of 10, 176-7, 191, 211
St. Barnabas, church of 114
St. Briocq 86, 288
Ste. Appoline, chapel of 114, 160
Ste. Clair (932) 157, 169
St. Fagan's Folk Museum 32
St. George 5, 32, 34, 45, 138, 150, 170, 175, 180, 211-2, 214 222
St. George's Esplanade 131
St. Helier 7, 19, 112
St. John, Lamb of 222
St. Julian, chapel of 119, 131
St. Magloire 7
St. Magloire (996) 47, 50-1
St. Malo 7-8, 19, 152, 220
St. Martin, church of 9, 211
St. Pierre-du-Bois, church of 9, 176
St. Sampson 8
St. Sampson, church of 9, 16, 168, 170, 211
Saint's Farm 36, 60, 64, 84, 123, 174, 181-2, 204, 277
Saint's Road 10
St. Saviour, church of 9, 134, 152, 173, 178, 276
St. Thomas 61
St. Tugual 7
La Salerie 85, 131
Saline Bay 4
Salomon 7
3, Salter Street 82, 165
Sandstone 106
Sandwich 113
Sark 7, 40
Sarlat 12
Sarre House, L'Erée 33
Sausmarez Manor 89, 123, 138, 183, 193
Scandinavia 6
Schnar 77
Scotland 14, 199
Sécage 77
La Seigneurie 56, 175, 185, 261
Seine 8

INDEX

Settle 77–8, 165–6, 268
Settlement patterns 9–10
Sheppard's 130
Shrubwood 54
Les Simons 54, 56, 198
Sixtus V 118
The Slaughterhouse 221
Small-parlour houses 115–7, 121, 161, 204
Sod ridge 40
Solar 73
Southampton 14, 16–17, 113, 116–7, 127, 183, 188, 248, 250, 296
Spain 6, 17, 173
Squint, 68
Stephen, King 112, 146
Stevens, Joan 216
Surrey 78
Swanage stone 5

La Table de cuisine 78
Tangela 93
La Tanière 88
La Tanque 78
Les Taudevins 54
Le Terpied 78
Terracing of dwellings 10
Terre battue 11, 29
Le Tertre (601) 37
Le Tertre (1026) 34, 47, 60–1, 63–5, 77, 169, 174, 176, 181, 198, 227, 259, 275, 290, 295
Thatching 12
Thatch ties 95
Thetford 68
Thoume family 221
Thoume, Thomas 221
Les Tilleuls 36, 47, 50–1, 90, 176, 181
Torteval Church 9
Toulouse 14
La Tour Beauregard 114–5, 119, 128–9
La Tourelle 148
La Tour Gand 114–5, 121
Tours 8–9
Le Tourtel 88, 90, 149, 175, 181, 198, 233, 264

Tower Hill 126
Town Church 9, 16, 140, 152, 160, 168–9, 172, 174, 193, 199, 211, 214, 220, 249
Town Hospital 86, 176, 260
Town wall 114
Trano, Battle of 8, 151
Le Tranquesous 11, 13
Tréguier 116–7, 154, 211, 249
La Trinité 114
Le Truchon 76
Le Truchot 129–30
Tudor contracts 18
Tupper family 130
Tyquet, Colas 145

United Club 124

Valcanville 86
Vale Castle 113, 169
Vale Church 9, 168, 170, 211, 218
Vale Priory 64
Les Vallettes 223
Le Vallon 220–1
Le Vallon Cottage 223
Valognes 61, 86
Le Varclin, district 108
Le Varclin 185
Le Variouf, district 44
Le Variouf (184) 107–8
Le Variouf de Haut 32
Les Vardes Farm Hotel 68, 192
Le Vauquiédor Manor 195, 261, 283, 288
Vaux Douit 104
Vazon 4
Venetian galleys 113
Venetian window 106, 124, 183
Venice 173
Les Vicheries 5
Vicomte de Carentan 114
La Vieille Maison, La Ville Amphrey 182
La Vieille Maison de la Villocq 54, 56

Les Vieilles Galliennes 74, 236
La Vieille Sous L'Eglise 41, 59, 75, 85, 182, 198, 203, 210
Les Vieilles Salines 197
Le Vieux Porte 104
Vikings 8
Le Vilaine 78
La Ville Amphrey 27, 38
Ville-au-Roi Manor 156, 181, 193–4, 203, 253
La Ville Durand 61
Les Villets (196) 26, 38
Les Villets Farm 47, 50
Les Villets, district 261
La Villette (123) 35, 204
La Villette (124) 36, 175, 180, 193, 264
La Villiaze 86, 89–90, 141, 198
Le Villocq (581) 170, 173, 175
Les Vinaires 75
Vinaires, Rue des 93
Vitré 116, 220
La Vrangue Manor 89, 141

Wales 7–8, 11, 22, 24, 30, 42, 57, 77, 115, 151, 153
Warehouses 129
Warwick, Duke of 17
Warwick, The Kingmaker 113
Wight, Isle of 17, 113
Wig stand 78
William the Conqueror 146
Williams, D. Trevor 112
Wilson, John 116
Winchelsea 113
Wine trade 15, 17, 68, 113
Wissant 14
Wisteria 26, 88, 198, 222, 277
Wooden shoulders 107, 189–90
Woodlands 128
Wool trade 17
Wyatt's 121

Yorkshire 78

LIST OF SUBSCRIBERS

Laurence Adkins, M.A.
Mrs. Lois M. Ainger
Mr. & Mrs. John R. Allan
Mr. V. J. Amy
Mr. G. R. Andrews (Andros)
Miss Wendy M. Angell
Mrs. G. T. A. Armitage
Miss J. F. Arthur
Mrs. M. H. Atkinson

Mr. H. Bachelet
Mr. John Bainbridge
Miss G. M. Barnett
Mr. K. J. Barton, M.Phil., F.S.A., F.M.A.
Les Beauchamps School Library
Mr. & Mrs. H. E. Bean
Mrs. L. M. Beeson
Miss C. Bell
Mrs. P. M. Best
Mr. & Mrs. J. D. Bichard
Mr. & Mrs. G. V. F. Birch
Mr. & Mrs. K. W. Bishop
Mr. E. A. Bisson
Mr. Maurice B. Bisson
Mrs. M. Bizet
Mrs. V. E. Blad
Mr. John Blaise
T. G. Blake, Esq.
Mrs. E. Blampied
Mr. G. P. Blampied
Mr. R. H. Blanchford, O.B.E., G.M., L.F.I.B.A.
E. H. Bodman (Mr.)
Mrs. Eileen M. Bostle
Mr. Stephen R. Bott
Mr. M. H. Le Boutellier
Mr. Ralph Henry Bowring
Mr. K. G. Bradford
Mr. & Mrs. F. Bramhall
Mr. R. N. Brehaut
Mrs. P. Brehaut
Brennans Estate Office
Mr. and Mrs. A. T. Brock
Mr. and Mrs. A. H. T. Broderick
Mr. A. H. J. Brouard, A.I.B.
Mr. A. M. Brouard
Mr. H. A. Brouard
Mr. H. W. Brouard
Mr. & Mrs. I. F. Brouard
Mr. & Mrs. N. J. Brouard
Mr. & Mrs. P. J. Brouard
Mr. & Mrs. R. A. Brouard
Mr. I. Browning
Mr. F. N. Browning
Miss G. Browning
Mr. G. J. Browning
Mrs. B. A. Buckley
Dr. J. C. Bulstrode
Miss P. K. Burgess
Mrs. A. G. Burns
Mr. G. I. Burr
Miss Burrard

Major General F. G. Caldwell
Mr. Richard G. Carey
Mr. & Mrs. De V. G. Carey
Mr. & Mrs. Marcel G. Cariou
Mr. & Mrs. W. J. Carman
Mrs. P. J. Carpenter
Mr. & Mrs. P. R. Castle
Channel Islands Galleries Ltd., of Trinity Square
Mr. & Mrs. C. B. Chantry
Miss K. M. Le Cheminant

His Excellency Air Chief Marshal Sir Peter Le Cheminant, G.B.E., K.L.B., D.F.C.
Mrs. M. J. Chepmell
Mrs. J. Cherry
Mr. W. J. Chick
Mr. Edward Choppen
Mrs. Violet Church
Mr. & Mrs. A. Carson Clark
Lieutenant Colonel H. W. Clark
Mr. Raymond Clark
Mr. & Mrs. R. J. T. Clark
Mr. D. E. H. Closs
Deputy G. G. le Cocq
The Reverend Canon and Mrs. Cogman
Mr. & Mrs. S. A. Coker
Mrs. H. R. Cole
Mrs. A. M. Collas
The Revd. Canon V. J. Collas, M.A.
Theda Malberb-Tanner Connell
Dr. Francis Coningsby
Mr. Brian R. Le Conte
D. A. Le Conte
Mr. D. O. Le Conte
Miss D. C. Cook
Dr. D. E. Coombe
Mr. & Mrs. L. S. Coomer
Bee Leng Cotterill
David Cotterill
Mr. & Mrs. John Court
Henry G. Coutanche
Mr. Pierre Coutanche
Mr. & Mrs. G. Le M. Le Couteur
Mr. D. D. Cranch
Mr. D. G. Creasey
Mr. & Mrs. J. C. Cross
Mr. J. L. Curtis, B.D.S.

Mr. & Mrs. H. R. Dally
Mrs. H. P. Davey
Mr. & Mrs. J. E. David
Rachel M. David
Mrs. Isobel de M. Davidson, F.I.S.T.
Mr. & Mrs. A. J. Davies
Miss B. U. Davis
Mrs. K. Davis
Group Captain L. C. Deane, D.S.O., D.F.C.
Mr. & Mrs. J. L. F. Denning
Mr. W. J. Denning
Mrs. W. J. Denning
The Misses N. A. & K. Ogier Dennis
Mrs. Mollie Despointes
Dr. J. R. Dickson
Mrs. Lilian A. Domaille
Miss Lucy Domaille
Mr. Jonathan Dorey
Mrs. Katharine Dorey
Mr. R. E. Dorey
Mr. Rupert Dorey
Mr. Thomas Dorey
Mr. John Dowding
Michael J. Dowding
Mr. & Mrs. E. S. Down
Mr. & Mrs. Nicholas Drake
Mr. Guy Dunell
Mr. & Mrs. G. J. Dunster
Mr. Robin Dupré
John Dymock

Mr. & Mrs. D. Edmonds
Mr. & Mrs. N. F. Elliot

Mrs. Phyllis M. Elliott
Mr. & Mrs. W. C. Elliott
J. E. English
Maurice English
Dr. J. Erskine
Mr. & Mrs. A. E. Evans
Mr. A. H. Ewen

Dr. D. F. Falla
Mr. & Mrs. Don Falla
Mrs. L. E. Falla
Mr. Michael Anthony Falla
Mr. P. J. Falla
Mr. & Mrs. V. J. Falla
Mr. D. M. Feak
Mr. & Mrs. R. A. Ferneyhough
Mr. B. J. M. Ferguson
Mr. I. B. Fisher
Joan Cohu de Lisle Fisher (Mrs.)
M. L. Fitzgerald
Mrs. Renee P. Fitzgerald
Mr. Neil F. Forster
Mrs. Jayne Foster
Mr. & Mrs. G. W. B. Foulds
Frances M. Fox
Mr. B. G. Frampton

Mrs. Anne Gale
Mr. A. G. C. Le Gallez
Miss P. M. Le Gallez
Mr. & Mrs. B. J. Gardiner
Mr. & Mrs. Derek A. Gardiner
Mr. H. E. de Garis
Mrs. Marie de Garis
Mr. W. J. Gaudion
Dr. C. J. Gavey
Mrs. Christine M. Gavey
Mr. Geoffrey P. Gavey
Mr. James A. Gavey
Mr. Michael E. Gavey
Mrs. Joan Gay
Mr. & Mrs. A. Geary
Mr. & Mrs. J. M. Gillingham
Mr. & Mrs. D. U. Girard
Mr. Peter J. Girard
Mrs. M. L. E. Godfrey
Mrs. J. E. Godwin
Mr. J. D. Goodwin
Mrs. V. J. Gollop
Mr. & Mrs. A. H. Goss
Margaret Graham
Mrs. D. F. Gregg
Mr. Dermott Griffith
Mrs. Betty Grut
Mr. J. & Mrs. M. Guerin
Mr. L. E. Guilbert
Mr. P. E. Guilbert
Dr. Susan Guille
Guille-Allès Library and Museum

Mr. I. J. Hall
Mr. E. J. Hamel
Mr. A. Hamon
Dr. D. P. G. Hamon, Ph.D., B.Sc.
Lawrence Harding
M. J. & R. Harding
Mr. B. P. Hardwick
Molly E. Harris
Dr. P. R. Harris
Mr. P. de B. C. Hart
Mrs. Joan Heath
Mr. J. S. Heaume
Mr. R. L. Heaume
Miss Jane Henderson
Mr. & Mrs. T. J. Henderson

Mr. & Mrs. R. C. Hendry
Mr. C. M. H. Herpe
Capt. G. C. Hocart, D.S.C., R
Colonel Archibald Hope of Luffness
Mrs. Anne V. Hopkins
Mrs. M. G. Hughes
Mrs. R. B. Hunter
Mr. Hutt, T.G., M.A.
The Islands' Insurance Company Limited

Mr. J. M. Jackson
Mrs. Rosemary Jagger
Mr. Lester James
Mr. Ian L. Jameson
Mr. Nigel Jee
Mr. & Mrs. C. H. Jehan
Mrs. Renée Jehan
The Earl of Jersey
B. R. de Jersey
Mrs. Diana de Jersey
P. C. de Jersey
Captain and Mrs. B. K. Johns
Mr. Peter Johnston
Barry Jones
Dr. E. D. Jones, C.B.E., F.S.A F.L.A., Aberystwyth
Mrs. M. Jordan

Mr. & Mrs. Jack Keen
Mrs. J. S. Kemp
Mr. & Mrs. D. A. Kempthorn
Mr. A. R. Klein
Mr. & Mrs. K. Kenyon
Jurat R. A. Kinnersley, T.D.,
Timothy Knight
Katharine Konig
Mr. & Mrs. L. Konyn
Mrs. F. J. El Korashy

La Mare du Cartaret Seconda School
Mr. J. W. Le Lacheur
Drs. D. C. & E. H. Laidlow
Mrs. C. A. Lainé
Dr. Derek C. Lainé
Miss D. N. Lainé
Mr. & Mrs. J. A. Lainé, Les Hougues, St. Sampson's
Frances Rosemary Lammas
Mr. Dudley H. Langlois
A. C. Lanoe
Mr. Christian Lapeyre
Mrs. Lawrence
Mr. & Mrs. E. R. Lawson
Mr. R. Lempriere
Mr. E. J. T. Lenfesty
Advocate J. N. Van Leuven
Mr. R. E. K. Levett
Mr. K. G. H. Lewis
Mr. D. W. Lewry
Mr. & Mrs. E. M. Lihou
Mrs. S. Lintell
Mr. & Mrs. John G. Lipscomb
Mr. J. N. de Lisle
Mr. & Mrs. B. T. E. Livesey
Mr. and Mrs. E. Lockett
Mr. & Mrs. Nicholas Long
Mr. & Mrs. R. Long
Mrs. Lilian M. Lucas
V. E. Luff, M.B.E.
Mr. Eric Fellowes Lukis
Mr. J. P. Lynas

Mrs. F. G. C. Macartney
Mr. Colin J. McCathie
Major T. A. McCathie
Mrs. G. M. McCave
Dr. & Mrs. I. N. McCave
Mr. David McClintock
Mr. A. J. McDade
Mrs. Edith M. McGhee
Mr. I. MacRae
Col. R. C. Mace
Mr. & Mrs. G. R. Mahy
Mr. D. E. Maindonald
Mrs. Iris Maingard
J. W. Maingay
Edward Francis Brehaut
 Malherb-Tanner
Mrs. J. G. M. Mansell
Mr. Peter S. Mansell
Mr. R. D. de la Mare, O.B.E.
Mr. C. F. A. Marmoy
J. Marr, Esq., B.Sc.(Econ.)
Mr. Patrick Fanshawe Martin
Mrs. R. J. Marquis
Mr. M. B. Marshall
Mr. P. Martel
Mr. & Mrs. P. W. Martel
Martel Maides Le Pelley & Moy,
 Estate Agents Auctioneers and
 Valuers
Mrs. Peronelle Martin
Mr. & Mrs. J. A. Meader
Miss D. C. Meldrum
Richard N. Mauger
Mr. W. F. Mauger
Marie-Louise Mendham, B.A.
Colin Le Messurier
Miss M. L. Le Messurier
Mr. P. N. Le Messurier
Mr. Hubert Le Mesurier
Mr. Alan Middleton
Mrs. Sheila Middleton
Mr. Robin Millard
Mr. & Mrs. D. A. Miller
Reverend Paul Miller
Mrs. M. N. Mimmack
Mr. M. Le Moignan
Mr. I. R. Monins
Mrs. D. P. E. Mooney
Miss N. C. Moore
Mrs. P. Denise Moore
Mr. Richard Moorman
Mr. R. S. Morgan
Mrs. A. E. Morris
Mr. & Mrs. J. E. Morris
Mr. & Mrs. W. A. Morton
Rafaela and Martin Mottram
Mr. C. M. Mould
Mrs. J. E. Moullin
Tessa Munro
Mrs. D. J. Murray

Miss I. M. Naftel
Mr. William Keith Neal
Mr. Trevor Nicholls
Mr. Hardwick Nichols
Mr. & Mrs. Christopher Nicole
Mr. & Mrs. G. V. B. Nicholson
Lt. Col. T. V. Nicholson, O.B.E.,
 E.R.D.
Mr. J. R. Nicolle
Mr. & Mrs. Brian Norman
Mr. L. H. Norman
Mr. M. R. Norman
Mr. R. L. Norman
Miss T. M. Norman
Miss A. M. J. Le Noury

Mrs. A. M. Le Noury
Mr. M. M. Le Noury

Mrs. A. M. Ogier
Mr. and Mrs. N. M. Ogier
Conseillier Thomas Daniel Ogier
Mrs. Frances O'Sullivan
Mr. David J. Ozanne
Major E. H. Ozanne
Mr. John G. Ozanne
Miss J. R. Ozanne
Miss R. A. Ozanne
Mr. & Mrs. R. N. Ozanne
Mr. & Mrs. T. J. Ozanne

Major and Mrs. R. A. Paddock
Miss Annette Le Page
Mrs. D. K. Le Page
F. Le Page, Esquire
G. R. Le Page, President
 Chamber of Commerce
Mr. & Mrs. H. Le Page
Dr. K. E. Le Page
Mrs. R. J. Le Page
Mrs. W. M. Le Page
Mr. & Mrs. Eric J. Paint
Mr. G. A. Paint, La Houguette,
 S. Pierre-du-Bois
Mr. & Mrs. Dick Palmer
Mr. Southcombe Parker (L.D.S.)
Mrs. Lenore Parkes
Miss Muriel R. Parkinson
Dr. & Mrs. Tom W. Parsons
Professor John Le Patourel
Mrs. Patricia Paxton
R. C. Payne
Dr. T. N. D. Peet
Mrs. Dorothy W. Le Pelley
Mr. Paul R. Le Pelley
Mr. A. E. Phillips
Mr. & Mrs. A. H. Pike
Mrs. M. D. G. Pike
Mr. Roger A. P. Pinckney
Mrs. K. R. Pipet
Jurat and Mrs. D. P. Plummer
Dr. N. Le Poidevin
Stephen E. F. and Mrs. Mary L.
 Le Poidevin
Col. H. W. Poat
Miss Julia du Port
Major and Mrs. Roland Porter
Mr. and Mrs. A. L. Prevel
Mr. & Mrs. R. M. Priaulx
Priaulx Library
Dave Prigent
Miss H. M. Procktor
Purdy Bros.
Miss M.E. de Putron
Mr. T.J. de Putron
R.A. de Putron F.C.A.

Mr. C. J. Rabey
Miss Rachel D. Rabey
Mrs. Ruth A. Randell
Mr. Charles Ray
Mr. W. Norman Read
Mr. & Mrs. R. C. Reed
Mr. & Mrs. R. C. Reed
Mr. Brian T. Rees
Mr. Kenneth C. Renault
Mr. and Mrs. H. A. Renier
Mr. & Mrs. F. J. Renouf
Dr. John Renouf
Mr. Rowan W. J. Revell
Mr. & Mrs. J. P. Robert
Mr. & Mrs. N. Robert
Alick Jean Robilliard (Mr.)
Ann Robilliard
Miss Enid Robilliard

Mr. J. N. Robilliard
W. A. Robilliard
Miss Y. J. Robilliard
Mr. & Mrs. H. N. Robin
Mr. & Mrs. M. Robins
Mr. G. W. S. Robinson
Mr. & Mrs. I. F. S. Robinson
John B. S. Robinson
Mrs. O. M. Robinson
Mr. Malcolm Robson
Mr. Charles Michael Roger
Mr. & Mrs. R. L. Rogers
Mr. & Mrs. A. R. P. Rose
Gwen E. L. Rougier
Mr. & Mrs. E. Rouillard
Mr. J. F. Roussel
Dr. O. N. Roussel
Mr. Robin Roussel
Mrs. D. Routh
Jonathan Rowe
Mr. K. E. E. Rowe
Louise Rowe
Mr. & Mrs. Richard Rowe
Mr. Phillip E. Rowe
Mr. & Mrs. G. R. Rowland
The Revd. Richard E. Ruggle
Mr. & Mrs. C. E. V. Ryan

St. Sampson's Secondary Modern
 School (Library) Guernsey
Mr. A. R. Salmon
Mr. B. L. Salmon
Viscountess Sandon (Grand-
 daughter of the late Dr.
 William Mansell-MacCulloch)
Mrs. Margaret Sarchet
Mr. D. A. G. Sarre
Mr. & Mrs. L. W. Sarre
B. A. E. Saunders
Miss Rosemary De Sausmarez
Mr. & Mrs. John & Lydia
 Le Sauvage
Mr. J. C. W. Sauvary
Captain the Revd. Cuthbert
 Le Messurier Scott
Mr. and Mrs. P. J. Scott
Mr. Derek B. Selvidge
Mrs. E. W. Sharp
Mr. David Shayer
Mrs. Aimée Shepherd
Mr. & Mrs. M. A. Sherfield
Mrs. K. E. M. Silten
Miss Mary Sims
Mr. G. H. C. Smith
Mr. & Mrs. R. Smith
Mrs. N. M. Alderson Smith
Jeremy C. S. F. Smithies Esq.
John A. Smyth, B.Sc.
States of Guernsey Ancient
 Monuments Committee
Robert Staig, Guernsey
P. H. & B. E. Steer
Mrs. Joan Stevens
Mr. Philip Stevens
Mr. Harry R. Stranger
Mr. John G. Stranger
Mrs. Jaqueline Stuckey
Mr. A. Le Sueur
M.-C. Swann
Dr. S. C. M. Sweet
Mr. K. W. Syvret

Mr. & Mrs. K. E. Tayler
Mr. & Mrs. Richard H. Taylor
Mrs. S. Taylor
Captain & Mrs. F. G. Thatcher
Mr. & Mrs. S. G. Thomas
Mr. Donald Thompson

Michael Le Tissier, Esq.
R. J. Le Tissier
Mr. Ronald Le Tissier
Mr. L. C. Le Tocq
Mr. & Mrs. S. A. Le Tocq
Mr. W. T. Le Tocq
Miss M. E. Tooley
Dr. & Mrs. P. H. Tooley
Mr. T. G. Torode
Mr. W. F. Torode
Miss Doris M. Tostevin
Elizabeth M. Tostevin
Mr. J. C. Tostevin, c/o La Couture,
 St. Piere du Bois, Guernsey
Mr. John M. Tostevin
Miss S. Le Q. Tostevin
Marlene Tostevin
Mr. M. W. Tostevin
Mrs. D. G. Towner
Dr. & Mrs. C. J. Toynton
Mr. H. Travers
Mr. & Mrs. P. E. Tripp
Lt. Col. and Mrs. La Trobe-
 Bateman (Sark)
Mr. A. Tucker
Dr. & Mrs. J. B. Tucker
Mr. R. J. Tucker
Miss G. Tullier
Mr. & Mrs. R. Tummon
Mr. and Mrs. F. Turian

Mr. & Mrs. John D. Uden
Mrs. Helen Uttley

Mr. H. C. Vaudin
Mr. & Mrs. Godfrey Vises
Mr. & Mrs. A.J. Voûte

Mr. R. S. Waite, F.R.I.C.S.
D. W. Walden
Miss Margaret Waller
Mrs. J. de V. G. Wallis
Mrs. M. E. Walter
Mrs. Diane J. Ward
Neville C. Watchurst
Mrs. S. C. Robins-Watson
Mr. W. Watson
Mrs. J. D. Way
Weald & Downland Open Air
 Museum, Singleton, Sussex
Dr. B. P. Webber
Mrs. Anne Wheeler
Mr. R. F. Whidborne
Mr. B. B. White
Mrs. B. H. White
Mr. D. J. B. White
Mr. & Mrs. J. H. Whomersley
Mrs. R. Wilkes
Mrs. R. H. Baynton-Williams
Mr. & Mrs. Geoffrey D. Williams
Mr. & Mrs. M. J. Wilson
Dowager Countess Wimborne
Miss Odette Winter
Mrs. M. Wood
Mrs. P. M. Wood
Mr. & Mrs. Philip S. Wood
Lt. Col. Patrick A. Wootton
Mrs. R. Worsley
D. L. Wright
Mr. Paul Wright
Mr. & Mrs. C. P. T. Wrinch

Mr. & Mrs. A. Yabsley
Mr. A. G. Yeaman
Mrs. E. R. Yeaman
Mr. I. B. Yeaman
Mr. P. D. Youngs